Mia's
MATH
SERIES

PRECALCULUS

Mia's Precalculus

발 행	2022년 8월 31일 초판 1쇄
	2024년 7월 15일 초판 2쇄
저 자	소미혜
발행인	최영민
발행처	헤르몬하우스
주 소	경기도 파주시 신촌로 16
전 화	031-8071-0088
팩 스	031-942-8688
전자우편	hermonh@naver.com
출판등록	2015년 3월 27일
등록번호	제406-2015-31호

ⓒ 소미혜 2022, Printed in Korea.

ISBN   979-11-92520-05-6 (53410)

- 책 값은 뒤 표지에 있습니다.
- 헤르몬하우스는 피앤피북의 임프린트 출판사입니다.
- 이 책의 어느 부분도 저작권자나 발행인의 승인 없이 무단 복제하여 이용할 수 없습니다.
- 파본 및 낙장은 구입하신 서점에서 교환하여 드립니다.

✤ 저자직강 인터넷 강의는 SAT, AP No.1 인터넷 강의 사이트인 마스터프랩 (www.masterprep.net) 에서 보실 수 있습니다.

Why? Mia's Precalculus

'이해하기 쉬운 개념
+
다양한 example 문제
+
심화 응용 문제'

그동안의 Precalculus 교재에서는 볼 수 없었던 삼중 그물망 구조로 Precalculus에 필요한 모든 토픽 및 개념과 실전 능력을 한 번에 잡는다!

스스로 빈칸을 채워가며 개념을 꼼꼼히 공부할 수 있도록 설계한 교재

그저 그런 교재가 아니다!
지난 10년간 현장에서 수많은 학생들에게 결과로 증명된 학교 GPA 최적의 교재

Preface

Precalculus의 뜻을 살펴보면 '이전의(before)~'의 뜻을 가진 'pre'와 미분(differentiation)과 적분(Integration)을 배우며 수학의 꽃이라 불리는 calculus(미적분학)가 합쳐져서 '미적분학을 배우기 전에 꼭 필요한 내용의 과목'이라고 해석할 수 있습니다. 실제로 precalculus에서의 내용을 마스터 해야만 다음 단계의 수학 calculus를 순조롭게 들을 수 있습니다.

또한, AMC, AIME 등과 같은 미국고등수학경시대회들은 precalculus를 시험범위에 포함시키고 있습니다. 이 때문에 precalculus는 미국고등심화수학을 배우기 전에 꼭 통과해야 하는 관문이고, 저자는 precalculus야말로 미국고등학교 수학의 '핵심'이라 생각합니다. 이를 위해 학생들이 쉽고 재미있게 공부할 수 있고, 기본기를 튼튼하게 다질 수 있는 다양한 문제들이 담긴 나만의 precalculus 교재를 제작하기 시작했습니다.

교재 제작을 위해 수많은 precalculus textbook들의 내용과 문제들을 연구하였습니다. 그리고 학원 및 개인지도를 통해 알게 된 국내외 많은 국제학교/외국인학교에 재학중인 학생들의 Precalculus GPA 관리를 지도하면서 각 학교 선생님들의 가르치는 방식과 내용들을 벤치마킹(Benchmarking) 하였습니다. 또한 학생들이 어려워하는 부분들을 분석하고, 학생들의 의견을 참고하며 교재를 지속적으로 개선해서 교재의 수준을 향상시켰습니다. 이렇게 완성된 교재를 통해 매년 평균 95% 이상의 학생들이 학교 GAP에서 A 이상을 맞는 성과를 얻을 수 있었습니다.

지금까지의 노하우를 모두 담은 강의와 교재를 더 많은 학생들과 나누고 싶어 책으로 출판하게 되었습니다. 아울러 이 책을 함께 만들기 위해 애써준 사랑하는 남편TY와 잘생긴 아들 주원이, 그 동안 함께해 준 고마운 학생들, 그리고 헤르몬하우스 관계자 여러분과 마스터프렙의 권주근 대표님께 감사의 마음으로 드립니다. 그리고 무엇보다도 소중한 기회를 주신 하나님께 감사와 찬양을 올려드립니다.

Mia Mihye So

Mia's Precalculus의 특징

1. 교재 내용, 문제에 대한 쉽고 명쾌한 Mia쌤의 설명, 해설강의는 유학 인터넷 강의 전문 사이트인 마스터프렙 (www.masterprep.net)에 마련되어 있습니다.

2. '이해하기 쉬운 개념 + 다양한 example 문제 + 심화 응용 문제' 삼중 그물망 구조로 개념과 실전연습을 한번에 잡아줍니다. 어려운 개념들을 쉽게 배우고 다양한 example 문제로 연습을 한 뒤, 배운 개념에 대한 심화 응용 문제(Expand Knowledge 문제)로 실전에 적용하는 연습까지 완벽한 개념정리를 완성시킬 수 있습니다. 학교 GPA 관리를 위해 공부하는 학생들은 필수내용들은 반드시 공부하고 심화응용문제(Expand Knowledge 문제)는 선택적으로 공부하면 됩니다.

3. 스스로 빈칸을 채워가며 개념을 꼼꼼하게 공부할 수 있게 설계하였습니다. 빈칸의 답은 페이지 하단에 배치하여 학생들이 필요 시 바로 참고할 수 있습니다.

4. 이해하기 쉽고 친근한 이미지를 활용하여 어려운 수식을 빠르게 이해할 수 있도록 작성하였습니다. 꼭 암기해야 할 개념, 공식은 shade 박스 안에 정리하였습니다.

이 책을 통해 학생들이 precalculus라는 과목이 쉽지 않지만 충분히 doable하다는 것을 깨닫고, 문제를 해결했을 때의 즐거움을 느끼며, 깊이 있는 문제들을 다루면서 사고력과 응용력이 한층 더 깊어지길 바랍니다.

◆ 기호 정리

* (star): 심화 응용 문제

$\mathbb{R}$: Real numbers $\cap$: and
$\mathbb{Z}$: Integers ∞ : infinity
$\mathbb{N}$: Natural numbers $\therefore$: Therefore
$\cup$: or $\because$: Since

저자 소개

Mia(소미혜) 선생님은 지난 13년 이상을 유학 수학 현장에서 다양한 학생들과 호흡하면서 최적화된 미국 수학 및 국제학교 수학에 대한 솔루션을 제공해온 수학 전문가이다.

압구정 미국수학 전문강사라는 타이틀이 위의 노력들을 통해서 자연스럽게 얻게 된 선생님의 별칭이다.

미국에서 인증된 수학전문강사(Texas 8-12 미국수학교사자격증 content exam + PPR exam 통과)로 관련된 전문자격증을 소지하고 있으며, 특히, 해외 엄마들 사이에 입 소문난 실력파 강사이다.

Precalculus, AP calculus AB BC, AP Statistics, SAT 1 2 math, IB Math 등에서 13년 이상의 경력을 가지고 있다. 또한 한국 수능수학 강의 경력도 4년 이상을 가지고 있어서 한국 수학과 미국/국제학교 수학에 대해서 모두 정통한 수학 전문가이다.

- 8-12 Texas Mathematics Teacher Certificate (content exam + PPR exam 통과)
- (현) No.1 유학 인터넷 강의 사이트 마스터프렙(www.masterprep.net) 수학강사
- (전) IBAdvance IB, sat 수학대표강사
- (전) 해커스유학 미국수학강사
- (전) PSU Edu AP, SAT 수학강사
- 미국텍사스고등학교, 국내국제고등학교 수학교사 경력 6년.
- 수능수학강의 경력 4년
- 용인외대부고, 경기외고, KIS, 제주KIS, SIS, 청라달튼, 브랭섬홀, 일본, 싱가포르, 베트남 국제학교 등의 학생들의 온라인/오프라인 개인지도
- College Board certification for AP Calculus AB, BC
- College Board certification for AP Statistics

Contents

1. Functions

1.1 Quadratic Functions 12
1.2 Function 26
1.3 Analyzing Functions 37
1.4 Piecewise Functions 45
1.5 Transforming Function 53
1.6 Composing Function 69
1.7 Inverse Function 75

2. Polynomial and Rational Functions

2.1 Polynomial Functions 90
2.2 Diving Polynomials 102
2.3 Real Zeros of Poly 111
2.4 Fundamental Theorem of Algebra 117
2.5 Rational Function 128
2.6 Polynomial and Rational Inequalities 145

3. Exponential and Logarithmic Functions

3.1 Exponential Function 158
3.2 Compound Interest 167
3.3 Logarithmic Function 173
3.4 Properties of Logarithm 184
3.5 Exp and Log Equations and Inequalities 193
3.6 Exponential Growth and Modeling 206

4. Trigonometry Definition and Graphs

4.1 Angles in Radian 214
4.2 Trigonometry of Right Triangles 228
4.3 Trigonometry of Any Angles 236

  4.4 Trigonometry in Unit Circle 244
  4.5 Trigonometric Graphs for Sin, Cos 249
  4.6 Trigonometric Graphs for Others 262

5. Trigonometry Identities

  5.1 Inverse Trigonometry Function 272
  5.2 Basic Trigonometric Identities 283
  5.3 Verifying Trigonometric Identities 291
  5.4 Sum and difference Identities 297
  5.5 Double-Angle Identity 304
  5.6 Half-Angle and Product-Sum Identities 314

6. Trig Equations and Geometry Triangles

  6.1 Basic Trigonometric Equations 324
  6.2 More Trigonometric Equations 330
  6.3 The Law of Sines 336
  6.4 The Law of Cosines 344
  6.5 Area of Triangles 350

7. Polar coordinate and Complex number

  7.1 Polar Coordinates 358
  7.2 Graphs of Polar Equations 366
  7.3 Complex Numbers and De Moivre's Theorem 376
  7.4 Parametric Equations 388

8. Vector

  8.1 Vector Basics 396
  8.2 Vectors in Two Dimensions 404

Contents

8.3 The Dot Product 413
8.4 Three-Dimensional Coordinate 425
8.5 Vectors in Three Dimensions 430
8.6 The Cross Product 438

9. Conic Section

9.1 Conic Sections and Parabolas...................................... 448
9.2 Ellipses 454
9.3 Hyperbolas 461
9.4 Transformation of Conics... 467
9.5 Rotation of Conics... 479

10. Matrix and System of Equation

10.1 Systems of Linear Equations in Several Variables...... 486
10.2 Algebra of Matrices 495
10.3 Inverse and Matrix Equation...................................... 502
10.4 Partial Fractions 510

11. Sequence and Series

11.1 Sequence and Sigma Notation 518
11.2 Arithmetic Sequence and Series............................... 526
11.3 Geometric Sequence and Series................................ 533
11.4 Applications of Sequence and Series......................... 542
11.5 Binomial Expansion 547
11.6 Mathematical Induction 556

Answers

Part 1
Functions

1.1 Quadratic Functions
1.2 Function
1.3 Analyzing Functions
1.4 Piecewise Functions
1.5 Transforming Function
1.6 Composing Function
1.7 Inverse Function

Mia's Precalculus
1.1 Quadratic Functions

1. Graph of Quadratic

※ Standard Form:

$y = ax^2 + bx + c$

a>0   a<0   a=2   a=0.5

a : shape of the parabola c : y intercept

※ Factored Form:

zeros

$y = a(x-p)(x-q)$

zeros(=①_____)

at ②_____

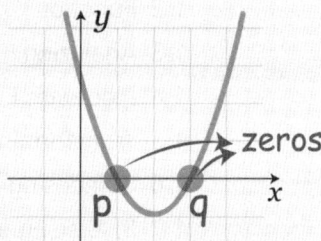

※ Vertex Form:

vertex

$y = a(x-h)^2 + k$

vertex at ③_____

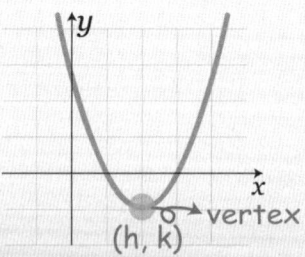

Blank : ① =roots = x intercept   ② $x = p$ or $x = q$ ③ (h, k)

EXAMPLE 1. Graph the functions briefly.

① $y = 2(x+3)(x-1)$

② $y = -(x+2)(x+5)$

③ $y = -3(x+1)^2 - 1$

④ $y = 0.5(x+1)^2 - 4$

⑤ $y = -x(x+1)$

⑥ $y = 2x(x-2)$

⑦ $y = \dfrac{1}{2}(x+4)^2$

⑧ $y = 2(x-2)^2$

2. Finding Zeros of Quadratic

The quadratic function $y = ax^2 + bx + c$ has zeros where $ax^2 + bx + c = \boxed{①}$.

We can find the zeros by;

① Factoring

② Graph on the calculator (look for the x-intercepts)

③ Use quadratic formula!

$$x = \frac{-b \pm \sqrt{b^2 - 4ac}}{2a}$$ Quadratic Formula

EXAMPLE 2. Find the x intercept and graph the function.

① $y = 2x^2 - 14x - 36$ ② $y = -2x^2 - 2x + 24$

③ $y = 2x^2 + 11x + 5$ ④ $y = 3x^2 - 5x + 2$

⑤ $y = 64 - x^2$ ⑥ $y = x^2 - 4$

Blank : ① 0

⑦ $y = 2x^2 + 10x + 11$ ⑧ $y = 2x^2 - 7x + 4$

3. Finding Vertex of Quadratic

We can find the vertex of the quadratic function $y = ax^2 + bx + c$ by;

① Complete the square!
ex)

$y = \boxed{2x^2 + 4x} - 5$ (complete the square) Factor out a from x^2, x terms

$= 2(x^2 + 2x \;\boxed{①}\; \boxed{②}) - 5$ To complete the square
: Take the half and square!

$= 2(x + 1)^2 \;\boxed{③}\; - 5$

so the vertex is ④ _____

② Easily, just use $x = \boxed{⑤}$, and plug into quadratic to find y.

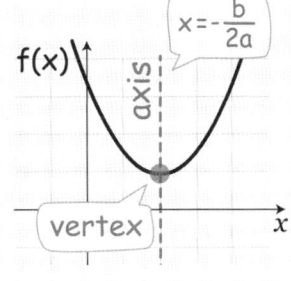

③ Take the average of two zeros and plug into quadratic to find y.

Whenever you're asked for the minimum or the maximum of a quadratic, find the vertex.

Blank : ① +1 ② -1 ③ -2 ④ (-1, -7) ⑤ $-\dfrac{b}{2a}$

Part 1 Functions 15

EXAMPLE 3. Find the vertex. Find the maximum or minimum.

① $y = x^2 + 6x + 8$

② $y = x^2 + 4x - 7$

③ $y = 2x^2 + 4x + 15$

④ $y = -5x^2 - 20x - 30$

⑤ $y = -2x^2 - 16x$

⑥ $y = 20x - 2x^2$

⑦ $y = -x^2 - 3x + 1$ ⑧ $y = 2x^2 - 2x + 3$

EXAMPLE 4. The height h of a baseball t seconds after being hit is given by $h(t) = -16t^2 + 80t + 3$.

a) At what time does the ball reaches its maximum height?

b) What is the maximum height that the baseball reaches?

4. Quadratic Inequalities

$f(x) \geq 0$: When is $f(x)$ above or on the x axis?

$f(x) < 0$: When is $f(x)$ below the x axis?

Inequalities	Graph	Solutions
$(x-2)(x-5) > 0$	zeros at 2 and 5	①
$(1-x)(x+3) \geq 0$	-3 to 1	②
$x^2 \leq 1$	-1 to 1	③

☺ Shortcut : As long as $a > 0$ (open up) for quadratic $ax^2 + bx + c$,

quadratic >0 or ≥ 0 is the ④_____ part of two zeros.

quadratic <0 or ≤ 0 is the ⑤_____ part of two zeros.

EXAMPLE 5. Solve the inequalities numerically.

① $x^2 + 7x \geq -12$ ② $x^2 \geq 16$

Blank : ① x<2 or x>5   ② -3≤x≤1   ③ -1≤x≤1   ④ outside   ⑤ inside

③ $36 < x^2$

④ $x^2 - 9x + 14 > 0$

⑤ $x^2 + 4x + 2 \leq 0$

⑥ $x^2 < 7 - 4x$

⑦ $132 - x - x^2 > 0$

⑧ $-x^2 - 4x - 3 \geq 0$

⑨ $x^2 - 4x + 4 > 0$

⑩ $x^2 - 6x + 9 \geq 0$

⑪ $x^2 - 2x + 1 \geq 0$

⑫ $x^2 - 8x + 16 > 0$

⑬ $x^2 - 10x + 25 \leq 0$

⑭ $x^2 + 2x + 1 < 0$

5. Discriminant

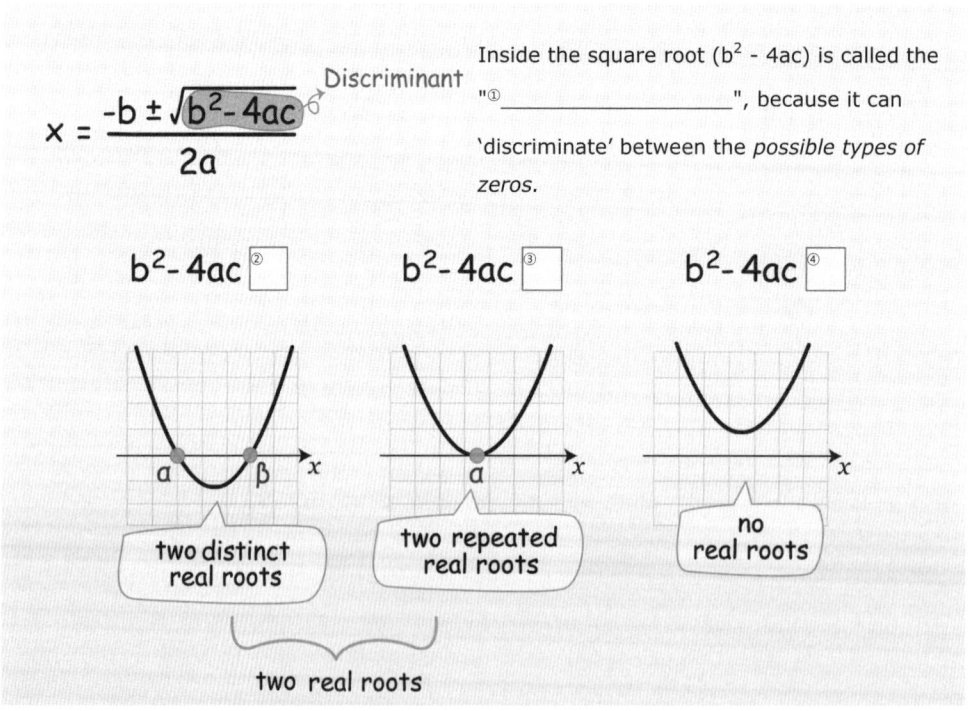

Inside the square root ($b^2 - 4ac$) is called the "① _____", because it can 'discriminate' between the *possible types of zeros*.

Blank : ① discriminant ② >0 ③ =0 ④ <0

EXAMPLE 6. Use the discriminant to determine the number and type of solutions for the equation.

① $9x^2 - 3x - 8 = -10$

② $2x^2 = 10x + 5$

③ $9x^2 + 6x + 6 = 5$

④ $4x^2 = 8x - 4$

⑤ $-6x^2 - 6 = -7x - 9$

⑥ $-4x^2 - 4x = 6$

EXAMPLE 7. Find the set of values of k for which the equation $2x^2 - x + k = 0$ has equal roots.

EXAMPLE 8. For the quadratic equation $kx^2 + (k+3)x = 1$ find the value of k which the equation has two real roots.

6. Systems of linear and Quadratic

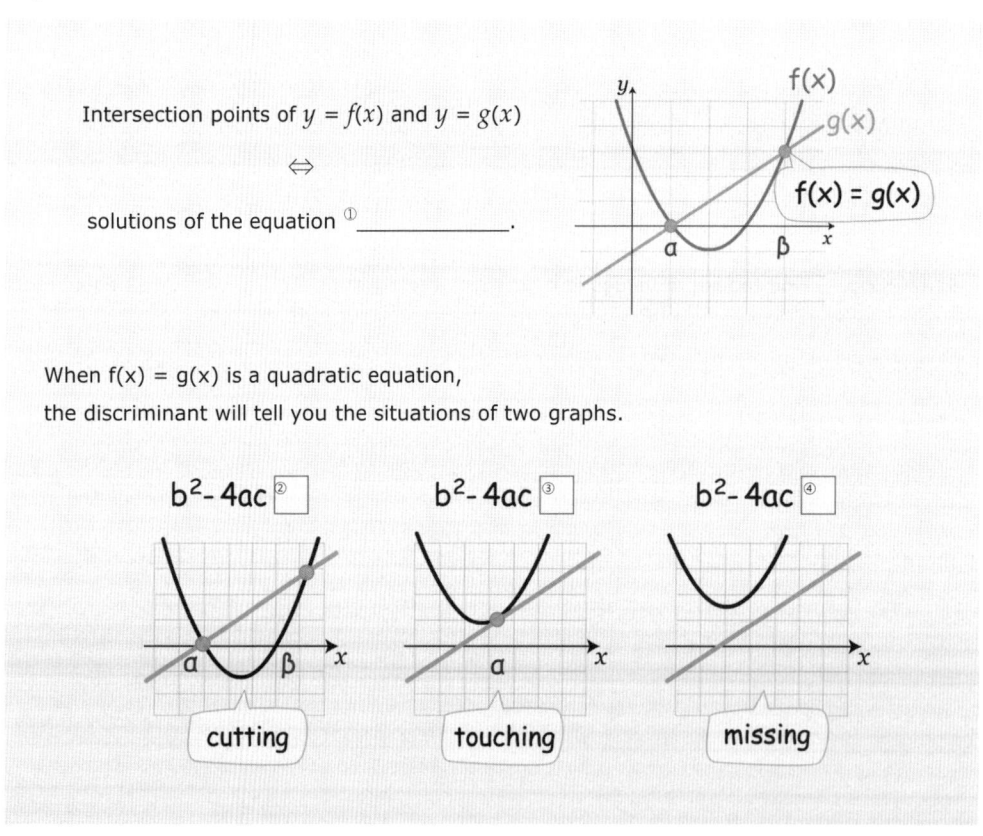

Intersection points of $y = f(x)$ and $y = g(x)$

$\Leftrightarrow$

solutions of the equation ①_____.

When f(x) = g(x) is a quadratic equation,
the discriminant will tell you the situations of two graphs.

$b^2 - 4ac$ ② cutting
$b^2 - 4ac$ ③ touching
$b^2 - 4ac$ ④ missing

Blank : ① f(x) = g(x) ② >0 ③ =0 ④ <0

EXAMPLE 9. Find the coordinates of the points of intersection between the line $2x - y = 1$ and the parabola $y = x^2 - 3x + 5$.

EXAMPLE 10. Find the values of m for which the lines $y = mx + 1$ are tangents to the curve with equation $y = x^2 - 4x + 2$.

EXAMPLE 11. Determine the value of k such that $g(x) = 3x + k$ intersects the quadratic function $f(x) = 2x^2 - 5x + 3$ twice.

7. Expand Knowledge

EXAMPLE 12. *A quadratic function passes through the point $(a-2,0)$ and $(a+6,0)$. Find the x coordinate of the vertex in terms of a.

EXAMPLE 13. *Find the maximum value of $\dfrac{1}{(x^2-8x+26)^4}$.

EXAMPLE 14. *A rectangle is bounded by the x-axis and the y-axis with a vertex on line $y = -x + 6$ as shown. What is the largest area of the rectangle?

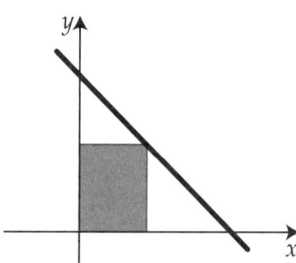

EXAMPLE 15. *At 10:00, Jay is 5 km due south of the train station and walking toward the station at 2 km per hour. At the same time, May is 2 km due east of the train station and running east away at 3 km per hour. After how many hours will they be closest to each other?

EXAMPLE 16. *A shop sells about 100 t-shirts each month for $8 each. The shop owner estimates that for each $2 increase in the price, he will sell about 10 fewer t-shirts per month. How much should the owner charge for each mug in order to maximize the monthly income from their sales?

(Let x = the number of $2 price increases.)

Mia's Precalculus
1.2 Functions

1. Relation

x → [f] → y or f(x)

A ①_____ is a set of pairs of input and output values.

It ②_____ an input to an output.

You can write a relation in many ways..such as

| Mapping | Table | Order Pairs | Graph |

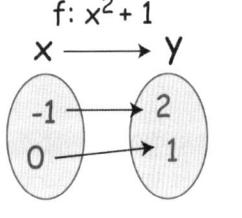
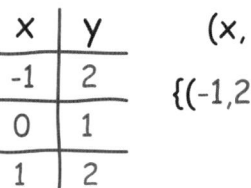
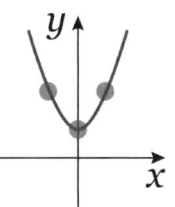

2. Function

※ Function

x → [f] → y or f(x)

A **function** is a special relation
where ③_____ **input** has ④_____ **output**.

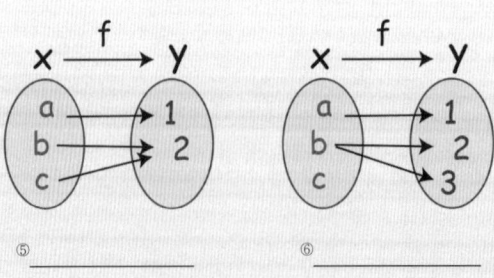

Blank : ① relation ② relates ③ each ④ one ⑤ function ⑥ Not a function

Input (=①_____ =②_____ variable) is the set of X.

Output (=③_____ =④_____ variable) is the set of Y.

Easy way to check if a relation is a function?

① different ⑤____ coordinate

② ⑥_____ test

Not a function !   Function !

If a vertical line crosses the curve twice or more, then it is NOT a function.

※ Evaluating (E-'*value*'-ate) Functions

$$f(x) = x^2 + 1$$

$$f(@) = @^2 + 1$$

$$f(2x) = \boxed{}$$

"x" is Just a Place-Holder

☺ $(2x)^2 \ne 2x^2$

EXAMPLE 1. Determine whether each relation is a function or not.

① 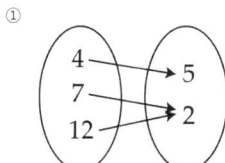   ②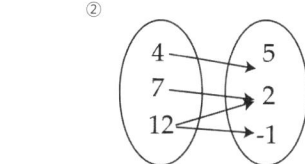

Blank : ① domain   ② independent   ③ range   ④ dependent   ⑤ x   ⑥ vertical line   ⑦ $(2x)^2+1$

③ $\{(2,-3),(-1,4),(3,5),(8,-11)\}$ ④ $\{(-1,3),(0,1),(2,-3),(-1,0)\}$

⑤ $\{(0,2),(-1,3),(12,-30),(0,4),(2,3)\}$ ⑥ $\{(1,2),(2,1),(4,4),(0,4),(3,4)\}$

⑦ 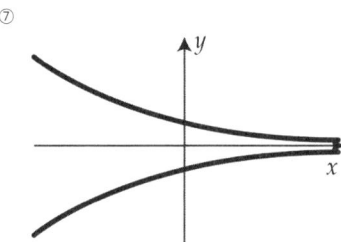   ⑧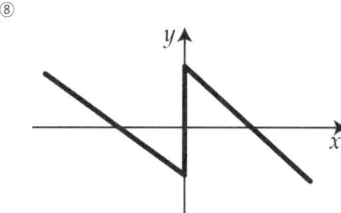

⑨ 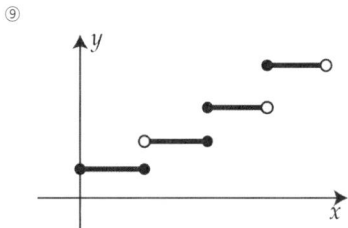   ⑩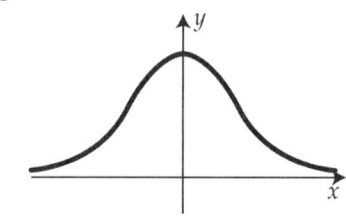

⑪ 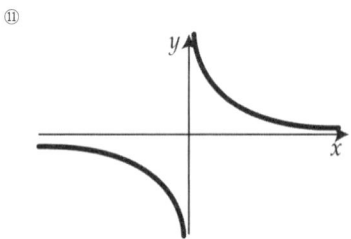   ⑫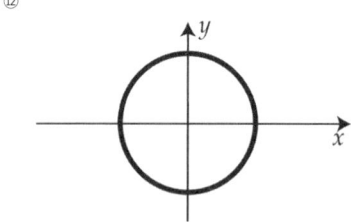

EXAMPLE 2. Evaluate $f(2)$, $f(2+h)$, and $\dfrac{f(2+h)-f(2)}{h}$ for given function.

① $f(x) = x^2 + 1$

② $f(x) = 2x - 1$

③ $f(x) = \dfrac{x}{x+1}$

④ $f(x) = \dfrac{1}{x-1}$

⑤ $f(x) = \sqrt{x+1}$

3. Domain and Range

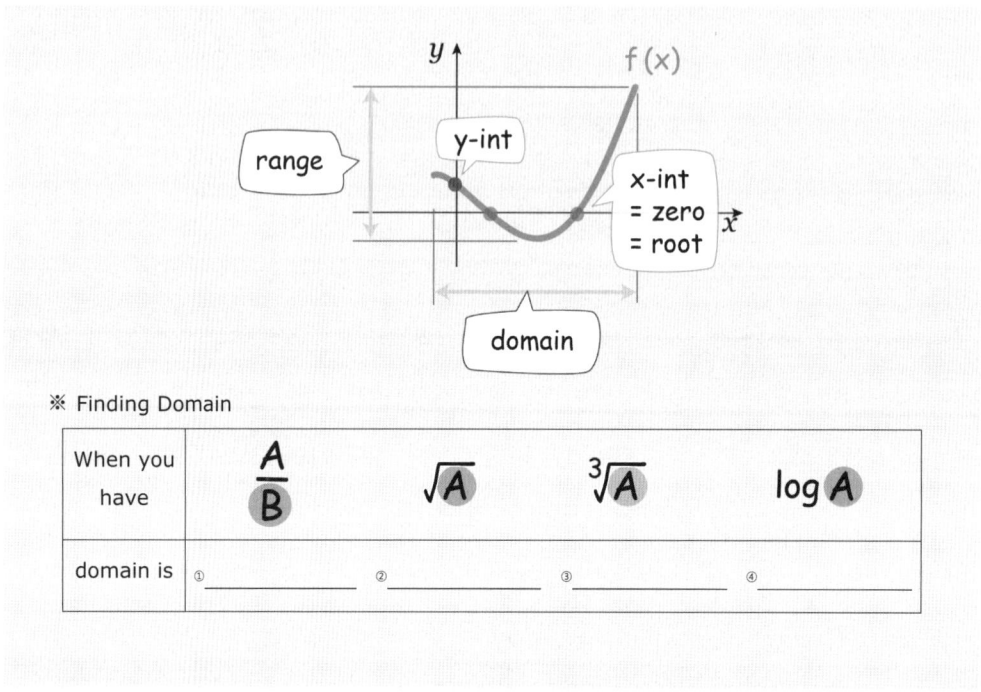

※ Finding Domain

When you have	$\dfrac{A}{B}$	$\sqrt{A}$	$\sqrt[3]{A}$	$\log A$
domain is	①	②	③	④

EXAMPLE 3. Find the domain of each of the following functions:

① $f(x) = x^2 + 5x$ 　　　　　② $h(x) = \sqrt{4-3x}$

③ $g(x) = \dfrac{3x}{x^2 - 4}$ 　　　　　④ $f(x) = \dfrac{x+4}{x^2 - 5x - 6}$

Blank : ① B≠0 　② A≥0 　③ all real numbers (R) 　④ A>0

30　Mia's Precalculus

⑤ $f(x) = \dfrac{x}{x^2+4}$

⑥ $f(x) = \dfrac{x-1}{x^2+2x+3}$

⑦ $F(x) = \dfrac{\sqrt{3x+12}}{x-5}$

⑧ $g(x) = \dfrac{\sqrt{x-2}}{x-7}$

⑨ $f(x) = \dfrac{(2x-1)^2}{\sqrt{x-5}}$

⑩ $f(x) = \dfrac{x^2}{\sqrt{x-1}}$

⑪ $f(x) = \sqrt{x^2-3x-4}$

⑫ $f(x) = \sqrt[3]{x^2-4}$

⑬ $f(x) = \dfrac{2}{\sqrt{4-x^2}}$

⑭ $f(x) = \dfrac{2}{\sqrt[3]{x^2-5}}$

⑮ $f(x) = \dfrac{1}{x-2} + \sqrt{x+3}$

⑯ $f(x) = \log_3(x-3)$

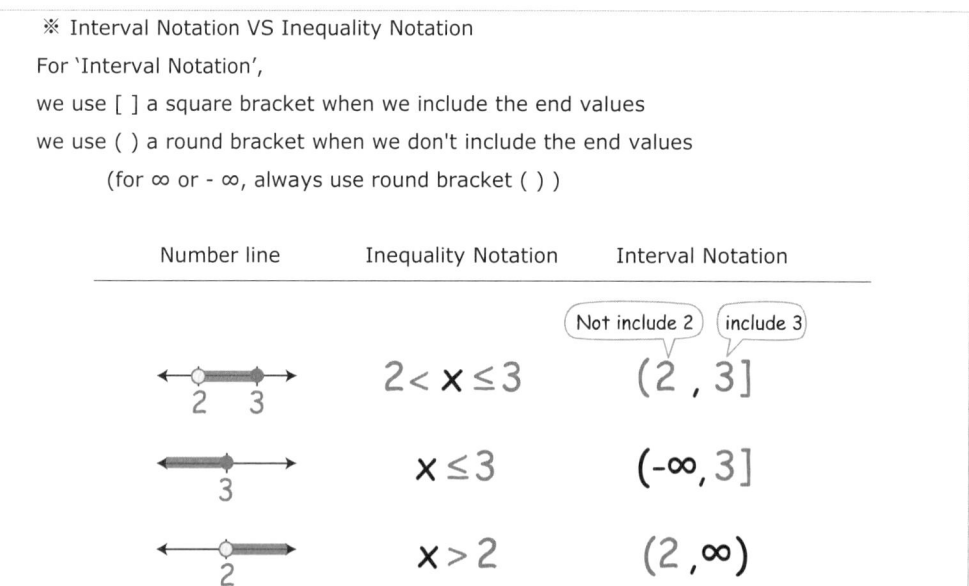

EXAMPLE 4. For each of the following graphs, find the domain and range:

①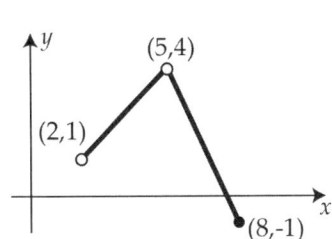

②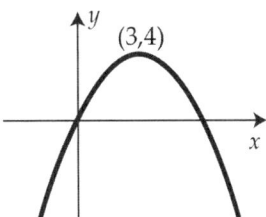

③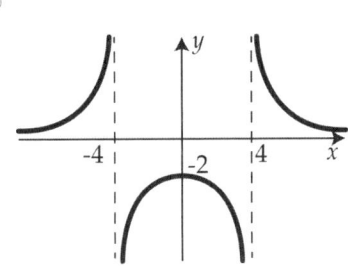

④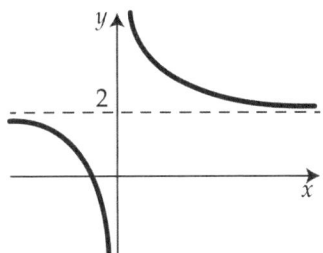

4. Implicit VS Explicit Function

Explicit: The dependent variable(y) and independent variable(x) are separated on opposite sides.	**Implicit**: The dependent variable(y) and independent variable(x) are not separated on opposite sides.
"y = function of x".	"function of y and x = something else".
$y = \pm\sqrt{4-x^2}$ 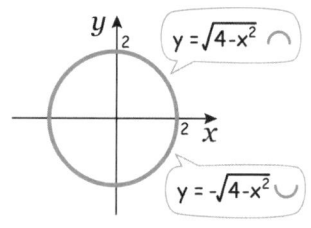	$x^2 + y^2 = 4$ 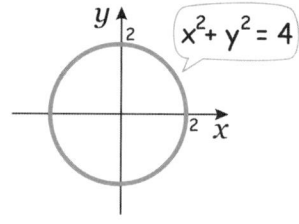

EXAMPLE 5. Convert the given implicit function to explicit function. Determine whether the equation defines y as a function of x.

① $x^2 + 2y = 4$

② $x^2 y - y = 1$

③ $x^2 + (y+2)^2 = 4$

④ $\dfrac{x^2}{4} - \dfrac{y^2}{9} = 1$

⑤ $x-y^3=0$

⑥ $x-y^4=0$

5. Expand Knowledge

EXAMPLE 6. * Find the domain of the function

$$f(x)=\frac{1}{x^2-2x+3}-\frac{3^{\sqrt{x+1}}}{x-2}+x^2+\sqrt{3-x}$$

EXAMPLE 7. *Find $f(x)$ when;

① $f(x+1) = 4x^2 + x$

② $f(2x) = x^2 - 1$

③ $f(2x-1) = \ln 4x$

EXAMPLE 8. * If $f(x^2 - 2x) = 2x^2 - 4x + 5$, then what is $f(8)$ =?

Mia's Precalculus
1.3 Analyzing Functions

1. Even and Odd Functions

Even function

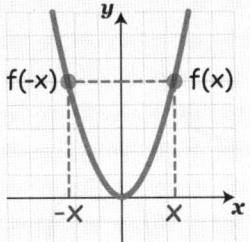

Odd function

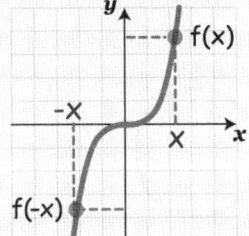

$f(-x) = f(x)$

symmetric over ①_____

ex) $y = x^2$

$y = x^4 - 3x^2 + 3$

$y = \cos x$

$y = |x|$

$f(-x) = -f(x)$

symmetric over ②_____

ex) $y = x^3$

$y = x^7 - 8x^5 + x$

$y = \sin x$

$y = \tan x$

EXAMPLE 1. Determine whether each of the following functions is even, odd, or neither.

①
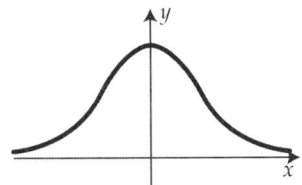

②
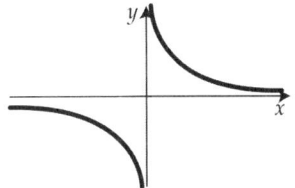

Blank : ① y axis ② origin

③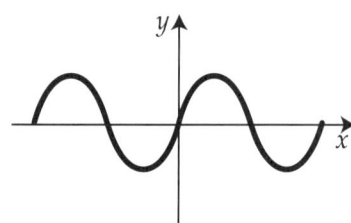

④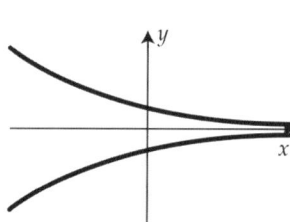

⑤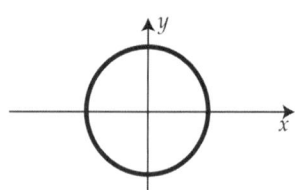

⑥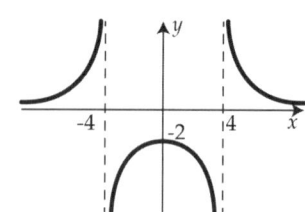

⑦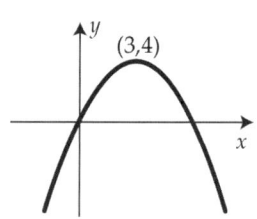

EXAMPLE 2. Determine whether each of the following functions is even, odd, or neither.

☺ Tip☞ Find ①_____ ,

If you get the ②_____ function back (=f(x)) the function is **even**.

If *all of the signs are changed* (= -f(x)) the function is **odd**.

① $f(x) = -x^4 + 2x^2 - 5$ ② $f(x) = x^5 + 3x^3 - x$

Blank : ① f(-x)   ② original

③ $f(x) = -3x^7 + x$ ④ $f(x) = x^{100} + 2x^{10} - 8$

⑤ $f(x) = -6x^4 + 2x - 8$ ⑥ $f(x) = 3x^{10} + x + 7$

⑦ $g(x) = |x| + 2$ ⑧ $g(x) = \sqrt{x-2}$

⑨ $h(x) = \sqrt[3]{x}$ ⑩ $f(x) = \sqrt[3]{x^2 + 2}$

⑪ $f(x) = -\dfrac{x^3}{x^2 + 2}$ ⑫ $g(x) = \dfrac{x}{|x|}$

⑬ $g(x) = x\left|x^2 - 2\right|$

⑭ $h(x) = |x - 2|$

2. Increasing and Decreasing

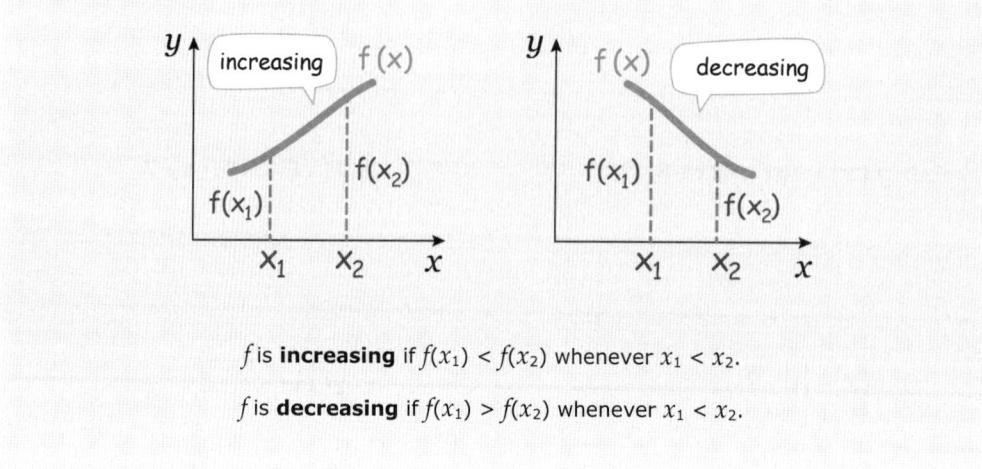

f is **increasing** if $f(x_1) < f(x_2)$ whenever $x_1 < x_2$.

f is **decreasing** if $f(x_1) > f(x_2)$ whenever $x_1 < x_2$.

3. Maximum and minimum

1) Relative (Local) maximum and minimum

① _____ Maximum (=Local Maximum)

The <u>height of the function at 'c'</u> is greater than (or equal to) the height anywhere else *in certain interval*.

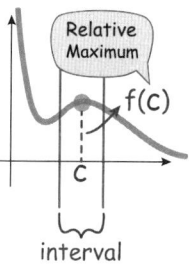

② _____ Minimum (=Local Minimum)

The <u>height of the function at 'c'</u> is less than (or equal to) the height anywhere else *in certain interval*.

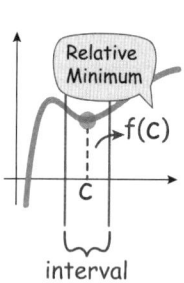

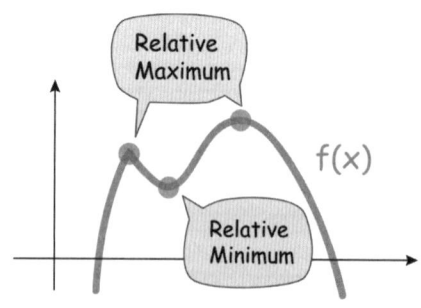

Blank : ① relative   ② relative

2) Absolute(Global) maximum and minimum

The maximum or minimum *over the entire function or given interval* is called
① _____ maximum or minimum.

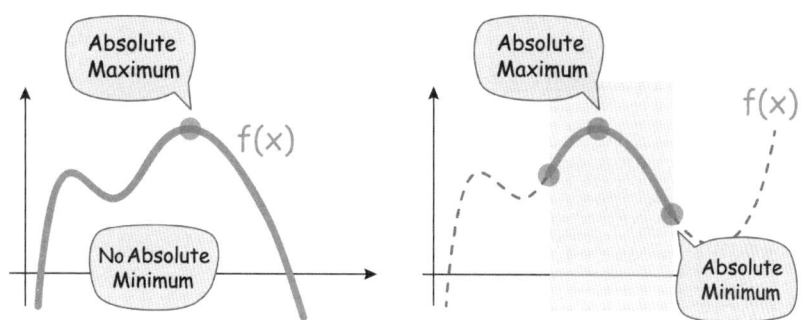

● *note*   The plural of Maximum is ② _____

The plural of Minimum is ③ _____

Maxima and Minima are collectively called ④ _____

EXAMPLE 3. Using the graph of f(x) given;

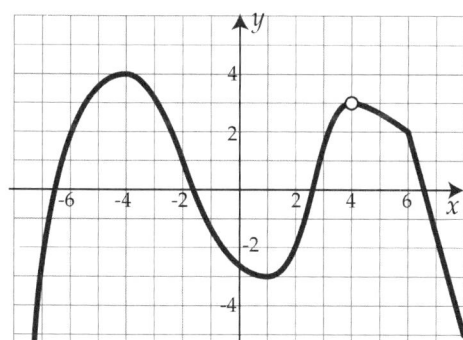

① Find the relative extrema, if they exist.

Blank : ① Absolute ② Maxima ③ Minima ④ Extrema

② Find the absolute extrema, if they exist.

③ Find the interval where $f(x_1) < f(x_2)$ whenever $x_1 < x_2$.

4. Average rate of change

The line that crosses two points on a curve is called a
①_____ line.

The **slope of the**② _____ **line** will be ;

③_____

We call it the '④_____ rate of change'.

※ Average Rate of Change

> The **slope of the secant line**
> that goes through two points **a** and **b**
> =Average rate of change =
> $$\frac{f(b) - f(a)}{b - a}$$

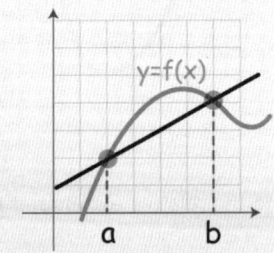

Blank : ① secant ② secant ③ $\frac{f(b) - f(a)}{b - a}$ ④ Average

EXAMPLE 4. Find the average rate of change over the given interval.

① $f(x) = x^2 + 3x$, [2, 6]

② $f(x) = 2x^2 - 4x + 3$, [-2, 5]

③ $f(x) = \dfrac{x+3}{x}$, [1, 7]

④ $f(x) = \dfrac{x+5}{x-4}$, [1, 7]

⑤ $f(x) = \sqrt{x+4}$, [5, 8]

⑥ $f(x) = \sqrt{x-1}$, [2, 6]

5. Expand Knowledge

EXAMPLE 5. *$f(x)$ is an even function and $g(x)$ is an odd function. Determine whether each of the following function $h(x)$ is even, odd, or neither.

① $h(x) = f(x)g(x)$

② $h(x) = f(x) + g(x)$

③ $h(x) = [g(x)]^2$

④ $h(x) = f(f(x))$

⑤ $h(x) = g(g(x))$

EXAMPLE 6. *If $f(x)$ is an even function and $g(x)$ is an odd function, $f(3) = 1$ and $g(2) = -3$, then $f(-3) + g(-2) =$

Mia's Precalculus
1.4 Piecewise Functions

1. Thirteen Basic Functions

Constant function
$$y = c$$
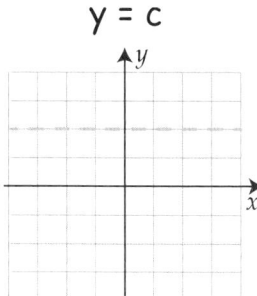

Linear function
$$y = x$$
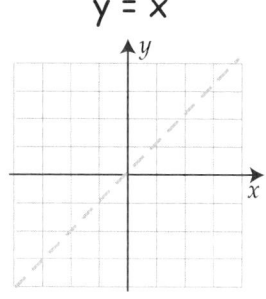

Quadratic function
$$y = x^2$$
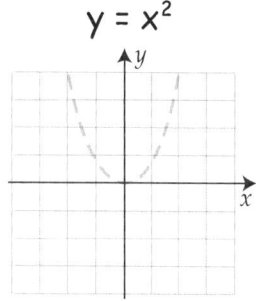

Cubic function
$$y = x^3$$
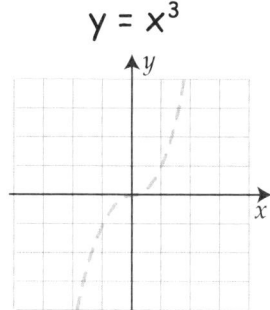

Square root function
$$y = \sqrt{x}$$
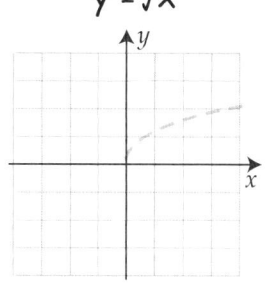

Cube root function
$$y = \sqrt[3]{x}$$
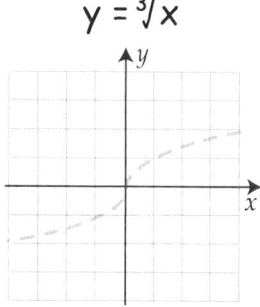

Reciprocal function
$$y = \frac{1}{x}$$
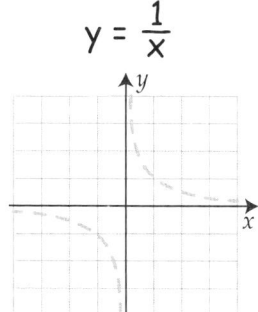

Absolute value function
$$y = |x|$$
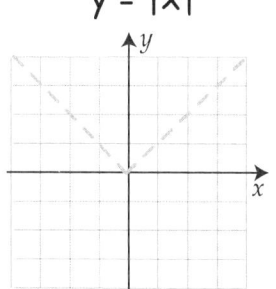

Exponential and Logarithmic function
$$y = 2^x \quad y = \log_2 x$$
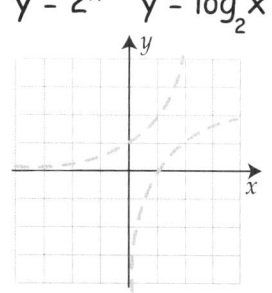

Part 1 Functions 45

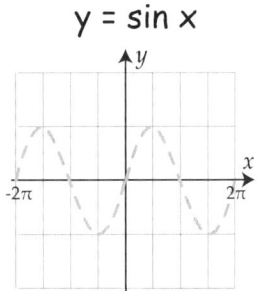
Sine function
y = sin x

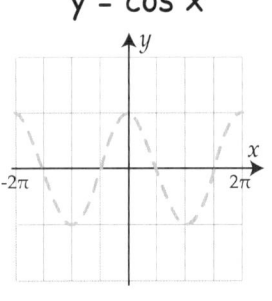
Cosine function
y = cos x

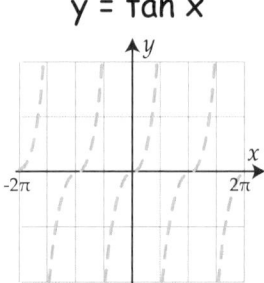
Tangent function
y = tan x

Which one satisfy $f(-x) = f(x)$?

Which one satisfy $f(-x) = -f(x)$?

2. Continuity

Continuous Function: a single unbroken graph.
                (that you could draw without lifting your pen from the paper)

Discontinuity: a graph which is not continuous

When we have;

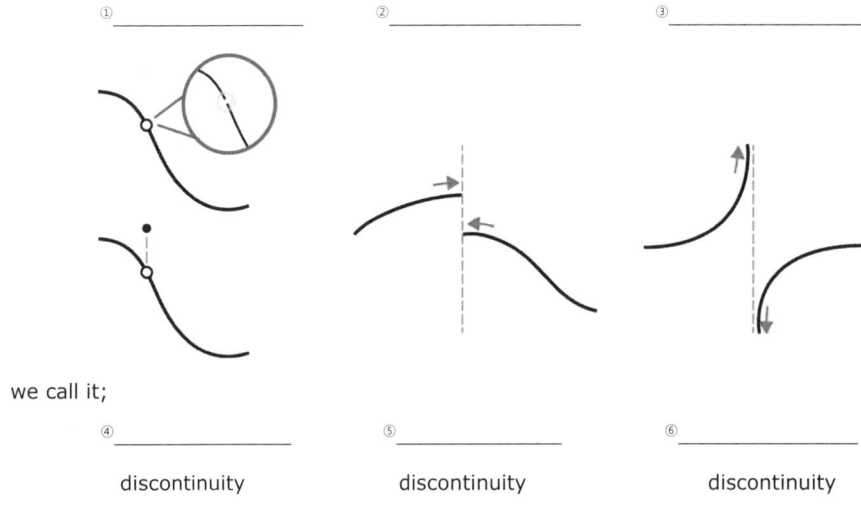

we call it;

④ _____   ⑤ _____   ⑥ _____
    discontinuity   discontinuity   discontinuity

Blank : ① hole ② gap ③ asymptotes ④ removable ⑤ jump ⑥ infinite

3. Piecewise-defined Functions

: a function made up in pieces.

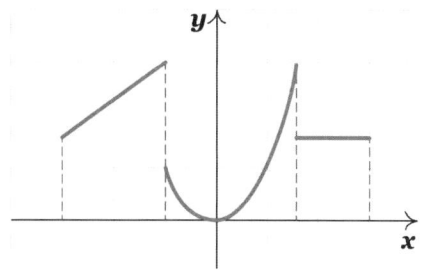

EXAMPLE 1. Graph the function. State the domain and range. Is it continuous? If not, what kind of discontinuity it is?

① $f(x) = \begin{cases} 4, & \text{if } x \leq 1 \\ x, & \text{if } x > 1 \end{cases}$

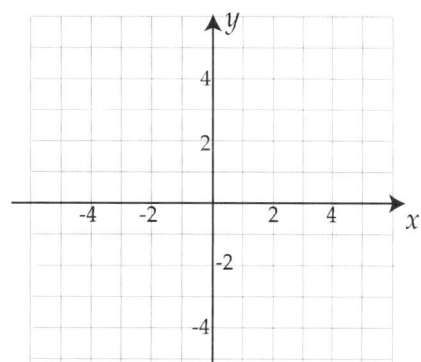

② $h(x) = \begin{cases} \sqrt{x}, & \text{if } x \geq 4 \\ x-2, & \text{if } x < 4 \end{cases}$

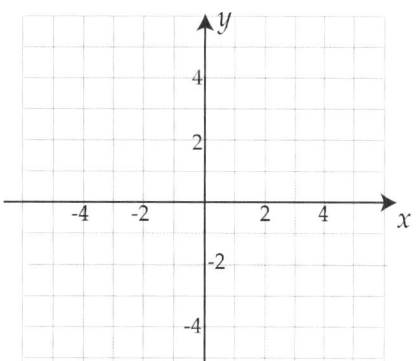

③ $g(x) = \begin{cases} 3, & \text{if } x = 0 \\ \sqrt[3]{x}, & \text{if } x \neq 0 \end{cases}$

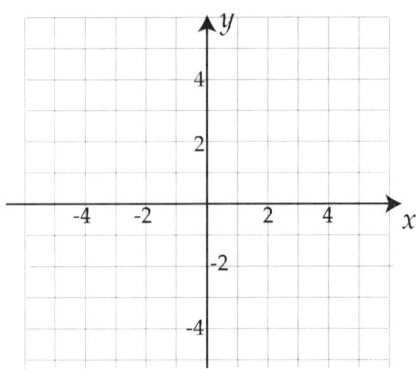

④ $f(x) = \begin{cases} x, & \text{if } x < 0 \\ 2, & \text{if } x = 0 \\ x^2, & \text{if } x > 0 \end{cases}$

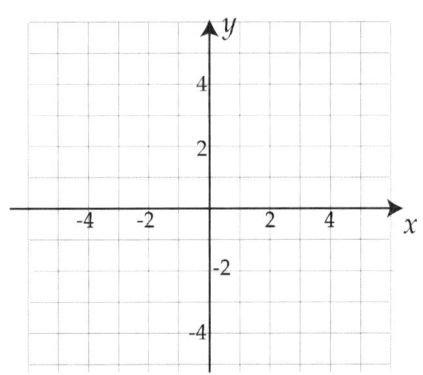

EXAMPLE 2. Give a rule for the piecewise-defined function.

①

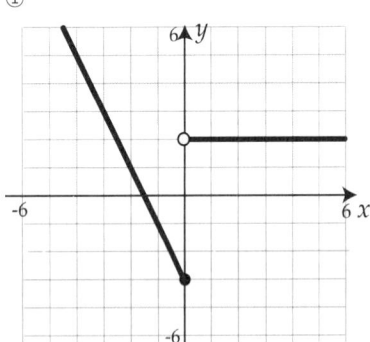

②

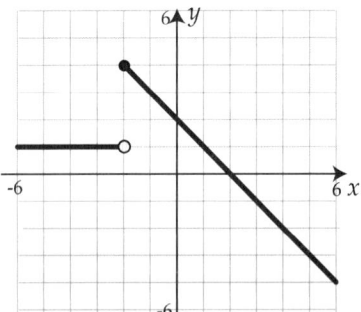

③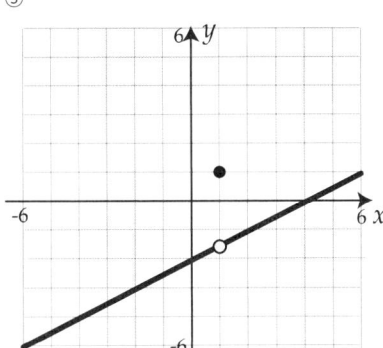

④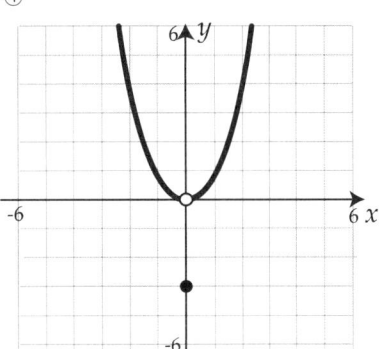

⑤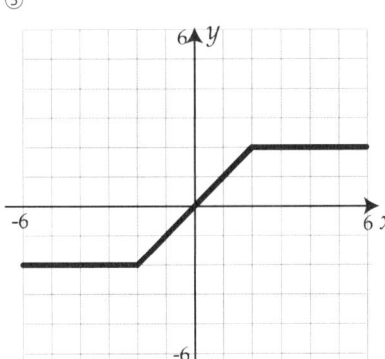

EXAMPLE 3. Evaluate the function.

① Find $f(0)$, $f(1)$, and $f(3)$ if $f(x) = \begin{cases} 2, & \text{if } x \leq 1 \\ x, & \text{if } x > 1 \end{cases}$

② Find $g(27)$, $g(-2)$, and $g(0)$ if $g(x) = \begin{cases} \dfrac{1}{x}, & \text{if } x < 0 \\ \sqrt[3]{x}, & \text{if } x \geq 0 \end{cases}$

③ Find $f(-4)$, $f(1)$, and $f(2)$ if $f(x) = \begin{cases} -2x+1, & \text{if } x < 1 \\ 2, & \text{if } x = 1 \\ x^2, & \text{if } x > 1 \end{cases}$

EXAMPLE 4. For what value of b will f(x) be continuous?

$$f(x) = \begin{cases} -x+4, & x > 3 \\ 2-\sqrt{x-b}, & x \leq 3 \end{cases}$$

4. Greatest Integer Function

$y = [x]$: the greatest integer that is less than or equal to x.

ex) [2.5] = ①_____

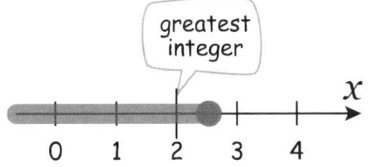

x	[x]
1	②
1.2	
1.5	
1.9	
2	
2.2	

-domain: ③_____

-range: ④_____

EXAMPLE 5. Evaluate.

① [2.1] ② [3.5]

③ [5] ④ [−3]

⑤ [−3.1] ⑥ [−6.5]

Blank : ① 2   ② 1,1,1,1,2,2   ③ All real Numbers (R)   ④ All integers (Z)

EXAMPLE 6. $f(x) = |x| + [x]$, what is $f(-2.5) = ?$

5. Expand Knowledge

EXAMPLE 7. * If a piecewise defined function f(x) is

$$f(x) = \begin{cases} [x] & , x \text{ is irrational} \\ x^2 & , x \text{ is rational} \end{cases}$$

, then what is $f(\sqrt{3}) + f(\sqrt{4}) + f(\sqrt{5}) = ?$

EXAMPLE 8. * If a piecewise defined function f(x) is

$$f(x) = \begin{cases} x+1 & , x \leq 2 \\ f(x-2) & , x > 2 \end{cases}$$

, then what is $f(1) + f(8) = ?$

Mia's Precalculus

1.5 Transforming Function

1. Transformation of the function

※ Translation

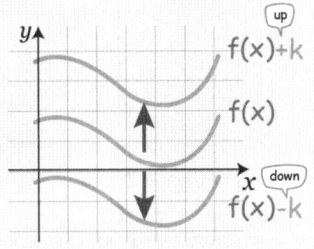

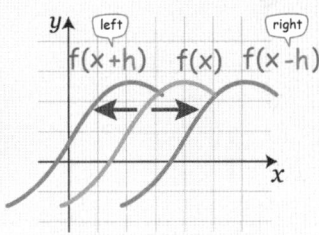

$$y = f(x) + k$$

: Vertically Shifted

① _____ k units

(k>0)

$$y = f(x - h)$$

: Horizontal Shift

to the ② _____ h units

(h>0)

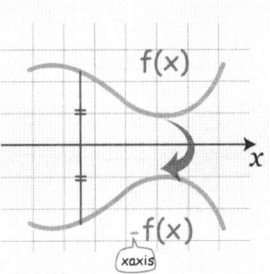

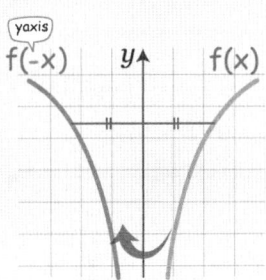

$$y = -f(x)$$

: reflected over ③ _____ -axis

$$y = f(-x)$$

: reflected over ④ _____ -axis

Blank : ① up ② right ③ x ④ y ⑤ 2 ⑥ shrink ⑦ 1/2 ⑧ 1/2 (=0.5) ⑨ stretch ⑩ 2

EXAMPLE 1. $f(x)$ is given. Graph the transformed function

① $y = f(x+2) - 3$

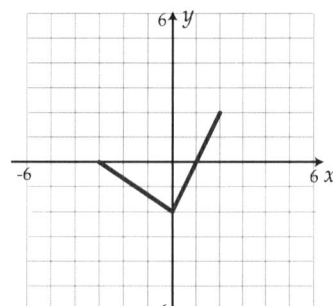

② $y = \sqrt{x-1} + 2$

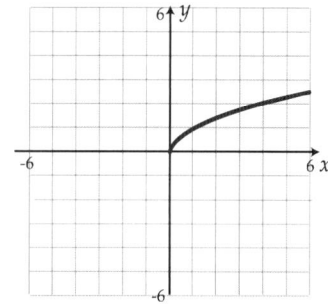

③ $y = -f(x) - 1$

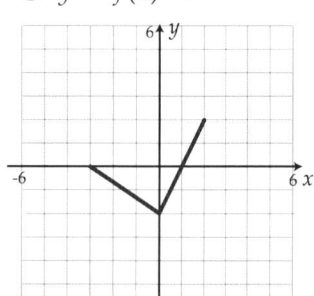

④ $y = \sqrt{-x} + 2$

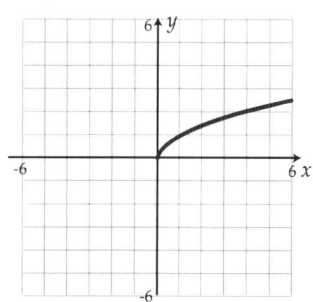

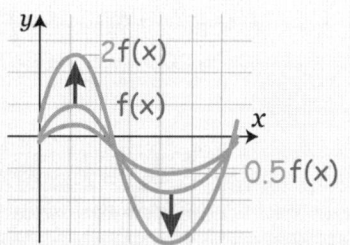

$y = 2f(x)$
: vertically stretch
by the factor ⑤_____

$y = 0.5\,f(x)$
: vertically shrink
by the factor ⑧_____

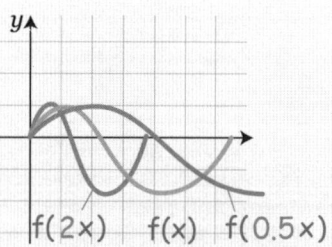

$y = f(2x)$
: horizontally ⑥_____
by the factor ⑦_____

$y = f(0.5\,x)$
: horizontally ⑨_____
by the factor ⑩_____

EXAMPLE 2. Graph the transformed function

① $y = \dfrac{f(x)}{2}$

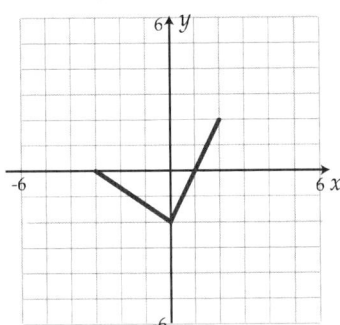

② $y = 2\sqrt{x}$

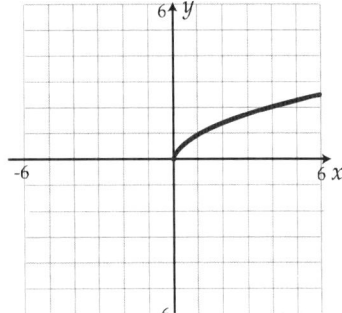

③ $y = f(2x)$

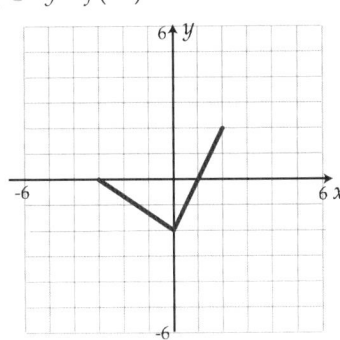

④ $y = \sqrt{\dfrac{x}{3}}$

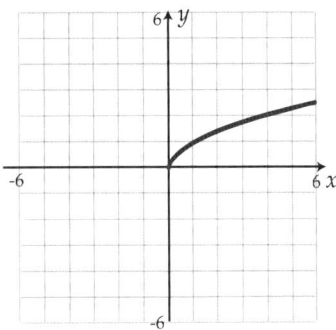

⑤ $y = f\left(\dfrac{x}{2}\right) - 1$

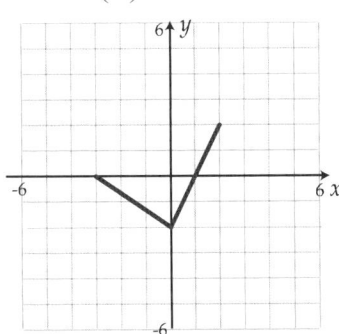

⑥ $y = 1 + \sqrt{2x}$

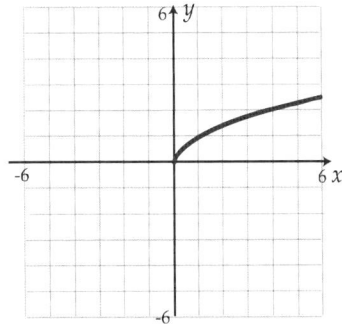

2. Transformation of the function

$y = f(x)$	original function (parent function)
$y = f(x) + k$	Vertically Shifted up k units
$y = f(x) - k$	Vertically Shifted down k units (k>0)
$y = f(x + h)$	Horizontal Shift to the left h units
$y = f(x - h)$	Horizontal Shift to the right h units (h>0)
$y = -f(x)$	reflected over x-axis
$y = f(-x)$	reflected over y-axis
$y = af(x),\ a > 1$	vertically stretch by the factor a
$\quad\quad 0 < a < 1$	vertically shrink by the factor a
$y = f(bx),\ b > 1$	horizontally shrink by the factor $1/b$
$\quad\quad 0 < b < 1$	horizontally stretch by the factor $1/b$

★ Few things to Remember

1) Order of Transformation is determined by order of operations.
   Reflect or stretch or compress → translation (shifting)

2) When you have $a\,f(bx+c) + d$? ①_____

☺ All in one (If a, b > 1, c, d > 0)

$$y = f(x) \;\longrightarrow\; y = -a\,f(-b(x+c)) + d$$

- refl. by x axis
- ver. stretch by a
- refl. by y axis
- hor. stretch by $1/b$
- Left c units
- Up d units

Blank: ① change to $a\,f\!\left(b\!\left(x + \dfrac{c}{b}\right)\right) + d$ (factor b out from bx+c)

EXAMPLE 3. Graph the transformed function

① $y = 2f(x) - 2$

② $y = f(x-1) + 3$

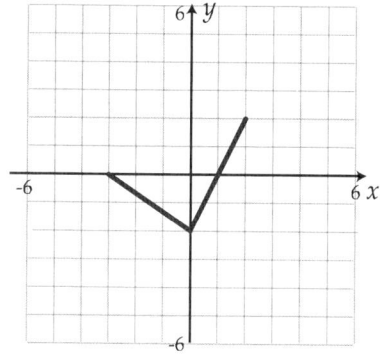
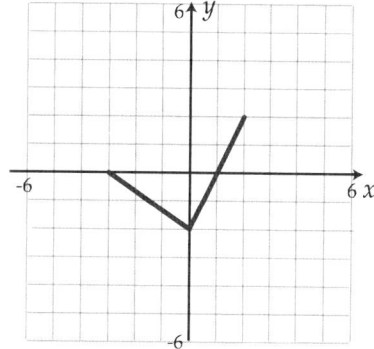

③ $y = f(-x-1)$

④ $y = f(-x+2)$

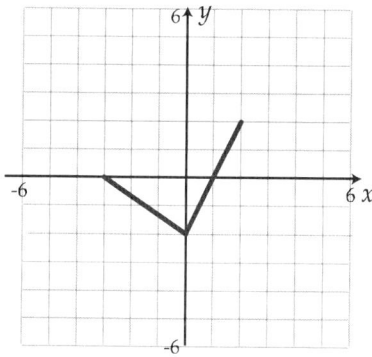
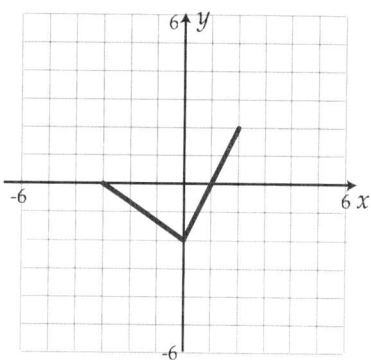

⑤ $y = -f(2x-4)$

⑥ $y = f(2x+2)$

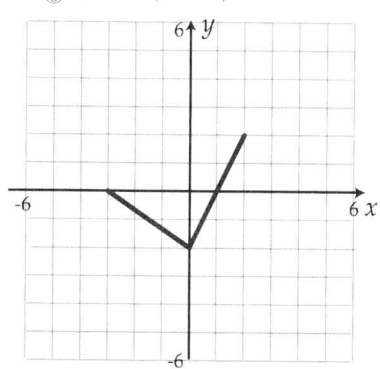
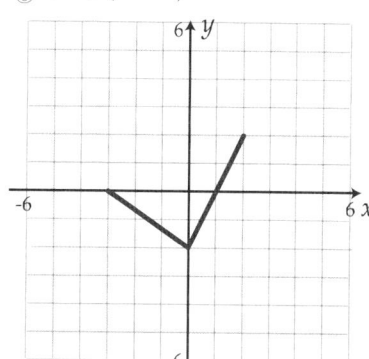

⑦ $y = f(0.5x+1)$

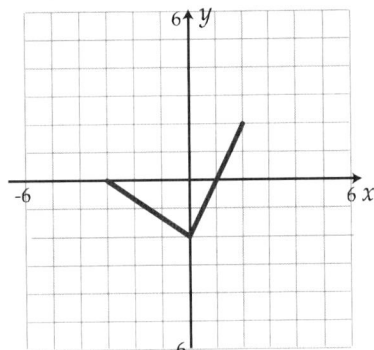

⑧ $y = f(0.5x)+1$

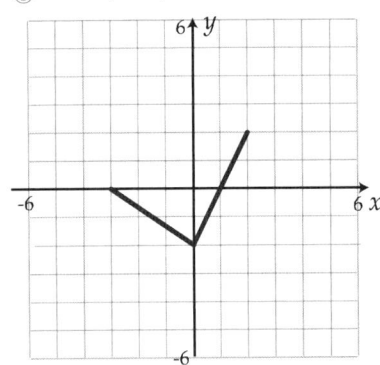

EXAMPLE 4. Graph the Function

① $f(x) = -x^2 + 4$ ② $f(x) = -\sqrt{-x} + 2$ ③ $f(x) = -2\sqrt[3]{x} - 2$

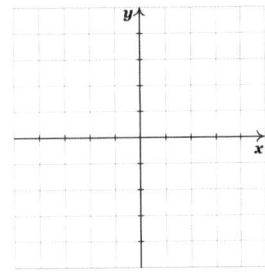 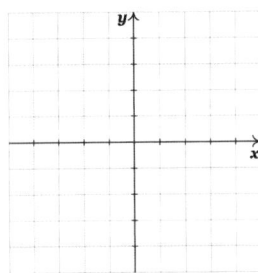 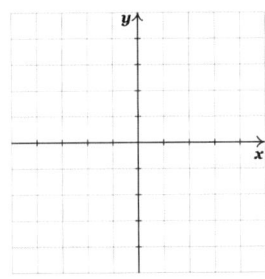

④ $f(x) = -(x-2)^3 - 1$ ⑤ $f(x) = -2\sqrt{3-x} - 1$ ⑥ $f(x) = |2-x| + 3$

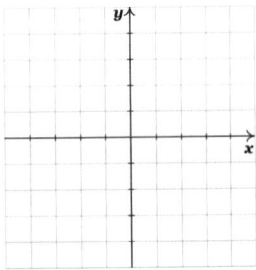 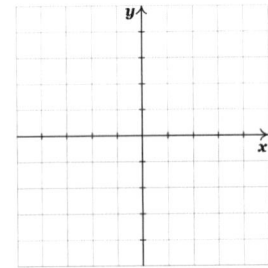 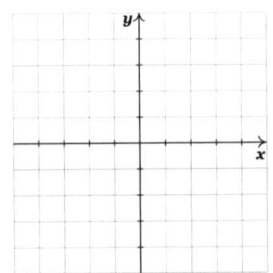

⑦ $f(x) = |2x - 4|$

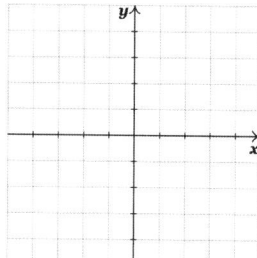

⑧ $f(x) = \sqrt{-3x - 18}$

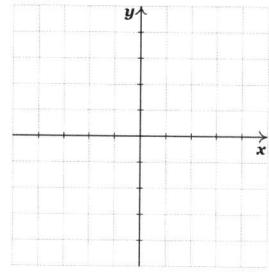

⑨ $f(x) = -\dfrac{1}{x-2} + 3$

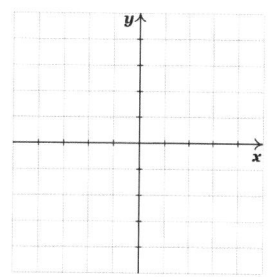

⑩ $f(x) = 1 - \dfrac{1}{x+2}$

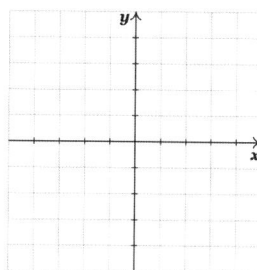

⑪ $f(x) = 2e^{-x-1} + 3$

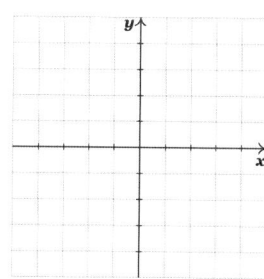

⑫ $f(x) = e^{2-x}$

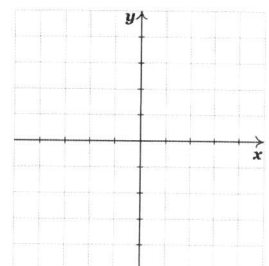

⑬ $f(x) = \log(0.5x + 1) + 2$

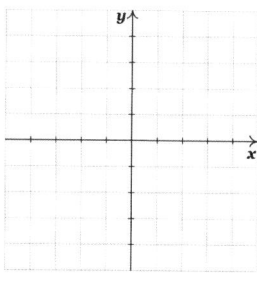

⑭ $f(x) = \log(2x + 1)$

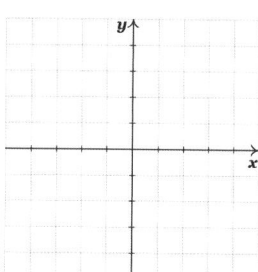

$e \approx 2.71...$ and e^x has a similar shape with 2^x.
(We will learn this more is Chapter 3)

EXAMPLE 5. * The point $A(4, -2)$ is on $f(x)$. Write the coordinates of the image of A on

① $2f(x)$

② $\dfrac{1}{2}f(x)$

③ $\dfrac{1}{2}f(x-2)$

④ $2f(x+1)$

⑤ $f(2x-2)$

⑥ $f(2x)-3$

⑦ $f(-x-1)$

⑧ $f(-x+2)$

3. Absolute Value transformations

The definition of absolute value is :

$$|x| = \begin{cases} \boxed{①} & , x \geq 0 \\ \boxed{②} & , x < 0 \end{cases}$$

"flip back to positive"

EXAMPLE 6. Express the given function as a piecewise function.

① $f(x) = |x-2|$ 　　　　　　　　② $f(x) = |2-x|$

③ $f(x) = \dfrac{|x-1|}{x-1}$ 　　　　　　　④ $f(x) = \dfrac{|x|}{x}$

⑤ $f(x) = |x^2 - 3x - 4|$ 　　　　　　⑥ $f(x) = |x^2 - x|$

Blank : ① x　② -x

⑦ $f(x) = |3-x| + x + 2$

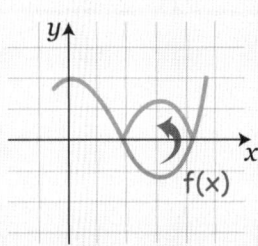

$y = |f(x)|$
: Fold up along the x axis

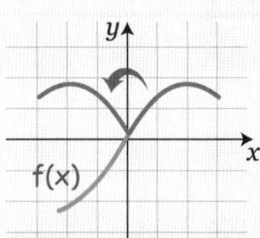

$y = f(|x|)$
: copy the right side and create a mirror image on the left
(like 'decalcomanie')

EXAMPLE 7. Graph the transformed function

① $y = |f(x)|$

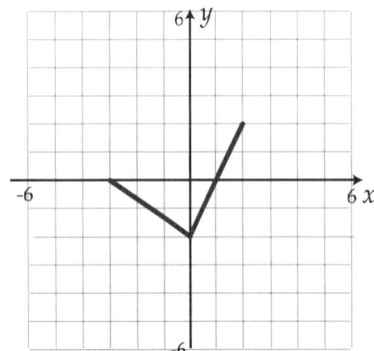

② $y = f(|x|)$

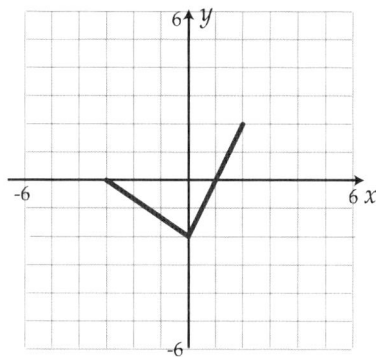

③ $y = |f(|x|)|$

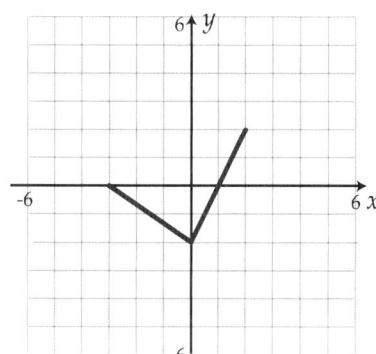

EXAMPLE 8. Graph the following Functions.

① $y = |x|(|x| - 2)$ ② $y = |x(x-2)|$

③ $y = |8 - x^3|$ ④ $y = 8 - |x^3|$

⑤ $y = |x^2 - 1| - 1$

4. Expand Knowledge

EXAMPLE 9.* If $f(x) = \sqrt{x} + 2$, find the function $g(x)$ which shows the graph of $f(x)$ after;

> vertical change : change of f(x) (= y)
> horizontal change : change of only x

① shifted horizontally left 3 followed by a shifted vertically down 4.

② shifted vertically up 5 followed by a shifted horizontally right 2.

③ shifted vertically up 4 followed by a vertical shrink of scale factor $\frac{1}{2}$.

④ vertical stretch of scale factor 2 followed by a shifted horizontally left 1.

⑤ shifted horizontally right 1 and vertically down 2 followed by a horizontal shrink of scale factor $\frac{1}{2}$

⑥ horizontal stretch of scale factor 2 followed by shifted vertically down 3 and horizontally left 2

⑦ shifted horizontally left 2 followed by a reflection through the y axis followed by a vertical stretch of scale factor 3.

⑧ vertical stretch of scale factor 2 followed by reflection through the x axis and followed by a shifted horizontally left 2.

⑨ reflection through the x axis and horizontal shrink of scale factor $\frac{1}{3}$ followed by a shifted horizontally right 1 and vertically down 1.

EXAMPLE 10. *Describe the transformation which transform the graph of $y = x^2 - 4x + 5$ to the graph of $y = 3x^2 + 24x + 45$.

EXAMPLE 11. *When $f(x) = 3x^2 + 18x + 26$, $f(x-a)$ is an even function. Find the value of a.

EXAMPLE 12. *When $y = x^2 + x + 2$ is shifted to the right 2 units and up 2 units, then the graph is tangent to the line $y = 2x + k$. What is the value k?

EXAMPLE 13. * Find the x of the intersection of $y = x^2 - 7|x| + 10$ and $y = 4$.

Mia's Precalculus
1.6 Composing Functions

1. Composite Functions

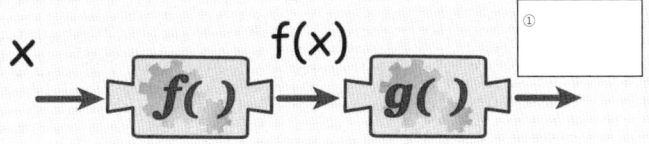

The result of f is sent through another function g.

Composition of g and f : $(g \circ f)(x) = g(f(x))$

outer function — inner function — composed with

We read it 'g composed with f'.

EXAMPLE 1. $f(x) = 2x + 3$ and $g(x) = \sqrt{x}$, then what is

① $(f \circ g)(x)$ ② $(g \circ f)(x)$

③ $(f \circ f)(x)$ ④ $(g \circ g)(x)$

Blank : ① g(f(x))

⑤ $(g \circ f)(3)$ ⑥ $(f \circ g)(1)$

⑦ $(f \circ f \circ g)(x)$

EXAMPLE 2. Use the table to find;

x	1	2	4	10	12
$f(x)$	-4	6	11	3	13

x	-5	-4	3	10	11
$g(x)$	4	10	6	2	12

① $(f \circ g)(-5)$ ② $(g \circ f)(1)$

③ $(f \circ g \circ f)(4)$ ④ $(f \circ g \circ g)(-4)$

EXAMPLE 3. Use the table to find;

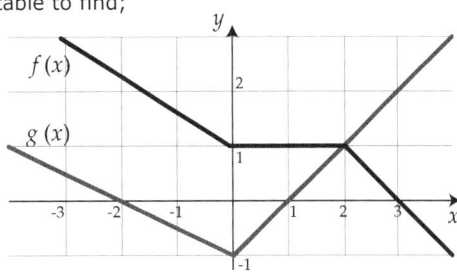

① $(f \circ g)(-2)$　　　　　　　② $(g \circ f)(1)$

③ $(g \circ f \circ f)(2)$　　　　　　④ $(f \circ g \circ f)(2)$

EXAMPLE 4. Find $(f \circ g)(x)$ and $(g \circ f)(x)$. Find the domain of each composite function.

☺ Tip ☞ You must find the intersection of

　　　　Domain of ①_____ function and domain ②_____ function!

　　　ex) Domain of $(f \circ g)(x)$ = domain of ③_____ ∩ domain of ④_____

① $f(x) = \dfrac{x}{x+3},\ g(x) = \dfrac{2}{x}$　　　　② $f(x) = \dfrac{2}{x},\ g(x) = \dfrac{4}{x+4}$

Blank : ① composite　② inner　③ (f ∘ g)(x)　④ g(x)

③ $f(x)=\sqrt{x}$, $g(x)=\sqrt{1-x}$ ④ $f(x)=\sqrt{x}$, $g(x)=\sqrt{x-2}$

⑤ $f(x)=x^2$, $g(x)=\sqrt{x}$ ⑥ $f(x)=x^2$, $g(x)=\sqrt{x-3}$

EXAMPLE 5. For a given function h(x), find its decomposition into simpler functions $h(x)=f(g(x))$. (There can be more than one answer)

① for $h(x)=\sqrt{x^2+1}$ ② for $h(x)=\dfrac{1}{(x^3+x+1)^2}$

③ for $h(x)=(x+1)+2\sqrt{x+1}+3$ ④ for $h(x)=(x-3)^2+2(x-3)-5$

2. Expand Knowledge

EXAMPLE 6. *If $(f \circ g)(x) = 16x+1$ and $f(x) = 4x+5$, find $g(x)$.

EXAMPLE 7. * If $(f \circ g)(x) = 16x+1$ and $g(x) = 4x+5$, find $f(x)$.

EXAMPLE 8. *If $(f \circ g)(x) = \dfrac{10x+1}{3}$ and $g(x) = 5x+2$, find $f(x+1)$.

EXAMPLE 9. * Graph of $f(x)$ is given below. Find the number of distinct x that satisfies $(f \circ f)(x) = 4$.

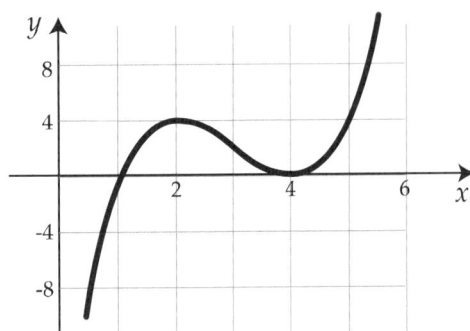

EXAMPLE 10. * Given that we can denote

$$\underbrace{f \circ f \circ f \circ \cdots \circ f}_{n \text{ times}} \text{ as } f^n,$$

then if $f(x) = 1 + x$, then what is $f^{10}(x)$?

EXAMPLE 11. *Given that we can denote

$$\underbrace{f \circ f \circ f \circ \cdots \circ f}_{n \text{ times}} \text{ as } f^n,$$

then if $f(x) = \dfrac{x}{1-x}$, then what is $f^{30}(x)$?

Mia's Precalculus

1.7 Inverse Function

1. One to One Function

※ One-to-one Function

: every member of "X" has **its own unique** matching member in "Y".

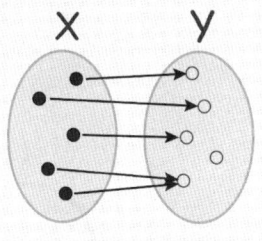

① _____   ② _____

To be a 'One to one function';

① ③ _____ has to be different!   ($f(x_1) \neq f(x_2)$ whenever $x_1 \neq x_2$)

② Satisfy the ④ _____ test and ⑤ _____ test

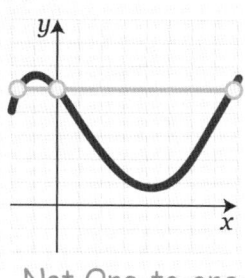
Not One-to-one function !

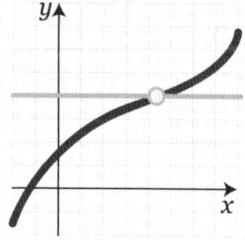
One-to-one Function !

If a horizontal line crosses the curve twice or above,
then it is NOT one to one function.

Blank : ① function But NOT One-to-one   ② One-to-one function   ③ x, y   ④ vertical line   ⑤ horizontal line

EXAMPLE 1. Determine whether it is a one-to-one function, just a function, or not a function.

① $\{(3,-1),(2,2),(-1,-11),(5,-12)\}$ ② $\{(3,-1),(-1,2),(3,-11),(5,-12)\}$

③ $\{(-2,0),(3,-.5),(1,9),(2,0)\}$ ④ $\{(0,1),(1,2),(3,4),(5,1)\}$

⑤ $\{(2,2),(2,1),(2,.5),(2,.5)\}$ ⑥ $\{(1,2),(2,3),(3,4),(4,5)\}$

⑦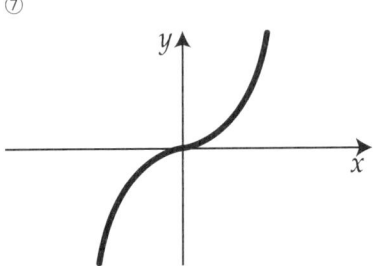

⑧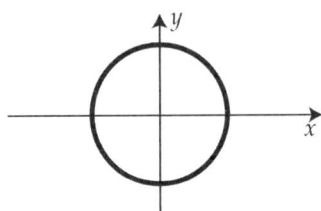

⑨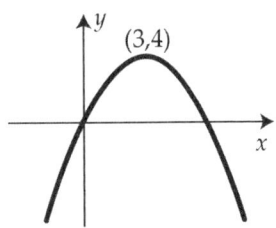

⑩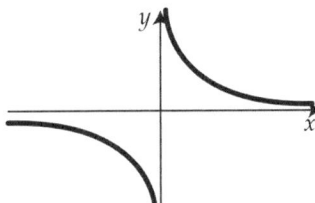

⑪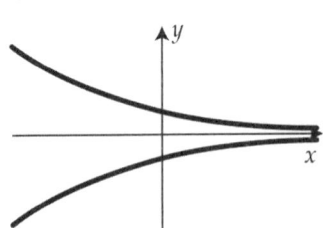

⑫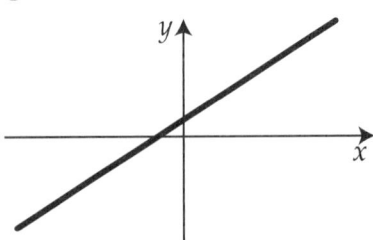

2. Inverse Function

※ Inverse function

When we **switch input(x) and output(y)** of a function $f(x)$,

we will have ① _____ which is the "② _____ Function of $f(x)$"

- If $f(a) = b$, then ③ _____.   ex) $f(2) = 5 \Leftrightarrow 2 = f^{-1}(5)$

- $f^{-1}(x) \neq \dfrac{1}{f(x)}$ (-1 is not a power, it is a 'inverse' notation)

$f^{-1}(x)$?? We switch x and y.

EXAMPLE 2. Use the table to find;

x	1	2	4	10	12
$f(x)$	-4	6	11	3	13

x	-5	-4	3	10	11
$g(x)$	4	10	6	2	12

Blank : ① $f^{-1}(x)$ ② inverse ③ $a = f^{-1}(b)$

① $f(2)$ ② $g(-4)$

③ $f^{-1}(3)$ ④ $g^{-1}(12)$

⑤ $(f \circ g^{-1})(2)$ ⑥ $(g^{-1} \circ f^{-1})(6)$

⑦ $(f \circ f^{-1})(11)$ ⑧ $(g^{-1} \circ g)(-4)$

EXAMPLE 3. Use the table to find;

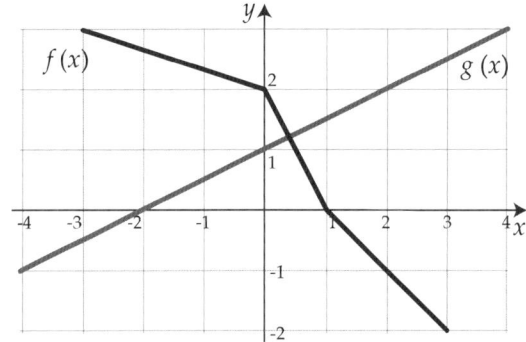

① $f(2)$ ② $g(0)$

③ $f^{-1}(2)$ ④ $g^{-1}(0)$

⑤ $(f^{-1} \circ g)(-2)$ ⑥ $(f^{-1} \circ g)(0)$

⑦ $(g^{-1} \circ f)(2)$ ⑧ $(g \circ f^{-1})(-1)$

⑨ $(f \circ f^{-1})(-1)$ ⑩ $(g \circ g^{-1})(-1)$

3. Finding the Inverse Algebraically

※ How to find the inverse function
① Write $y = f(x)$.
② **Switch x and y.**
③ Solve for y.

EXAMPLE 4. Find the inverse of a function.

① $f(x) = 6x + 7$

② $f(x) = \dfrac{4}{x}$

③ $f(x) = \dfrac{1}{2}(2x-3)^3 + 2$

④ $f(x) = 2\sqrt[3]{x+1}$

⑤ $f(x) = x^2 + 1, \ x \geq 0$

⑥ $f(x) = x^2 + 1, \ x < 0$

⑦ $f(x) = (x-2)^2 + 3, \ x \leq 2$

⑧ $f(x) = 2(3-x)^2, \ x \leq 3$

⑨ $f(x) = \dfrac{2x+6}{-7x-3}$ ⑩ $f(x) = \dfrac{-3x+4}{x-2}$

⑪ $f(x) = \dfrac{2}{3+x}$ ⑫ $f(x) = \dfrac{-3x}{x+2}$

※ Inverse of Rational Functions shortcut

$$y^{-1} = \left(\dfrac{ax+b}{cx+d}\right)^{-1} = \dfrac{dx-b}{-cx+a}$$

Switch a, d and negate (put -) on b, c.

EXAMPLE 5. Find the inverse function and determine whether the inverse represents a function.

① $f = \{(6, 0), (-1, 1), (-3, 2), (-5, 3)\}$

② $g = \{(-7, 5), (-5, 7), (6, 5), (-6, 9)\}$

> Only **ONE-TO-ONE function** has an inverse function!
> If f is NOT a one-to-one?
> Restrict the domain(cut the graph) and make a one to one!

EXAMPLE 6. Does the function have an inverse function? If not, then restrict its domain and find the inverse of the function with the restricted domain.

① $y = (x-2)^3$ ② $y = \sqrt{x-2}$

③ $y = (x+2)^2 - 1$ ④ $y = (x-1)^2 + 2$

⑤ $*y = |x+1|$

⑥ $*y = x^2 + 2x + 2$

4. Facts about Inverse Function

1. If $f(a) = b$, then ①_____.

2. Only **ONE-TO-ONE function** has an <u>inverse function</u>!
   If f is NOT a one-to-one?
   Restrict the domain(cut the graph) and make a one to one!

3. The domain of f is the ②_____ of f^{-1}

   and the range of f is the ③_____ of f^{-1}.

4. If the point (a, b) lies on graph of f ,

   then the point ④_____ must lie on the graph of f^{-1}.

5. $(f \circ f^{-1})(x) =$ ⑤_____ and $(f^{-1} \circ f)(x) =$ ⑥_____.

6. f^{-1} is a reflection of the graph of f in the line ⑦_____.

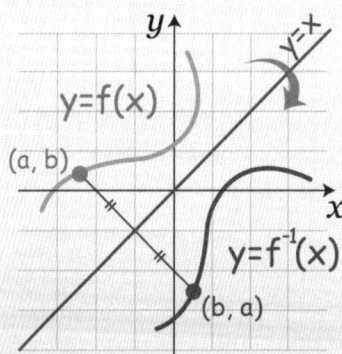

Blank : ① $a = f^{-1}(b)$ ② range   ③ domain   ④ (b, a)   ⑤ x   ⑥ x   ⑦ y = x

82 Mia's Precalculus

EXAMPLE 7. Draw the graph of the inverse function $f^{-1}(x)$.

①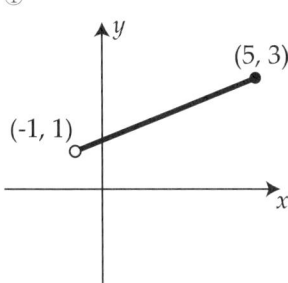

②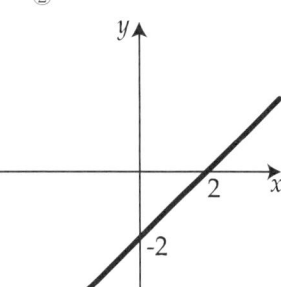

③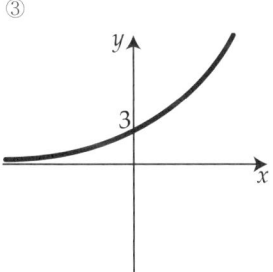

④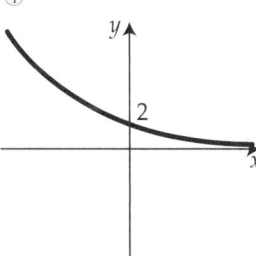

⑤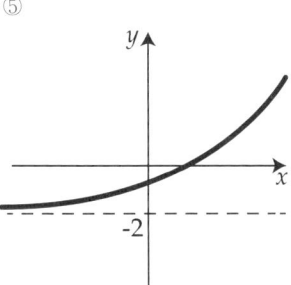

⑥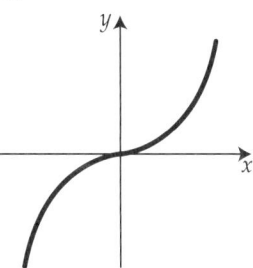

⑦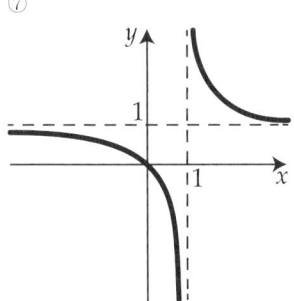

⑧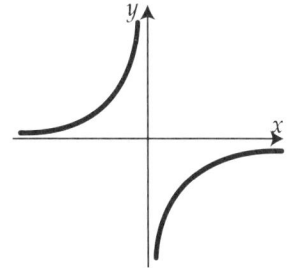

EXAMPLE 8. Does the function have an inverse function? If not, then restrict its domain and graph the inverse of the function with the restricted domain.

①
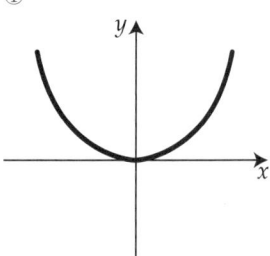

②
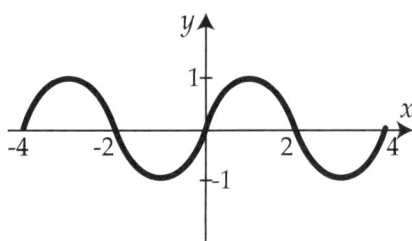

EXAMPLE 9. Determine i) the domain of the function, ii) the range of the function, iii) the domain of the inverse, and iv) the range of the inverse.

> ☺ Tip ☞ $f^{-1}(x)$?? We **switch x and y**.
>
> = switch ① _____ and ② _____.

① $f(x) = \dfrac{3x+1}{x+2}$

Blank : ① domain ② range

② $f(x) = x^2, x < 0$

③ $f(x) = \sqrt{x+2}$

④ $f(x) = x^3 + 2$

5. Self-Inverse Function

A function that satisfy

$f(x) = f^{-1}(x)$ or $f(f(x)) = x$

is called **self-inverse function**.

To be a self-inverse function, the function should be symmetrical about the line y=x.

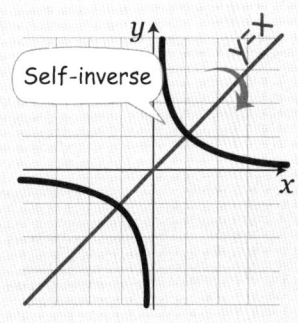

EXAMPLE 10. Find the function which satisfies $f(x) = f^{-1}(x)$.

a) $y = x$

b) $y = -x$

c) $y = 2x$

d) $y = -x + 2$

e) $y = -2x$

f) $y = \dfrac{1}{x}$

g) $y = -\dfrac{1}{x}$

h) $y = \dfrac{2}{x-1} + 1$

i) $y = \dfrac{1}{x-1}$

6. Expand Knowledge

EXAMPLE 11. * A piecewise function f(x) is given. Determine a so that f(x) has an inverse.

$$f(x) = \begin{cases} ax, & x \geq 0 \\ -x^2, & x < 0 \end{cases}$$

EXAMPLE 12. * If a function $f(2x-1)=4x+3$ is defined for all real numbers, then what is the inverse function of f(x)?

EXAMPLE 13. * If $f\left(\dfrac{x+1}{x-1}\right)=2x$, then what is $f^{-1}(6)=?$

EXAMPLE 14. * Find the inverse function for $f(x)=\dfrac{x^2-4}{2x^2+1}$, $x<0$.

Part 2
Polynomial and Rational Functions

2.1 Polynomial Functions
2.2 Diving Polynomials
2.3 Real Zeros of Poly
2.4 Fundamental Theorem of Algebra
2.5 Rational Function
2.6 Polynomial and Rational Inequalities

Mia's Precalculus
2.1 Polynomial Functions

1. Polynomial

poly- means ① _____

-nomial means ② _____

※ A **polynomial** function of degree n :

$$P(x) = \underbrace{\underset{\text{Leading Coefficient}}{a_n} x^{\overset{\text{Degree}}{n}}}_{\text{Leading Term}} + a_{n-1}x^{n-1} + \cdots + a_1 x + \underbrace{a_0}_{\text{Constant Term}}$$

where n is a nonnegative integer and $a_n \neq 0$.

$a_n, a_{n-1}, \ldots, a_1, a_0$ is called the **coefficients**.

a_0 is called the **constant coefficient** or **constant term**.

$a_n x^n$ is the **leading term** and a_n is the **leading coefficient**.

ex)

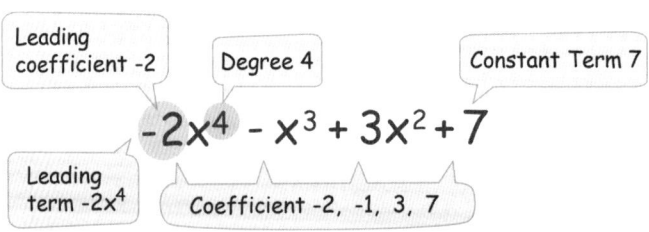

$-2x^4 - x^3 + 3x^2 + 7$

- Leading coefficient -2
- Degree 4
- Constant Term 7
- Leading term $-2x^4$
- Coefficient $-2, -1, 3, 7$

Blank : ① many ② terms

Degree of Polynomial: highest power that appears

Polynomial or not?
  ① no division by a variable.
  ② Coefficient is a ①_____.
  ③ exponents can only be nonnegative integers (②_____)

EXAMPLE 1. Determine which of the following is polynomial function. For those that are, state the degree.

① $f(x) = 2 - 3x^4$

② $f(x) = \sqrt{x}$

③ $g(x) = \dfrac{x}{x^2 - 1}$

④ $f(x) = -7$

⑤ $k(x) = -2x^3(x-1)^2$

⑥ $f(x) = \dfrac{x}{3}$

⑦ $h(x) = \sqrt[3]{x^2}$

⑧ $k(x) = \pi$

Blank : ① real number   ② 0,1,2,3,...

2. Shape of Polynomial Functions

Each graph, based on their degree, has a different shape and characteristics.

when a > 0	when a < 0
Linear function y = ax + b	
Quadratic Function y = ax² + bx + c	
Cubic Function y = ax³ + bx² + cx + d	
Quartic Function y = ax⁴ + bx³ + cx² + dx + e	

We can find ;

End Behavior when degree is odd : a > 0 ①_____ a < 0 ②_____

End Behavior when degree is even : a > 0 ③_____ a < 0 ④_____

Number of turning point of cubic Function : ⑤_____

Number of turning point of quartic Function : ⑥_____

> ※ Degree and Turning points
>
> If $f(x)$ is a polynomial function of degree n,
> then the graph of $f(x)$ has at most ⑦_____ turning points.

Blank : ① ↓↑ (down to up) ② ↑↓ (up to down) ③ ↑↑ (both up) ④ ↓↓ (both down) ⑤ 2 or 1 ⑥ 3,2 or 1 ⑦ n-1

3. Graphing Polynomial

1) End behavior Model

※ The **end behavior** (shape of the end of graph)

of polynomial $P(x) = a_n x^n + a_{n-1} x^{n-1} + \ldots + a_1 x^1 + a_0$ is determined by

*the leading term*①_____.

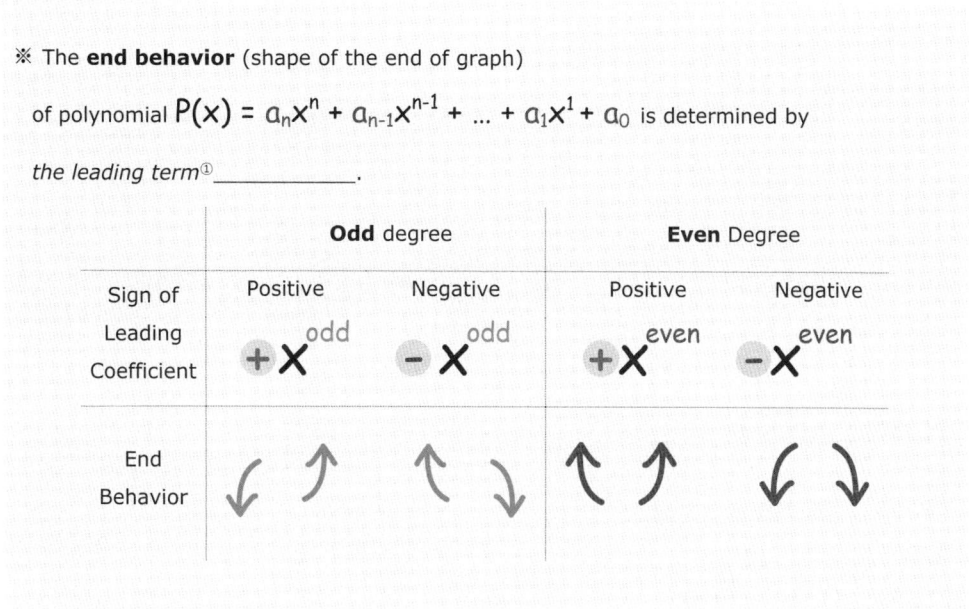

EXAMPLE 2. Determine the end behavior for each graph.

As $x \to \infty$ means when x gets bigger(go to the right),

as $x \to -\infty$ means when x gets smaller (go to the left)

$y \to \infty$ means the graph is going ②_____.

$y \to -\infty$ means the graph is going ③_____.

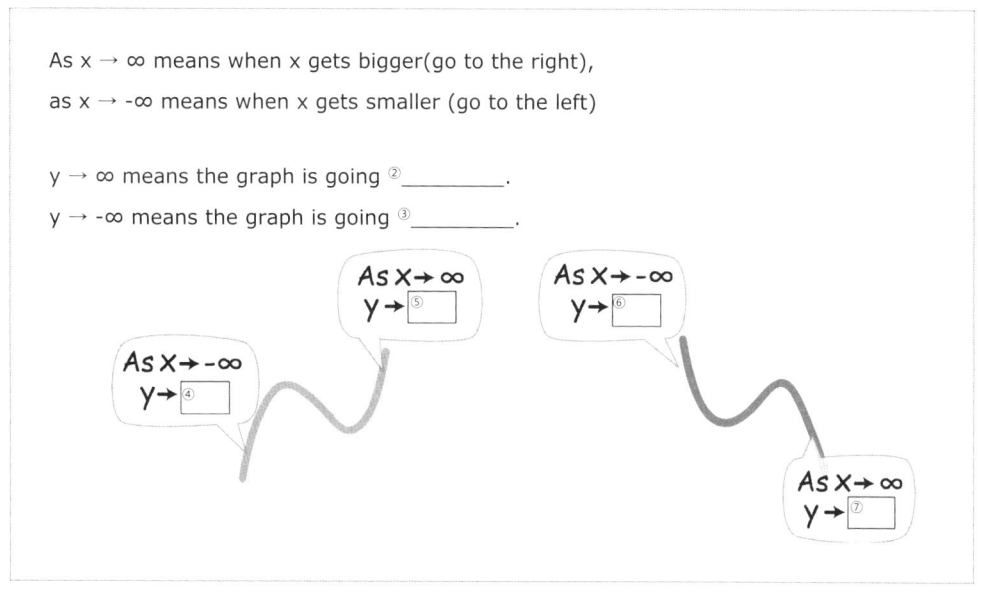

Blank : ① $a_n x^n$ ② up ③ down ④ $-\infty$ ⑤ ∞ ⑥ ∞ ⑦ $-\infty$

① $f(x) = 4(x+4)(x+3)^3$

② $f(x) = -(x-3)^2(x-1)^3$

③ $f(x) = -2x^3(x^2-2)^2$

④ $f(x) = 0.5x(x+4)^3(x^2-2)^2$

⑤ $f(x) = -2(x-3)^2(x^2+4)^3$

⑥ $f(x) = 3x^2(x^3-2)^3(x^2+1)$

2) Zeros of Polynomial

① When we have a ①_____ **form** of a polynomial,

then we can find the zeros(=roots = x intercept) using *zero product property*.

$$X \cdot Y = 0 \text{ then } X = 0 \text{ or } Y = 0$$

② Multiplicity: how often a root appears.

ex) $(x-1)^2$: The root(zero) x = 1 appears twice, so the multiplicity is ②____.

Odd multiplicity	**Even** multiplicity
$(x-r)^{odd}$	$(x-r)^{even}$
③_____ the x axis at r.	④_____ the x axis at r.

ex)

$$P(x) = -2(x-1)^2 (x+2)^3$$

(multiplicity)

P(x) ⑤(crosses/touches) at x = 1, and ⑥(crosses/touches) at x = -2.

Blank : ① factored ② 2 ③ cross ④ touch ⑤ touches ⑥ crosses

③ Shape of the graph near zero
  : 3 or more multiplicities <u>flattens out</u> near zero.

$(x-r)^{odd}$ $(x-r)^1$ or $(x-r)^{3 \text{ or more}}$ or

$(x-r)^{even}$ $(x-r)^2$ or $(x-r)^{4 \text{ or more}}$ or

2) Finding y-intercepts

For every polynomial function, <u>constant</u> term is the y-intercept.
(or plug in x = 0)

EXAMPLE 3. For the polynomial,
a) determine the end behavior,
b) determine whether the graph crosses or touches the x-axis at each x-intercept.
c) find the y intercept.
d) Sketch the graph briefly.

① $f(x) = (x-2)(x+3)(2x-1)$ ② $f(x) = (x+1)^2(x-2)$

③ $f(x) = -2x^2(x-2)$ ④ $f(x) = -2x^3(x-2)^2$

⑤ $f(x) = -2(x+2)^2(x-1)^4$ ⑥ $f(x) = (x-1)^2(x-5)^3$

⑦ $f(x) = -2x^2(x-1)^3(x+6)^4$ ⑧ $f(x) = x(x-\sqrt{3})^3(x-2)^4$

⑨ $f(x) = x^3(x+2)^3(x-3)^4$

⑩ $f(x) = -2x^2(x+1)^3(x-3)^2$

⑪ $f(x) = x(x^2+1)(x^2-5)$

⑫ $f(x) = x^3(x^2+2x+3)(x+2)$

⑬ $f(x) = (x-1)^2(x^2+2x+5)^3$

⑭ $f(x) = -x(x-1)^2(x^2+3x+3)$

EXAMPLE 4. Factor the polynomial and use the factored form to find the zeros. Then sketch the graph.

$$a^2 - b^2 = (a \bigcirc b)(a \bigcirc b)$$

$$a^3 - b^3 = (a \bigcirc b)(a^2 \bigcirc ab \bigcirc b^2)$$
$$a^3 + b^3 = (a \bigcirc b)(a^2 \bigcirc ab \bigcirc b^2)$$

① $f(x) = x^3 - x^2 - 2x$ 　　　　② $f(x) = x^4 + 2x^3 - 8x^2$

③ $f(x) = x^3 + x^2 - x - 1$ 　　　　④ $f(x) = x^3 - 2x^2 - 4x + 8$

⑤ $f(x) = -2x^4 - x^3 + 3x^2$ 　　　　⑥ $f(x) = x^5 + 8x^2$

Blank : ① + −　② − + +　③ + − +

⑦ $f(x) = x^4 + x^3 - x - 1$

EXAMPLE 5. Find lowest order polynomial equation for each of these graphs.

①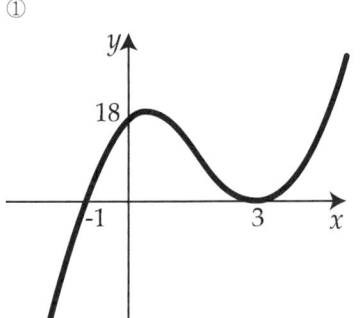

②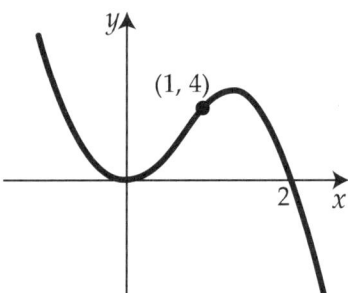

③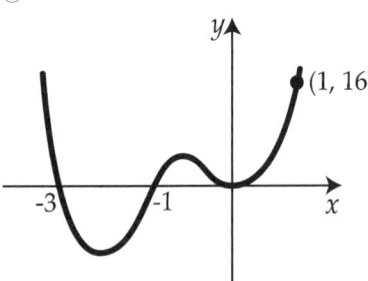

④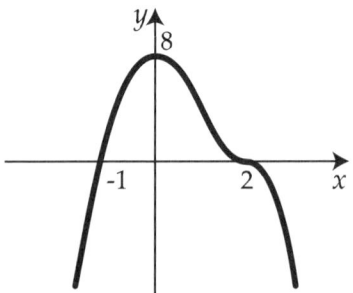

⑤

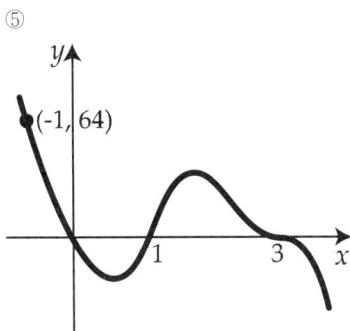

4. Expand Knowledge

EXAMPLE 6. *When a is a real number, m is odd and n is even, what could be the graph of $y = a(x-2)^m(x+1)^n$?

EXAMPLE 7. * Sketch the graph of $y = -(x-a)^2(x-b)$ where $a < b$. How many solutions does the equation $-(x-a)^2(x-b) = k$ have when $k < 0$?

Mia's Precalculus

2.2 Dividing Polynomials

1. Dividing Polynomial

When you divide a polynomial P(x) by another polynomial D(x), we get a quotient polynomial ①_____ and a remainder polynomial ②_____.

$$D(x) \overline{\smash{\big)}\, P(x)} \quad \begin{array}{c} Q(x) \\ \vdots \\ R(x) \end{array}$$

We can rewrite this as;

dividend → P(x) = D(x)·Q(x) + R(x)
          divisor   Quotient   Remainder

or

dividend → $\dfrac{P(x)}{D(x)}$ = Q(x) + $\dfrac{R(x)}{D(x)}$
divisor →

Notice that the **degree of the remainder** is always *less than* the **degree of the divisor**.

2. Long Division of Polynomial

This is a method similar to division for *Numbers*.

Divide $2x^3 - 7x^2 + 5$ by $x - 3$.

※ **Be sure that**

Rewrite the polynomial P(x) from highest to lowest exponent.

When you have a missing term, include the missing terms with a coefficient of ③_____.

Blank : ① Q(x)   ② R(x)   ③ 0

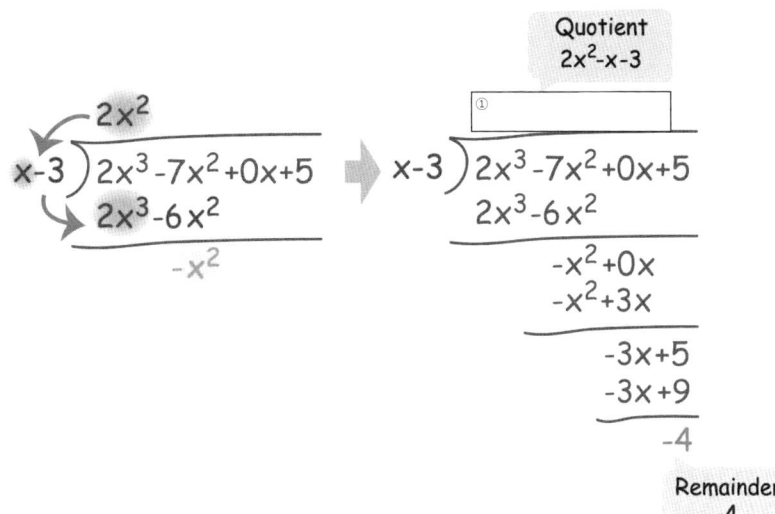

You can write the result as ;

② _____

EXAMPLE 1. Use long division to perform the division.

① $\dfrac{x^3 - 9x^2 + 27x - 27}{x^2 - 3}$ ② $\dfrac{x^3 + 6x + 2}{x^2 - 2x + 2}$

Blank : ① $2x^2 - x - 3$ ② $2x^2 - x - 3 + \dfrac{-4}{x-3}$

③ $\dfrac{4x^3 - 3}{x + 5}$

④ $\dfrac{3x^4 - 5x^3 - 10x + 2}{x^2 + x + 2}$

3. Synthetic Division

Synthetic division is a quick method of dividing polynomials;
it can be used *only* when we divide a polynomial by ①_____.

Divide $2x^3 - 7x^2 + 5$ by $x - 3$ using synthetic division.

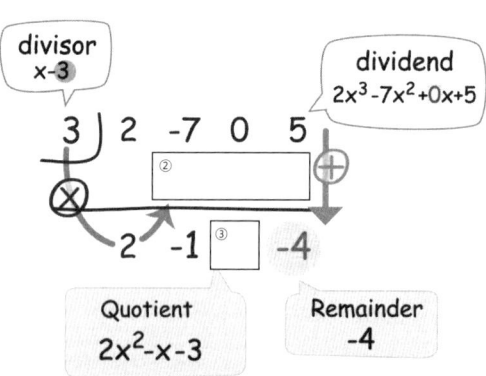

Blank : ① x − c (linear)   ② 6 -3 -9   ③ -3

EXAMPLE 2. Use synthetic division to perform the division.

① $\dfrac{x^3 - 9x^2 + 27x - 27}{x - 3}$

② $\dfrac{3x^3 + 5x^2 - 4x + 1}{x + 4}$

③ $\dfrac{x^3 - 8x + 2}{x + 2}$

④ $\dfrac{5x^3 + x^2 - 3}{x + 3}$

⑤ $\dfrac{x^4 - 5x^2 - 10}{x - 4}$

⑥ $\dfrac{2x^4 - 10x^3 + 8}{x - 2}$

⑦ $\dfrac{2x^3 + 4x^2 - 2x + 3}{2x - 1}$

⑧ $\dfrac{6x^3 - 10x^2 + 5x + 2}{2x - 3}$

4. The Remainder Theorem

When you divide a polynomial $P(x)$ by $(x-c)$, the remainder R will be ① _____ .

☺ Proof:

The polynomial $P(x)$ can be expressed as; ② _____

And when we plug in $x=c$; ③ _____

EXAMPLE 3. Find the remainder using remainder theorem.

Just calculate ④ _____ !

① $\dfrac{2x^3 - 3x^2 + 9x + 1}{x-2}$

② $\dfrac{x^3 - x^2 + x + 5}{x+1}$

③ $\dfrac{x^{10} + 3x^7 - 7x + 6}{x-1}$

④ $\dfrac{x^{117} + 3x^{10} - 3x + 1}{x+1}$

Blank : ① $P(c)$ ② $P(x) = (x - c) \cdot Q + R$ ③ $P(c) = (c - c) \cdot Q + R \Rightarrow R = P(c)$ ④ $P(c)$

EXAMPLE 4. For each polynomial, evaluate $P(c)$.

① $P(x) = 5x^4 + 30x^3 - 40x^2 - 36x + 14$.
Find $P(-7)$.

② $P(x) = 2x^4 - 21x^3 - 30x^2 + 8x - 100$.
Find $P(12)$.

③ $P(x) = 3x^3 + 4x^2 - 2x - 1$.
Find $P\left(\dfrac{2}{3}\right)$.

④ $P(x) = x^3 - x + 1$.
Find $P\left(\dfrac{1}{4}\right)$.

EXAMPLE 5. If the polynomial $f(x) = 2x^3 - kx^2 - 5x + 2$ is divided by $x - 2$, the remainder is 2. What is the value of k?

5. Factor Theorem

When you divide a polynomial $P(x)$ by $(x-c)$, what happen when remainder is 0? ①

> When $P(c) = 0$,
> then $(x-c)$ is the **factor** of the polynomial P.
> then polynomial P is **divisible by** $(x-c)$.

EXAMPLE 6. Use the Factor Theorem to determine whether the function
$f(x) = x^4 + x^3 - 19x^2 + 11x + 30$ has a factor;

① $x-1$ ② $x+1$

③ $x-2$ ④ $x+2$

⑤ $x-3$

Blank : ① $P(x) = (x - c) \cdot Q \Rightarrow (x - c)$ is factor of $P(x)$.

EXAMPLE 7. If a polynomial P(x) = $x^2 + kx - 8$ has a factor of $x+3$, then what is the value of constant k?

EXAMPLE 8. If the polynomial $f(x) = 2x^3 - kx^2 - 5x + 2$ is divisible by $x-2$, what is the value of k?

6. Expand Knowledge

EXAMPLE 9. *When you divide the polynomial $x^3 - px^2 + qx + 2$ by $x^2 - 3x + 2$ the remainder is 2. Find p and q.

EXAMPLE 10. *When you divide the polynomial $x^3 + ax^2 - bx + 3$ by $x^2 - 1$, the remainder is $x - 1$. Find a and b.

EXAMPLE 11. *The polynomial $x^2 - (k+1)x - 4$ has a factor $(x - k + 1)$. Find k.

Mia's Precalculus

2.3 Real Zeros of Polynomial

1. The Rational Zeros Theorem

The **possible rational zeros** of the polynomial

$P(x) = a_n x^n + a_{n-1} x^{n-1} + \ldots + a_1 x^1 + a_0$ is

$$\text{Possible Rational Zeroes of } P(x) = \frac{\text{Factors of constant term } (a_0)}{\text{Factors of Leading Coefficient } (a_n)}$$

ex) Find the possible rational zeros of $f(x) = 2x^3 + x^2 - 13x + 6$.

$$\text{possible Rational Zeros of } f(x) = \frac{\text{factor of } \textcircled{1}}{\text{factor of } \textcircled{2}} = \frac{\textcircled{3}}{}$$

EXAMPLE 1. List the possible rational zeros of the polynomial function.

① $f(x) = 6x^4 + 4x^3 - 3x^2 + 2$ ② $f(x) = 2x^4 - 5x^2 + 5x - 8$

③ $f(x) = 5x^4 + 6x^3 - 2x^2 - 8$ ④ $f(x) = 4x^3 - 2x^2 + x + 7$

Blank : ① 6 ② 2 ③ $\pm 1, \pm 2, \pm 3, \pm 6, \pm \frac{1}{2}, \pm \frac{3}{2}$

2. Descartes' Rule of Signs

Descartes rule of signs determines the *'possible'* number of positive and negative zeros

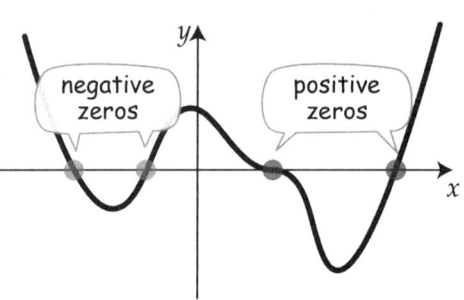

First, rewrite the polynomial P(x) from highest to lowest exponent (ignore any missing terms) Then, count how many times there is a change of sign.

※ Descartes' Rule of Sign
Number of positive roots equals the number of sign changes of P(x) , or minus even integers (-2, -4, ..).
Number of negative roots equals the number of sign changes of P(-x) , or minus even integers.

$$P(x) = +2x^5 -3x^4 -3x^3 +4x^2 -x -1$$

3 Sign changes : 3 or 1 positive roots

$$P(-x) = -2x^5 -3x^4 +3x^3 +4x^2 +x -1$$

2 Sign changes : 2 or 0 negative roots

EXAMPLE 2. Use Descartes' Rule of Signs to determine how many positive and how many negative real zeros the polynomial can have.

① $P(x) = -x^3 - x^2 - x + 2$ ② $P(x) = x^4 - 3x^3 + 2x^2 - x - 3$

③ $P(x) = x^5 + 2x^3 - x^2 + 5x - 1$ ④ $P(x) = 3x^7 - 8x^5 + 4x^4 - 4x^3 - 4x^2 + 2$

3. Finding All Rational Zeros

EXAMPLE 3. Factor the polynomial $f(x) = 2x^3 + x^2 - 13x + 6$, and find all real zeros.

i) Find the *first zero*

(Using possible rational zeros, find the first number that makes f = 0)

$f(1) =$

$f(-1) =$

$f(2) =$

ii) Divide (using synthetic division)

iii) Repeat and find all zeros

EXAMPLE 4. Factor the polynomial and find all real zeros.

① $P(x) = x^3 + 3x^2 - 4x - 12$

② $P(x) = 2x^3 + 5x^2 + x - 2$

③ $P(x) = 2x^3 + 4x^2 + 5x + 3$

④ $P(x) = 2x^3 - 7x^2 + 9x - 6$

⑤ $P(x) = x^4 - 11x^2 - 18x - 8$

⑥ $P(x) = x^4 + 8x^3 + 14x^2 - 8x - 15$

4. Intermediate-Value Theorem

※ Intermediate Value Theorem

If f is a function that is continuous on $[a,b]$, and k is a number btwn f(a) and f(b), then there is at least one number c on $[a,b]$ such that $f(c) = k$.

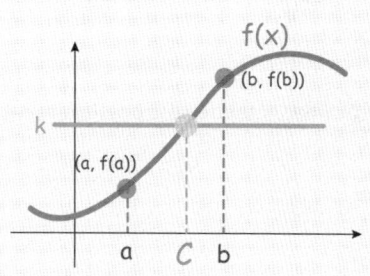

EXAMPLE 5. Use intermediate value theorem to prove the following.

① Show that $f(x) = 2x^3 - 6x + 1$ has a zero in the interval $[1,2]$.

② Show that $f(x) = x^{13} + 5x - 3$ has a zero in the interval $[0,1]$.

③ Show that $f(x) = 4x^3 - 3x + 1$ has a value x that satisfy $f(x) = 2$ in the interval $[0,2]$

EXAMPLE 6. The table below shows selected values of a continuous function f. For [0, 10],

x	0	1	3	4	6	7	9	10
$f(x)$	-2	1	7	3	1	-2	3	1

① what is the fewest possible number of zeros?

② what is the fewest possible number of x where $f(x) = 2$?

Mia's Precalculus
2.4 Fundamental Theorem of Algebra

1. Complex Number

In algebra 2, we've learned about complex number.

A **complex Number** is a combination of a ①_____ number and an ②_____ number.

$a + bi$ — real part, imaginary part, $\sqrt{-1}$
complex number

ex) $3+2i$, -2 (imaginary part is 0), $-3i$ (real part is 0) ...

Conjugate of $a + bi$ is③ _____.

2. Fundamental Theorem of Algebra

We have two different roots (=zeros)

① real roots and ② imaginary roots (roots with imaginary number i)

All together we call it **complex roots.**

complex roots
- real roots (no i) = x intercept $2, 0.5, \sqrt{3}$ ...
- imaginary roots (with i) $2i + 3, -4i$ ...

※ Fundamental Theorem of Algebra

① Every polynomial equation has at least one **complex roots.**

② Any polynomial of **degree n** has **n complex roots.**

Blank : ① real ② imaginary ③ a − bi

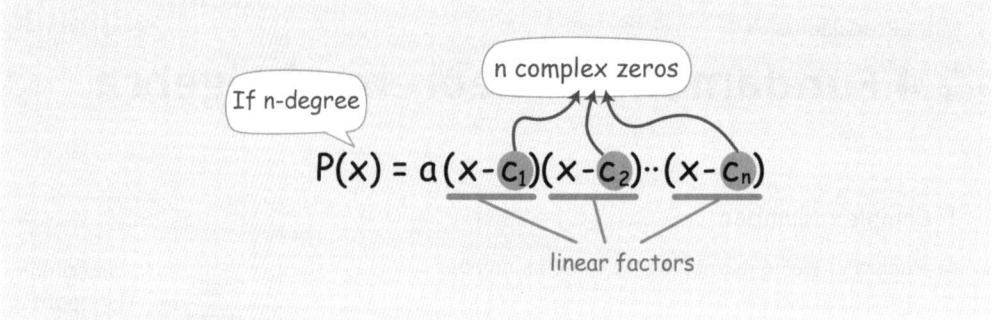

EXAMPLE 1. Determine the number of distinct real roots and imaginary roots for each function.

> You can see your real roots in the graph (= ①_____)
> but you cannot see your imaginary roots in your graph.

① Degree 2

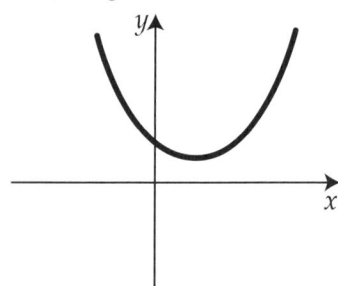

② Degree 2

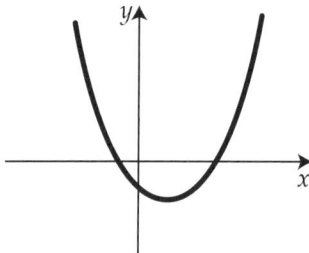

③ Degree 3

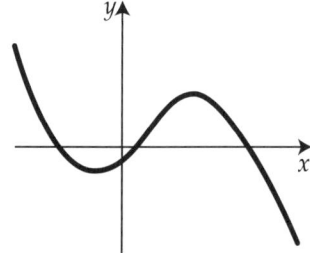

④ Degree 3

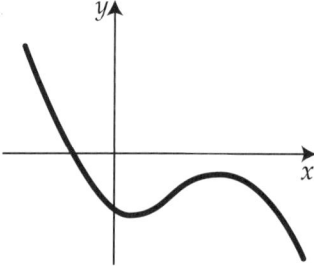

Blank : ① x intercept

⑤ Degree 3

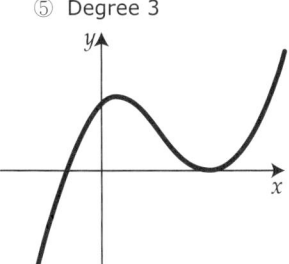

⑥ Degree 4

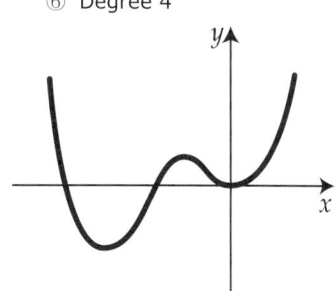

⑦ Degree 4

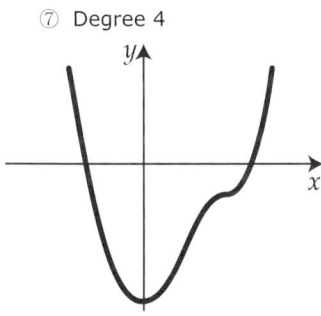

⑧ Degree 6

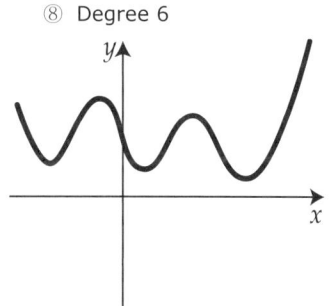

⑨ Degree 5

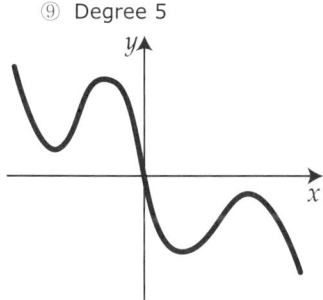

⑩ Degree 5

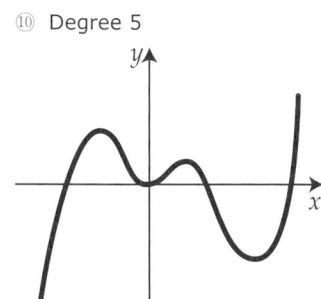

If we factor the polynomial **completely**, then we will find the *imaginary zeros*.

EXAMPLE 2. Factor f(x) completely and find all complex zeros.

① $f(x) = x^3 + x$ 　　　　　　　　　② $f(x) = x^4 + 4x^2$

③ $f(x) = x^3 + 5x^2 + 10x + 8$ 　　　　④ $f(x) = x^3 - 3x^2 + 5x - 3$

⑤ $f(x) = x^3 - 3x^2 + 2x - 6$ 　　　　⑥ $f(x) = x^4 + 9x^2 + 8$

⑦ $f(x) = x^4 + 4x^2 - 32$

3. Conjugate Zeros Theorem

※ Conjugate Zeros Theorem

Complex Roots always come in pairs!

When $a + bi$ is the root, $a - bi$ is also the root.

EXAMPLE 3. Write a polynomial function of least degree with integer coefficients that has the given zeros.

① $1 + 2i$ ② $3 + i$

③ -2, 2 + i

④ -1, 3i

⑤ −2, i, −2i

EXAMPLE 4. The polynomial $f(x) = x^3 - 7x^2 + 25x - 39$ has one zero as $2 - 3i$, find the other zeros.

4. Sums and products of roots of polynomials

When we have a polynomial of degree n

$$P(x) = a_n x^n + a_{n-1} x^{n-1} + \ldots + a_1 x^1 + a_0$$

Sum of the roots: $-\dfrac{a_{n-1}}{a_n}$ Product of the roots: $(-1)^n \dfrac{a_0}{a_n}$

ex) $P(x) = ax^2 + bx + c = 0$

Sum of the roots: ① _____

Product of the roots: ② _____

ex) $P(x) = ax^3 + bx^2 + cx + d = 0$

Sum of the roots: ③ _____

Product of the roots: ④ _____

EXAMPLE 5.   What is the sum and the product of a polynomial function?

① $P(x) = 2x^2 - 4x - 5$ ② $P(x) = x^2 + 3x - 7$

③ $P(x) = -x^3 + 3x^2 - 4x + 1$ ④ $P(x) = 2x^3 - 7x^2 + 3x - 2$

⑤ $P(x) = x^4 - 13x^2 + 36$ ⑥ $P(x) = \pi x^7 - 5x^5 + 3x^3 - 5x + \pi$

Blank : ① $-\dfrac{b}{a}$ ② $\dfrac{c}{a}$ ③ $-\dfrac{b}{a}$ ④ $-\dfrac{d}{a}$

⑦ $P(x) = 3x^7 - 5x^6 + 3x^2 + x$ ⑧ $P(x) = -x^5 - x^4 + x^3 + x^2$

EXAMPLE 6. If the roots of a quadratic equation $2x^2 + 5x - 4 = 0$ are α and β, what is the value of $\dfrac{1}{\alpha} + \dfrac{1}{\beta}$?

EXAMPLE 7. A quartic equation $x^4 + ax^3 + 15x^2 - 18x + b = 0$ has real coefficients and two of its roots are $3i$ and $1 - 2i$. Find the values of a and b.

EXAMPLE 8. The polynomial $f(x) = x^3 - 7x^2 + 25x - 39$ has one zero as $2 - 3i$, find the other zeros. (Hint: Use the sum of the root formula.)

EXAMPLE 9. Given that $1 - i\sqrt{6}$ is a root of the function $f(x) = x^3 + x^2 + x + 21$, find the remaining roots. (Hint: Use the sum of the root formula.)

If we know two roots of a quadratic equation, then the equation will be

$$a[\,x^2 - (\text{Sum of roots})x + (\text{Product of roots})\,] = 0$$

EXAMPLE 10. The equation $4x^2 + bx + c = 0$ has roots -4 and 1. Find the values of b and c.

EXAMPLE 11. If one of the roots of a quadratic equation $f(x) = 0$ is $-3 + 2i$, what is the quadratic equation?

5. Expand Knowledge

EXAMPLE 12. *The quadratic equation $x^2 - 4x + 7 = 0$ has roots p and q. Find a quadratic equation with integer coefficients and roots p^2 and q^2.

EXAMPLE 13. *The quadratic equation $2x^2 - 4x + 9 = 0$ has roots p and q. Find a quadratic equation $ax^2 + bx + c$ with integer coefficients and roots $p+1$ and $q+1$.

EXAMPLE 14. * If one of the roots of $mx^2 + (4m-1)x + k = 0$ is $-1 + 2i$, where m and k are real numbers, then what is the value of k?

Mia's Precalculus

2.5 Rational Functions

1. Rational Function

Rational Function:

① _____ of two polynomials

Rational Function

$R(x) = \dfrac{P(x)}{Q(x)}$

Ratio of two Polynomials

2. Reciprocal Function $y = \dfrac{1}{x}$

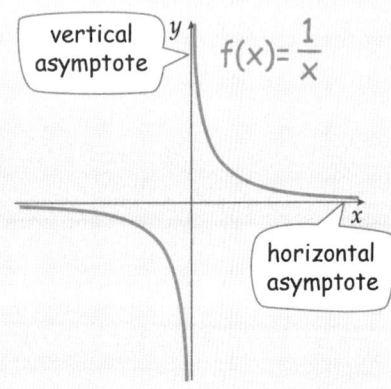

vertical asymptote

$f(x) = \dfrac{1}{x}$

horizontal asymptote

※ Reciprocal Function $y = \dfrac{1}{x}$

- domain: ② _____
- range: ③ _____
- intercept: ④ _____
- even or odd? ⑤ _____
- Horizontal Asymptote? ⑥ _____
- Vertical Asymptote? ⑦ _____

EXAMPLE 1. Graph the rational function using transformation.

① $R(x) = \dfrac{3}{x-1} + 2$

② $R(x) = \dfrac{4}{x+2} - 1$

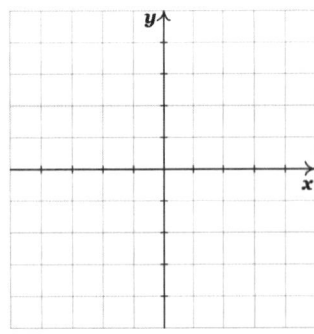

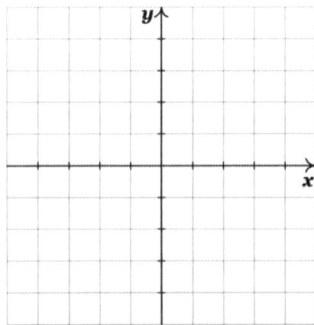

③ $R(x) = -\dfrac{1}{x+1} + 1$

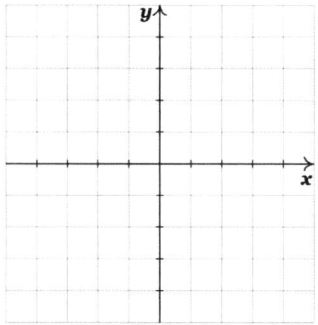

④ $R(x) = -\dfrac{2}{x} - 1$

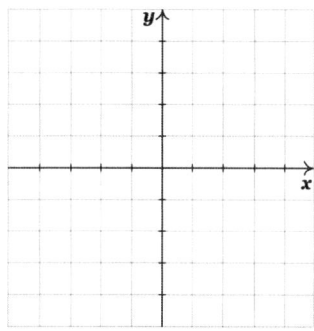

⑤ $R(x) = \dfrac{3x+2}{x-1}$

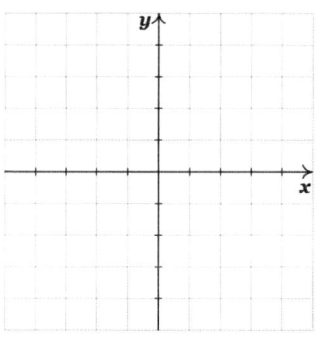

⑥ $R(x) = \dfrac{2x-1}{x+1}$

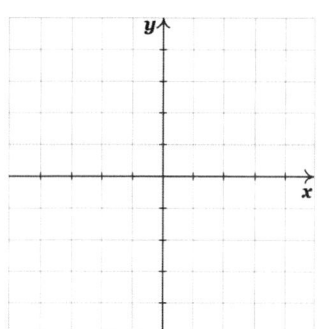

Blank : ① ratio ② All real numbers x ≠ 0 ③ All real numbers y ≠ 0 ④ none ⑤ odd ⑥ y = 0 ⑦ x = 0

3. Definition of Asymptotes

① _____ : A line that a curve approaches as it goes towards infinity

☺ *Notation:* $x \to 2$ means x approaches to (get closer to) 2. ($\neq x = 2$)

$x \to \infty$ means x gets bigger and bigger.

'Vertical' Asymptote :

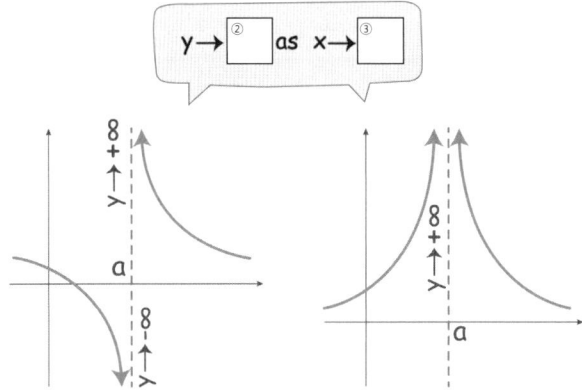

'Horizontal' Asymptote :

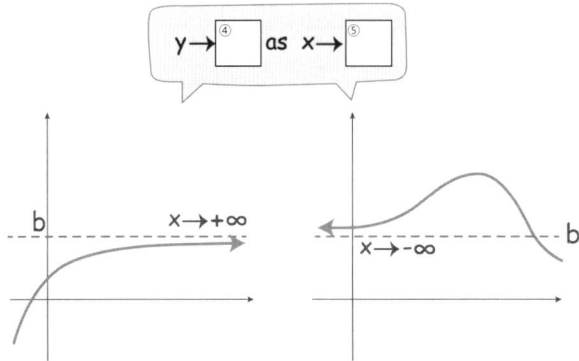

Blank : ① asymptotes ② $\pm\infty$ ③ a ④ b ⑤ $\pm\infty$

4. Graphing Rational Functions

1) Finding the Domain and Asymptotes

※ Rational Functions

Rational Function: $R(x) = \dfrac{P(x)}{Q(x)}$ — Ratio of two Polynomials

① Finding domain : ①_____ (②Reduce / Do not reduce)

② Vertical Asymptotes : ③_____ (④Reduce / Do not reduce)

③ Hole: When you **reduce (x-h)** from the top and the bottom,
then there will be a hole at ⑤_____.

④ Horizontal or Oblique (=slant) Asymptotes
 : ⑥_____ the degrees of the top and the bottom

Deg of Top < Bottom $\dfrac{2x+3}{3x^2+1}$ ⑦

Deg of Top = Bottom $\dfrac{2x^2+3}{3x^2+1}$ ⑧ → ratio of the leading coefficient

Deg of Top > Bottom (1 greater) $\dfrac{3x^2+3}{3x+1}$ $y = x - \dfrac{1}{3}$ oblique asymptote

Deg of Top > Bottom (2,3.. greater) $\dfrac{2x^3+3}{3x+1}$ ⑨

Blank : ① $Q(x) \neq 0$ ② Do not reduce ③ $Q(x) = 0$ ④ Reduce ⑤ $x = h$ ⑥ compare ⑦ $y = 0$ ⑧ $y = \dfrac{2}{3}$ ⑨ none

You can find oblique asymptote by

using ①_____ _____.

> oblique asymptote $y = x - \frac{1}{3}$

$$\begin{array}{r} x - \frac{1}{3} \\ 3x+1 \overline{\smash{\big)}\, 3x^2 + 0x + 3} \\ \underline{3x^2 + 1x} \\ -1x + 3 \\ \underline{-1x} \quad \vdots \end{array}$$

EXAMPLE 2. Find the domain, any asymptotes, and hole of the rational function.

> Key☞ Factor out and reduce to the lowest term
> EXCEPT for the domain.

① $R(x) = \dfrac{3x}{x+4}$

② $R(x) = \dfrac{3x+5}{2x-6}$

③ $R(x) = \dfrac{2x^2 - 5x - 3}{x^3 - 2x^2 - 3x}$

④ $R(x) = \dfrac{2x^2 - 5x - 12}{12x - 3x^2}$

Blank : ① long division

⑤ $R(x) = \dfrac{x^4 - 16}{x^2 - 2x}$

⑥ $R(x) = \dfrac{x-3}{3x^2+1}$

⑦ $R(x) = \dfrac{6x^2 + 7x - 5}{3x^4 + 5}$

⑧ $R(x) = \dfrac{x^4 - 2x^2 + 1}{x^2 - x}$

⑨ $R(x) = \dfrac{x^3 - 4x^2 + 4}{x^2 - 2x + 1}$

⑩ $R(x) = \dfrac{x^3}{x^2 - 5x - 14}$

⑪ $R(x) = \dfrac{x^3 - 8}{x^2 - 5x + 6}$

2) Finding intercepts

Remember, make sure the rational expression is in ① _____ terms! (Reduce!)

x-intercepts : we let ② _____.

y-intercepts: we let ③ _____.

EXAMPLE 3. Find the x-intercept and y-intercept

① $R(x) = \dfrac{3x+5}{x-6}$

② $R(x) = \dfrac{x^2 - 4x + 4}{x^2 - 2x + 1}$

③ $R(x) = \dfrac{x^3}{x^2 - 5x - 14}$

④ $R(x) = \dfrac{x^3 - 8}{x^2 - 5x + 6}$

⑤ $R(x) = \dfrac{x^4 - 16}{x^2 - 2x}$

⑥ $R(x) = \dfrac{2x^2 - 5x - 3}{x^3 - 2x^2 - 3x}$

Blank : ① lowest ② y = 0 ③ x = 0

3) Behavior near vertical asymptotes

$y = \dfrac{(2x-1)(x+4)}{(x-1)(x+2)}$ has a vertical asymptotes at ① _____, _____.

We need to know whether $y \to \infty$ or $y \to -\infty$ on each side of each vertical asymptote. To determine the sign of y near the vertical asymptotes, we use test values.

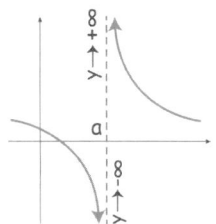

ex) around vertical asymptote x = 1

for right side of x = 1, let's use ② _____ (a test value close to the right side of 1)

$$y = \dfrac{(2(1.1)-1)((1.1)+4)}{((1.1)-1)((1.1)+2)}$$ whose sign is ③ ▢/▢ = ④ ▢

for left side of x = 1, let's use ⑤ _____ (a test value close to the left side of 1)

$$y = \dfrac{(2(0.9)-1)((0.9)+4)}{((0.9)-1)((0.9)+2)}$$ whose sign is ⑥ ▢/▢ = ⑦ ▢

ex) around vertical asymptote x = -2

So we can conclude that;

	x = -2			x = 1	
the sign of $\dfrac{(2x-1)(x+4)}{(x-1)(x+2)}$	$\dfrac{(-)(+)}{(-)(-)}$	$\dfrac{(-)(+)}{(-)(+)}$	$\dfrac{(+)(+)}{(-)(+)}$	$\dfrac{(+)(+)}{(+)(+)}$
	$-\infty$	$+\infty$	$-\infty$	$+\infty$

Blank : ① x = 1 , x = -2   ② 1.1   ③ ++/++   ④ +∞   ⑤ 0.9   ⑥ ++/-+   ⑦ -∞

5. Sketch the Graph (follow the guideline!)

Factor and Reduce	$y = \dfrac{2x^3+7x^2-4x}{x^3+x^2-2x} = \dfrac{x(2x-1)(x+4)}{x(x-1)(x+2)} = \dfrac{(2x-1)(x+4)}{(x-1)(x+2)}$
Vertical asymptote	$y = \dfrac{(2x-1)(x+4)}{\underbrace{(x-1)(x+2)}_{=0 \quad =0}}$ $\quad x = 1, \; x = -2$
Horizontal asymptote	$y = \dfrac{\overset{Degree!}{2x^2+7x-4}}{x^2+x-2}$ $\quad y = 2$
y-intercept	$y = \dfrac{(\overset{\to 0}{2x}-1)(x+4)}{(x-1)(x+2)} \to \dfrac{-4}{-2}$ $\quad (0, 2)$
x-intercept	$y = \dfrac{\overset{=0}{(2x-1)}\overset{=0}{(x+4)}}{(x-1)(x+2)}$ $\quad \left(\dfrac{1}{2}, 0\right) \; (-4, 0)$
Behavior near vertical asymptote	$\begin{array}{c|c\|c\|c\|c} & \multicolumn{2}{c}{x=-2} & \multicolumn{2}{c}{x=1} \\ \hline \text{the sign of } \dfrac{(2x-1)(x+4)}{(x-1)(x+2)} & \dfrac{(-)(+)}{(-)(-)} & \dfrac{(-)(+)}{(-)(+)} & \dfrac{(+)(+)}{(-)(+)} & \dfrac{(+)(+)}{(+)(+)} \\ & -\infty & +\infty & -\infty & +\infty \end{array}$
holes	Where $x = 0$
Graph	(graph showing rational function with vertical asymptotes at $x=-2$ and $x=1$, horizontal asymptote at $y=2$, x-intercepts at -4 and $\tfrac{1}{2}$, hole at $(0, 2)$)

Mia's Precalculus

EXAMPLE 4. Analyze the given rational function. Graph the function.

① $f(x) = \dfrac{2x}{(x-3)(x+4)}$

Domain

Vertical asymptote

Horizontal asymptote

x-intercept

y-intercept

② $f(x) = \dfrac{x-3}{x^2 - 6x - 16}$

Domain

Vertical asymptote

Horizontal asymptote

x-intercept

y-intercept

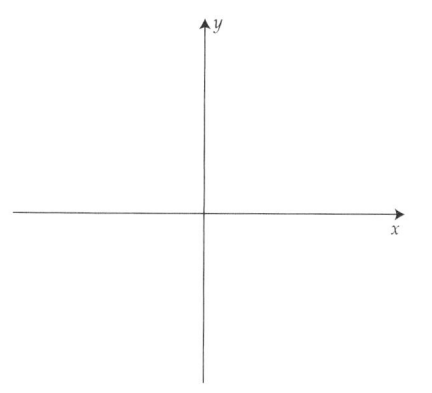

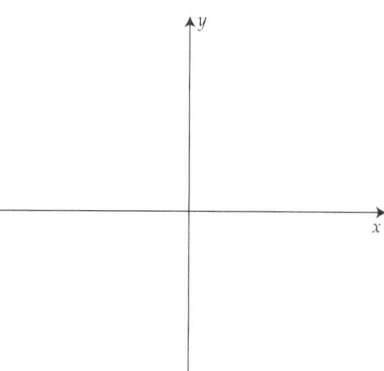

③ $f(x) = \dfrac{4}{x^2 - 4}$

Domain

Vertical asymptote

Horizontal asymptote

x-intercept

y-intercept

④ $f(x) = \dfrac{x - 3}{(x - 2)(x + 3)}$

Domain

Vertical asymptote

Horizontal asymptote

x-intercept

y-intercept

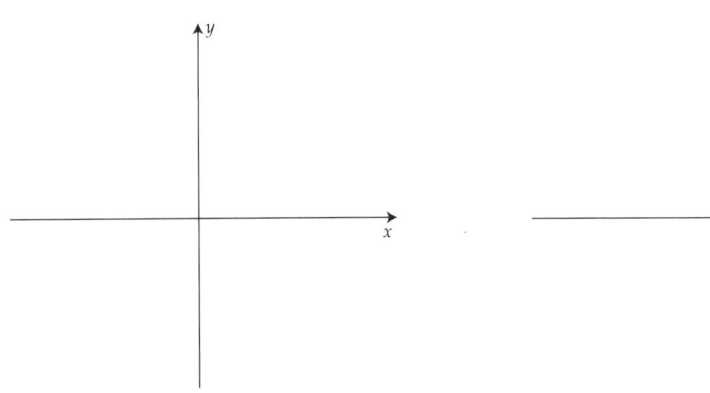

⑤ $f(x) = \dfrac{x^2 + x - 12}{x^2 - x - 6}$

Domain

Vertical asymptote

Horizontal asymptote

x-intercept

y-intercept

⑥ $f(x) = \dfrac{x^2 + 3x - 4}{x^2 + 2x - 8}$

Domain

Vertical asymptote

Horizontal asymptote

x-intercept

y-intercept

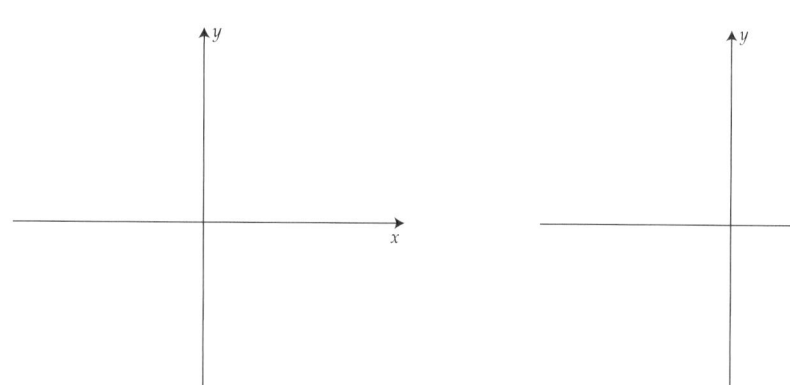

⑦ $f(x) = \dfrac{x^3 + 3x^2 - 18x}{x^2 - 36}$

Domain

Vertical asymptote

Horizontal asymptote

x-intercept

y-intercept

⑧ $f(x) = \dfrac{x^3 - 27}{x^2 - 6x + 9}$

Domain

Vertical asymptote

Horizontal asymptote

x-intercept

y-intercept

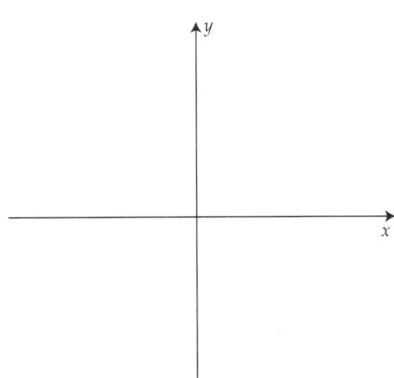

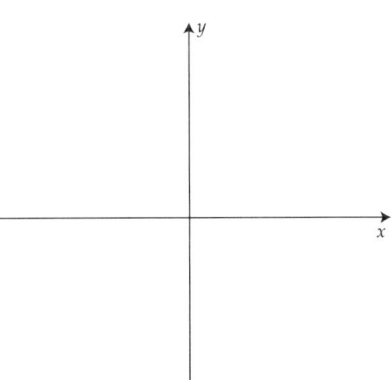

⑨ $f(x) = \dfrac{x^2 - 16}{x + 2}$

Domain

Vertical asymptote

Horizontal asymptote

x-intercept

y-intercept

⑩ $f(x) = \dfrac{x^2 - 4}{x - 1}$

Domain

Vertical asymptote

Horizontal asymptote

x-intercept

y-intercept

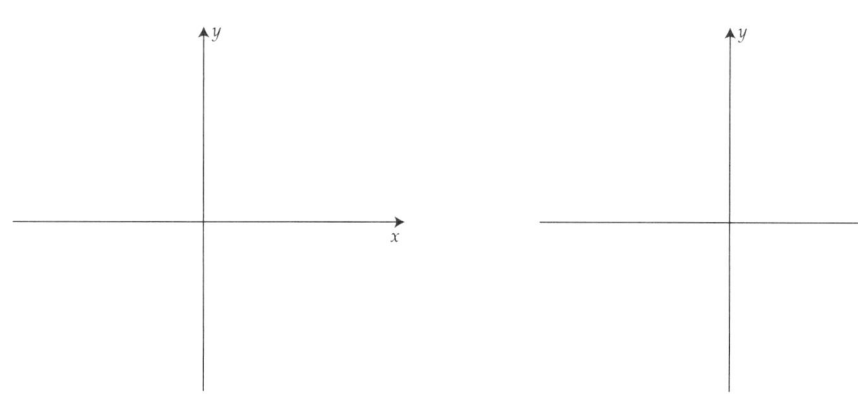

⑪ * $f(x) = \dfrac{x^2 - 4x - 5}{x^2 + 5}$

Domain

Vertical asymptote

Horizontal asymptote

x-intercept

y-intercept

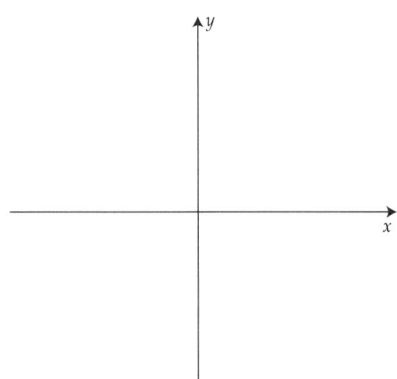

EXAMPLE 5. What is the difference between $y = \dfrac{x^2-1}{x+1}$ and $y = x-1$?

EXAMPLE 6. Match the graph of the rational function with its equation.

A. $f(x) = \dfrac{(x+2)(x-3)}{x+4}$

B. $f(x) = \dfrac{-2}{x^2+1}$

C. $f(x) = \dfrac{x+2}{(x-4)(x-8)}$

D. $f(x) = \dfrac{(x+2)(x-8)}{(x-4)(x-8)}$

①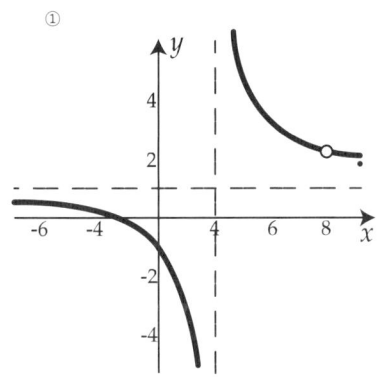

②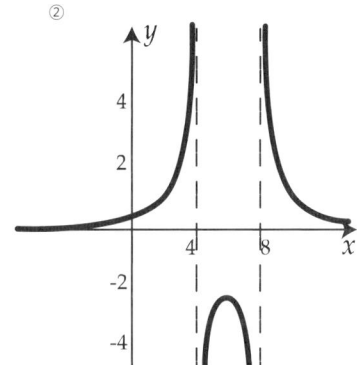

③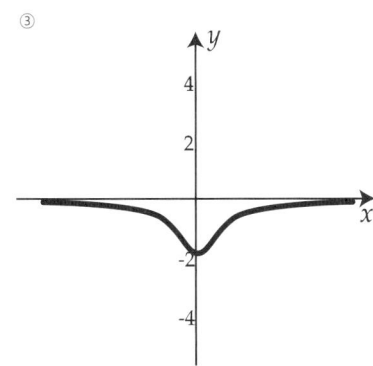

④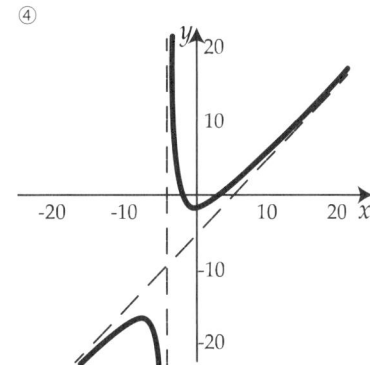

6. Expand Knowledge

EXAMPLE 7. *If the vertical asymptote rational function $R(x) = \dfrac{x^2 - 3x + b}{(x-1)(x+1)}$ is $x = -1$, what is the value of b?

EXAMPLE 8. *If the vertical asymptote rational function $R(x) = \dfrac{x^3 + 2x^2 - bx + 3}{(x-1)(x+1)}$ is $x = -1$, what is the value of b?

Mia's Precalculus

2.6 Polynomial and Rational Inequalities

1. Polynomial Inequalities Graphically

When we solve inequalities we try to find ①_____ or ②_____(s) of what the inequality sign says.

※ Solving Inequalities

$f(x) = g(x)$: When is the graph of **f(x)** ③_____ the **g(x)**?

$f(x) > g(x)$: When is the graph of **f(x)** ④_____ the **g(x)**?

$f(x) < g(x)$: When is the graph of **f(x)** ⑤_____ the **g(x)**?

$f(x) > 0$: When is the graph of **f(x)** ⑥_____ the ⑦_____?

For example, using the graph of f(x) and g(x), we can find out

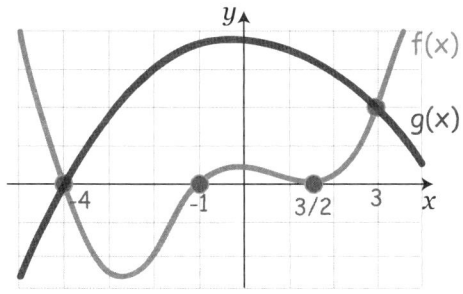

1) f(x)>0

2) f(x)≥0

3) f(x)≤0

4) f(x) = g(x)

5) f(x) ≤ g(x)

Blank : ① intervals ② values ③ intersect ④ above ⑤ below ⑥ above ⑦ x axis

Part 2 Polynomial and Rational Functions 145

EXAMPLE 1. Solve the given inequality using the graph.

①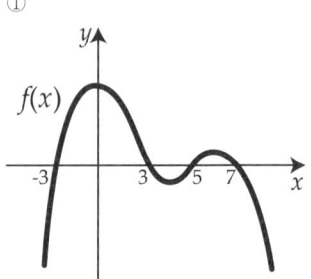

$f(x) > 0$

②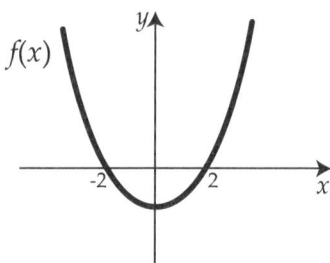

$f(x) \geq 0$

③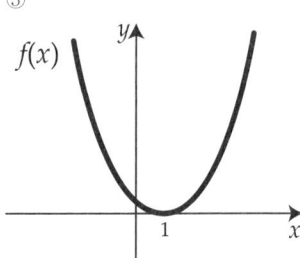

$f(x) \leq 0$

④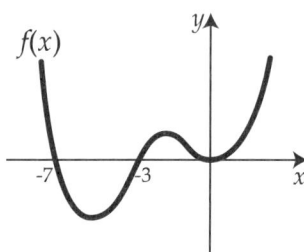

$f(x) \leq 0$

⑤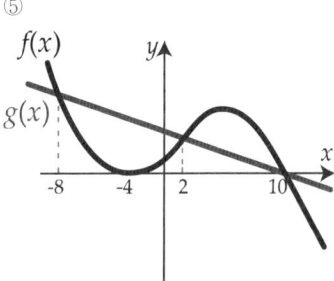

(i) $f(x) > 0$

(ii) $f(x) > g(x)$

⑥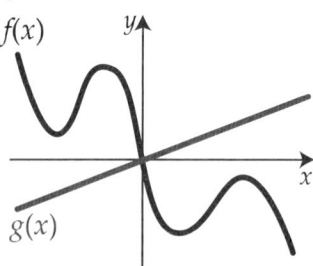

(i) $f(x) < 0$

(ii) $f(x) \geq g(x)$

⑦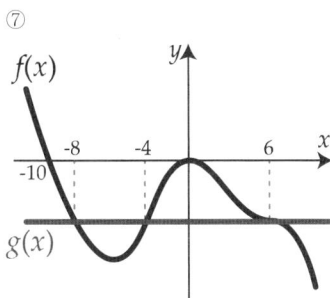

(i) $f(x) \geq 0$

(ii) $f(x) \leq g(x)$

⑧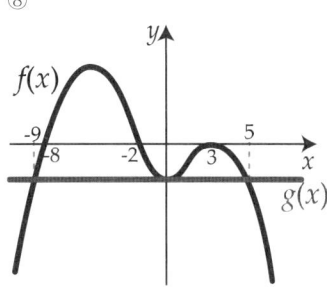

(i) $f(x) \leq 0$

(ii) $f(x) > g(x)$

2. Polynomial Inequalities Numerically

We want to solve $(x+4)(x+1)(2x-3)^2 \geq 0$

① Factor the polynomial.
② Find the **real zeros** (where f(x) = 0) and build up the intervals.
③ Pick a **test points** from each intervals
④ Determine if f is **positive**(f > 0) or **negative**(f < 0) on that interval by plugging in the test points.

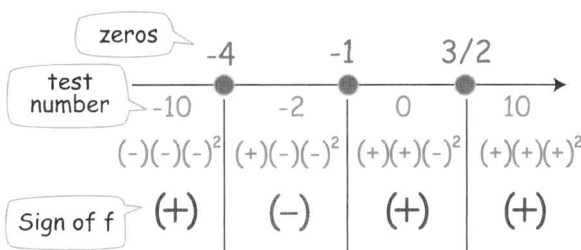

Determine whether the zeros include or not in my answer.

⑤ Read the inequality and find the appropriate interval(s).

Solution will be $(-\infty, -4] \cup [-1, \infty)$.

EXAMPLE 2. Solve the inequalities.

> If the multiplicity is **Odd**, the sign will **Change** around zeros.
> If the multiplicity is **Even**, the sign will **stay the same** around zeros.

① $(x+1)(x-3)(x-5)<0$

② $x(2x-1)(x+2)>0$

③ $x(x-1)(x+2)^2 >0$

④ $x^2(3-x)(x-2)^3 <0$

⑤ $x(1-x)(x+1)^2(x-3)^4 \geq 0$

⑥ $x^3(x-2)^2(x+2)^3(x-3)^4 \geq 0$

⑦ $x^3(x+1)^2(x^2+1) \geq 0$

⑧ $(x-1)(x+1)^2(x^2+3) \leq 0$

⑨ $x^4 - 13x^2 + 36 > 0$ ⑩ $x^3 - 7x^2 - 18x > 0$

⑪ $x^4 < 36x^2$ ⑫ $x^3 \geq 5x^2$

⑬ $2x^3 + 17x^2 - 2x - 80 > 0$ ⑭ $x^3 + 5x^2 - 4x - 20 \geq 0$

3. Rational Function Inequalities Graphically

Same thing goes with rational functions.

For example, using the graph of $P(x) = \dfrac{x}{(x-4)(x+4)}$

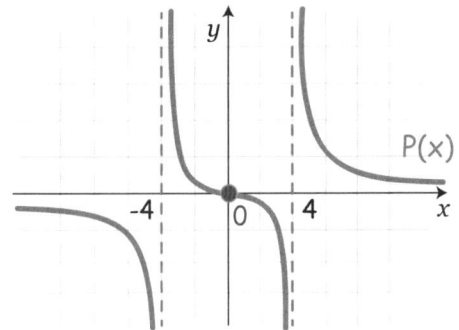

we can find out

1) $P(x) > 0$

2) $P(x) \geq 0$

3) $P(x) \leq 0$

EXAMPLE 3. Solve the given inequality using the graph.

①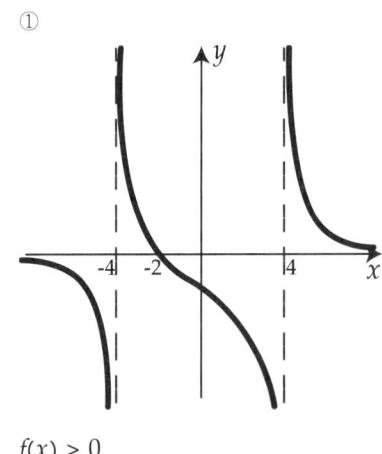

$f(x) > 0$

②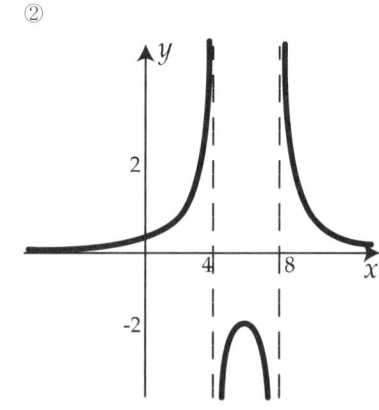

$f(x) \geq 0$

③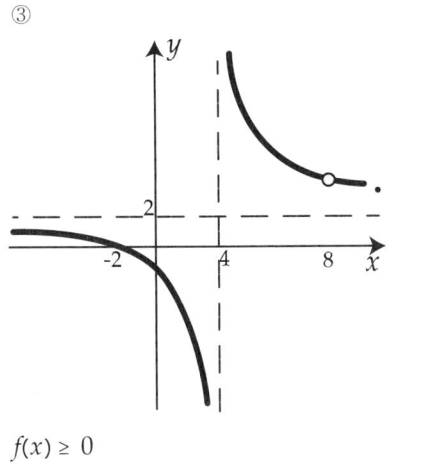

$f(x) \geq 0$

④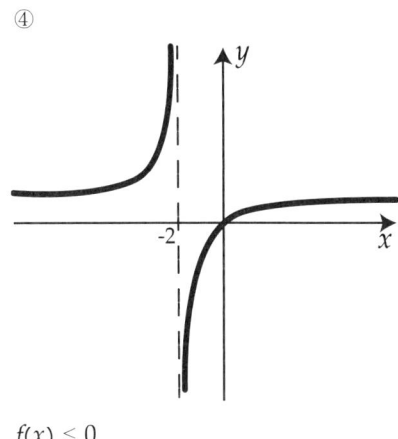

$f(x) \leq 0$

4. Rational Function Inequalities Numerically

For rational inequality $\dfrac{f(x)}{g(x)} \geq 0$, then we multiply ① _____ on both sides.

(NOT $g(x)$, since $g(x)$ could be positive or negative).

$$\dfrac{f(x)}{g(x)} \geq 0 \quad \xrightarrow{\text{multiply } g(x)^2} \quad f(x)\,g(x) \geq 0,\ g(x) \neq 0$$

Do the same thing for $\dfrac{f(x)}{g(x)} \leq 0$, $\dfrac{f(x)}{g(x)} > 0$, $\dfrac{f(x)}{g(x)} < 0$.

We want to solve $\dfrac{x}{(x-4)(x+4)} \geq 0$

① Change it into ②_____.

② Find the **real zeros** and build up the intervals.

③ Pick a **test points** from each intervals

④ Determine if f is **positive**(f > 0) or **negative**(f < 0) on that interval by plugging in the test points.

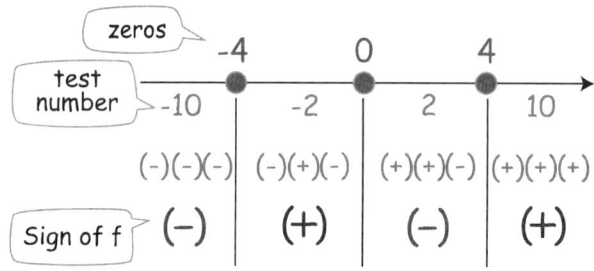

⑤ Read the inequality and find the appropriate interval(s).
Do not forget to **EXCLUDE the undefined x** in your answer.

Solution will be $(-4, 0] \cup (4, \infty)$

EXAMPLE 4. Solve the inequality.

① $\dfrac{x-7}{x+1} \geq 0$

② $\dfrac{x-4}{x+5} > 0$

Blank : ① $g^2(x)$ ② $x(x-4)(x+4) \geq 0$, $x \neq 4, -4$

③ $\dfrac{x-9}{x+6} > 1$

④ $\dfrac{x+28}{x+9} < 2$

⑤ $\dfrac{(x+1)^2(x-3)^3}{(x+2)(x+3)} \geq 0$

⑥ $\dfrac{(x+1)^2(x-2)^4}{(1-x)^3} > 0$

⑦ $\dfrac{(x-1)(3-x)}{(x-2)^2} < 0$

⑧ $\dfrac{x^2(x-12)(x+2)^2}{x-7} \leq 0$

⑨ $\dfrac{x^2-4}{x} < 0$

⑩ $\dfrac{x^2-4}{x^2} \geq 0$

⑪ $\dfrac{3x}{5-x} \leq x$

⑫ $\dfrac{8x}{7-x} < x$

⑬ $\dfrac{12}{x-5} \leq \dfrac{10}{x-1}$

5. Expand Knowledge

EXAMPLE 5. * Find the domain of $y = \sqrt{\dfrac{x}{x^2 - 16}}$.

EXAMPLE 6. * Find the domain of $y = \sqrt[3]{\dfrac{x}{25 - x^2}}$.

EXAMPLE 7. * Solve $\dfrac{x^2 - 4x - 5}{|x+2|} < 0$.

EXAMPLE 8. * Solve $\dfrac{x(x-2)^3(x-7)}{|x-1|} \leq 0$.

Part 3
Exponential and Logarithmic Functions

3.1 Exponential Function
3.2 Compound Interest
3.3 Logarithmic Function
3.4 Properties of Logarithm
3.5 Exp and Log Equations and Inequalities
3.6 Exponential Growth and Modeling

Mia's Precalculus
3.1 Exponential Function

1. Properties of Exponents

If a and b are positive numbers,

$x^a \cdot x^b = x^{\boxed{①}}$ Multiplication Law

$\dfrac{x^a}{x^b} = x^{\boxed{②}}$ Division Law

$(x^a)^b = x^{\boxed{③}}$ Power Law

$(xy)^a = x^a y^a$ Power of a Product Law

$\left(\dfrac{x}{y}\right)^a = \dfrac{x^a}{y^a}$ Power of a Quotient Law

$x^0 = \boxed{④}$ Zero Exponent ($x \neq 0$)

$x^{-a} = \boxed{⑤}$, $\dfrac{1}{x^{-a}} = \boxed{⑥}$ Negative Exponent ($x \neq 0$)

$\left(\dfrac{x}{y}\right)^{-a} = \boxed{⑦}$

$x^{\frac{a}{b}\{root\}} = \boxed{⑧}$ Fractional Exponent

$x^{\frac{1}{2}} = \underline{}$ $x^{\frac{1}{3}} = \underline{}$

$(-1)^n \begin{cases} \boxed{⑪}, \text{n is odd} \\ \boxed{⑫}, \text{n is even} \end{cases}$

Blank : ① a+b   ② a−b   ③ ab   ④ 1   ⑤ $\dfrac{1}{x^a}$ ⑥ x^a ⑦ $\dfrac{y^a}{x^a}$ ⑧ $\sqrt[b]{x^a}$ ⑨ $\sqrt{x}$ ⑩ $\sqrt[3]{x}$ ⑪ −1   ⑫ 1

EXAMPLE 1. Simplify.

① $\dfrac{3^{n-2} \cdot 9^{2-n}}{3^{2-n}}$

② $\dfrac{2^{n-3} \times 8^{n+1}}{2^{2n-1} \times 4^{2-n}}$

③ $\dfrac{x^{-1} + y^{-1}}{x^{-1} y^{-1}}$

④ $\dfrac{x^{-1} y^{-1}}{x^{-1} + y^{-1}}$

⑤ $\sqrt{x\sqrt{x}}$

⑥ $\sqrt{a\sqrt{a\sqrt{a}}}$

⑦ $\sqrt{\sqrt[3]{a} \times a^3}$

⑧ $\sqrt[3]{a\sqrt{a}}$

⑨ $\sqrt[4]{\dfrac{\sqrt[3]{x}}{\sqrt{x}}}$

⑩ $\sqrt{\dfrac{\sqrt[4]{x}}{\sqrt[3]{x}}}$

⑪ $(a^{\frac{1}{2}} + b^{\frac{1}{2}})(a^{\frac{1}{2}} - b^{\frac{1}{2}})$

⑫ $(a^{\frac{1}{3}} - b^{\frac{1}{3}})(a^{\frac{2}{3}} + a^{\frac{1}{3}}b^{\frac{1}{3}} + b^{\frac{2}{3}})$

EXAMPLE 2. Factor or simplify.

① $2^{n+3} + 2^n$ 　　　　　　　　　② $2^{n+3} + 8$

③ $2^{3+n} + 2^{2+n}$ 　　　　　　　④ $\dfrac{2^{m+3} + 2^m}{9}$

⑤ $36^x - 11(6^x) + 18$ 　　　　　⑥ $4^x - (2^x) - 6$

⑦ $9^x + 3^{x+1} - 4$ 　　　　　　⑧ $25^x - 5^{x+1} - 6$

⑨ $9^x - 4^x$ 　　　　　　　　　⑩ $25 - 16^x$

⑪ $\dfrac{6^n}{3^n}$ 　　　　　　　　　⑫ $\dfrac{8^n}{2^n}$

2. Exponential Function

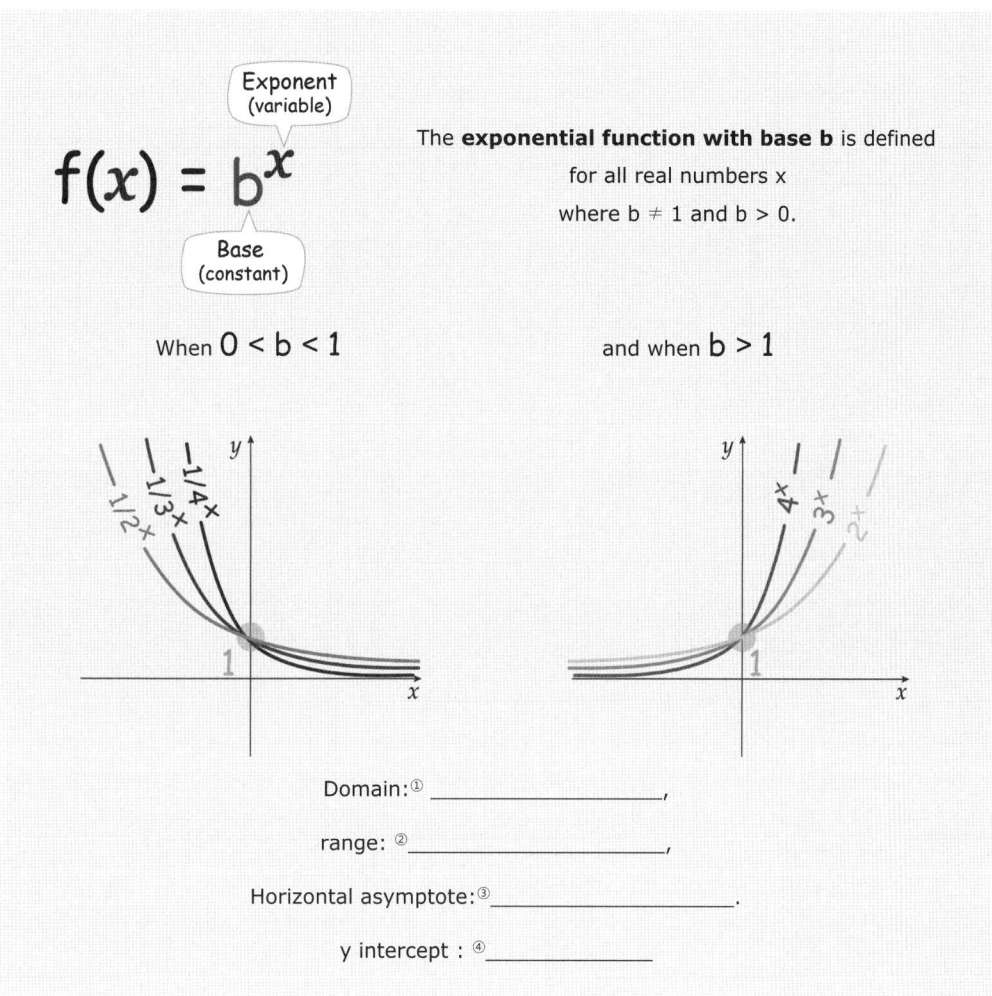

$f(x) = b^x$

Exponent (variable)
Base (constant)

The exponential function with base b is defined for all real numbers x where $b \neq 1$ and $b > 0$.

When $0 < b < 1$ and when $b > 1$

Domain: ① _____,

range: ② _____,

Horizontal asymptote: ③ _____.

y intercept : ④ _____

Blank : ① $(-\infty, \infty)$ ② $(0, \infty)$ ③ $y = 0$ ④ $(0, 1)$

EXAMPLE 3. Graph the function. State the domain, range, and asymptotes.

① $f(x) = 2^{x+2}$

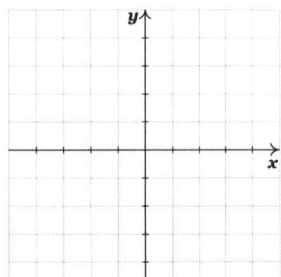

② $f(x) = (0.75)^x$

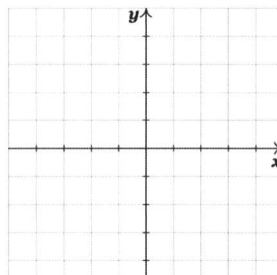

③ $f(x) = 4^{x-1} - 2$

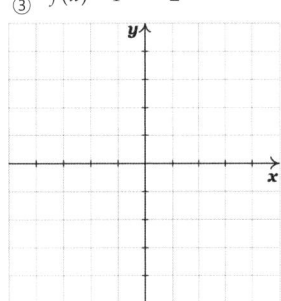

④ $f(x) = -2^{-x} + 1$

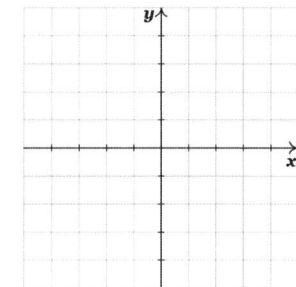

⑤ $f(x) = -0.5^x + 1$

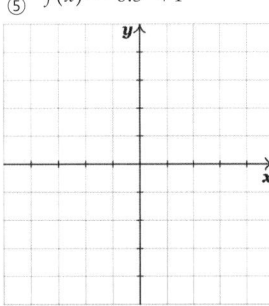

⑥ $f(x) = 2\left(\dfrac{1}{3}\right)^x - 2$

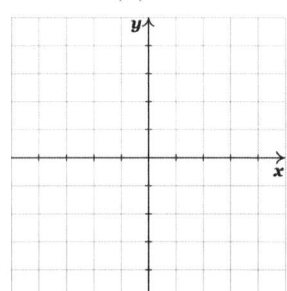

3. Euler Number

The number e is a famous (①rational/irrational) number, and is one of the most important numbers in mathematics.

$$e = 2.71828182845...$$

It is called ②_____ number (after Leonhard Euler).

e is found in many interesting areas (ex) compound interest, exponential growth...), so it is worth learning about.

* Euler Number

n	$\left(1+\dfrac{1}{n}\right)^n$
1	2.00000
2	2.00000
5	2.48832
10	2.59374
100	2.59374
1000	2.71692
10000	2.71815

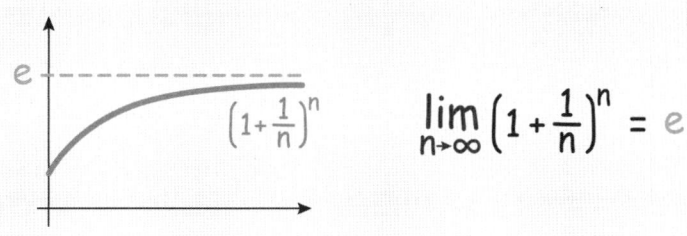

$$\lim_{n \to \infty} \left(1+\dfrac{1}{n}\right)^n = e$$

'lim' means approaching!

Blank : ① irrational   ② Euler

EXAMPLE 4. Use transformation to graph the function. Determine the horizontal asymptote of the function.

① $f(x) = e^{-x}$

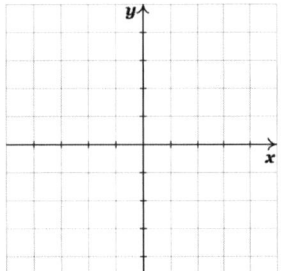

② $f(x) = 1 - e^{2+x}$

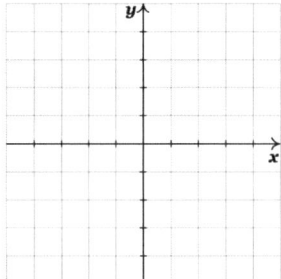

③ $f(x) = -e^{x+2} - 1$

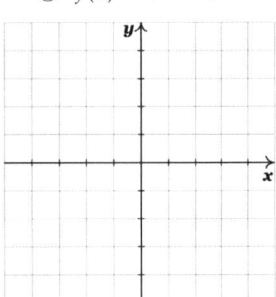

④ $f(x) = e^{-x} - 3$

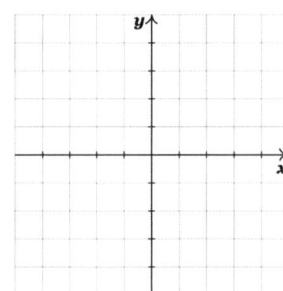

⑤ $f(x) = e^{1-x} - 2$

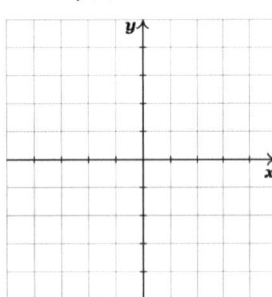

⑥ $f(x) = e^{2-x}$

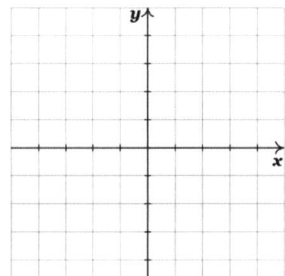

⑦ $f(x) = 2e^x - 3$

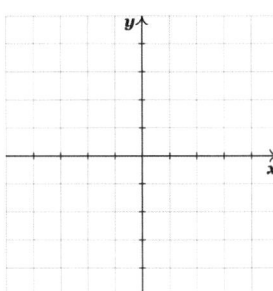

⑧ $f(x) = \dfrac{1}{2}e^{x-1}$

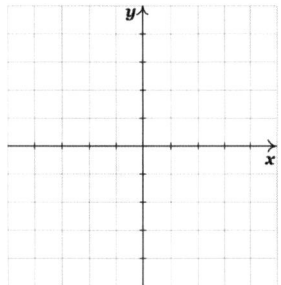

4. Expand Knowlegde

EXAMPLE 5. * For $a > 0, a \neq 1$,

$$\dfrac{\sqrt{\sqrt{\sqrt{a}}}}{\sqrt[4]{\sqrt[4]{a}}} = a^k.$$

What is the value of k?

EXAMPLE 6. * Find the value of $(3^{\frac{1}{4}} - 1)(3^{\frac{1}{4}} + 1)(3^{\frac{1}{2}} + 1)(3+1)(3^2+1)$.

EXAMPLE 7. * The graph of $y = 3^x$ and $y = 3^{x-a}$ is given. If a rectangle with area of 81 is drawn using the point $(a, 0)$ as shown. What is the value of a?

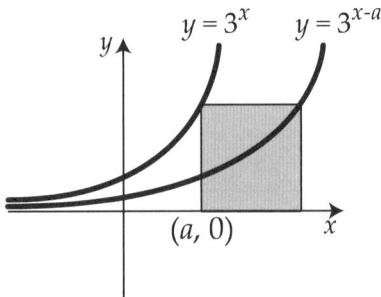

EXAMPLE 8.   * Which of the following describes the property of $y = a^x$, where $a > 0, a \neq 1$.

I. $f\left(\dfrac{1}{x}\right) = \dfrac{1}{f(x)}$

II. $f\left(\dfrac{x}{y}\right) = f(x) - f(y)$

III. $f(xy) = f(x) + f(y)$

IV. $f(x - y) = \dfrac{f(x)}{f(y)}$

V. $f(x + y) = f(x) f(y)$

VI. $f(nx) = [f(x)]^n$

3.2 Compound Interest

Mia's Precalculus

1. Compound Interest

Simple interest means the interest on principal (initial money) only.

$1,000 is invested at annual interest rate 10% with simple interest;

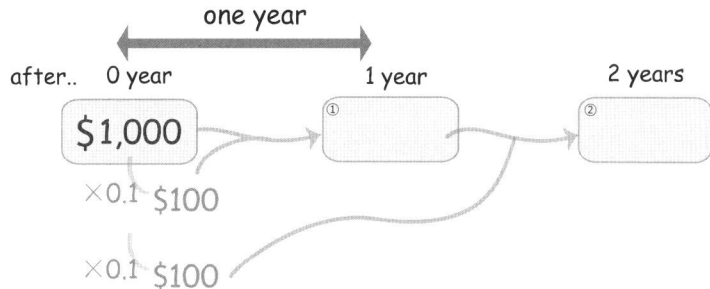

Compound interest means interest on principal (initial money) and interest previously earned.

$1,000 is invested at annual interest rate 10% compounded *annually*;

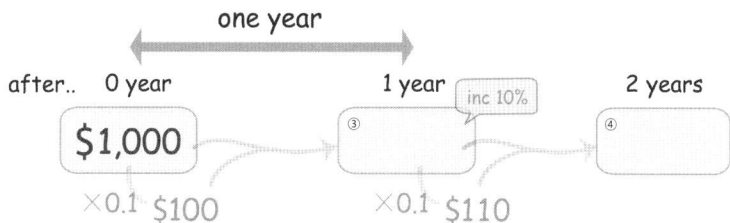

Blank : ① $1100   ② $1200   ③ $1100   ④ $1210

Part 3 Exponential and Logarithmic Functions

1) Compounded Annually

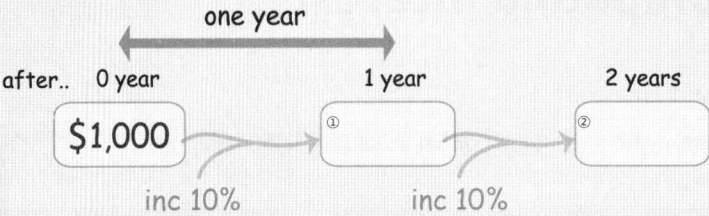

If a **principal P** is invested at a fixed annual **interest rate r** *compounded annually* calculated at the end of each year, then **after t years** the value of the investment is

$$\text{New} = P(1+r)^t$$

(rate) (time(yr)) (principal)

2) Compounded n times a year

$1,000 is invested at annual interest rate 10% compounded *semiannually* (2 times a year);

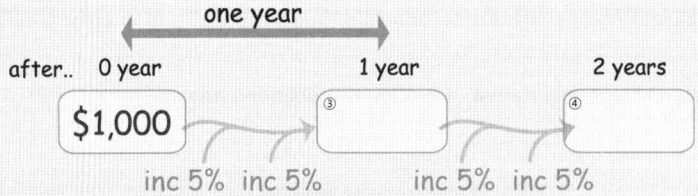

we **"split" the interest,** and give **more "often"**!

If a **principal P** is invested at a fixed annual **interest rate r** *compounded n times a year* calculated at the end of each year, then **after t years** the value of the investment is

$$\text{New} = P\left(1+\frac{r}{n}\right)^{tn}$$

(compound n times a year)

Blank : ① $1000(1+0.1)$ ② $1000(1+0.1)^2$ ③ $1000(1+0.05)^2$ ④ $1000(1+0.05)^4$

ex)

	"split" the interest, give more "often"
Annually (once a year)	$P(1+r)^t$
Semiannually (twice a year, n=2)	$P\left(1+\dfrac{r}{①}\right)^{t\times ②}$
Quarterly (4 times a year, n=4)	$P\left(1+\dfrac{r}{③}\right)^{t\times ④}$
Monthly (12 times a year, n=12)	$P\left(1+\dfrac{r}{⑤}\right)^{t\times ⑥}$

3) Compounded Continuously

If it is *compounded continuously* (when n is a large number) we use a special formula.

$$\text{New} = Pe^{rt}$$

(principal, rate, time(yr))

☺ Proof:

$$P\left(1+\frac{r}{n}\right)^{nt} = P\left[\left(1+\frac{r}{n}\right)^{\frac{n}{⑦}}\right]^{t\,⑧} = P\left[\left(1+\frac{1}{m}\right)^{⑨}\right]^{t\,⑩}$$

When m is a big number the formula will be Pe^{rt}.

Blank : ① 2 ② 2 ③ 4 ④ 4 ⑤ 12 ⑥ 12 ⑦ r ⑧ r ⑨ m ⑩ r

☺ All in one

Compounded Annually	$New = P(1+r)^t$ (rate, time(yr), principal)
Compounded n times a year	$New = P\left(1+\dfrac{r}{n}\right)^{tn}$ (compound n times a year)
Compounded Continuously	$New = Pe^{rt}$ (rate, time(yr), principal)

EXAMPLE 1. Find the new amount that result from the investment.

① $1,000 invested at 9% compounded annually after a period of 8 years

② $1,000 invested at 12% compounded semiannually after a period of 3 years

③ $14,000 invested at 14% compounded monthly after a period of 13 years

④ $480 invested at 9% compounded quarterly after a period of 5 years

⑤ $12,000 invested at 6% compounded continuously after a period of 4 years

⑥ $4,000 invested at 0.5% compounded continuously after a period of 7 years

---

Increased by r% each year (or month, ...) : $P(1+r)^t$

Decreased by r% each year (or month, ...) : $P(1-r)^t$

EXAMPLE 2. The population of Smallville in the year 1890 was 2400. Assume the population increased at a rate of 0.2% per year. Estimate the population in 1925.

EXAMPLE 3. The 2000 population of Jacksonville was 32,000 and was decreasing at the rate of 0.01% each year. At that rate, estimate the population after 3 years.

EXAMPLE 4. Jonas has a savings account that earns 3 percent interest compound semiannually. She has $1000 in her account, what was her deposit before 18 months?

EXAMPLE 5. Jay will be buying a used car for $20,000 in 3 years. How much money should he ask his parents for now so that, if he invests it at 3% compounded continuously, he will have enough to buy the car?

EXAMPLE 6. What rate of interest compounded annually is required to double an investment in 3 years?

Mia's Precalculus
3.3 Logarithmic Function

1. Logarithm

A **logarithm** is another way of writing an ①_____.

A logarithm gives you the power(exponent) a base must be raised to produce a given number.

Logarithmic function with base b **is defined by**

$$b^x = a \quad \Leftrightarrow \quad \log_b a = x$$

(base) (exponent) (value) ③ ④

Remember, $b \neq 1$, $b > 0$, and a **has to be** ⑤_____.

We can read it as : 'log base b of a is equal to x'

※ Special Logarithm

⑥_____ log   ⑧_____ log

(Common Log)   (Natural Log)

$\log_{10} x =$ ⑦ ☐ $\log_e x =$ ⑨ ☐

Blank : ① exponent ② base ③ value ④ exponent ⑤ positive (a>0) ⑥ Common ⑦ log x ⑧ Natural ⑨ ln x

Part 3 Exponential and Logarithmic Functions

EXAMPLE 1.   Find x using the definition of log.

> **What power**(exponent) a base must be raised to produce a given number?

① $\log_{10} 100{,}000 = x$ ② $\log_2 32 = x$

③ $\log_{10} 0.01 = x$ ④ $x = \log_5 \dfrac{1}{25}$

⑤ $\log_2 \dfrac{1}{4} = x$ ⑥ $x = \log_{1/2} 2$

⑦ $\log_{16} 4 = x$ ⑧ $\log_2 \sqrt{2} = x$

⑨ $4 = \log_x 625$ ⑩ $\log_x 4 = -1$

⑪ $\log_5 x = 3$ ⑫ $-2 = \log_{1/2} x$

⑬ $\log_{(x-1)} 5 = 1$

EXAMPLE 2. Find the domain.

> Remember : If $y = \log_b a$, then $a > 0$.

① $\log(x+8)$ 　　　　　　　　　　② $\ln(2-x)$

③ $\log_5(2x^2 + 9x - 5)$ 　　　　　　④ $\ln(x^2 + 3x + 2)$

⑤ $\log_5\left(-\dfrac{2}{x+2}\right)$ 　　　　　　⑥ $\log_5\left(\dfrac{1}{x+2}\right)$

⑦ $\log_5\left[\dfrac{(1+x)(3+x)^2}{1-x}\right]$ 　　⑧ $\log_5\left[\dfrac{(x-1)(x+2)}{x-2}\right]$

2. Basic Properties of Logarithms

$\log_b 1 = \boxed{①}$

$\log_b b = \boxed{②}$

$\log_b b^x = x$ 　　　ex) $\log_2 2^x = $ ③____, $\log 10^2 = $ ④____, $\ln e^y = $ ⑤____

$b^{\log_b x} = x$ 　　　ex) $2^{\log_2 3} = $ ⑥____, $10^{\log x} = $ ⑦____, $e^{\ln 4} = $ ⑧____

EXAMPLE 3. Evaluate the logarithm using basic log properties.

① $\log_2 8$ 　　　　　　　　　　　② $\log_3 \sqrt{3}$

③ $6^{\log_6 11}$ 　　　　　　　　　　④ $\log_5 1$

⑤ $\log 100$ 　　　　　　　　　　　⑥ $\log \sqrt[5]{10}$

⑦ $\log \dfrac{1}{1000}$ 　　　　　　　　　⑧ $10^{\log 6}$

⑨ $10^{\log 5^2}$ 　　　　　　　　　　⑩ $\log \dfrac{1}{\sqrt{10}}$

⑪ $e^{\ln 4}$ 　　　　　　　　　　　⑫ $\ln \sqrt{e}$

⑬ $\ln e$ 　　　　　　　　　　　⑭ $\ln e^5$

⑮ $\ln e^{kt}$

⑯ $\ln(\log 10^{e^2})$

Blank : ① 0 ② 1 ③ x ④ 2 ⑤ y ⑥ 3 ⑦ x ⑧ 4

EXAMPLE 4. Change into an equivalent expression.

To get rid of the LOG, you need ① _____

To get rid of the BASE, you need ② _____

$\log_2 8 = 3 \rightarrow \boxed{{}_{③}}\log_2 8 = {}_2{}^3 \rightarrow \boxed{{}^{④}}$

$2^3 = 8 \rightarrow \boxed{{}^{⑤}}2^3 = \log_2 8 \rightarrow \boxed{{}^{⑥}}$

	Exponential Form	Logarithmic Form
①		$\log 1000 = 3$
②	$5^x = 4000$	
③		$\ln \dfrac{1}{8} = x$
④		$\log_3 27 = 3$
⑤	$e^{1/2} = x$	
⑥	$10^x = 2$	
⑦		$\ln x^y = 2$
⑧	$10^{2x} = 5$	
⑨	$2^{x^2-x} = 3$	
⑩	$e^{4x^2} = 7$	
⑪		$y = \log(x^2 - 4x)$

Blank : ① base   ② log   ③ 2   ④ $8 = 2^3$ ⑤ $\log_2$ ⑥ $3 = \log_2 8$

EXAMPLE 5. Find the inverse.

① $y = 2^{x-1}$

② $y = 5^x + 3$

③ $y = 3e^x - 2$

④ $y = 3(10^{x-2})$

⑤ $y = \log_5 x$

⑥ $y = \log_7 x + 5$

⑦ $y = \ln(x+2)$

⑧ $y = 2\log x - 3$

⑨ $y = 3\log x + 2$

⑩ $y = \ln(x-1) + 1$

⑪ $y = \dfrac{1}{2}\log_3(x-1) + 2$

⑫ $y = \dfrac{\ln(x+2) - 1}{2}$

3. Graph of Log

Logarithm and exponential function are ①_____,
so we can draw the log graph
by taking the exponential function and reflecting across the ②_____.

$y = \log_b x$ When $0 < b < 1$ $y = \log_b x$ and when $b > 1$

Domain: ③_____,
range: ④_____,
Vertical asymptote: ⑤_____.
x intercept : ⑥_____

EXAMPLE 6.   Graph the function and find the asymptotes.
① $y = \log_3 x + 3$ ② $y = \ln(x + 3)$

Blank : ① inverse   ② y = x   ③ (0, ∞)   ④ (-∞, ∞)   ⑤ x = 0   ⑥ (1, 0)

③ $y = \ln(-x+3)$

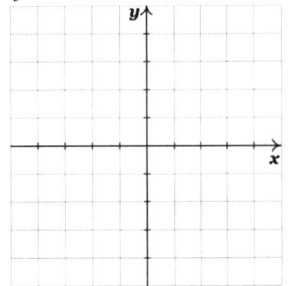

④ $y = \log_{0.3}(2-x)$

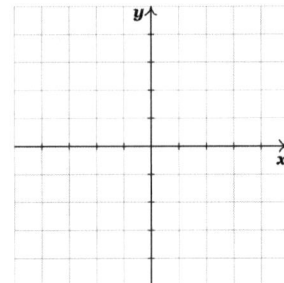

⑤ $y = \log_{0.2}(x-1)$

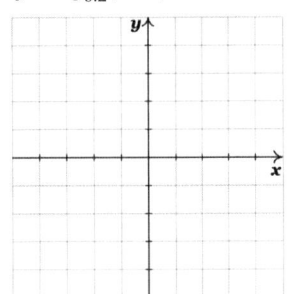

⑥ $y = -\log_3(-x) + 2$

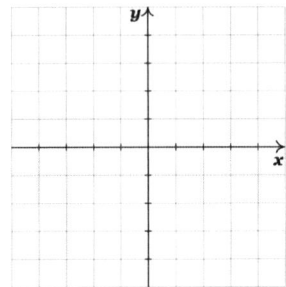

⑦ $y = 2\log x$

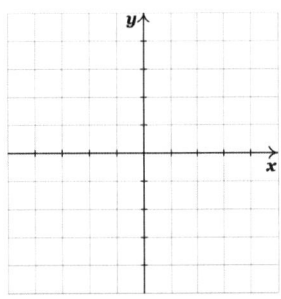

⑧ $y = \log(2x)$

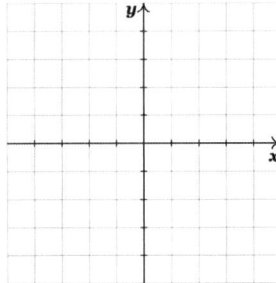

⑨ $y = \ln(0.5x) - 1$

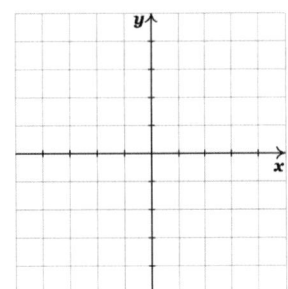

⑩ $y = 0.5\log x + 2$

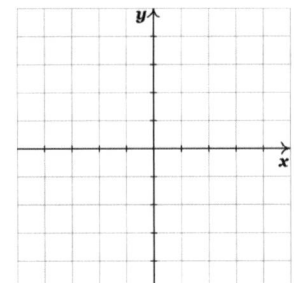

⑪ $y = |\log x|$

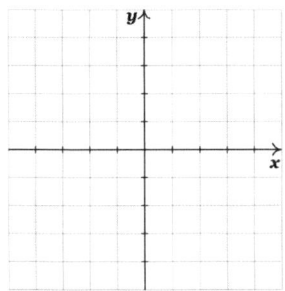

⑫ $y = \log|x|$

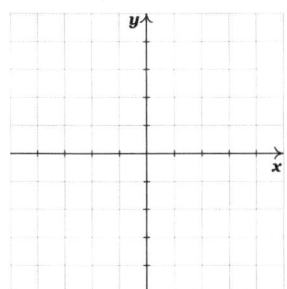

4. Expand Knowledge

EXAMPLE 7. * Evaluate each expression.

① $\ln\left[\ln\left(e^{e^7}\right)\right]$

② $10^{\log e^{\ln x^2}}$

③ $4\log_3 3^{\log 100}$

④ $e^{\log_3 3^{\ln 3}}$

EXAMPLE 8. * Find the domain of the function $y = \sqrt{\ln(x-2)}$.

EXAMPLE 9. * Find the domain of the function $y = \log_2(\log x)$.

EXAMPLE 10. * Find the domain of the function $y = \ln(\ln(\ln x))$.

EXAMPLE 11. * Find the inverse of the function $y = \dfrac{2^x}{1-2^x}$.

EXAMPLE 12. * The graph below shows $y = f(x)$, where $f(x) = x + \ln x$. Find the solution of $f(x) = f^{-1}(x)$. (Hint: Use the graph of $f(x)$ and $f^{-1}(x)$)

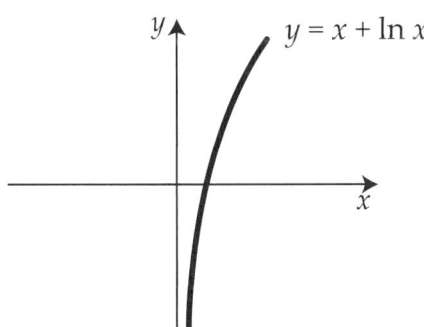

Mia's Precalculus

3.4 Properties of Logarithms

1. Properties of Logarithms

※ Properties of Log ($x, y > 0, b > 0, b \neq 1$)

$$\log_b xy = \log_b x + \log_b y \quad \text{Product Property}$$

$$\log_b \frac{x}{y} = \log_b x - \log_b y \quad \text{Quotient Property}$$

$$\log_b x^n = n \log_b x \quad \text{Power Property}$$

$$\log_{b^n} x = \frac{1}{n} \log_b x$$

$$\log_b x = \frac{\log_c x}{\log_c b} \quad \text{Change of Base}$$

EXAMPLE 1. Use the properties of logarithms to simplify the expression.

① $\log 3 + \log 10$

② $\log_3 24 - \log_3 8$

③ $3\ln 2 + \ln 6 - 2\ln 3$

④ $\log 32 - 2\log 4 - \dfrac{1}{3}\log 8$

⑤ $2\ln xy - 3\ln y - \dfrac{1}{2}\ln z$

⑥ $2\ln(xy) - 4\ln(xz) + 3\ln(xz)$

⑦ $\log 2x + 2(\log x - \log y)$

⑧ $2(\log_5 x + 2\log_5 y - 3\log_5 z)$

⑨ $2\log_6(x-1) - \log_6(x^2-1)$

⑩ $\log(x^2 - 2x - 3) - \log(x+1)$

⑪ $\dfrac{\log 9}{\log 2} \cdot \dfrac{\log 8}{\log 27}$

⑫ $\dfrac{\log 8}{\log 4}$

⑬ $\log_4 23 \cdot \log_{23} 16$

⑭ $\log_2 3 \cdot \log_3 4 \cdot \log_4 5$

⑮ $\log_4 10 \div \log_4 5$

⑯ $\log_5 23 \div \log_8 23$

⑰ $e^{2\ln 5}$

⑱ $10^{3\log x}$

⑲ $10^{2(\log 30 - \log 5)}$

⑳ $5^{2\log_5 4 - 3\log_5 2}$

㉑ $\log_2 x + \log_4 x$

㉒ $\log_4 x + \log_8 x$

EXAMPLE 2. Expand the given log. Given $a = \log x$, $b = \log y$ and $c = \log z$, find an expression in terms of a, b, and c for

① $\log xy^3$

② $\log(xy)^3$

③ $\log x^2 y \sqrt[3]{z}$

④ $\log 100\sqrt{xy}$

⑤ $\log\left(\dfrac{10y^2}{\sqrt{z}}\right)$

⑥ $\log \dfrac{\sqrt{x}}{y^3 z}$

⑦ $\dfrac{\log x^3}{\log y^2}$

⑧ $\log \sqrt{x\sqrt{y}}$

⑨ $\log_{xy} \sqrt[3]{z\sqrt{x}}$ ⑩ $\log_x \sqrt{yz}$

EXAMPLE 3. Write $\log_{13} \dfrac{10}{\sqrt[5]{x^2(4x+1)^3}}$ in expanded form.

EXAMPLE 4. Write $\log(x^2 - y^2)$ in expanded form.

EXAMPLE 5. What is $\log_2 3 \times \log_3 4 \times \log_4 5 \times \ldots \times \log_{63} 64$?

EXAMPLE 6. True or false?

I. $\log(x+y) = \log x + \log y$

II. $\log x \cdot \log y = \log(x+y)$

III. $\log x + \log y = \log xy$

IV. $\dfrac{\log x}{\log y} = \log x - \log y$

V. $\log x - \log y = \log \dfrac{x}{y}$

VI. $\log(x-y) = \log \dfrac{x}{y}$

VII. $(\log x)^2 = 2\log x$

VIII. $\log \dfrac{1}{x} = -\log x$

EXAMPLE 7. Which one is different from others?

$\log_3 14 \quad \log_3 2 + \log_3 7 \quad \dfrac{\log 14}{\log 3} \quad \dfrac{\ln 14}{\ln 3} \quad \log_3 2 \cdot \log_3 7 \quad \dfrac{1}{2}\log_3 196$

2. Expand Knowledge

EXAMPLE 8.   *Solve the problem.

① What transformation is required to go from the graph of $y = \ln x$ to the graph of $y = \ln(x^2)$?

② What transformation is required to go from the graph of $y = \ln x$ to the graph of $y = \log x$?

EXAMPLE 9. *Simplify the followings. (Hint: $n! = 1 \cdot 2 \cdot 3 \cdots n$)

① $\log_5(\log_2 3) + \log_5(\log_3 4) + \log_5(\log_4 5) + \ldots + \log_5(\log_{31} 32)$

② $2^{\log_2 1 + \log_2 2 + \log_2 3 + \ldots + \log_2 10}$

③ $\log_2(2\cdot 2^2 \cdot 2^3 \cdot 2^4 \cdots 2^{10})^2$

④ $(\log_2 2)(\log_2 2^2)(\log_2 2^3)\cdots(\log_2 2^{10})$

EXAMPLE 10.   *Let $f(x) = \ln(x+1) + \ln 4$.

(a)   Find $f^{-1}(x)$.

(b)   Find the range of $f^{-1}(x)$.

EXAMPLE 11.   *If $y = \ln x - \ln(x+2) + \ln(x^2 - 4)$, express x in terms of y.

EXAMPLE 12. * For $1<x<4$, write each logarithmic expression in increasing order.
$$A = \log_2 x^2, \quad B = (\log_2 x)^2, \quad C = \log_2(\log_2 x), \quad D = \log_4 x$$

EXAMPLE 13. * Which of the following describes the property of $y = \log x$.

I. $f\left(\dfrac{1}{x}\right) = \dfrac{1}{f(x)}$

II. $f\left(\dfrac{x}{y}\right) = f(x) - f(y)$

III. $f(xy) = f(x) + f(y)$

IV. $f(x-y) = \dfrac{f(x)}{f(y)}$

V. $f(x+y) = f(x)f(y)$

VI. $[f(x)]^n = nf(x)$

VII. $f(x^n) = nf(x)$

Mia's Precalculus

3.5 Exp and Log Equations and Inequalities

1. Logarithmic Equations

EXAMPLE 1. Solve the equation.

> You must CHECK your Answer!!
> Type1. If you want to get rid of the log,
> raise both sides to be power of that base!

① $\log_5(x+1) = 2$

② $2\ln(x-2) = 3$

③ $\ln\left(\log_3\left(\dfrac{2}{x-1}\right)\right) = 1$

④ $\log_2(\log_3 x) = 2$

⑤ $\log_3 x + \log_3(x-24) = 4$

⑥ $\log_2 x - \log_2(x-1) = 3$

⑦ $\log(x^2+9) = 1 + 2\log x$

⑧ $2\log(x-2) - \log x = 0$

⑨ $\log_3 x + \log_9 x = 2$

⑩ $\log_{16} x - \log_{32} x = 0.5$

Type2. Use the one to one property.

If $\log_b x = \log_b y$, then $x = y$.

---

⑪ $\log_8 2 + \log_8 x = \log_8 7$

⑫ $\log_2(x+5) = \log_2 x + \log_2 5$

⑬ $\ln(x-2) + \ln(2x-3) = 2\ln x$

⑭ $\log_3 x + \log_3(x+3) = \log_3 4$

⑮ $\log x - \log(x+2) = \log(x+6)$

⑯ $\ln(5x^2+4) = 2\ln 3x^2 - \ln(2x^2-1)$

⑰ $\ln(3x^2-4) + \ln(x^2+1) = \ln(2+6x^2)$

⑱ $\log(4+x) - \log(x-4) = \log 5$

Type 3. Make a Substitution!

⑲ $\left(\log x\right)^2 = \log x^4 - 3$　　　　　⑳ $2(\log x)^2 = \log x^3 + 5$

㉑ $4\log_4 x = 9\log_x 4$　　　　　㉒ $4\log_x 10 + \log_{10} x = 5$

EXAMPLE 2. Solve the following simultaneous equations
$$xy = 3$$
$$2\log_3 x - \log_3 y = 2$$

2. Solving Exponential Equation

EXAMPLE 3. Solve the equation using log.

> Type1. Make the base same if you can.

① $3(2^x) = 24$

② $5\left(\dfrac{1}{2}\right)^x = 20$

③ $32^{x-1} = 4^{x+2}$

④ $\left(\dfrac{5}{4}\right)^{4x} = \left(\dfrac{16}{25}\right)^{9-x}$

⑤ $\left(\dfrac{9}{16}\right)^{3x-2} = \left(\dfrac{4}{3}\right)^{x-4}$

⑥ $49^{\frac{x}{3}} = 7^{x-4}$

> Type2. If you want to bring exponent x down,
> take 'log' on both sides!

⑦ $2^x = 3$

⑧ $3^{x+1} = 8$

⑨ $3e^{2x} = 15$

⑩ $2e^{3x-1} = 14$

⑪ $5^{x-2} = 3^{3x+1}$

⑫ $11^{x-1} = 7^{2x+1}$

⑬ $7^{1-2x} = 2^x$

⑭ $4^{x-3} = 6^{2x}$

> Type3. Make a substitution!

⑮ $2e^{2x} - e^x = 6$

⑯ $e^{2x} - 15e^x = -56$

⑰ $3^{2x+1} - 11 \times 3^x = 4$

⑱ $5^{2x} - 5^{x+1} + 4 = 0$

⑲ $e^x + 5e^{-x} = 6$

⑳ $e^x - 6e^{-x} = 1$

㉑ $3e^{5x} - 10e^{3x} - 8e^x = 0$ ㉒ $2e^{6x} + e^{3x} - 1 = 0$

㉓ $3xe^x + x^2 e^x = 0$

3. Application

EXAMPLE 4. If you deposit $5000 into an account paying 6% annual interest compounded annually, how long until there is $8000 in the account?

EXAMPLE 5. If you deposit $8000 into an account paying 7% annual interest compounded quarterly, how long until there is $12400 in the account?

EXAMPLE 6. At 3% annual interest compounded continuously, how long will it take to double your money?

4. Exponential and Logarithmic Inequalities

※ Property of Inequality for Exponential and Logarithmic Functions

If $b > 1$, then $b^x > b^y$ if and only if $x > y$.

If $b > 1$, then $\log_b x > \log_b y$ if and only if $x > y$.

(But remember! When you have log A, A part should be ① _____.)

EXAMPLE 7. Solve the inequalities.

① $2^{x-1} > 3$

② $e^{2x+1} < 2$

③ $2 < 10^x \leq 4$

④ $8 \leq 3^x < 27$

⑤ $xe^x - 3e^x < 0$

⑥ $2^x x^2 - 2^x(2x+3) < 0$

Blank : ① positive

⑦ $\log_2 2x < 2$

⑧ $\log(2x-1) < 0$

⑨ $\log_2(3x+1) < 4$

⑩ $\ln x - 2 > 3$

⑪ $2\ln x - 1 \geq 5$

⑫ $\dfrac{1}{2} < \log x < 2$

⑬ $2 \leq \log_3 x \leq 3$

5. Expand Knowledge

EXAMPLE 8.   * Solve $x^{\ln x} = e^{(\ln x)^4}$.

EXAMPLE 9. * Solve $x^{\log_4 x} = x$.

EXAMPLE 10.   * Solve $\log_x(2x^2 + 8x) = 3$.

EXAMPLE 11. * Solve $\log(\log x) + \log(\log x^3 - 2) = 0$

EXAMPLE 12. * Solve $\ln(x-3) + \ln(x+4) < 3\ln 2$

EXAMPLE 13. * Find the exact solution of the equation $2^{3x-2} \times 3^{2x-3} = 36^{x-1}$.

Mia's Precalculus
3.6 Exponential Growth and Modeling

1. Exponential Growth and Decay Model (Halving or doubling)

A single cell amoeba *doubles* every 4 days. If there were 5 cells initially what is the population of the amoeba after t days?

0 days	after 4 days	after 8 days	...	after t days?
5	5·(2)	①		②

after t days, we will get : ③ _____

※ Exponential Growth Model (Doubling or Halving)

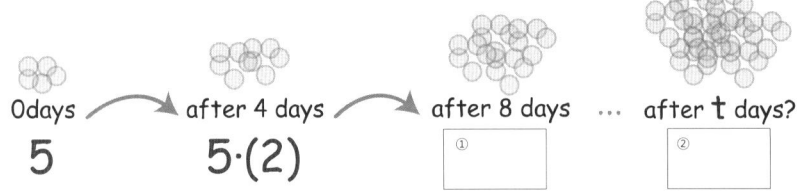

Doubling every n days   Halving every n days:
(or other time units)   = Half life is n days
                               (or other time units)

$$\text{New} = P(2)^{\frac{t}{n}} \quad \text{Doubling time} \qquad \text{New} = P\left(\frac{1}{2}\right)^{\frac{t}{n}} \quad \text{Halving time}$$

where P is the initial value, t is the time (with same time units with n).

Blank : ① $5·2^2$ ② $5·2^{t/4}$ ③ $5·2^{t/4}$

EXAMPLE 1. Find the exponential function that satisfies the given conditions.

① Initial population = 1078,
   doubling every 8 hours

② Initial mass = 420 g,
   halving once every 26 years

③ Initial mass = 416 g,
   halving once every 23 days

④ Initial population = 1081,
   doubling every hour

EXAMPLE 2. Under ideal conditions a certain bacteria population doubles every three hours. Initially there are 1000 bacteria.

(a) Find a model for the bacteria population after t hours.

(b) How many bacteria are in the colony after 15 hours?

(c) When will the bacteria count reach 200,000?

EXAMPLE 3. A single cell amoeba doubles every 9 days. About how long will it take one amoeba to produce a population of 400?

EXAMPLE 4. The half-life of a certain radioactive substances is 20 days. There are 45g present initially.
(a) Express the amount of substance remaining as a function of time t.

(b) Find the amount of substance remaining after 26 days.

EXAMPLE 5. The half-life of a certain radioactive substances are 7 days. There are 23g present initially. When will there be 25% remaining?

EXAMPLE 6. A certain radioactive isotope has a half-life of approximately 1900 years. How many years to the nearest year would be required for a given amount of this isotope to decay to 30% of that amount?

2. Exponential Growth/decay

In our world, a lot of things grow (or decay) exponentially.
(not forever, but at least for a while)

So we have a generally useful formula:

※ Exponential Growth/decay Model (Relative Growth Rate)

A population that experiences exponential growth increases according to the model

$$\text{New} = Pe^{rt}$$

where P is the initial value, t is the time, r is the relative growth rate.

(If $r > 0$, then it is ① _____

If $r < 0$, then it is ② _____)

Blank : ① exponential growth ② exponential decay

EXAMPLE 7. The initial bacterium count in a culture is 600. A biologist later makes a sample count of bacteria in the culture and finds that the relative rate of growth is 30% per hour.

(a) Find a function that models the number of bacteria after t hours.

(b) What is the estimated count after 10 hours?

(c) When will the bacteria count reach 80,000?

(d) Sketch the graph of the function.

EXAMPLE 8. The population of rabbits is increasing according to the law of exponential growth. In an experiment, it was observed that there were 200 rabbits after the second day and 1000 rabbits after the fourth day. How many rabbits were there in the original population?

EXAMPLE 9. In a research experiment, the population of a city is growing according to exponential model. If the growth rate per year is 4% of the current population, how long will it take for the population to double?

3. Logistic Growth

That growth can't go on forever as they will soon run out of available food.

In many real life applications,
the growth is now always unlimited,
but **may have a limit** (= ① _____).

※ Logistic growth

$$\text{New} = \frac{L}{1+Ce^{-kt}} \quad (\text{Limit} = L)$$

※ Facts about logistic curve;

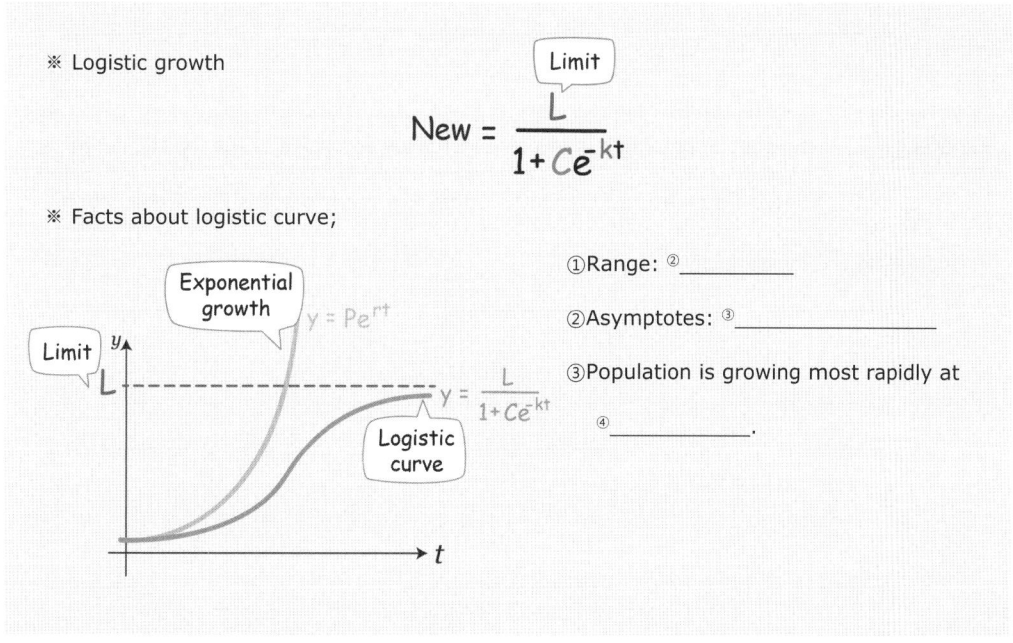

① Range: ② _____

② Asymptotes: ③ _____

③ Population is growing most rapidly at
④ _____.

Blank : ① carrying capacity   ② $0 < y < L$ ③ $y = 0, y = L$ ④ $y = \dfrac{L}{2}$

EXAMPLE 10. The spread of a disease through a college of 6000 students can be modeled with the logistic equation $y = \dfrac{6000}{1+590e^{-0.1t}}$, where y is the number of people infected after t days. The college will cancel class when 60% or more students are infected.

(a) How many people are infected when the disease is spreading the fastest?

(b) After how many days will the college cancel classes?

EXAMPLE 11. If the population of fish in the lake increases according to the logistic curve $P = \dfrac{10{,}000}{1+10e^{-t/3}}$, where t is measured in months. After how many months is the population increasing the most rapidly?

Part 4
Trigonometry Definition and Graphs

4.1 Angles in Radian
4.2 Trigonometry of Right Triangles
4.3 Trigonometry of Any Angles
4.4 Trigonometry in Unit Circle
4.5 Trigonometric Graphs for Sin, Cos
4.6 Trigonometric Graphs for Others

Mia's Precalculus
4.1 Angles In Radian

1. Radian

We can measure *the size of the angle* by using *two units*,

①_____ and ②_____.

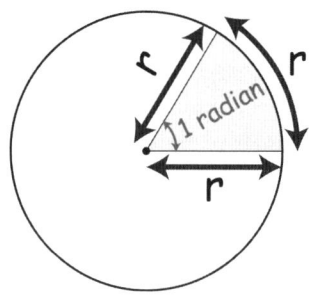

'**Radian**' is the angle made by taking the ③_____ and **wrapping it along the edge** of a circle

※ Facts about Radian and Degree

① *1 Radian* is about 57.2958°.

② The unit of *degree* is '°'.

　The unit of *radian* is ④_____ or ⑤_____.

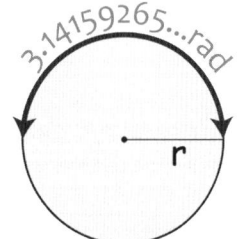

③ There are ⑥_____ radians in a half circle

　And also ⑦_____° in a half circle

　So, ⑧_____ = ⑨_____°

※ Radian and Degree

$$180° = \pi \text{ (rad)}$$

Blank : ① degree　② radian　③ radius　④ rad　⑤ none　⑥ π　⑦ 180　⑧ π　⑨ 180

2. Converting Angles

Converting Degree → Radian

$$\text{Degree}° \times \frac{\pi}{180°}$$

Converting Radian → Degree

$$\text{Radian} \times \frac{180°}{\pi}$$

EXAMPLE 1. Convert degrees into radians, and radians into degrees.

① $90°$

② $100°$

③ $-135°$

④ $150°$

⑤ $\dfrac{\pi}{3}$

⑥ $\dfrac{5\pi}{3}$

⑦ $-\dfrac{4\pi}{3}$

⑧ $-\dfrac{\pi}{12}$

⑨ $\dfrac{2}{3}$

⑩ 7

☺ Memorize!

Degrees	0°	30°	45°	60°	90°	180°	270°	360°
Radians	①	②	③	④	⑤	⑥	⑦	⑧

Blank : ① 0 ② $\dfrac{\pi}{6}$ ③ $\dfrac{\pi}{4}$ ④ $\dfrac{\pi}{3}$ ⑤ $\dfrac{\pi}{2}$ ⑥ π ⑦ $\dfrac{3\pi}{2}$ ⑧ 2π

3. Angles in Standard position

When an angle is in "**standard position**", its vertex is at the Origin.

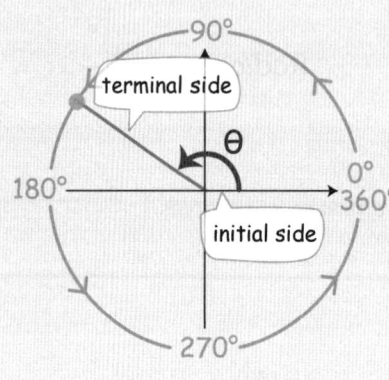

positive angle

negative angle

A **positive angle** goes
Counter Clock Wise (CCW)
from the X-axis
(upward and to the left).

A **negative angle** goes
Clock Wise (CW)
from the X-axis
(downward and to the left).

EXAMPLE 2. Draw a circle for each part and mark the points corresponding to the following angles.

① $\theta = -120°$

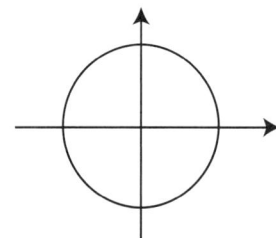

② $\theta = 720°$

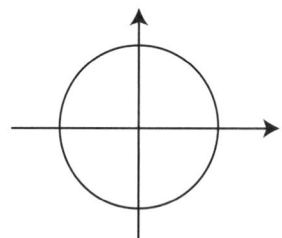

③ $\theta = \dfrac{5\pi}{4}$

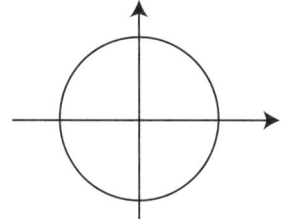

④ $\theta = \dfrac{5\pi}{2}$

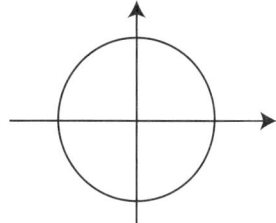

⑤ $\theta = -\dfrac{7\pi}{6}$

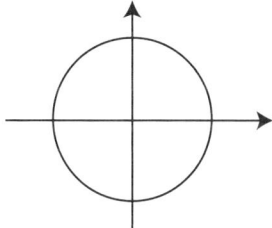

⑥ $\theta = \dfrac{11\pi}{6}$

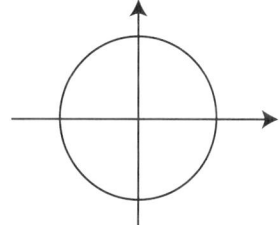

⑦ $\theta = \dfrac{17\pi}{6}$

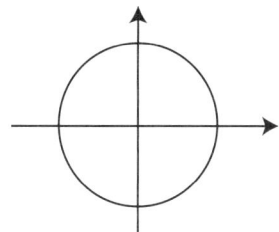

⑧ $\theta = -\dfrac{10\pi}{3}$

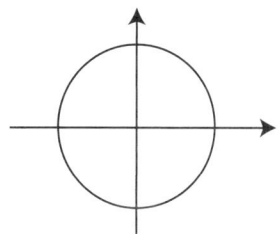

⑨ $\theta = -\dfrac{5\pi}{3}$

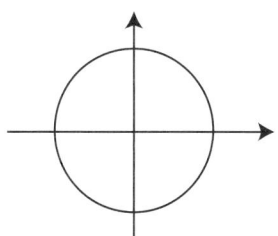

⑩ $\theta = -\dfrac{7\pi}{4}$

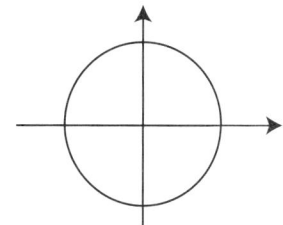

EXAMPLE 3. Fill in the blanks with appropriate angle.

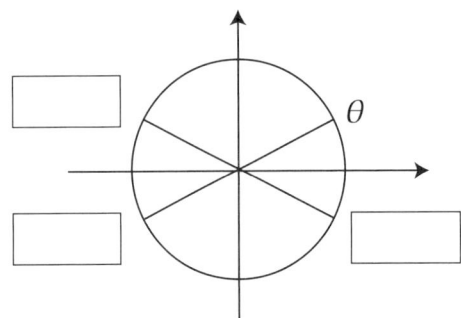

EXAMPLE 4. The measure of an angle in standard position is given. Find two positive angles and two negative angles that are coterminal with the given angle.

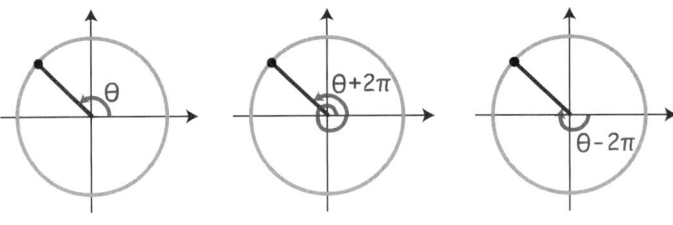

Coterminal angles are the angles that have the same terminal sides.
We can find the coterminal angle by adding or subtracting 360° or 2π to it.

① $120°$

② $-145°$

③ $\dfrac{4\pi}{3}$

④ $-\dfrac{3\pi}{4}$

4. Arc Length and Area of Sector

※ Formulas for Arc Length and Sector Area

If θ is a central angle (in *RADIAN*) in a circle of radius r, the arc length S and the area of sector A is;

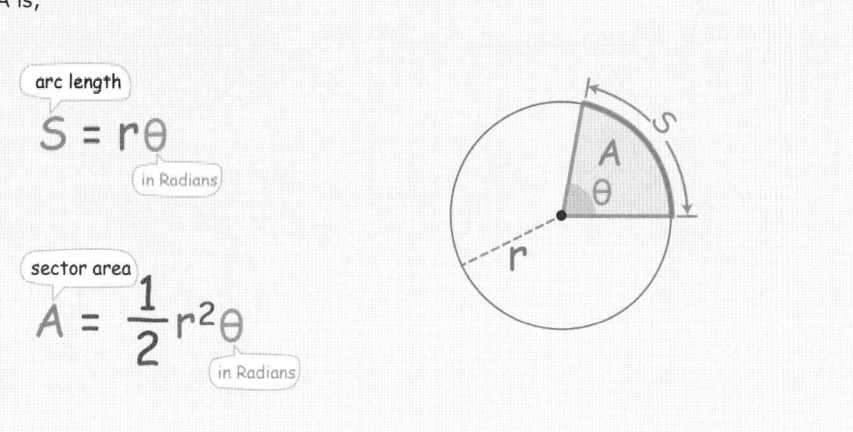

In geometry, we have learned that "the ratio of the measures of the angles equals the ratio of the corresponding lengths of the arcs subtended by these angles".

So, we can set;

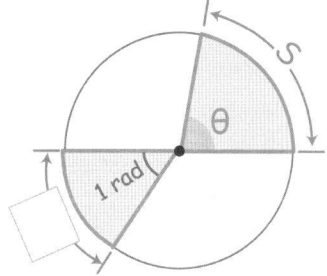

$$\frac{S}{①} = \frac{②}{③}$$

$$S = ④$$

The ratio of the area of the sector to the area of the whole circle is the same as the ratio of angle θ to a full turn.

So, we can set;

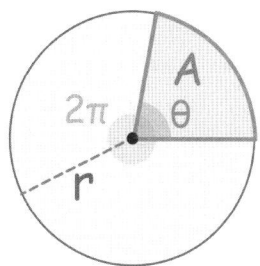

$$\frac{A}{⑤} = \frac{⑥}{⑦}$$

$$A = ⑧$$

Blank : ① θ   ② r   ③ 1   ④ rθ   ⑤ θ   ⑥ πr²   ⑦ 2π   ⑧ $\frac{1}{2}r^2\theta$

EXAMPLE 5. Find the arc length and the area of the sector.

①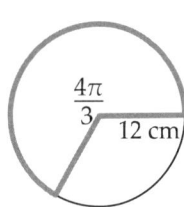

②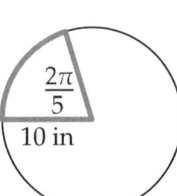

③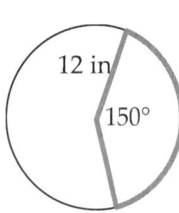

④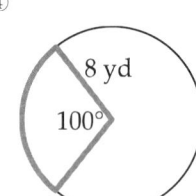

⑤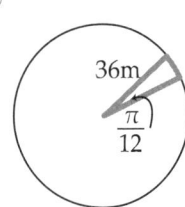

⑥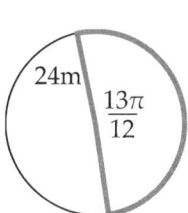

EXAMPLE 6. Find the measure of angle θ in radians

①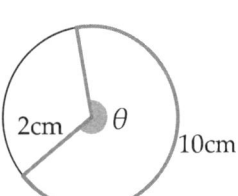

②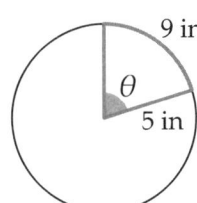

③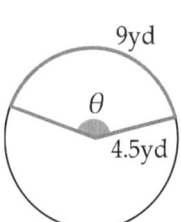

④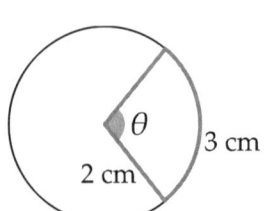

EXAMPLE 7. Two points, A and B, lie on the circumference of a circle of radius r cm. The minor arc AB has length 10 cm and subtends an angle of 2 at the center of the circle.

(a) Find the value of r.

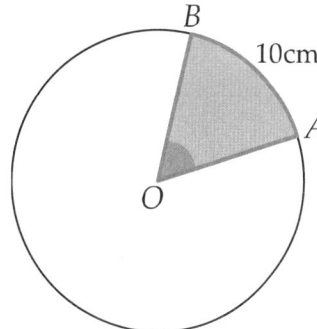

(b) Find the length of the major arc AB.

(c) Calculate the perimeter of the shaded region.

EXAMPLE 8. A sector of a circle has perimeter 12 cm and angle at the centre θ = 50°. Find the radius of the sector.

EXAMPLE 9. Find the area swept by the wiper blade shown, if the total length of the windshield wiper is 25 inches.

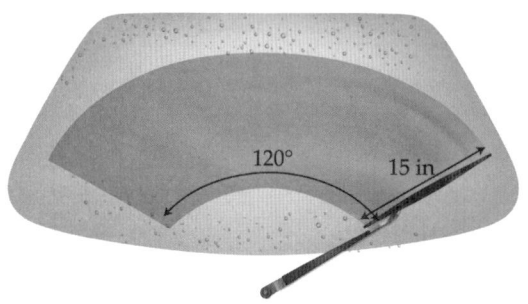

5. Angular Speed and Linear Speed

An object traveling in a circular motion has BOTH **linear** and **angular** speed.

1) Angular Speed and Linear Speed

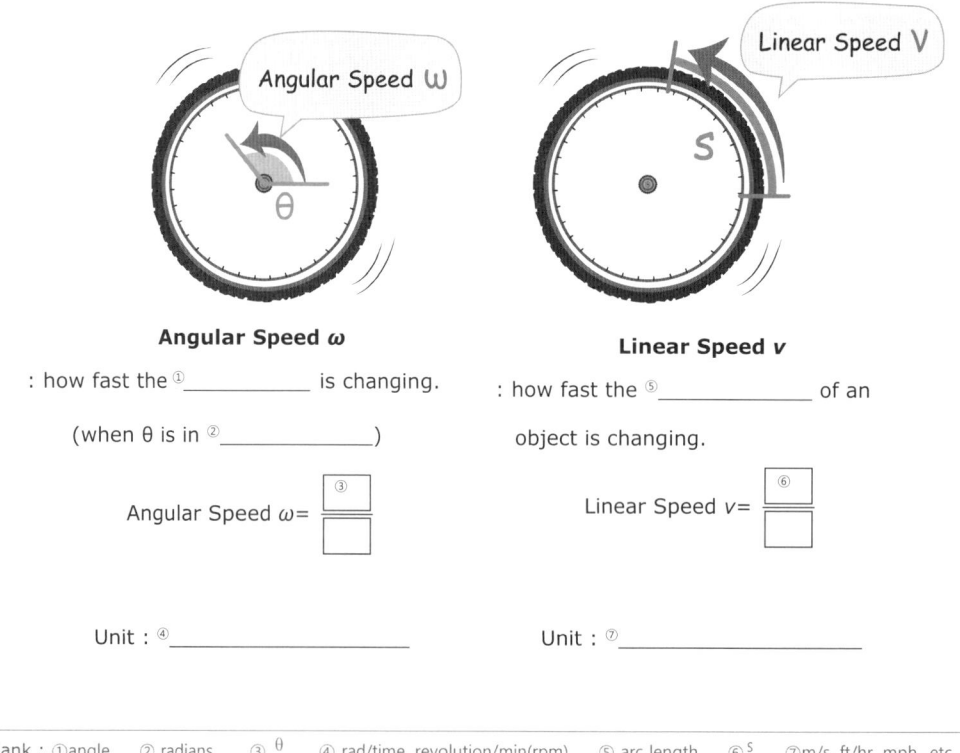

Angular Speed ω

: how fast the ①_____ is changing.

(when θ is in ②_____)

Angular Speed $\omega = \dfrac{\boxed{③}}{\boxed{}}$

Unit : ④_____

Linear Speed v

: how fast the ⑤_____ of an object is changing.

Linear Speed $v = \dfrac{\boxed{⑥}}{\boxed{}}$

Unit : ⑦_____

Blank : ①angle ②radians ③$\dfrac{\theta}{t}$ ④rad/time, revolution/min(rpm) ⑤arc length ⑥$\dfrac{s}{t}$ ⑦m/s, ft/hr, mph...etc

222 Mia's Precalculus

2) Relation between Angular Speed w and Linear Speed v

The linear speed is dependent on the radius of the circle and how fast the object is rotating (ω).

$$\text{Linear Speed } v = \frac{S}{t} = \frac{\boxed{①}}{t} = r\frac{\boxed{②}}{t} = r\boxed{③}$$

※ Formulas for Angular Speed and Linear Speed

Angular Speed
$$\omega = \frac{\theta}{t}$$

Linear Speed
$$v = \frac{S}{t} = r\omega$$

Where θ is angle in radians, S is arc length, r is radius

EXAMPLE 10. A ball on the end of a string is spinning around a circle with a radius of 7 cm. If in 3 sec a central angle of $\frac{1}{3}$ radian has been covered,

① What is the angular speed of the ball?

② What is the linear speed of the ball?

EXAMPLE 11. A wheel is rotating at 8 radians per sec, and the wheel has a 12in diameter. What is the speed of a point on the rim?

Blank : ① rθ   ② θ   ③ w

3) Revolution

> ※ **1 revolution** around the circle = ①_____ radians

EXAMPLE 12. A turntable rotates at 10 revolutions per minute.
① What is its angular speed in radians per minute?

② What is its angular speed in radians per second?

EXAMPLE 13. The radius of the tires of a car is 3 ft, and they are revolving at the rate of 24 revolutions per minute. How fast is the car traveling in miles per hour? (1mi = 5280ft)

EXAMPLE 14. A thread is being pulled off a spool at the rate of 60 cm per sec. Find the radius of the spool if it makes 120 revolutions per min.

Blank : ① 2π

EXAMPLE 15. Each tire of an automobile has a diameter of 6 feet. How many revolutions per minute (rpm) does a tire make when the automobile is traveling at a speed of 60 ft per sec.

6. Expand Knowledge

EXAMPLE 16. * A sector OAB has a radius of r and central angle θ in radian. If θ is increased by 20% and r is decreased by 20%. What is the percent change in the area of sector?

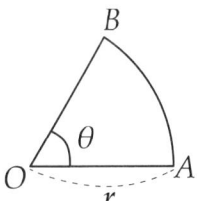

EXAMPLE 17. * The figure below shows an equilateral triangle ABC with side 6 in, and three arcs with centers at the vertices of the triangle. Calculate the perimeter of the figure.

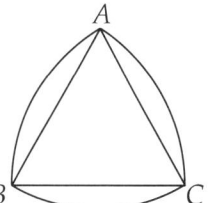

EXAMPLE 18. *A cone in made by rolling a piece of paper as shown in the figure.

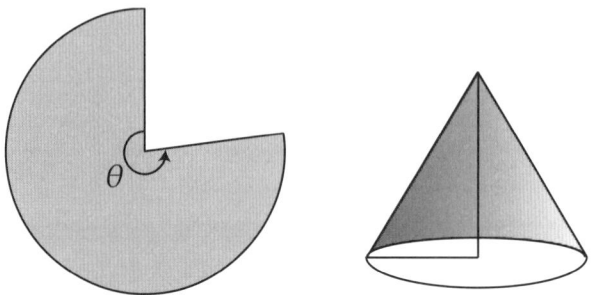

If the cone has a height 4 cm and base diameter 6 cm, find the size of the angle marked θ.

EXAMPLE 19. * A sheep is tied to a pole which is 3m from a long fence. The length of the rope is 6m. Find the area which the sheep can feed on.

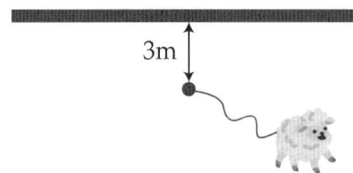

EXAMPLE 20.   * The belt fits tightly around two pulleys which have radii 8 cm and 2 cm, respectively. The distance of the centers of each pulley is 12cm. (The figure is not drawn in scale)

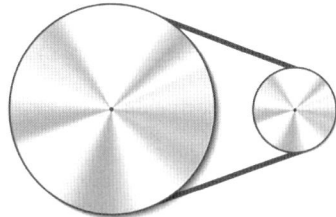

(a) What is the length of the belt? (Ignore the thickness of the belt.)

(b) The smaller pulley rotates 30 times in 12 seconds. Find the angular speed of each pulley in radians per second.

> Linear speed of the belt is ①_____ around all pulleys.

Blank : ①same

Mia's Precalculus
4.2 Trigonometry of Right Triangles

1. Trigonometry of Right Triangle (Definition 1)

A **right-angled triangle** has names for each side:

① _____ side is adjacent to the angle,

② _____ side is opposite the angle,

and the longest side is the ③ _____.

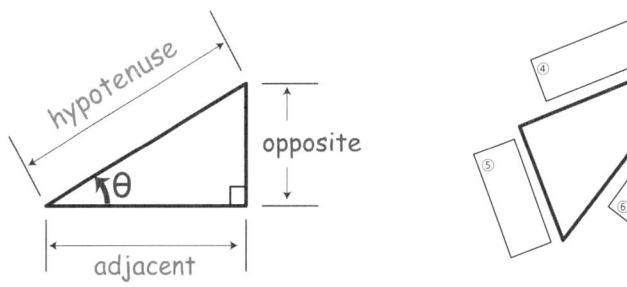

There are **Six Trigonometric Functions**

which tells you the ⑦ _____ of the ⑧ _____ of a right triangle.

※ Trigonometry Function of Acute Angles

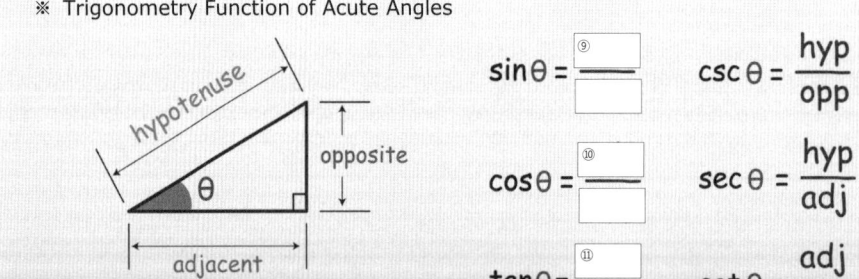

$$\sin\theta = \frac{⑨\quad}{\quad} \qquad \csc\theta = \frac{hyp}{opp}$$

$$\cos\theta = \frac{⑩\quad}{\quad} \qquad \sec\theta = \frac{hyp}{adj}$$

$$\tan\theta = \frac{⑪\quad}{\quad} \qquad \cot\theta = \frac{adj}{opp}$$

Blank : ① adjacent ② opposite ③ hypotenuse ④ adjacent ⑤ opposite ⑥ hypotenuse ⑦ ratio ⑧ two sides
⑨ $\frac{opp}{hyp}$ ⑩ $\frac{adj}{hyp}$ ⑪ $\frac{opp}{adj}$ ⑫ reciprocal

How to remember? Think

"Soh Cah Toa"

csc ("cosecant"), sec("secant"), cot ("cotangent") are the ⑫_____ of sin("sine"), cos("cosine"), and tan("tangent") respectively.

EXAMPLE 1. Find the exact values of the given trigonometric ratios of the angle θ in the triangle.

①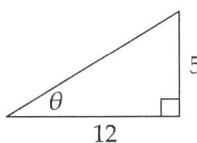

All trig ratios;

②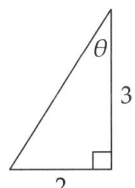

All trig ratios;

③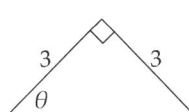

sin θ =

sec θ =

tan θ =

④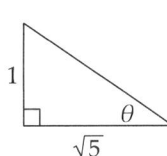

csc θ =

cos θ =

cot θ =

⑤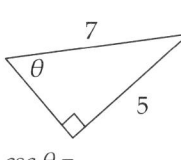

csc θ =

cos θ =

cot θ =

⑥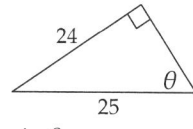

sin θ =

sec θ =

tan θ =

EXAMPLE 2. Assume that $0 < \theta < \dfrac{\pi}{2}$ and $a, b > 0$ satisfying the given conditions. Evaluate the indicated trigonometric function.

① $\sin\theta = \dfrac{3}{4};\quad \cos\theta$

② $\sin\theta = \dfrac{1}{3};\quad \cot\theta$

③ $\csc\theta = \dfrac{a}{b};\quad \cos\theta$

④ $\sec\theta = a;\quad \cot\theta$

⑤ $\tan\theta = a;\quad \sec\theta$

EXAMPLE 3. Express x and y in terms of trigonometric ratios of θ.

①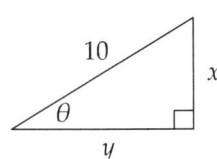

②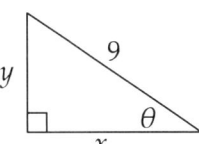

③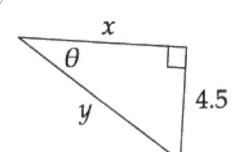

④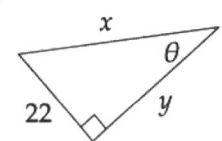

2. Special values of the trigonometric functions

※ Special Values of Trigonometry Function

	0°	30°	45°	60°	90°
	0	π/6	π/4	π/3	π/2
sin	0	$\frac{\sqrt{1}}{2}$	$\frac{\sqrt{2}}{2}$	$\frac{\sqrt{3}}{2}$	1
cos	1	$\frac{\sqrt{3}}{2}$	$\frac{\sqrt{2}}{2}$	$\frac{\sqrt{1}}{2}$	0
tan	0	$\frac{1}{\sqrt{3}}$	1	$\sqrt{3}$	und

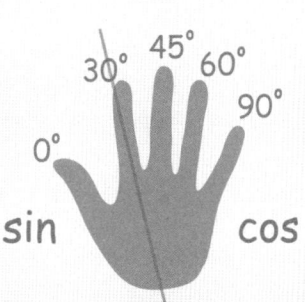

EXAMPLE 4. Memorize the table and then find the trig ratio.

① $\sin 60°$

② $\sin 45°$

③ $\cos 45°$

④ $\cos 30°$

⑤ $\tan \dfrac{\pi}{3}$

⑥ $\cos 0$

⑦ $\sin 0$

⑧ $\cos \dfrac{\pi}{3}$

⑨ $\tan \dfrac{\pi}{4}$

⑩ $\sin \dfrac{\pi}{6}$

⑪ $\tan \dfrac{\pi}{6}$

⑫ $\sin \dfrac{\pi}{2}$

⑬ $\sec \dfrac{\pi}{6}$

⑭ $\sec \dfrac{\pi}{4}$

⑮ $\csc \dfrac{\pi}{4}$

⑯ $\cot \dfrac{\pi}{6}$

⑰ $\cot \dfrac{\pi}{3}$

⑱ $\sec \dfrac{\pi}{3}$

3. Angle of Elevation and Depression

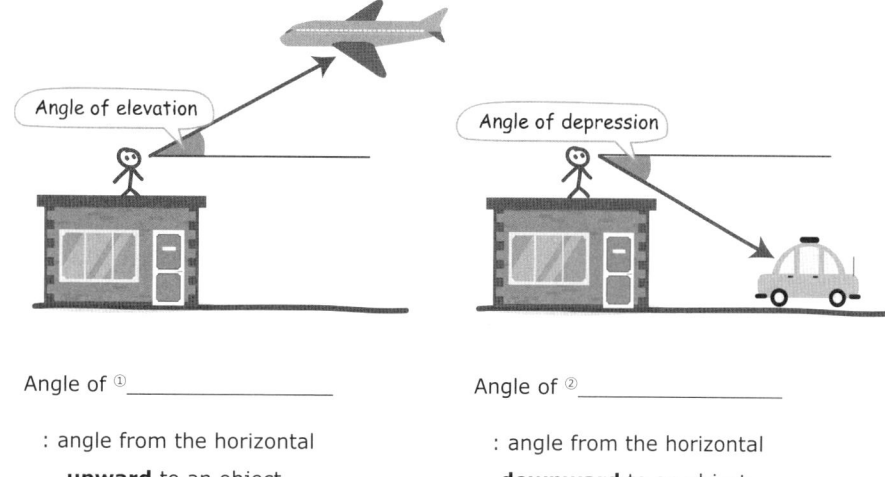

Angle of ① _____

: angle from the horizontal **upward** to an object.

Angle of ② _____

: angle from the horizontal **downward** to an object.

EXAMPLE 5. A giant redwood tree casts a shadow 200 ft long. Find the height of the tree if the angle of elevation of the sun is 57.6°.

EXAMPLE 6. An airplane is flying at a height of 2 miles above level ground. The angle of depression from the plane to the foot of the tree is 15°. What is the distance the plane must fly to be directly above the tree?

Blank : ① elevation ② depression

EXAMPLE 7. A 25ft ladder is leaning against a building making 35° angle with the ground. How far up the building does the ladder touch?

EXAMPLE 8. From a point on the ground 500 ft from the base of a building, an observer finds that the angle of elevation to the top of the building is 32° and that the angle of elevation to the top of a flagpole atop the building is 46°. Find the height of the building and the length of the flagpole.

EXAMPLE 9. Jay is standing 100 feet from the base of a tree, as shown in the figure. He measures the angle of elevation from the top of his head to the top of the tree to be 37°. If Jay is 6 feet tall, how tall is the tree?

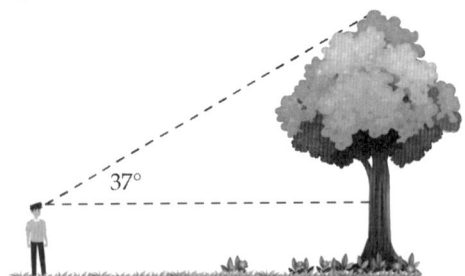

EXAMPLE 10. In traveling across flat land, you notice a mountain directly in front of you. Its angle of elevation (to the peak) is 3.5°. After you drive 13 miles closer to the mountain, the angle of elevation is 9°. Approximate the height of the mountain.

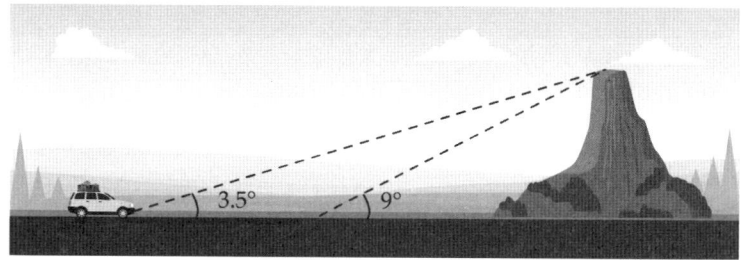

EXAMPLE 11. A Laser beam is to be directed toward the center of the circular disk in space, but the beam strays 0.05 degrees from its intended path. The disk has a radius of 100 feet and is situated 200 miles directly above the Earth where the laser is located. How many feet will the laser beam miss the edge of the disk? (5,280 feet = 1 mile)

Mia's Precalculus

4.3 Trigonometry of Any Angles

1. Trigonometry of Any Angles (Definition 2)

   Soh Cah Toa is only for the trigonometric ratios of an ①_____ angles.

   But what if we have an ②_____ angle?

   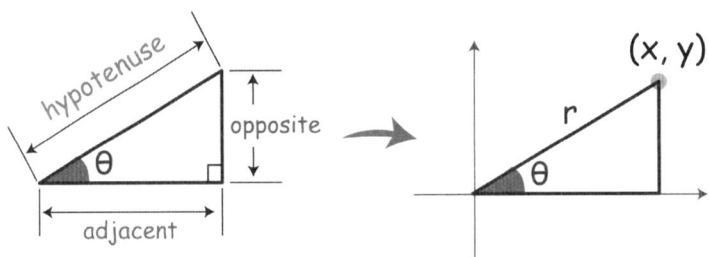

   If we place the triangle in the coordinate
   , we can find x, y, r instead of opp, adj , hyp.

   ※ Trigonometry Function of Any Angles

   If θ is in standard position, (x, y) is on the terminal side of θ,

   And r is the distance from (0, 0) to (x, y), then

   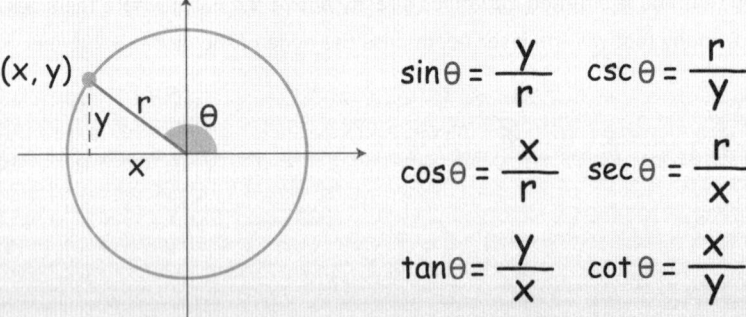

   $\sin\theta = \dfrac{y}{r}$ $\csc\theta = \dfrac{r}{y}$

   $\cos\theta = \dfrac{x}{r}$ $\sec\theta = \dfrac{r}{x}$

   $\tan\theta = \dfrac{y}{x}$ $\cot\theta = \dfrac{x}{y}$

   Remember! $r = \sqrt{\square^2 + \square^2}$ ③ is always ④_____.

Blank : ① acute   ② other (obtuse or negative..)   ③ $\sqrt{x^2 + y^2}$ ④ positive

EXAMPLE 1. Find the trigonometric functions of θ if the given point is on terminal side.

☺ Tip: You can use reference triangle (Drop a perpendicular line from the terminal side to the x-axis) and SOH CAH TOA!

①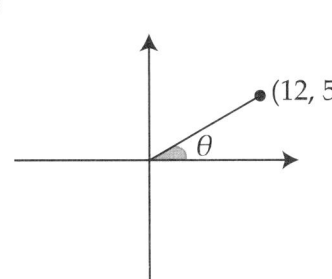

sin θ =

cos θ =

tan θ =

②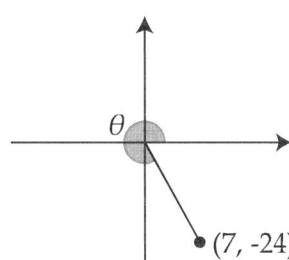

sin θ =

cos θ =

tan θ =

③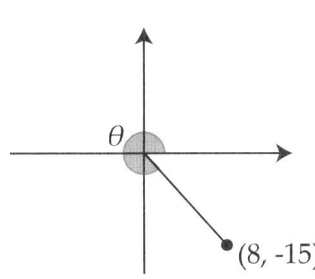

csc θ =

cos θ =

cot θ =

④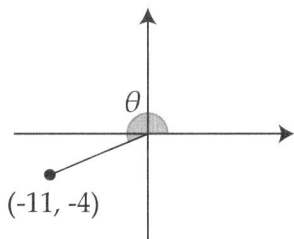

csc θ =

cos θ =

cot θ =

⑤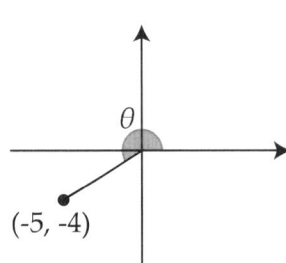

sin θ =

sec θ =

tan θ =

⑥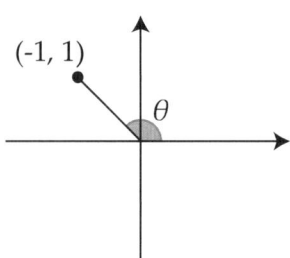

sin θ =

sec θ =

tan θ =

2. Trigonometry of Any Angles (Definition 3)

※ Signs of Trig Functions

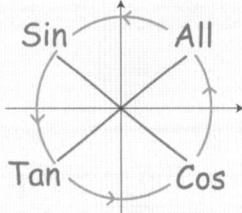

ARE **positive!!**

"Remember: **A**ll **S**tudents **T**ake **C**alculus*"*

EXAMPLE 2. Find the quadrant in which θ lies from the information given.

① $\sin\theta > 0$, $\cos\theta < 0$ ② $\tan\theta > 0$, $\sin\theta < 0$

③ $\tan\theta < 0$, $\sec\theta > 0$ ④ $\sec\theta < 0$, $\csc\theta > 0$

⑤ $\sin\theta > 0$, $\cot\theta > 0$ ⑥ $\cot\theta > 0$, $\csc\theta > 0$

⑦ $\csc\theta < 0$, $\sec\theta < 0$ ⑧ $\csc\theta < 0$, $\cot\theta < 0$

※ Reference Angle $\bar{\theta}$
: the **acute angle** between the terminal side of θ and x axis.

※ Reference triangle
: Drop a perpendicular line from the terminal side to the x-axis

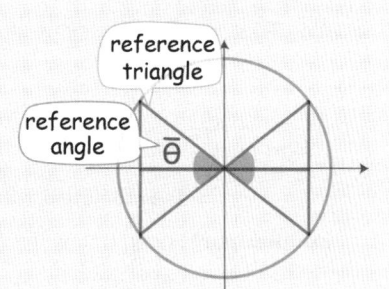

ex)

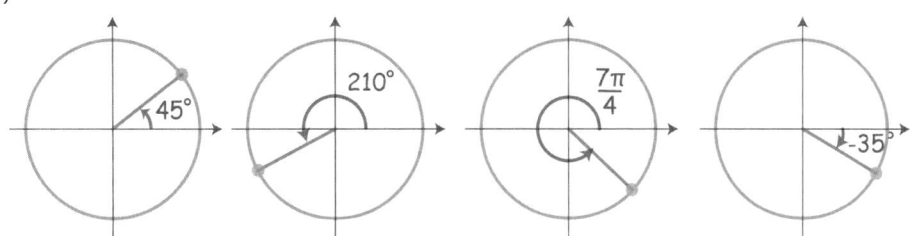

EXAMPLE 3. Find the reference number for each value of θ.

① $\theta = -300°$ ② $\theta = 315°$

③ $\theta = \dfrac{7\pi}{3}$ ④ $\theta = -\dfrac{\pi}{3}$

⑤ $\theta = -\dfrac{5\pi}{6}$ ⑥ $\theta = \dfrac{7\pi}{4}$

※ Evaluating Trigonometric Functions of Any Angles

Any trig function of θ can be written as ;

sign part is determined by ① _____

(see the quadrant in which the terminal side lies)

number part is determined by ② _____

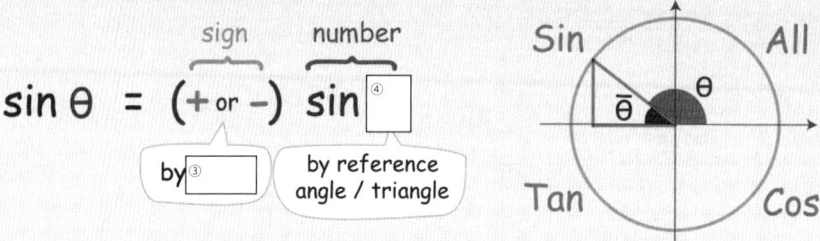

ex) $\tan 120° = $ ⑤ ____ $\tan$ _____ $\tan 210° = $ ⑥ ____ $\tan$ _____

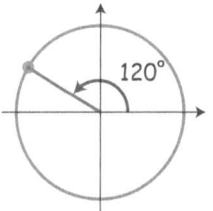   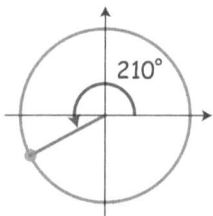

Blank : ① ASTC   ② reference angle $\bar{\theta}$ ③ ASTC   ④ $\bar{\theta}$ ⑤ −tan60°   ⑥ +tan 30°

EXAMPLE 4. Express the given trigonometric ratio as a function of its reference angle. Find the values of given trigonometric ratios.

① $\sin 225°$

② $\cos 150°$

③ $\tan(-210°)$

④ $\sec 300°$

⑤ $\sin \dfrac{3\pi}{4}$

⑥ $\cos \dfrac{11\pi}{3}$

⑦ $\cos \dfrac{5\pi}{4}$

⑧ $\tan \dfrac{11\pi}{6}$

⑨ $\cos\left(-\dfrac{4\pi}{3}\right)$

⑩ $\sin \dfrac{4\pi}{3}$

⑪ $\csc \dfrac{9\pi}{4}$

⑫ $\sec\left(-\dfrac{5\pi}{4}\right)$

⑬ $\cot\left(-\dfrac{17\pi}{6}\right)$

⑭ $\csc\left(-\dfrac{8\pi}{3}\right)$

EXAMPLE 5. Find the exact values of the given trigonometric functions of θ from the given information.

① $\sin\theta = -\dfrac{4}{5}$, θ is in quadrant III

Find $\cos\theta$, $\tan\theta$.

② $\tan\theta = -\dfrac{2}{7}$, θ is in quadrant II

Find $\sin\theta$, $\cos\theta$.

③ $\csc\theta = \dfrac{4}{3}$, $\dfrac{\pi}{2} \leq \theta \leq \pi$

Find $\sec\theta$, $\tan\theta$.

④ $\cot\theta = 2$, $\pi \leq \theta \leq \dfrac{3\pi}{2}$

Find $\sin\theta$, $\sec\theta$.

⑤ $\cos\theta = \dfrac{5}{13}$, $\sin\theta < 0$

Find $\sin\theta$, $\cot\theta$.

⑥ $\sec\theta = -\dfrac{7}{5}$, $\csc\theta < 0$

Find $\sin\theta$, $\cot\theta$.

3. Expand Knowledge

EXAMPLE 6. * Find the quadrant in which θ lies given that $\sin\theta\sec\theta<0$, $\cos\theta\cot\theta<0$.

EXAMPLE 7. * If $\dfrac{3\pi}{2}<\theta<2\pi$, simplify

$$\sin\theta+\cos\theta+\tan\theta+|\sin\theta|+|\cos\theta|+|\tan\theta|.$$

Mia's Precalculus
4.4 Trigonometry in Unit Circle

1. Trigonometry of Unit Circle (Definition 4)

Reminder ☺

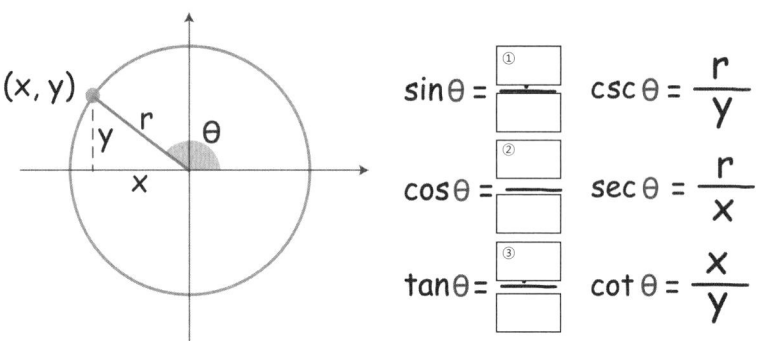

A '④_____' is a circle with radius ⑤____.

※ Sine and Cosine in Unit Circle

When θ is in standard position,

Let point (x, y) represent the point where the terminal side of the angle intersects the unit circle

(r = ⑥____).

Then

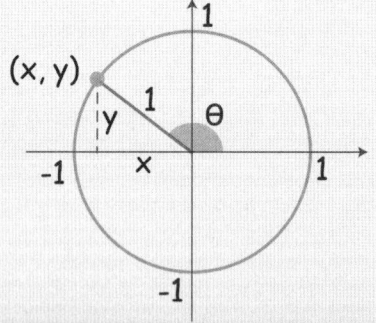

$$\sin\theta = y \quad \cos\theta = x \quad \tan\theta = \frac{y}{x}$$

Blank : ① $\frac{y}{r}$ ② $\frac{x}{r}$ ③ $\frac{y}{x}$ ④ unit circle ⑤ 1 ⑥ 1

For the whole circle we need values in every quadrant, with the correct plus or minus sign as per Cartesian Coordinates:

Note that cos is first and sin is second, so it goes (cos, sin):

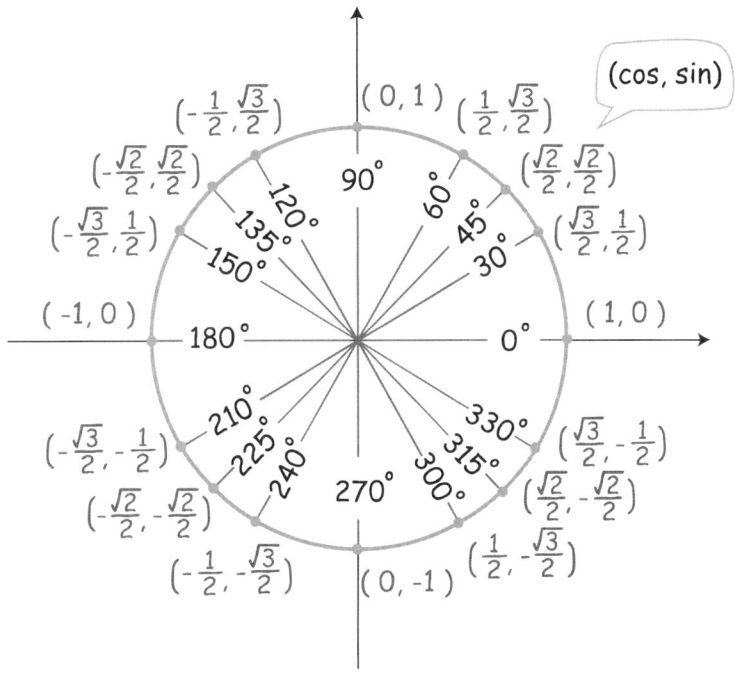

EXAMPLE 1. Find the exact value of each expression using unit circle.

① $\sin \dfrac{\pi}{3}$

② $\cos \dfrac{5\pi}{6}$

③ $\cos \dfrac{5\pi}{6}$

④ $\sin \dfrac{5\pi}{4}$

⑤ $\tan \dfrac{7\pi}{4}$

⑥ $\sin 120°$

⑦ $\sec\dfrac{7\pi}{6}$

⑧ $\cot\dfrac{13\pi}{6}$

⑨ $\cot 0$

⑩ $\sec\dfrac{3\pi}{4}$

⑪ $\sec\dfrac{10\pi}{3}$

⑫ $\csc 60°$

⑬ $\sin 2\pi$

⑭ $\tan 2\pi$

⑮ $\cos\dfrac{\pi}{2}$

⑯ $\sin\pi$

⑰ $\tan 7\pi$

⑱ $\sin(-8\pi)$

※ Facts form Unit circle

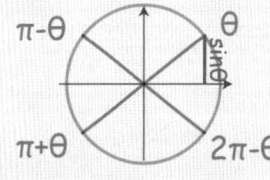

$\sin(\pi-\theta) = \sin\theta$
$\sin(\pi+\theta) = $ ①
$\sin(2\pi-\theta) = $ ②
$\sin(2\pi+\theta) = $ ③

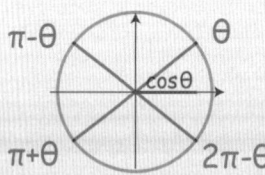

$\cos(\pi-\theta) = -\cos\theta$
$\cos(\pi+\theta) = $ ④
$\cos(2\pi-\theta) = $ ⑤
$\cos(2\pi+\theta) = $ ⑥

Blank : ① $-\sin\theta$ ② $-\sin\theta$ ③ $\sin\theta$ ④ $-\cos\theta$ ⑤ $\cos\theta$ ⑥ $\cos\theta$

EXAMPLE 2. Given the $\sin \theta = 0.6$, find the value of

① $\sin(\pi - \theta)$　　　　　　　　　② $\sin(\theta + \pi)$

③ $\sin(2\pi - \theta)$　　　　　　　　　④ $\sin(-\theta)$

EXAMPLE 3. Given the $\cos \theta = 0.4$, find the value of

① $\cos(\pi + \theta)$　　　　　　　　　② $\cos(\pi - \theta)$

③ $\cos(-\theta)$　　　　　　　　　　④ $\cos(2\pi - \theta)$

2. Expand Knowledge

EXAMPLE 4. * $\cos\theta + \cos(\pi - \theta) + \cos(\pi + \theta) + \cos(2\pi + \theta)$.

EXAMPLE 5. * A unit circle is divided into 10 equal angles. Let the ten terminal points are $A_1, A_2, \ldots, A_{10}$ as shown. If $\angle A_1 O A_2 = \theta$, what is $\sin\theta + \sin 2\theta + \ldots + \sin 10\theta$?

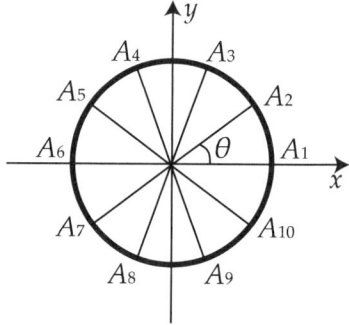

Mia's Precalculus

4.5 Trigonometric Graphs for Sin, Cos

1. Transformations of trigonometric graphs

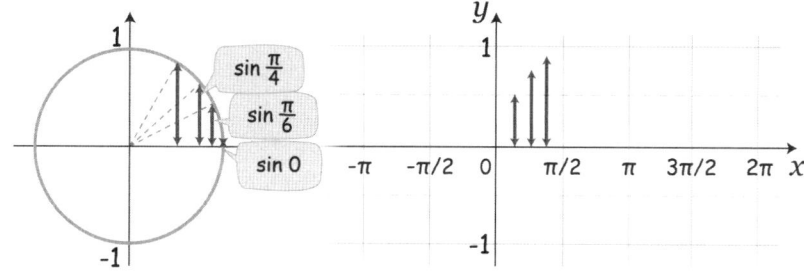

The **Sine Function** y = ①_____ has this 'wavy' up-down curve

which repeats every ②_____ radians and passes ③_____ (when x = 0).

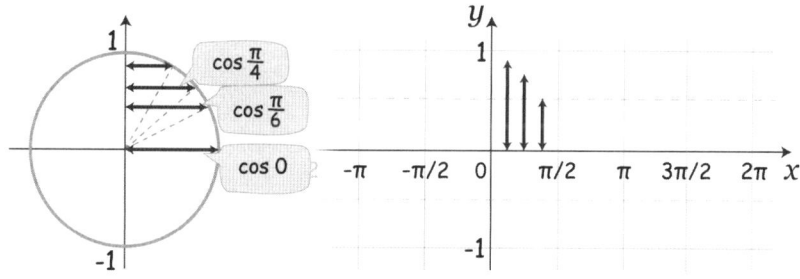

The **Cosine Function** y = ④_____ has this 'wavy' up-down curve

which repeats every ⑤_____ radians and passes ⑥_____ (when x = 0).

Blank : ① sin x   ② 2π ③ 0   ④ cos x   ⑤ 2π ⑥ 1
⑦ periodic   ⑧ repeats   ⑨ $\frac{max - min}{2}$ ⑩ [-1,1] , 1, 2π , origin , odd   ⑪ [-1,1] , 1, 2π , y axis , even

Part 4 Trigonometry Definition and Graphs

Trig functions are ⑦ _____ functions, because all possible y values ⑧ _____ **in the same sequence** over a given set of x values.

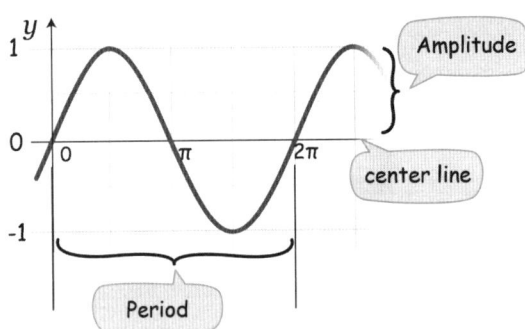

☺ Words

Amplitude: distance between the center line and the maximum point

(=half the distance from the max point to the min point=⑨ _____)

Period: length of x for which the graph repeats.

※ Graphs of Trigonometric Functions

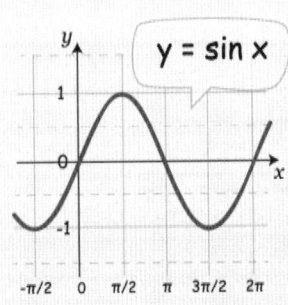

y = sin x

⑩ Domain: (-∞, ∞)

Range: _____

Amplitude: _____

Period: _____

Symmetry: _____ (odd/even)

y = cos x

⑪ Domain: (-∞, ∞)

Range: _____

Amplitude: _____

Period: _____

Symmetry: _____ (odd/even)

EXAMPLE 1. Evaluate using the graph of sin and cos.

① $\sin\dfrac{3\pi}{2}+\sin 2\pi$

② $\sin 5\pi+\sin\dfrac{\pi}{2}$

③ $\cos\dfrac{\pi}{2}+\cos 2\pi-\cos\pi$

④ $\cos\dfrac{3\pi}{2}-\cos\pi$

2. Transforming the Graph of Sine and Cosine

Let's look at how the **amplitude** and **period changes** as numbers of the function *change*.

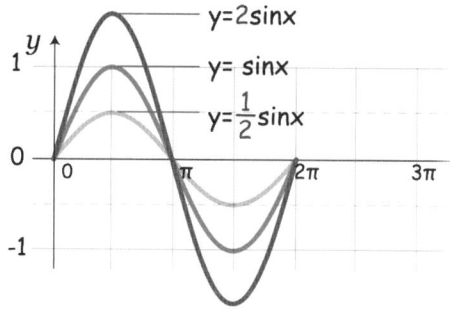

When the number **in front of sin x** changes.
the ① _____ changes,

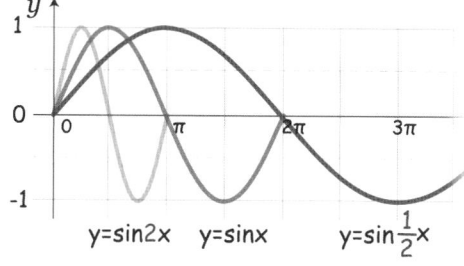

When the number **in front of x** changes.
the ② _____ changes,

Blank : ① amplitude ② period

※ Transformation of Sine and Cosine

$$y = A \begin{smallmatrix} \sin \\ \cos \end{smallmatrix} (B(x-C)) + D$$

Amplitude: ①_____   Period: ②_____

Translation : ③_____

EXAMPLE 2. Find the amplitude, period, translations and range of the function.

① $y = 4\sin\left(5x + \dfrac{\pi}{8}\right) + 3$ ② $y = -\sin\left(\dfrac{x}{3} - \pi\right) - 1$

③ $y = -\sin\left(\dfrac{1}{5}x + 3\right) + 2$ ④ $y = 4\cos(2x + 3\pi) - 2$

Blank : ① $|A|$ ② $\dfrac{2\pi}{B}$ ③ Left or right C units, up or down D units

⑤ $y = -\dfrac{1}{2}\cos\left(\dfrac{\pi x}{3} - \dfrac{\pi}{5}\right)$ ⑥ $y = -3\sin\left(\dfrac{3}{\pi}x + \pi\right) - 3$

EXAMPLE 3. Graph the function over a one-period interval.

① $y = 3\sin x$ ② $y = 2\cos x$

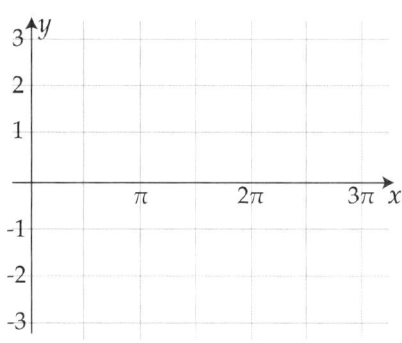 

③ $y = -2\sin x + 2$ ④ $y = 3\sin x - 1$

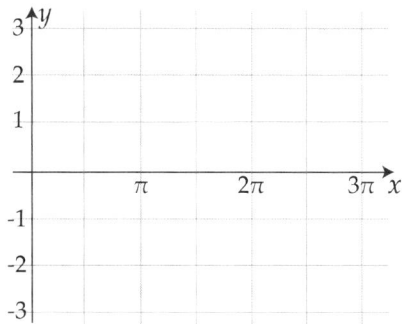 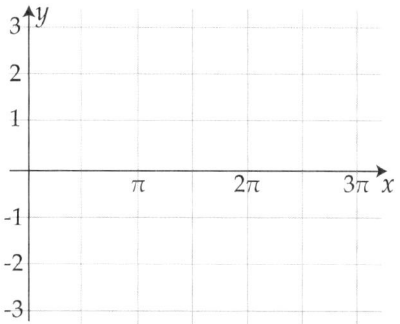

⑤ $y = \cos\left(x - \dfrac{\pi}{2}\right) + 2$

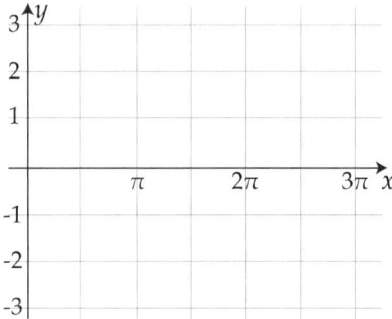

⑥ $y = 3\sin\left(x + \dfrac{\pi}{4}\right)$

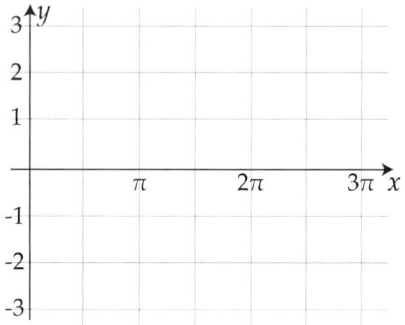

⑦ $y = 3\cos(2x)$

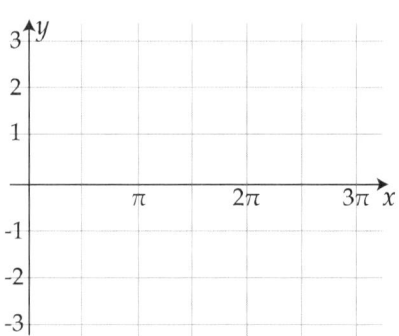

⑧ $y = 2\sin(2x) + 1$

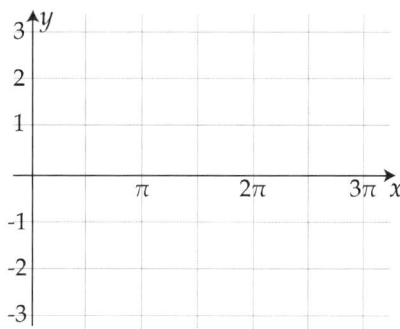

⑨ $y = 2\sin\left(\dfrac{x}{3}\right)$

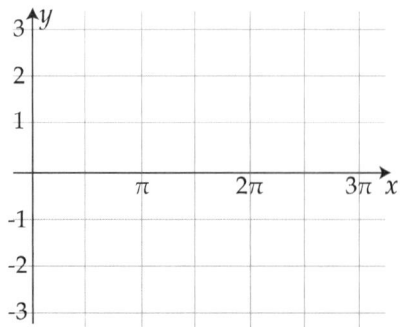

⑩ $y = -3\cos\left(\dfrac{x}{2}\right) - 1$

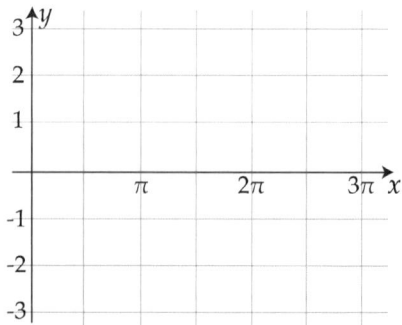

⑪ $y = -2\cos(\pi x)$

⑫ $y = -\sin\left(\dfrac{\pi x}{3}\right)$

EXAMPLE 4. The graph of one complete period of a sine or cosine curve is given. Write an equation that represents the curve.

①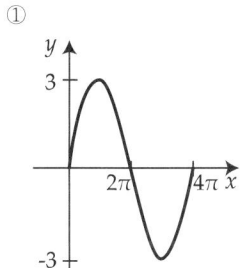

②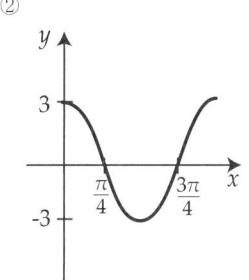

③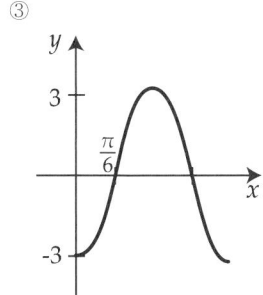

④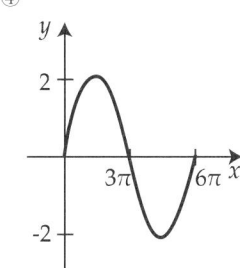

Part 4 Trigonometry Definition and Graphs

⑤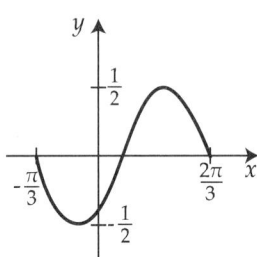

⑥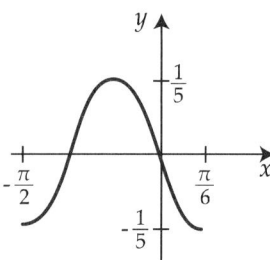

⑦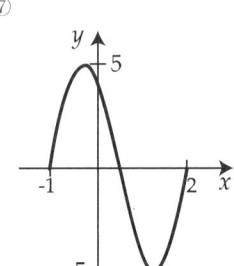

⑧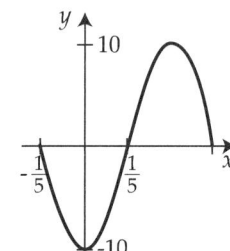

⑨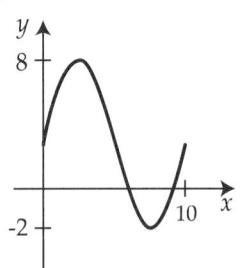

⑩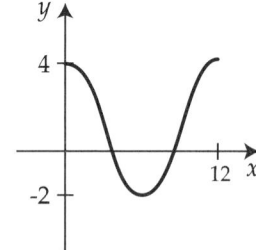

3. Modeling using trigonometric functions

EXAMPLE 5. The height of water in the harbor is 18 m at high tide, and 12 hours later at low tide, it is 10 m. The graph below shows how the height of water changes with time over 24 hours.

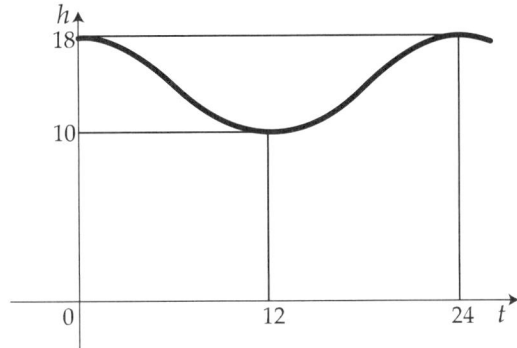

Find the equation for height (in meters) in terms of time (in hours).

EXAMPLE 6. The Ferris wheel with diameter 50ft makes one complete turn every 200 sec. The bottom of the wheel is 8ft above the ground and a seat A starts at the bottom of the wheel. Find an equation that describes the height of seat A with respect to time.

EXAMPLE 7. The following diagram shows a waterwheel with a bucket. The wheel rotates at a constant rate in an anticlockwise (counterclockwise) direction.

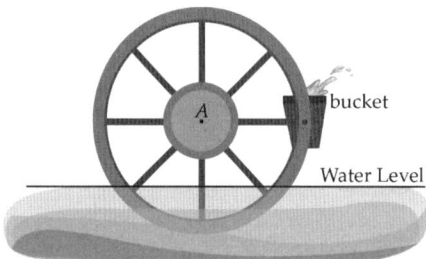

The diameter of the wheel is 8 m. The centre of the wheel, A, is 2 m above the water level. The water bucket turns at a rate of one rotation every 30 seconds. Find an equation that describes the height of the water bucket with respect to time.

EXAMPLE 8. A wright is attached to a spring suspended from a beam. At time t = 0, it is pulled down to a point 7cm above the ground and released. After than, is bounces up and down between its minimum height of 7 cm and a maximum height of 21 cm. It first reaches a maximum height 0.6 seconds after starting. Find an equation that describes its motion.

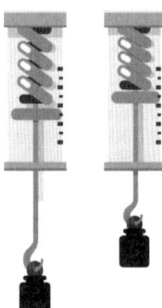

EXAMPLE 9. A pendulum is pulled back 20° off center and released to swing. It takes the pendulum a quarter of a second to reach other side. Determine a function that describes the angle of the pendulum with respect to time.
(Take t = 0 to be the time when the pendulum is at very right)

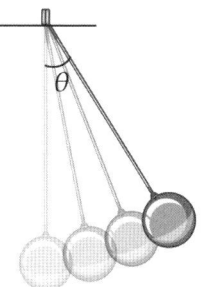

4. Expand Knowledge

EXAMPLE 10. * The graph shown has equation $y = C - A\sin\left(\dfrac{x}{B}\right)$. Find the values of A, B and C.

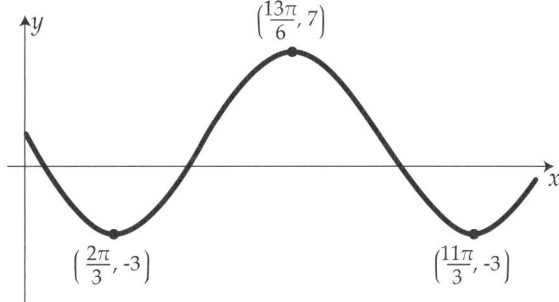

EXAMPLE 11. *The graph shown has equation $y = a\sin\left(bx - \dfrac{\pi}{6}\right) + c$. Find the values of a, b and c.

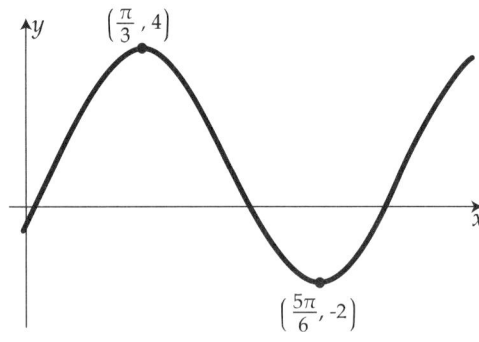

EXAMPLE 12. * Find the range of the function $f(x) = \dfrac{3}{5 + 2\sin x}$.

EXAMPLE 13. * Find the smallest positive value of x for which $\dfrac{1}{3 - \sin\left(x - \dfrac{\pi}{4}\right)}$ takes its maximum value.

※ Periodic Function

If a function f is periodic, where p is a positive number, called a period of f , then

$$f(x + p) = f(x)$$

EXAMPLE 14. * What is the period of $f(x-2)=f(x)$

EXAMPLE 15. * What is the period of $f(x+10)=f(x+4)$?

EXAMPLE 16. * If $f(x)=f(x+2)$ and $f(0)=1, f(1)=2$, then what is $f(1001)+f(1002)+f(1003)$?

Mia's Precalculus
4.6 Trigonometric Graphs for Others

1. The Graph of Tangent

　※ Graph of Tangent

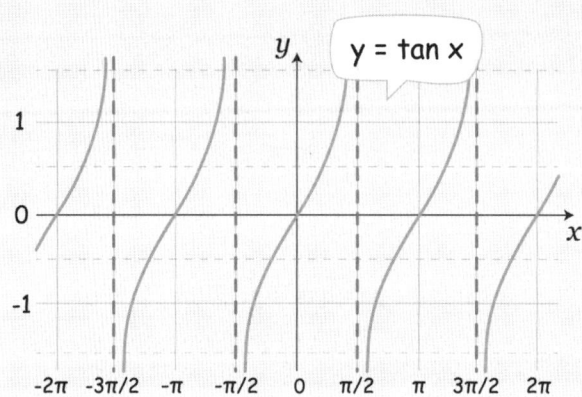

Domain: ①_____

Range: ②_____

Amplitude: ③_____

Period: ④_____

Symmetry: ⑤_____(odd/even)

$$y = A\tan(B(x-C)) + D$$

Period: ⑥_____　translation: ⑦_____

Blank : ① R, x ≠ $\frac{(2n-1)\pi}{2}$ (where n is integer)　② R(all real numbers)　③ none　④ π　⑤ origin (odd)
　⑥ $\frac{\pi}{B}$　⑦ Left or right C units,　up or down D units

EXAMPLE 1. Find the period and translation of given function.

① $y = -2\tan\left(2x - \dfrac{\pi}{4}\right) + 1$

② $y = 3\tan\left(\dfrac{x}{4} + \pi\right) + 3$

③ $y = 3\tan\left(\dfrac{1}{2}x - 2\right) - 5$

④ $y = 4\tan(3\pi x - \pi)$

EXAMPLE 2. Graph the function.

① $y = 3\tan x$

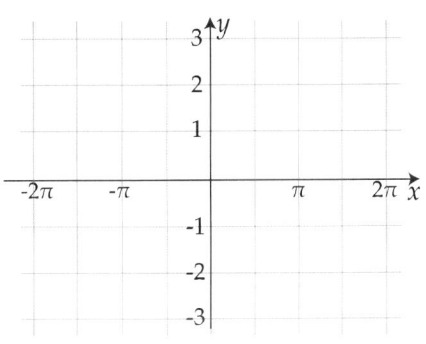

② $y = \tan 2x$

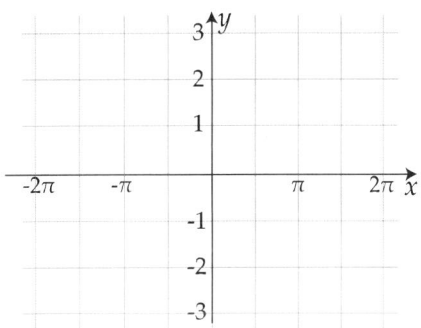

③ $y = -\tan\dfrac{x}{2}$

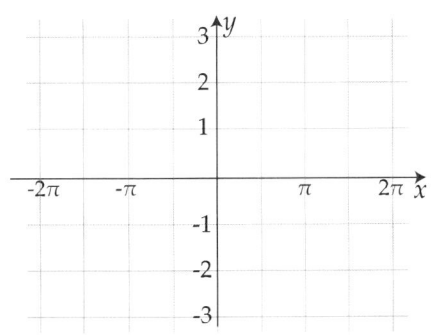

④ $y = \tan(x - \pi)$

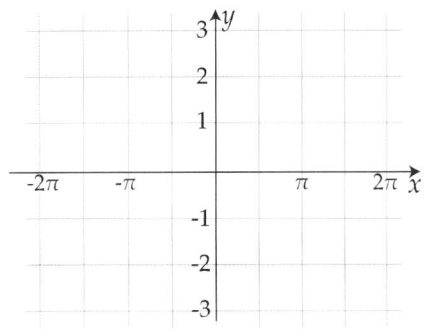

⑤ $y = \tan\left(x - \dfrac{\pi}{2}\right)$

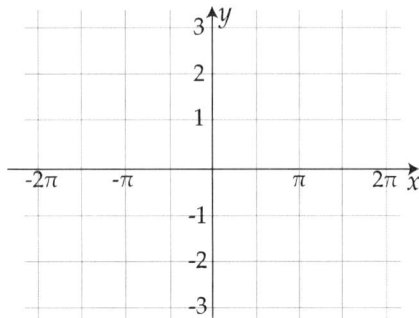

2. The Graph of Csc, Sec, and Cot

To sketch a reciprocal function;

$y = f(x)$	$y = \dfrac{1}{f(x)}$
0	①
vertical asymptote	
1	
-1	
Large and positive	
small and positive	
Large and negative	
small and negative	
Maximum point	
Minimum point	

Blank : ① und , 0 , 1 , -1 , small and positive , large and positive , small and negative , large and negative , min , max

1) Graph of y=csc(x)

Try to graph the reciprocal function of sin x.

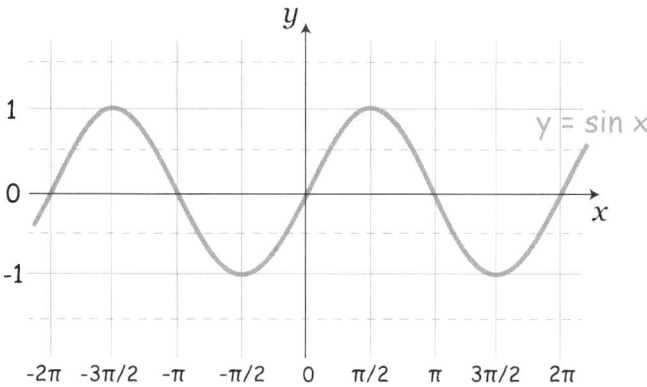

2) Graph of y=sec(x)

Try to graph the reciprocal function of cos x.

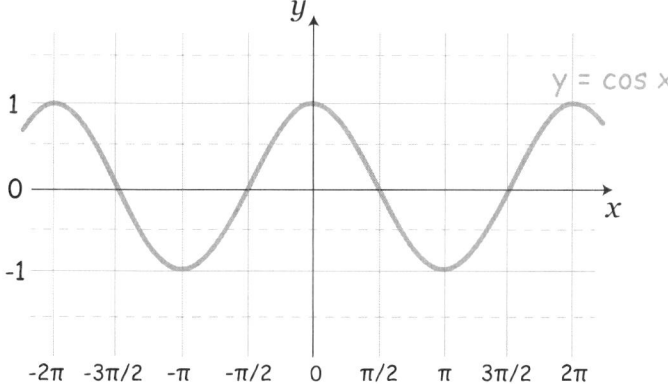

3) Graph of y=cot(x)

Try to graph the reciprocal function of tan x.

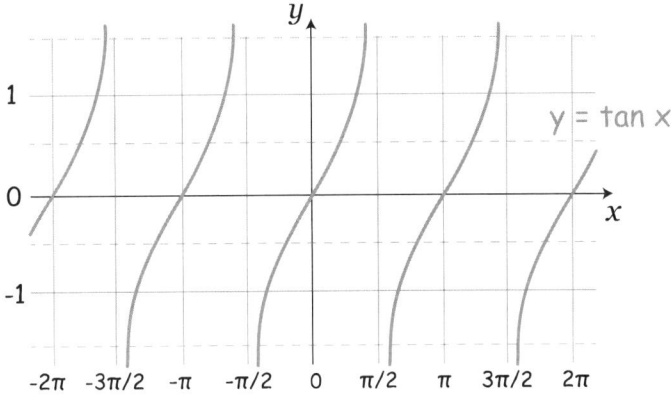

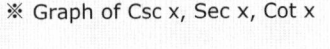

※ Graph of Csc x, Sec x, Cot x

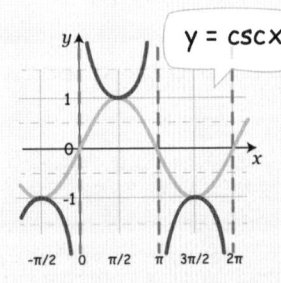
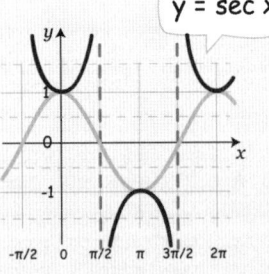
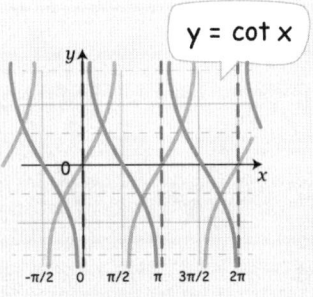

EXAMPLE 3. Graph the function.

① $y = 2\csc x$

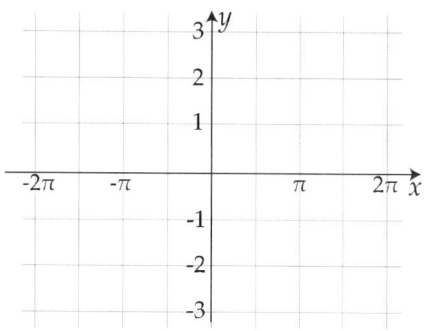

② $y = 0.5\sec x$

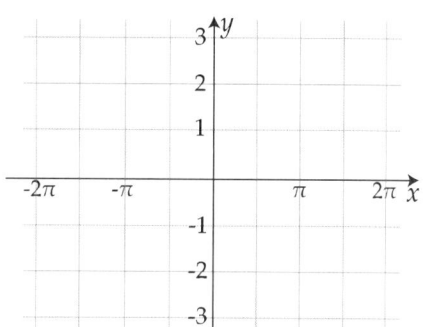

③ $y = \sec(0.5x)$

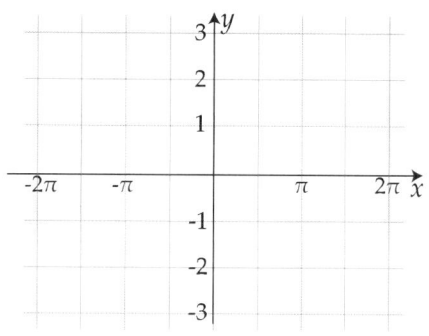

④ $y = \csc 2x$

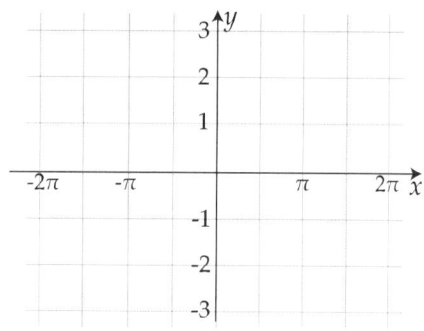

⑤ $y = \cot(x - \pi)$

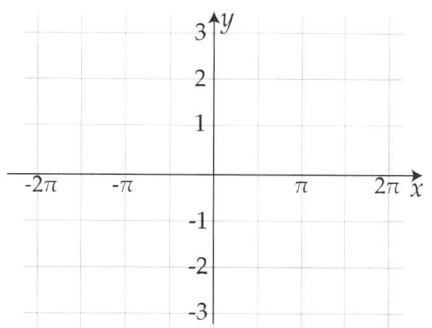

⑥ $y = \cot x + 1$

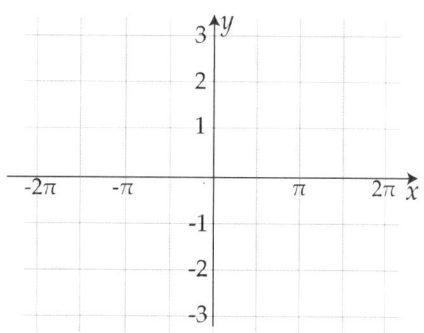

☺ ALL in one _ Graphs of trig functions

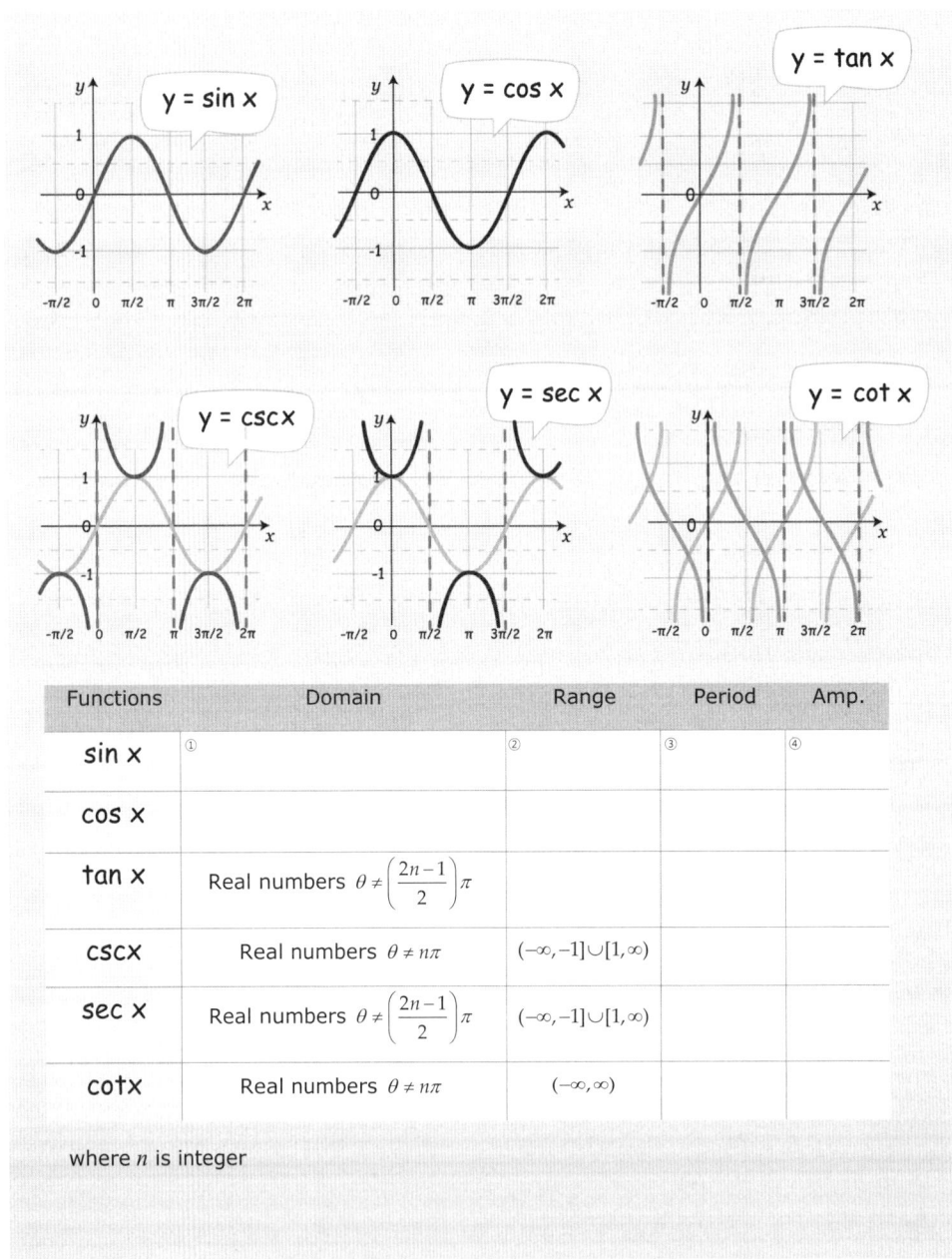

where n is integer

Blank : ① R, R   ② [-1, 1] , [-1, 1] , R   ③ 2π, 2π, π, 2π, 2π, π   ④ 1 , 1 , none , none , none , none

3. Expand Knowledge

EXAMPLE 4. * Write each value in increasing order.
$$A = \sin(1),\ B = \cos(1),\ C = \tan(1)$$

Part 5
Trigonometry Identities

5.1 Inverse Trigonometry Function
5.2 Basic Trigonometric Identities
5.3 Verifying Trigonometric Identities
5.4 Sum and difference Identities
5.5 Double-Angle Identity
5.6 Half-Angle and Product-Sum Identities

Mia's Precalculus
5.1 Inverse Trigonometry Function

1. Inverse Trig Function

※ Inverse Trigonometry function

The Sine function takes an ①_____ and gives us the ②_____.

Inverse Sine **sin⁻¹**(= **arcsin**) takes the ③_____ and gives us the ④_____.

$$\sin(30°) = \frac{1}{2} \quad \rightleftarrows \quad \begin{array}{l} 30° = \sin^{-1}\left(\frac{1}{2}\right) \\ 30° = \arcsin\left(\frac{1}{2}\right) \end{array} \quad \text{(Inverse Trig)}$$

EXAMPLE 1. Find the measure of the indicated angle to the nearest degree.

①
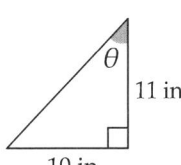
11 in, 10 in

②
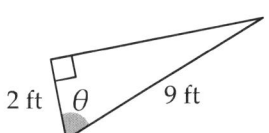
2 ft, 9 ft

③
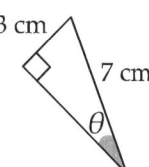
3 cm, 7 cm

④
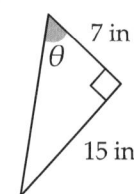
7 in, 15 in

Blank : ① angle ② ratio ③ ratio ④ angle

EXAMPLE 2. A 40-ft ladder leans against a building. If the base of the ladder is 12 ft from the base of the building, what is the angle formed by the ladder and the building?

EXAMPLE 3. Joshua observes a boat in the sea below him from a point 6 ft above a 45 ft cliff. He has been told that the distance from the boat to the base of the cliff is 60 ft. What is the angle of depression, in degrees, from Joshua to the boat?

2. Graph of Inverse Trig Function

☺ remind:

① Only **ONE-TO-ONE function** has an inverse function!

② Functions and their inverses are always symmetric about the line ① _____.

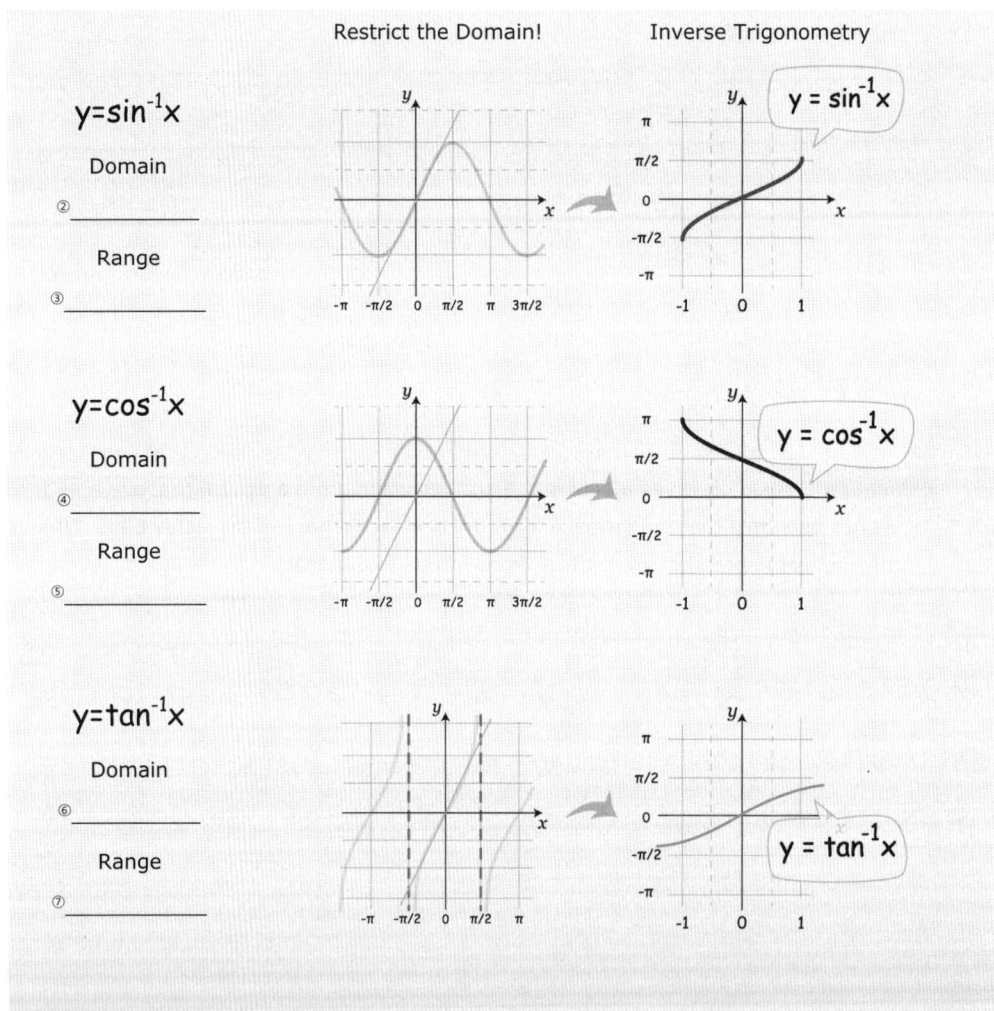

Blank: ① $y=x$ ② $[-1,1]$ ③ $\left[-\dfrac{\pi}{2}, \dfrac{\pi}{2}\right]$ ④ $[-1,1]$ ⑤ $[0,\pi]$ ⑥ $\mathbb{R}$ ⑦ $\left(-\dfrac{\pi}{2}, \dfrac{\pi}{2}\right)$

In unit circle:

$-\frac{\pi}{2} \leq \sin^{-1}x \leq \frac{\pi}{2}$ $0 \leq \cos^{-1}x \leq \pi$ $-\frac{\pi}{2} < \tan^{-1}x < \frac{\pi}{2}$

EXAMPLE 4. Evaluate in radians.

Inverse Trig gives you the ANGLE!

① $\sin^{-1}\left(\frac{1}{2}\right)$ ② $\arccos\left(\frac{\sqrt{3}}{2}\right)$

③ $\tan^{-1}(1)$ ④ $\arctan(0)$

⑤ $\arccos\left(\frac{\sqrt{2}}{2}\right)$ ⑥ $\sin^{-1}(1)$

☺ Tip: Notice that $\csc^{-1}A = \sin^{-1}\left(\frac{1}{A}\right)$

⑦ $\text{arccsc}(2)$ ⑧ $\text{arcsec}(1)$

⑨ $\cot^{-1}(\sqrt{3})$ ⑩ $\text{arccsc}\left(\frac{2\sqrt{3}}{3}\right)$

⑪ $\text{arcsec}(\sqrt{2})$ ⑫ $\text{arccot}(1)$

Part 5. Trigonometry Identities

☺ Tip: Notice that

$$\sin^{-1}(-A) = \underline{\quad①\quad}$$

$$\cos^{-1}(-A) = \underline{\quad②\quad}$$

$$\tan^{-1}(-A) = \underline{\quad③\quad}$$

⑬ $\cos^{-1}\left(-\dfrac{\sqrt{3}}{2}\right)$ ⑭ $\arcsin\left(-\dfrac{1}{2}\right)$

⑮ $\arctan\left(-\sqrt{3}\right)$ ⑯ $\tan^{-1}(-1)$

⑰ $\sin^{-1}\left(-\dfrac{\sqrt{2}}{2}\right)$ ⑱ $\cos^{-1}\left(-\dfrac{1}{2}\right)$

3. Evaluating Inverse Trigs (Type1)

☺ remind: $f^{-1}(f(x)) = f(f^{-1}(x)) = \underline{\quad④\quad}$

But if there is inverse trig or trig in your outer function, be careful with the range!

$$\boxed{⑤} \leq \sin(\sin^{-1}x) = x \leq \boxed{⑥}$$

$$\boxed{⑦} \leq \cos(\cos^{-1}x) = x \leq \boxed{⑧}$$

$$\boxed{⑨} < \tan(\tan^{-1}x) = x < \boxed{⑩}$$

Blank : ① $-\sin^{-1}A$ ② $\pi - \cos^{-1}A$ ③ $-\tan^{-1}A$ ④ x   ⑤ -1   ⑥ 1   ⑦ -1   ⑧ 1   ⑨ $-\infty$ ⑩ ∞

EXAMPLE 5. Find the exact value.

① $\sin(\sin^{-1} 0.5)$

② $\tan(\arctan 0.2)$

③ $\cos(\cos^{-1}(-0.4))$

④ $\cos(\cos^{-1} \pi)$

⑤ $\sin(\arcsin e)$

⑥ $\sin(\sin^{-1} 0.8)$

⑦ $\tan(\arctan 2)$

⑧ $\tan(\tan^{-1} 3)$

4. Evaluating Inverse Trigs (Type2)

$$\boxed{①} \leq \sin^{-1}(\sin x) = x \leq \boxed{②}$$

$$\boxed{③} \leq \cos^{-1}(\cos x) = x \leq \boxed{④}$$

$$\boxed{⑤} < \tan^{-1}(\tan x) = x < \boxed{⑥}$$

If the answer is NOT in the range, use ASTC and reference angle to find the angle that is IN THE RANGE.

Blank : ① $-\dfrac{\pi}{2}$ ② $\dfrac{\pi}{2}$ ③ 0   ④ π ⑤ $-\dfrac{\pi}{2}$ ⑥ $\dfrac{\pi}{2}$

ex) Find the exact value.

a) $\sin^{-1}\left(\sin\dfrac{\pi}{3}\right)$

b) $\cos^{-1}\left(\cos\dfrac{\pi}{3}\right)$

c) $\tan^{-1}\left(\tan\dfrac{\pi}{3}\right)$

d) $\sin^{-1}\left(\sin\dfrac{2\pi}{3}\right)$

e) $\cos^{-1}\left(\cos\dfrac{2\pi}{3}\right)$

f) $\tan^{-1}\left(\tan\dfrac{2\pi}{3}\right)$

g) $\sin^{-1}\left(\sin\dfrac{5\pi}{4}\right)$

h) $\cos^{-1}\left(\cos\dfrac{5\pi}{4}\right)$

i) $\tan^{-1}\left(\tan\dfrac{5\pi}{4}\right)$

j) $\sin^{-1}\left(\sin\dfrac{11\pi}{6}\right)$

k) $\cos^{-1}\left(\cos\dfrac{11\pi}{6}\right)$

l) $\tan^{-1}\left(\tan\dfrac{11\pi}{6}\right)$

EXAMPLE 6. Find the exact value.

① $\sin^{-1}\left(\sin\dfrac{\pi}{6}\right)$

② $\tan^{-1}\left(\tan\dfrac{\pi}{3}\right)$

③ $\cos^{-1}\left(\cos\dfrac{3\pi}{4}\right)$

④ $\cos^{-1}\left(\cos\left(-\dfrac{\pi}{3}\right)\right)$

⑤ $\tan^{-1}\left(\tan\left(-\dfrac{2\pi}{3}\right)\right)$

⑥ $\cos^{-1}\left(\cos\dfrac{4\pi}{3}\right)$

⑦ $\cos^{-1}\left(\cos\dfrac{7\pi}{4}\right)$

⑧ $\tan^{-1}\left(\tan\dfrac{11\pi}{6}\right)$

⑨ $\tan^{-1}\left(\tan\dfrac{7\pi}{3}\right)$

⑩ $\sin^{-1}\left(\sin\dfrac{10\pi}{3}\right)$

⑪ $\cos^{-1}\left(\cos\dfrac{7\pi}{5}\right)$

⑫ $\sin^{-1}\left(\sin\dfrac{5\pi}{8}\right)$

5. Evaluating Inverse Trigs (Type3)

EXAMPLE 7. Use a sketch to find the exact value.

> ☺ Tip: Use a sketch!

① $\sin\left(\tan^{-1}\dfrac{1}{2}\right)$ 　　　　　② $\tan\left(\cos^{-1}-\dfrac{1}{3}\right)$

③ $\cos\left(\arctan\left(-\dfrac{3}{4}\right)\right)$ 　　　　　④ $\cos\left(\sin^{-1}\left(-\dfrac{3}{5}\right)\right)$

⑤ $\tan\left(\cos^{-1}\left(-\dfrac{5}{13}\right)\right)$ 　　　　　⑥ $\sec\left(\cos^{-1}\left(-\dfrac{8}{17}\right)\right)$

EXAMPLE 8. Write the following as an algebraic expression in x, x > 0.

① $\tan(\arcsin x)$

② $\cos(\sin^{-1} x)$

③ $\sin(\sin^{-1} x)$

④ $\cos(\arccos x)$

⑤ $\cot(\cos^{-1} x)$

⑥ $\sec(\operatorname{arccot} x)$

⑦ $\sin\left(\tan^{-1} \dfrac{x}{\sqrt{5}}\right)$

⑧ $\cot\left(\cos^{-1} \dfrac{3}{\sqrt{x^2+9}}\right)$

⑨ $\sin\left(\sec^{-1} \dfrac{\sqrt{x^2+4}}{x}\right)$

6. Expand Knowledge

EXAMPLE 9. * Determine whether each function is odd, even, or neither.

① $y = \sin^{-1} x$

② $y = \cos^{-1} x$

③ $y = \tan^{-1} x$

EXAMPLE 10. * True or False.

① $\sin^{-1} x = \dfrac{1}{\sin x} = \csc x$

② $\tan^{-1} x = \dfrac{\sin^{-1} x}{\cos^{-1} x}$

③ $\cot^{-1} x = \dfrac{1}{\tan^{-1} x}$

EXAMPLE 11. * Give the domain and range of each composite function.

① $y = \sin(\cos^{-1} x)$

② $y = \tan(\sin^{-1} x)$

③ $y = \cos(\tan^{-1} x)$

Mia's Precalculus

5.2 Basic Trigonometric Identities

1. Fundamental Identities

※ Reciprocal Identities

$$\sin\theta = \frac{1}{\csc\theta} \qquad \cos\theta = \frac{1}{\sec\theta} \qquad \tan\theta = \frac{1}{\cot\theta}$$

$$\csc\theta = \frac{1}{\sin\theta} \qquad \sec\theta = \frac{1}{\cos\theta} \qquad \cot\theta = \frac{1}{\tan\theta}$$

※ Quotient Identities

$$\tan\theta = \frac{\sin\theta}{\cos\theta} \qquad \cot\theta = \frac{\cos\theta}{\sin\theta}$$

☺ Proof:

When $\sin\theta = \frac{y}{r}$ and $\cos\theta = \frac{x}{r}$,

then $\tan\theta = \frac{y}{x} = \dfrac{\frac{y}{\boxed{①}}}{\frac{x}{\boxed{②}}} = \boxed{③}$

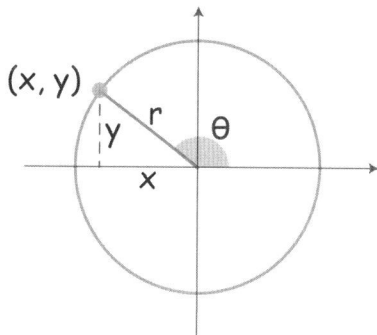

Blank : ① r   ② r   ③ $\dfrac{\sin\theta}{\cos\theta}$

Part 5. Trigonometry Identities

EXAMPLE 1. Simplify the given expression.

① $\tan x \cos x$

② $\cot x \tan x$

③ $\cot u \sin u$

④ $\dfrac{\sec \theta}{\csc \theta}$

⑤ $\dfrac{\csc \theta}{\cot \theta}$

※ Pythagorean Identities

$$\sin^2 \theta + \cos^2 \theta = 1$$
$$1 + \tan^2 \theta = \sec^2 \theta$$
$$1 + \cot^2 \theta = \csc^2 \theta$$

☺ Careful! $\sin^2 \theta = (\sin \theta)^2 \neq \sin \theta^2$

☺ Proof:

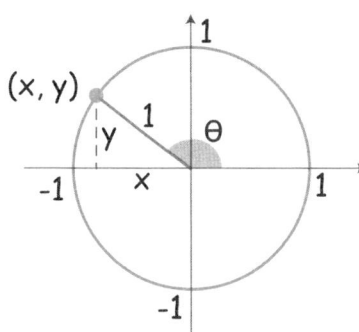

According to Pythagorean Theorem,

$$\sin^2\theta + \cos^2\theta = \boxed{①}$$

and if we divide everything by $\cos^2\theta$, then

$$\frac{\sin^2\theta}{\boxed{②}} + \frac{\cos^2\theta}{\boxed{③}} = \frac{1}{\boxed{④}}$$

$$\boxed{⑤} + 1 = \boxed{⑥}$$

EXAMPLE 2. Simplify the given expression.

① $\dfrac{1+\tan^2 x}{\csc^2 x}$

② $\dfrac{1-\cos^2\theta}{\sin\theta}$

③ $\dfrac{\cos x - \cos^3 x}{\sin^3 x}$

④ $\dfrac{\sin^2 x + \tan^2 x + \cos^2 x}{\sec x}$

⑤ $\dfrac{\sec\theta - \cos\theta}{\sin\theta}$

⑥ $\dfrac{1}{\cot^2\theta - \csc^2\theta}$

Blank : ① 1　② $\cos^2\theta$　③ $\cos^2\theta$　④ $\cos^2\theta$　⑤ $\tan^2\theta$　⑥ $\sec^2\theta$

※ Cofunction Identities

$$\sin\left(\frac{\pi}{2}-\theta\right) = \cos\theta \qquad \cos\left(\frac{\pi}{2}-\theta\right) = \sin\theta$$

$$\tan\left(\frac{\pi}{2}-\theta\right) = \cot\theta \qquad \cot\left(\frac{\pi}{2}-\theta\right) = \tan\theta$$

$$\csc\left(\frac{\pi}{2}-\theta\right) = \sec\theta \qquad \sec\left(\frac{\pi}{2}-\theta\right) = \csc\theta$$

(Complementary)

※ Odd-Even Identities

$$\sin(-\theta) = -\sin\theta \qquad \csc(-\theta) = -\csc\theta$$

$$\cos(-\theta) = \cos\theta \qquad \sec(-\theta) = \sec\theta$$

$$\tan(-\theta) = -\tan\theta \qquad \cot(-\theta) = -\cot\theta$$

☺ Proof:
From the figure;

$$\sin\theta = \frac{\boxed{①}}{\boxed{}} \qquad \cos\left(\frac{\pi}{2}-\theta\right) = \frac{\boxed{②}}{\boxed{}}$$

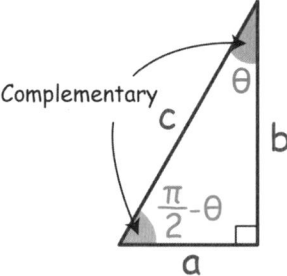

③ (even/odd) function: $f(-x) = f(x)$

④ (even/odd) function: $f(-x) = -f(x)$

Sin is ⑤(even/odd) function, *cos* is ⑥(even/odd) function, *tan* is ⑦(even/odd) function.

Blank : ① $\frac{a}{c}$ ② $\frac{a}{c}$ ③ even ④ odd ⑤ odd ⑥ even ⑦ odd

EXAMPLE 3. Simplify the given expression.

① $\sin x \csc(-x)$

② $\sec(-x)\sin\left(\dfrac{\pi}{2}-x\right)$

③ $\cos(-x)\csc\left(\dfrac{\pi}{2}-x\right)$

④ $\sec^2(-x)-\tan^2 x$

⑤ $\cot(-x)\tan(-x)$

⑥ $\sin^2(-x)+\sin^2\left(\dfrac{\pi}{2}-x\right)$

EXAMPLE 4. Use the even–odd properties to find the exact value of each expression.

① $\sin(-60°)$

② $\cos(-270°)$

③ $\tan(-\pi)$

④ $\csc\left(-\dfrac{\pi}{3}\right)$

⑤ $\cos\left(-\dfrac{\pi}{4}\right)$

⑥ $\tan\left(-\dfrac{\pi}{4}\right)$

⑦ $\cot\left(-\dfrac{\pi}{6}\right)$

EXAMPLE 5. Simplify the given expression.

① $\dfrac{\tan\left(\dfrac{\pi}{2}-x\right)\csc x}{\csc^2 x}$

② $\dfrac{1+\tan x}{1+\cot x}$

③ $\left(\sec^2 x+\csc^2 x\right)-\left(\tan^2 x+\cot^2 x\right)$

④ $\dfrac{\sec^2 u-\tan^2 u}{\cos^2 v+\sin^2 v}$

⑤ $\sin x\left(\tan x+\cot x\right)$

⑥ $\sin\theta-\tan\theta\cos\theta+\cos\left(\dfrac{\pi}{2}-\theta\right)$

⑦ $(\cot x-\csc x)(\cos x+1)$

⑧ $\dfrac{(\sec x-\tan x)(\sec x+\tan x)}{\sec x}$

⑨ $\dfrac{\tan x}{\csc^2 x} + \dfrac{\tan x}{\sec^2 x}$

⑩ $\sin x \cos x \tan x \sec x \csc x$

⑪ $\dfrac{\sec^2 x \csc x}{\sec^2 x + \csc^2 x}$

2. Expand Knowledge

EXAMPLE 6. *If $\sin\theta + \cos\theta = \dfrac{1}{2}$, then $\sin\theta\cos\theta = ?$

EXAMPLE 7. *If $\sin\theta + \cos\theta = \dfrac{1}{4}$, what is the value of $\tan\theta + \cot\theta$?

EXAMPLE 8. *If both the angles are acute and $\tan(3x+20°) = \cot(2x-40°)$, find x.

EXAMPLE 9. * What is $\sin^2 1° + \sin^2 2° + \sin^2 3° + \cdots + \sin^2 88° + \sin^2 89°$?

Mia's Precalculus
5.3 Verifying Trigonometric identities

1. Verifying Identities

EXAMPLE 5. Verify the identity.

Type1. Use Identities!
(Sometimes changing in terms of sin and cos will help.)

① $\cos^2 x - \sin^2 x = 1 - 2\sin^2 x$

② $\dfrac{\csc(-x)}{\sec(-x)} = -\cot x$

③ $(\tan x + \cot x)^4 = \csc^4 x \sec^4 x$

④ $\cot^2 x - \cos^2 x = \cot^2 x \cos^2 x$

Part 5. Trigonometry Identities

⑤ $\dfrac{\cos\theta \cot\theta}{1-\sin\theta} - 1 = \csc\theta$

⑥ $\dfrac{\tan x - \sin x}{\tan x \sin x} = \dfrac{\tan x \sin x}{\tan x + \sin x}$

⑦ $\dfrac{\csc x + \sec x}{\sin x + \cos x} = \csc x \sec x$

> Type2. Factoring could help.

⑧ $\dfrac{\sin^3 x + \cos^3 x}{\sin x + \cos x} = 1 - \sin x \cos x$

⑨ $\dfrac{\cot u - \tan u}{\cot^2 u - \tan^2 u} = \sin u \cos u$

⑩ $\dfrac{\sin^2 x - \cos^2 x}{(\sin x + \cos x)^2} = \dfrac{(\sin x - \cos x)^2}{\sin^2 x - \cos^2 x}$

| Type3. Combine the fractions! |

⑪ $\dfrac{1+\sin\theta}{\cos\theta} + \dfrac{\cos\theta}{1+\sin\theta} = 2\sec\theta$

⑫ $\dfrac{1}{\csc\theta+\cot\theta} + \dfrac{1}{\csc\theta-\cot\theta} = 2\csc\theta$

| Type4. Multiply or divide the top and the bottom by same things. |

⑬ $\dfrac{\sec x - 1}{\tan x} = \dfrac{\tan x}{\sec x + 1}$

⑭ $\dfrac{1+\sin x}{1-\sin x} = (\tan x + \sec x)^2$

⑮ $\dfrac{\tan x + \tan y}{1 - \tan x \tan y} = \dfrac{\cot x + \cot y}{\cot x \cot y - 1}$

Type5. Work each side separately!
---

⑯ $\dfrac{\csc x \sec x + 2}{\csc x \sec x} = (\sin x + \cos x)^2$

⑰ $\dfrac{\tan^2 x}{1+\sec x} = \dfrac{1-\cos x}{\cos x}$

2. Expand knowledge

EXAMPLE 2. * Verify $\ln|\sec\theta + \tan\theta| + \ln|\sec\theta - \tan\theta| = 0$

EXAMPLE 3. * If $0 < x < \dfrac{\pi}{2}$, verify $\log_2 \cos x + \log_2\left(\dfrac{\cos x}{1+\sin x} + \dfrac{1+\sin x}{\cos x}\right) = 1$

Mia's Precalculus
5.4 Sum and Difference Identities

1. Sum and Difference Identities

  ※ Sum and Difference Identities

  $$\sin(A \pm B) = \sin A \cos B \pm \cos A \sin B$$

  $$\cos(A \pm B) = \cos A \cos B \mp \sin A \sin B$$

  (switch sign)

  $$\tan(A \pm B) = \frac{\tan A \pm \tan B}{1 \mp \tan A \tan B}$$

EXAMPLE 1. Find the exact value of the expression without using calculator.

① $\sin(75°) = \sin\left(\boxed{}\right)$ 　　　② $\cos(75°) = \cos\left(\boxed{}\right)$

③ $\cos(15°) = \cos\left(\boxed{}\right)$ 　　　④ $\tan(75°) = \tan\left(\boxed{}\right)$

⑤ $\tan(105°) = \tan\left(\boxed{}\right)$

EXAMPLE 2. Find the exact value of the expression without using a calculator.

① $\sin 20° \cos 40° + \cos 20° \sin 40°$

② $\sin 215° \cos 95° - \cos 215° \sin 95°$

③ $\cos \dfrac{5\pi}{12} \cos \dfrac{\pi}{4} - \sin \dfrac{5\pi}{12} \sin \dfrac{\pi}{4}$

④ $\cos \dfrac{5\pi}{18} \cos \dfrac{2\pi}{9} - \sin \dfrac{5\pi}{18} \sin \dfrac{2\pi}{9}$

⑤ $\dfrac{\tan 40° + \tan 110°}{1 - \tan 40° \tan 110°}$

⑥ $\dfrac{\tan 80° - \tan(-40°)}{1 + \tan 80° \tan(-40°)}$

EXAMPLE 3. Verify the following.

① $\cos\left(x + \dfrac{\pi}{2}\right) = -\sin x$

② $\sin(x+y) + \sin(x-y) = 2\sin x \cos y$

③ $\dfrac{\cos(x+y)}{\cos(x-y)} = \dfrac{1 - \tan x \tan y}{1 + \tan x \tan y}$

EXAMPLE 4. Simplify $\tan\left(A+\dfrac{\pi}{4}\right)\tan\left(A-\dfrac{\pi}{4}\right)$.

EXAMPLE 5. Simplify $\dfrac{\tan(A+B)+\tan(A-B)}{1-\tan(A+B)\tan(A-B)}$.

EXAMPLE 6. Find the exact value of the expression.

① $\sin\left(\sin^{-1}\dfrac{3}{5}+\cos^{-1}\dfrac{1}{2}\right)$ ② $\cos\left(\sin^{-1}\dfrac{3}{5}-\tan^{-1}\dfrac{1}{3}\right)$

③ $\cos\left(\tan^{-1}\dfrac{4}{3}+\sec^{-1}\dfrac{13}{5}\right)$

④ $\sin\left(\cos^{-1}\dfrac{2}{3}+\cot^{-1}2\right)$

⑤ $\sin\left(\arcsin x+\arccos x\right)$

⑥ $\cos\left(\arccos x-\arctan x\right)$

2. Expand Knowledge

EXAMPLE 7. * The figure shown consists of three squares. Find the sum of the angles A and B.

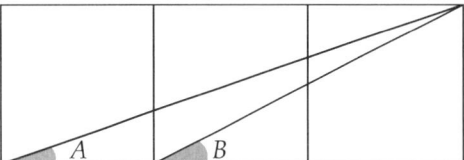

EXAMPLE 8. * Use the figure which shows two lines whose equations are $y = 5x - 5$ and $y = \dfrac{2}{3}x$. What is the acute angle between the two lines.

☺ Tip: If the angle between horizontal line and linear function $y = mx + b$ is θ,

then ① _____.

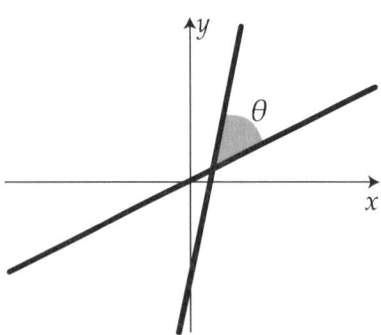

Blank : ① slope m = tan θ

EXAMPLE 9.* If $\cos^{-1}\left(\dfrac{4}{5}\right) = \alpha$ and $\cos^{-1}\left(\dfrac{2}{3}\right) = \beta$, what is $\cos(\alpha + \beta)$?

Mia's Precalculus
5.5 Double-Angle Identity

1. Double Angle Identity

From sum identity we can find; $\sin(\theta + \theta) = $ ① _____.

  ※ Double Angle Formulas

$$\sin(2\theta) = 2\sin\theta\cos\theta$$

$$\cos(2\theta) = \cos^2\theta - \sin^2\theta$$
$$= 1 - 2\sin^2\theta$$
$$= 2\cos^2\theta - 1$$

$$\tan(2\theta) = \frac{2\tan\theta}{1 - \tan^2\theta}$$

EXAMPLE 1. Find the exact value of the expression or simplify the expression using double identity.

① $\sin(120°) = \sin(\boxed{})$

② $\cos(120°)$

③ $2\sin 6\alpha$

④ $\sin 10B$

⑤ $\cos 4A$

⑥ $2\cos 8\beta$

⑦ $\tan 4C$

Blank : ① $\sin\theta\cos\theta + \cos\theta\sin\theta = 2\sin\theta\cos\theta$

EXAMPLE 2. Use a double-angle identity to simplify the expression.

① $4\sin A\cos A$

② $6\sin 2\beta \cos 2\beta$

③ $2\cos^2 3\alpha - 1$

④ $2\sin^2 2\beta - 1$

⑤ $\sin^2 2\theta - \cos^2 2\theta$

⑥ $2\cos^2 \dfrac{A}{2} - 1$

⑦ $4\sin^2 \dfrac{\beta}{2} - 2$

⑧ $\cos^2 3\theta - \sin^2 3\theta$

⑨ $\dfrac{2\tan 2\beta}{1-\tan^2 2\beta}$

⑩ $\dfrac{2\tan C}{1-\tan^2 C}$

EXAMPLE 3. Verify the following

① $\sin 4x = (4\sin x\cos x)(2\cos^2 x - 1)$

② $\cos 4x = 8\sin^4 x - 8\sin^2 x + 1$

③ $\dfrac{\sin 2x + \sin x}{1 + \cos 2x + \cos x} = \tan x$

④ $\tan 2x = \dfrac{2}{\cot x - \tan x}$

EXAMPLE 4. Find an expression for $\cos 4x$ in terms of $\cos x$.

EXAMPLE 5. Use the information given about the angle θ, $0 \leq \theta \leq 2\pi$, to find the exact value of the indicated trigonometric function.

① $\cos\theta = -\dfrac{8}{17}$, $\dfrac{\pi}{2} < \theta < \pi$,

Find $\sin(2\theta)$

② $\sin\theta = \dfrac{2\sqrt{6}}{5}$, $\tan\theta < 0$,

Find $\sin(2\theta)$

③ $\tan\theta = -\dfrac{11}{9}$, $\sin\theta < 0$,

Find $\cos(2\theta)$

④ $\cot\theta = \dfrac{3}{5}$, $\sin\theta < 0$,

Find $\cos(2\theta)$

EXAMPLE 6. Find the exact value of the expression. ($1 \le x \le 1$)

① $\sin\left(2\cos^{-1}\dfrac{5}{13}\right)$

② $\cos\left(2\tan^{-1}\dfrac{24}{7}\right)$

③ $\sec\left(2\tan^{-1}\dfrac{3}{4}\right)$

④ $\csc\left(2\sin^{-1}\dfrac{5}{6}\right)$

⑤ $\sin(2\arccos x)$

⑥ $\cos(2\arccos x)$

2. Power Reducing Formula

From $\cos(2\theta) =$ ①_____,

we can find; $\sin^2\theta =$ ② _____, $\cos^2\theta =$ ③ _____.

※ Power-Reducing Formulas

power reduce

$$\sin^2\theta = \frac{1}{2}[1-\cos(2\theta)] \quad \cos^2\theta = \frac{1}{2}[1+\cos(2\theta)]$$

$$\tan^2\theta = \frac{1-\cos(2\theta)}{1+\cos(2\theta)}$$

EXAMPLE 7. Use the power-reducing formulas to rewrite the expression in terms of the first power of the cosine.

① $(\cos x + 1)^2$ ② $(2 - \sin x)^2$

Blank : ① $\cos^2\theta - \sin^2\theta = 2\cos^2\theta - 1 = 1 - 2\sin^2\theta$ ② $\frac{1}{2}(1-\cos 2\theta)$ ③ $\frac{1}{2}(1+\cos 2\theta)$

③ $\sin^4 x$ ④ $\cos^4 x$

⑤ $\sin^2 x \cos^2 x$

3. Expand Knowledge

EXAMPLE 8.   *What is the period and amplitude of $y = 4\sin x \cos x - 1$?

EXAMPLE 9.* What is the period and amplitude of $y = \sin^2 x + 5$?

EXAMPLE 10. * A Circle with diameter $AB = 5$ is given. Two points C and D is on the circumference of the circle such that $AC = 4$, $2\angle CAB = \angle BAD$. Find the length of AD.

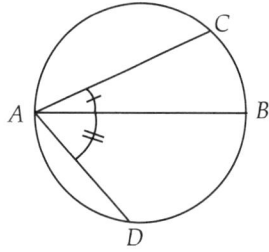

EXAMPLE 11. * For right triangle ABC as shown, point D is on the side $\overline{BC}$ so that $\angle BAD = \angle B$. What is $\cos(\angle ADC)$?

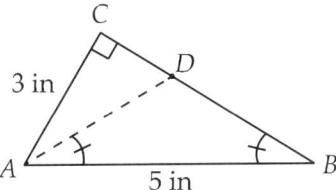

EXAMPLE 12. * From the top of mountain A which is 3km high, it is observed that the angle of elevation of the top of the mountain B is twice as much as the angle of depression of the base of the mountain B. When the distance between the base of mountain A and mountain B is 5km, what is the height of the mountain B?

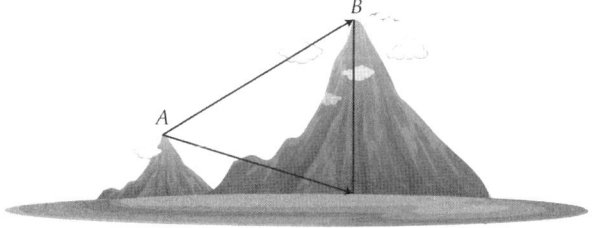

Mia's Precalculus

5.6 Half-Angle and Product-Sum Identities

1. Half Angle and Product-Sum Identities

※ Half-Angle Formulas

$$\sin\frac{\theta}{2} = \pm\sqrt{\frac{1}{2}[1-\cos\theta]} \qquad \cos\frac{\theta}{2} = \pm\sqrt{\frac{1}{2}[1+\cos\theta]}$$

$$\tan\frac{\theta}{2} = \frac{1-\cos\theta}{\sin\theta} = \frac{\sin\theta}{1+\cos\theta}$$

EXAMPLE 1. Find the exact value of the expression using half angle identities.

① $\sin(22.5°)$ \qquad ② $\cos(22.5°)$

③ $\cos(112.5°)$ \qquad ④ $\sin\left(\dfrac{\pi}{12}\right)$

⑤ $\cos\left(\dfrac{\pi}{12}\right)$

EXAMPLE 2. Use the information given about the angle θ, 0 ≤ θ ≤ 2π, to find the exact value of the indicated trigonometric function.

① $\sin\theta = \dfrac{5}{13}$, $\dfrac{\pi}{2} < \theta < \pi$,

Find $\sin\dfrac{\theta}{2}$

② $\cot\theta = -\dfrac{7}{24}$, $\dfrac{3\pi}{2} < \theta < 2\pi$,

Find $\cos\dfrac{\theta}{2}$

③ $\csc\theta = -\dfrac{5}{3}$, $\pi < \theta < \dfrac{3\pi}{2}$,

Find $\cos\dfrac{\theta}{2}$

※ Sum-to-Product Formulas

$$\sin A + \sin B = 2 \sin\left(\frac{A+B}{2}\right) \cos\left(\frac{A-B}{2}\right)$$

$$\sin A - \sin B = 2 \cos\left(\frac{A+B}{2}\right) \sin\left(\frac{A-B}{2}\right)$$

$$\cos A + \cos B = 2 \cos\left(\frac{A+B}{2}\right) \cos\left(\frac{A-B}{2}\right)$$

$$\cos A - \cos B = -2 \sin\left(\frac{A+B}{2}\right) \sin\left(\frac{A-B}{2}\right)$$

EXAMPLE 3. Use the sum-to-product formulas to write the sum or difference as a product.

① $\sin 5\theta - \sin 3\theta$

② $\sin 3\theta + \sin \theta$

③ $\cos 6\theta + \cos 4\theta$

④ $\cos 3\theta + \cos 9\theta$

⑤ $\cos\left(\theta + \dfrac{\pi}{2}\right) - \cos\left(\theta - \dfrac{\pi}{2}\right)$

※ Product-to-Sum Formulas

$$2\sin A \cos B = \sin(A+B) + \sin(A-B)$$

$$2\cos A \sin B = \sin(A+B) - \sin(A-B)$$

$$2\cos A \cos B = \cos(A+B) + \cos(A-B)$$

$$-2\sin A \sin B = \cos(A+B) - \cos(A-B)$$

EXAMPLE 4. Use the product-to-sum formulas to write the product as a sum or difference.

① $6\sin\dfrac{\pi}{4}\cos\dfrac{\pi}{2}$ 　　　　　② $4\cos\dfrac{\pi}{3}\sin\dfrac{5\pi}{6}$

③ $10\cos 75° \cos 15°$ 　　　　　④ $4\sin 3x \sin 2x$

EXAMPLE 5. Verify the following.

① $\dfrac{\sin(x+y)-\sin(x-y)}{\cos(x+y)+\cos(x-y)} = \tan y$

② $\dfrac{\sin x + \sin 2x + \sin 3x}{\cos x + \cos 2x + \cos 3x} = \tan 2x$

☺ Trigonometry Identities All in one

※ Reciprocal Identities

$$\sin\theta = \frac{1}{\csc\theta} \qquad \cos\theta = \frac{1}{\sec\theta} \qquad \tan\theta = \frac{1}{\cot\theta}$$

$$\csc\theta = \frac{1}{\sin\theta} \qquad \sec\theta = \frac{1}{\cos\theta} \qquad \cot\theta = \frac{1}{\tan\theta}$$

※ Quotient Identities

$$\tan\theta = \frac{\sin\theta}{\cos\theta} \qquad \cot\theta = \frac{\cos\theta}{\sin\theta}$$

※ Pythagorean Identities

$$\sin^2\theta + \cos^2\theta = 1$$
$$1 + \tan^2\theta = \sec^2\theta$$
$$1 + \cot^2\theta = \csc^2\theta$$

※ Cofunction Identities

$$\sin\left(\frac{\pi}{2}-\theta\right) = \cos\theta \qquad \cos\left(\frac{\pi}{2}-\theta\right) = \sin\theta$$

(Complementary)

$$\tan\left(\frac{\pi}{2}-\theta\right) = \cot\theta \qquad \cot\left(\frac{\pi}{2}-\theta\right) = \tan\theta$$

$$\csc\left(\frac{\pi}{2}-\theta\right) = \sec\theta \qquad \sec\left(\frac{\pi}{2}-\theta\right) = \csc\theta$$

※ Odd-Even Identities

$$\sin(-\theta) = -\sin\theta \qquad \csc(-\theta) = -\csc\theta$$
$$\cos(-\theta) = \cos\theta \qquad \sec(-\theta) = \sec\theta$$
$$\tan(-\theta) = -\tan\theta \qquad \cot(-\theta) = -\cot\theta$$

※ Sum and Difference Identities

$$\sin(A \pm B) = \sin A \cos B \pm \cos A \sin B$$

$$\cos(A \pm B) = \cos A \cos B \mp \sin A \sin B$$

(switch sign)

$$\tan(A \pm B) = \frac{\tan A \pm \tan B}{1 \mp \tan A \tan B}$$

※ Double Angle Formulas

$$\sin(2\theta) = 2\sin\theta\cos\theta$$

$$\cos(2\theta) = \cos^2\theta - \sin^2\theta$$
$$= 1 - 2\sin^2\theta$$
$$= 2\cos^2\theta - 1$$

$$\tan(2\theta) = \frac{2\tan\theta}{1 - \tan^2\theta}$$

※ Power-Reducing Formulas

power reduce

$$\sin^2\theta = \frac{1}{2}[1 - \cos(2\theta)] \quad \cos^2\theta = \frac{1}{2}[1 + \cos(2\theta)]$$

$$\tan^2\theta = \frac{1 - \cos(2\theta)}{1 + \cos(2\theta)}$$

※ Half-Angle Formulas

$$\sin\frac{\theta}{2} = \pm\sqrt{\frac{1}{2}[1-\cos\theta]} \qquad \cos\frac{\theta}{2} = \pm\sqrt{\frac{1}{2}[1+\cos\theta]}$$

$$\tan\frac{\theta}{2} = \frac{1-\cos\theta}{\sin\theta} = \frac{\sin\theta}{1+\cos\theta}$$

※ Sum-to-Product Formulas

$$\sin A + \sin B = 2\sin\left(\frac{A+B}{2}\right)\cos\left(\frac{A-B}{2}\right)$$

$$\sin A - \sin B = 2\cos\left(\frac{A+B}{2}\right)\sin\left(\frac{A-B}{2}\right)$$

$$\cos A + \cos B = 2\cos\left(\frac{A+B}{2}\right)\cos\left(\frac{A-B}{2}\right)$$

$$\cos A - \cos B = -2\sin\left(\frac{A+B}{2}\right)\sin\left(\frac{A-B}{2}\right)$$

※ Product-to-Sum Formulas

$$2\sin A\cos B = \sin(A+B) + \sin(A-B)$$

$$2\cos A\sin B = \sin(A+B) - \sin(A-B)$$

$$2\cos A\cos B = \cos(A+B) + \cos(A-B)$$

$$-2\sin A\sin B = \cos(A+B) - \cos(A-B)$$

Part 6
Trig Equations and Geometry Triangles

6.1 Basic Trigonometric Equations
6.2 More Trigonometric Equations
6.3 The Law of Sines
6.4 The Law of Cosines
6.5 Area of Triangles

Mia's Precalculus
6.1 Basic Trigonometric Equations

1. Solving Trigonometric Equations

☺ Reminder: We need ①_____ and ②_____ to evaluate $\cos\dfrac{4\pi}{3}=$ ③_____.

To solve the equation $\cos x = -\dfrac{1}{2}$, we need ④_____ and ⑤_____.

※ How to Solve a trig equation?
① Find the **reference angle**.
② Determine which **quadrants** your solutions lie in.
③ Express the solutions in standard form.

Case 1. i) Solve $\cos x = -\dfrac{1}{2}$ for $0 \leq x \leq 2\pi$.

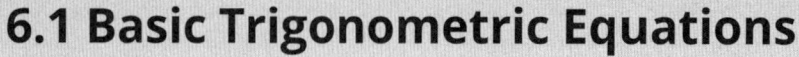

The reference angle is $\bar{x} = \boxed{⑥}$.

$\cos x$ is ⑦_____ in ⑧ ___, ___ quadrant.

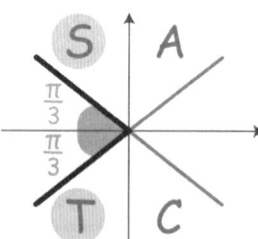

The solution is ⑨_____.

(Find all angles in the given interval is standard position)

Blank : ① ASTC ② reference angle ③ $-\dfrac{1}{2}$ ④ ASTC ⑤ reference angle ⑥ $\dfrac{\pi}{3}$ ⑦ negative ⑧ II, III ⑨ $\dfrac{2\pi}{3}, \dfrac{4\pi}{3}$

<u>Case 2.</u> ii) Solve $\cos x = -\dfrac{1}{2}$ for every x. (all solution)

Because the cosine function repeats its values every ① _____ units, we get

all solutions of the equation by adding integer multiples of ② _____ to these solutions:

　　　The solution is ③ _____.

EXAMPLE 1. Solve the equation i) when $0 \leq x \leq 2\pi$ and ii) for every x without GCD.

① $\sqrt{2}\sin x = -1$　　　　　　　　　　② $2\cos x - \sqrt{3} = 0$

③ $\sqrt{3}\tan x + 1 = 0$　　　　　　　　　④ $\tan x = 1$

Blank : ① 2π　② 2π (=$2\pi k$)　③ $\dfrac{2\pi}{3} + 2\pi k$, $\dfrac{4\pi}{3} + 2\pi k$ where k is integer

Part 6. Trig Equations and Geometry Triangles

⑤ $2\cos x - 1 = 0$ ⑥ $2\sin x + \sqrt{2} = 0$

EXAMPLE 2. Solve the equation i) when $0 \leq x \leq 2\pi$ and ii) for every x without GCD.

> When reference angle is 0 or 90°, using graph will be helpful.

① $\sin x = 1$ ② $\sin x = 0$

③ $\cos x = 0$ ④ $\cos x + 1 = 0$

EXAMPLE 3. Solve the equation when $0 \leq x \leq 2\pi$. You may answer in terms of inverse trig function.

> Inverse Trig only gives you ①_____.

① $\sin x = 0.8$

② $\tan x = 2.5$

③ $\cos x = -0.3$

④ $\sin x = -\dfrac{2}{3}$

⑤ $\tan x = -2$

Blank : ① reference angle

EXAMPLE 4. Solve the equation for $0 \leq x \leq 2\pi$.

Type 1. Factor the quadratic

① $2\cos^2 x + 11\cos x = -5$ ② $4\sin^2 x - \sqrt{3}\sin x = 2\sin^2 x$

③ $3\sin x \cos x = 2\sin x$ ④ $\sin x - 2\sin x \cos x = 0$

Type 2. Take the square root

⑤ $\tan^2 x - 1 = 0$ ⑥ $3\cot^2 x - 1 = 0$

EXAMPLE 5. Solve the equation $\sqrt{3}\tan x = -1$ when $0 \leq x \leq 4\pi$.

EXAMPLE 6. Solve the equation $\tan^2 x = 1$ when $-\pi \leq x \leq \pi$.

Mia's Precalculus

6.2 More Trigonometric Equations

1. More Trigonometric Equations

   EXAMPLE 1. Solve the equations when $0 \leq x \leq 2\pi$.

Type1. Use reciprocal trig ratio.

   ① $3\csc x = 6$

   ② $\cot^2 x = 3$

   ③ $3\cot^2 x + 4 = 7$

   ④ $\sec^2 x = 4$

Type2. Change into single trig equation.

   ⑤ $2\cos^2 x + 9\sin x = 3\sin^2 x$

   ⑥ $1 = 2\sin^2 x + \cos x$

⑦ $\tan^2 x \sec^2 x + 2\sec^2 x - \tan^2 x = 2$

⑧ $1 - \csc x = \cot^2 x$

Type3. Divide both sides by cos.

⑨ $\sin x = \cos x$

⑩ $\sqrt{3}\sin x = \cos x$

Type4. Use double angle identities.

⑪ $\cos 2x = \cos x$

⑫ $\sin 2x - \sin x = 0$

Type5. Square both sides. You MUST check the answer!

⑬ $\tan x = 1 - \sec x$ ⑭ $\csc x = \cot x + 1$

⑮ $\cos x = \sin x - 1$

2. Solving Trigonometric Equations Using Substitution

※ How to Solve a trig equation?
① Make a substitution for the angle part and adjust the INTERVAL!
② Find the **reference angle**.
③ Determine which **quadrants** your solutions lie in.
④ Express the solutions in standard form.

Solve $2\sin 2x + 1 = 0$ when $0 \leq x \leq 2\pi$.

Make a substitution $2x = A$.

Sign part **tells you** which quadrant (ASTC)   Number part **tells you** reference angle

$$\sin A = -\frac{1}{2}$$

When $0 \leq x \leq 2\pi$,   ①____ $\leq A \leq$ ②____.

The reference angle is $\overline{A} = \boxed{③}$.

$\sin A$ is ④_____ in ⑤____, ____ quadrant.

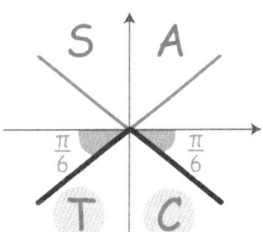

So $A =$ ⑥_____.

(Find all angles in the given interval is standard position)

The solution x is ⑦_____.

Blank : ① 0   ② 4π ③ $\dfrac{\pi}{6}$ ④ negative   ⑤ III, IV   ⑥ $\dfrac{7\pi}{6}, \dfrac{11\pi}{6}, \dfrac{19\pi}{6}, \dfrac{23\pi}{6}$ ⑦ $\dfrac{7\pi}{12}, \dfrac{11\pi}{12}, \dfrac{19\pi}{12}, \dfrac{23\pi}{12}$

EXAMPLE 2. Solve the equation for given interval.

① $2\cos 2x = 1$, $0 \le x \le 2\pi$

② $\cos 3x = -\dfrac{\sqrt{3}}{2}$, $0 \le x \le 2\pi$

③ $\sin\left(\dfrac{x}{2}\right) = \cos\left(\dfrac{x}{2}\right)$, $0 \le x \le 2\pi$

④ $\sin(2x) = \cos(2x)$, $0 \le x \le \pi$

⑤ $4\tan 2x = 2\sec^2 2x$, $0 \le x \le \pi$

⑥ $2\sin^2 2x + 1 = 3\sin 2x$, $0 \leq x \leq 2\pi$

⑦ $\sqrt{2}\sin\left(x + \dfrac{\pi}{4}\right) = 1$, $0 \leq x \leq 2\pi$

Mia's Precalculus

6.3 The Law of Sines

1. Law of Sines and Cosines

※ Law of Sines

Law of Sines shows that in any triangle the lengths of the sides are

① _____ to the sines of the corresponding opposite angles,

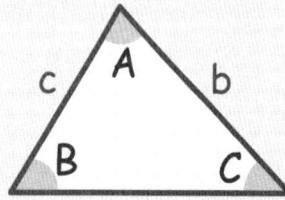

$a : b : c = \sin A : \sin B : \sin C$

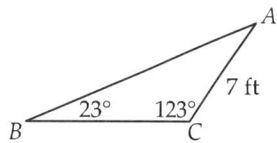 $= \dfrac{b}{\sin B} = \dfrac{c}{\sin C}$

EXAMPLE 1. Use the Law of Sines to find the measurement indicated.

① Find AB.

② Find AC

Blank : ① proportional   ② a   ③ sin A

③ Find AB.

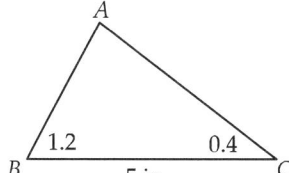

④ Find AC

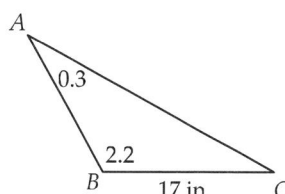

⑤ Find m∠C

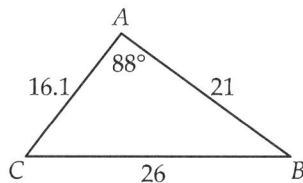

⑥ Find m∠C

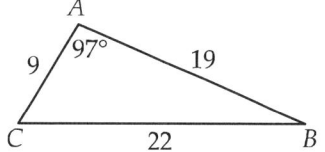

※ Ambiguous case (Tricky case) SSA triangle

When solving a **"Side, Side, Angle" triangle** we need to check carefully!
There might be no solution or there could be another possible answer!

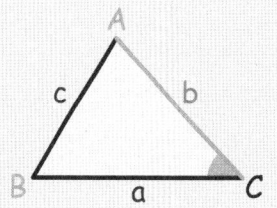

ex) Find ∠A. State the number of possible triangles that can be formed.

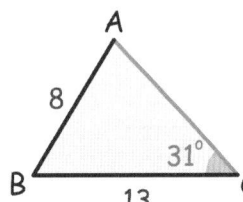

First, let's try to find ∠A.

$$\frac{\boxed{①}}{\sin 31°} = \frac{\boxed{②}}{\sin A}$$

∠A = ③ _____

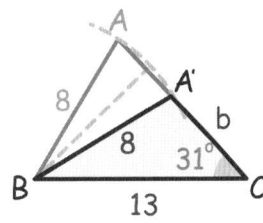

Is there any another possible answer?

By swinging side "8" left and right we can join up with side "b" in two possible locations.

In this case ∠A' = 180° - ④ _____

(since ABA' is isosceles triangle)

= ⑤ _____

EXAMPLE 2.   Find all possible angle of;

① m∠C

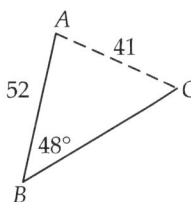

② m∠A

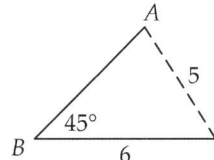

Blank : ① 8   ② 13   ③ 56.818°   ④ 56.818°   ⑤ 123.182°

338 Mia's Precalculus

③ $m\angle A$
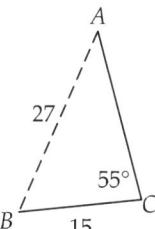

④ $m\angle B$
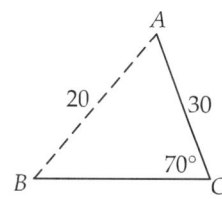

⑤ $m\angle C$
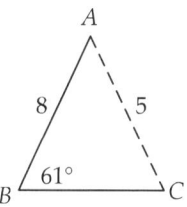

⑥ $m\angle A$
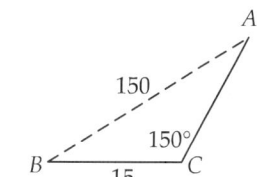

EXAMPLE 3. State the number of possible triangles that can be formed. Then solve the triangle.

> Solve the triangle : find the missing angles and sides.

① ∠C = 10°, c = 10, b = 20

② ∠A = 40°, a = 270, b = 580

③ ∠A = 120°, a = 25, b = 10

④ ∠B = 60°, b = 170, a = 180

EXAMPLE 4. For the figure below find $m\angle ADB$ and $m\angle C$ given $m\angle ADB > m\angle C$.

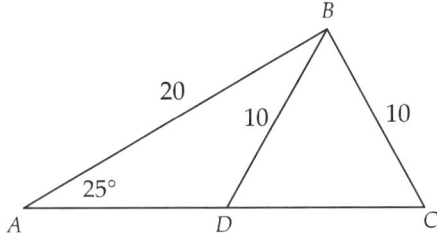

2. Expand Knowledge

EXAMPLE 5. * The triangle shown in the diagram has angles θ and 2θ. Find the value of θ in degrees.

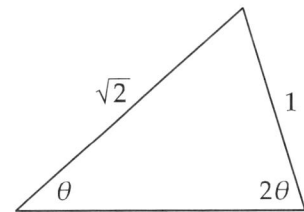

EXAMPLE 6. * In traveling across flat land, you notice a mountain directly in front of you. Its angle of elevation (to the peak) is 3.5°. After you drive 13 miles closer to the mountain, the angle of elevation is 9°. Approximate the height of the mountain. (Use *law of sine* to solve the problem)

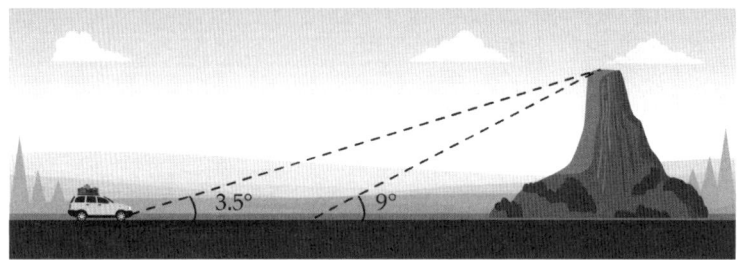

EXAMPLE 7. * Lighthouse B and C are 11.2 km apart in the shore. A boat starts at point A, which is 7 kilometers from B, and sails in a straight line toward C. When the boat is *once again* 7 kilometers from point B, how far is it from point C?

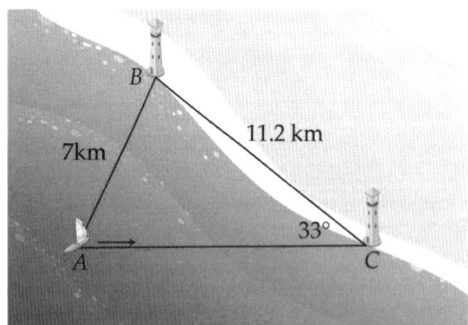

EXAMPLE 8. * From triangle ABC, angle $A : B : C = 1 : 2 : 3$. What is;

a) $\sin A : \sin B : \sin C$

b) $a : b : c$

Mia's Precalculus
6.4 The Law of Cosines

1. **Law of Cosines**

   We have two right triangles in $\triangle ABC$.

   $c^2 = h^2 + \boxed{①}^2$

   $b^2 = h^2 + \boxed{②}^2 = h^2 + \boxed{③}$

   By substitution,

   $b^2 = $ ④ _____

   And we know that $\cos B = \boxed{⑤}$ so it gives us $x = c \cos B$.

   Therefore $b^2 = $ ⑥ _____

   ※ **Law of Cosines**

   $a^2 = b^2 + c^2 - 2bc \cos A$
   $b^2 = a^2 + c^2 - 2ac \cos B$
   $c^2 = a^2 + b^2 - 2ab \cos C$

   Blank : ① x   ② (a-x)   ③ $a^2 - 2ax + x^2$ ④ $c^2 + a^2 - 2ax$ ⑤ $\dfrac{x}{c}$ ⑥ $c^2 + a^2 - 2ac \cos B$

☺ Using Law of Sine and Cosine Tip:

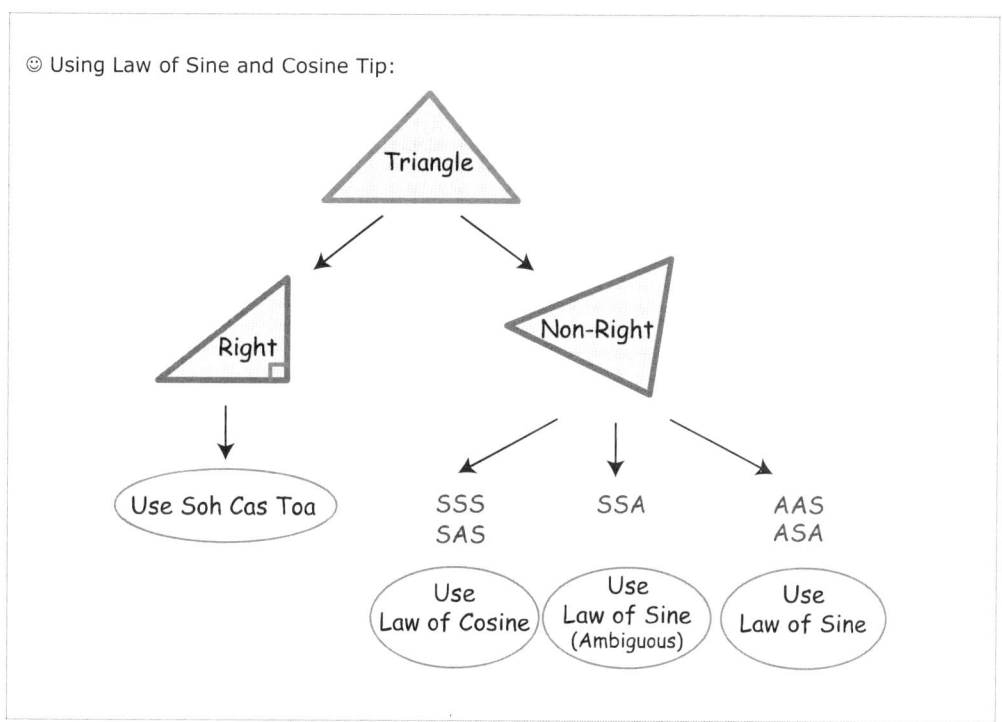

EXAMPLE 1. Use the Law of Cosines to find the measurement indicated.

① Find BA.

② Find AC

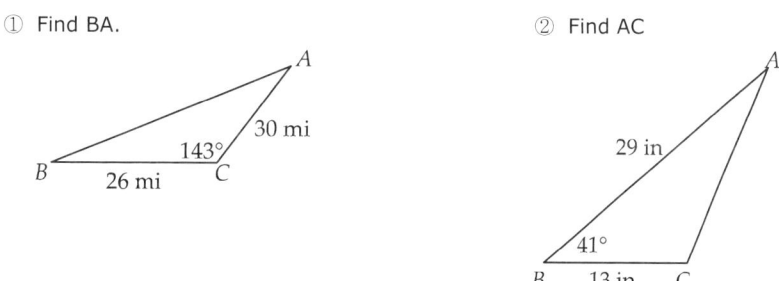

From $a^2 = b^2 + c^2 - 2bc \cos A$, if we solve for $\cos A$;

$$\cos A = \frac{b^2 + c^2 - a^2}{2bc}$$

③ Find m∠C

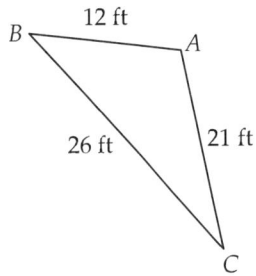

④ Find m∠A

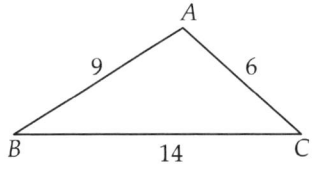

⑤ Find m∠B

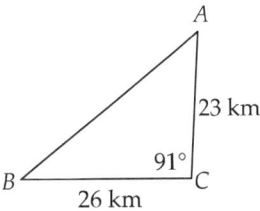

⑥ Find m∠C

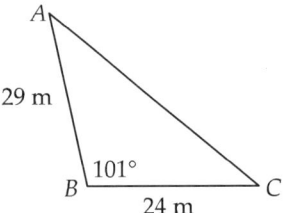

EXAMPLE 2. Triangle ABC is shown. Find the value of x.

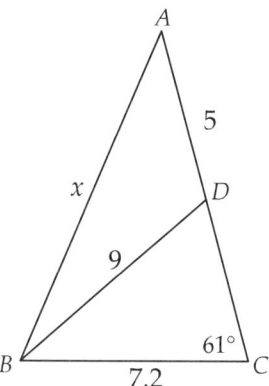

EXAMPLE 3. Triangle ABC is inscribed in a rectangular box whose sides are 1, 2, and 3 in long as shown. Find the measure of $\angle CAB$.

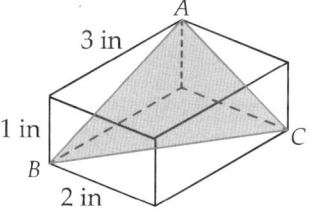

EXAMPLE 4. If a triangle has sides of lengths 3, 5, 7, what is the largest angle in the triangle?

2. Expand Knowledge

EXAMPLE 5. * State the number of possible triangles can be formed.
(Hint: Try to find the possible lengths of AC using law of Cosine)

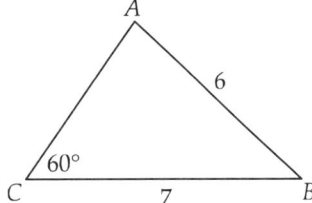

EXAMPLE 6. * Two observers A and B are positioned 20m apart on a horizontal ground. They are trying to measure the height of the tree CD as shown. Observer A looked up the tree and find out that the angle of elevation of the top of the tree is 48°. If CB = 32m and $\angle CBA = 80°$, find the height of the tree.

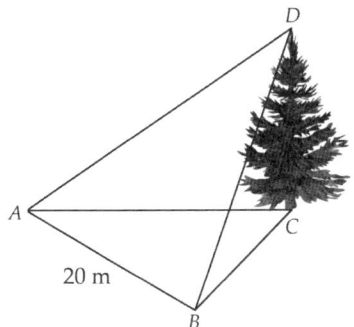

EXAMPLE 7. * From triangle ABC, $\sin A : \sin B : \sin C = 2 : 3 : 4$. What is $\angle A$?

Mia's Precalculus

6.5 Area of Triangles

1. Area of a Triangle (for SAS Triangle)

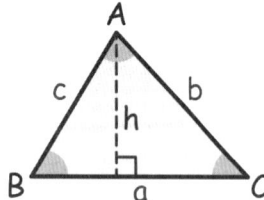

We know that the

Area of a triangle of $\triangle ABC =$ ① _____

Since $\sin C =$ ② , it gives us $h =$ ③ _____

Therefore Area of $\triangle ABC =$ ④ _____.

※ Area of a Triangle

When we have SAS Triangle (where A is ⑤ _____ angle of side c and b)

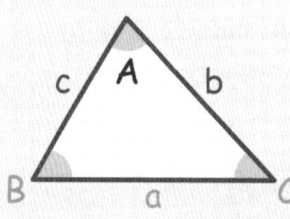

$$\triangle ABC = \frac{1}{2}bc\sin A$$
$$= \frac{1}{2}ac\sin B$$
$$= \frac{1}{2}ab\sin C$$

Blank : ① $\frac{1}{2}ah$ ② $\frac{h}{b}$ ③ $b\sin C$ ④ $\frac{1}{2}ab\sin C$ ⑤ included

EXAMPLE 1. Find the area of the triangle.

①

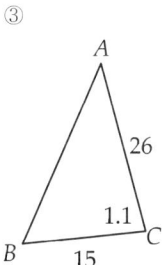

②

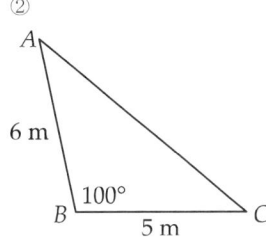

③

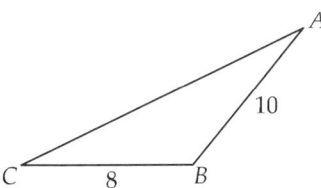

④

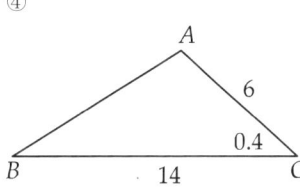

EXAMPLE 2. The area of the obtuse triangle shown in the diagram is 20 cm². Find the obtuse angle B in radian without using calculator.

EXAMPLE 3. From the diagram shown

(a) the perimeter of the shaded region
(b) the area of the shaded region

①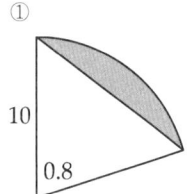

②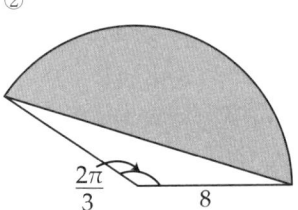

③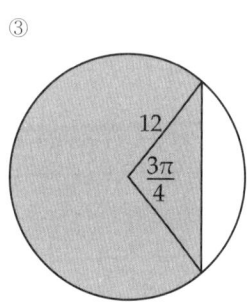

※ Area of segment in circle (when θ is in radians)

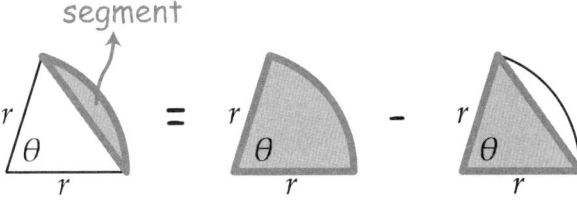

= ① _____ - ② _____

$$Segment\ Area = \frac{1}{2}r^2(\theta - \sin\theta)$$

EXAMPLE 4. Two equal circles of radius 6 is given. The center of one circle is on the circumference of the other. Find the exact area of the shaded region without using calculator.

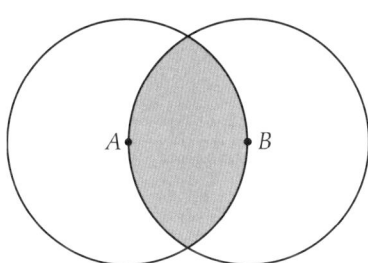

Blank : ① $\frac{1}{2}r^2\theta$ ② $\frac{1}{2}r^2\sin\theta$

2. Area of a Triangle (for SSS Triangle)

※ Area of a Triangle (Heron's Formula)

When we have SSS Triangle

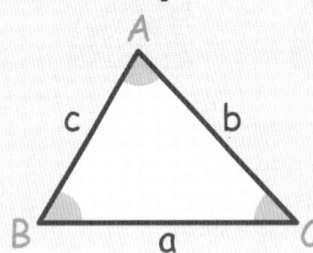

$$\triangle ABC = \sqrt{s(s-a)(s-b)(s-c)}$$

semiperimeter $s = \dfrac{a+b+c}{2}$

EXAMPLE 5. Find the area of the figure.

①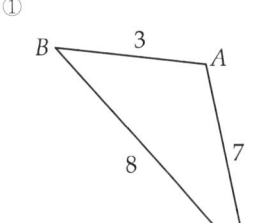

②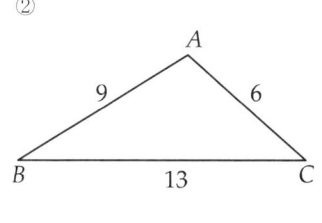

③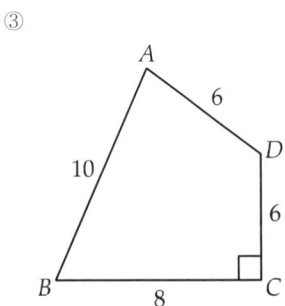

3. Expand Knowledge

EXAMPLE 6. * A semicircle with radius 4 is given. Let O be the center, C be the point on the circumference, and $\angle AOC = \theta$.

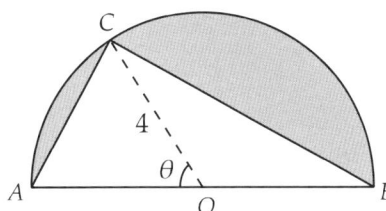

The total area of the shaded region is given by $8(\pi - a\sin\theta)$. Find a.

EXAMPLE 7. * A square $ABCD$ and a sector OAD are overlapped as shown. Find the expression for the shaded area in terms of r, θ, and trigonometric function.

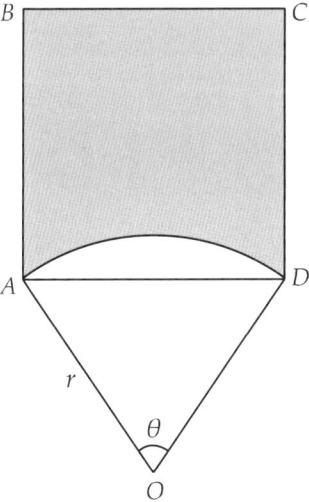

Part 7

Polar coordinate and Complex number

7.1 Polar Coordinates
7.2 Graphs of Polar Equations
7.3 Complex Numbers and De Moivre's Theorem
7.4 Parametric Equations

Mia's Precalculus

7.1 Polar Coordinates

1. Polar Coordinate

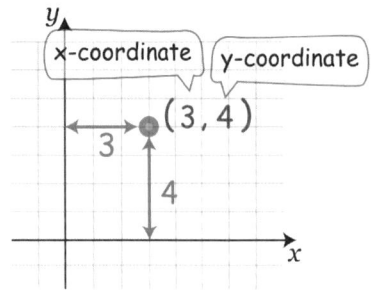
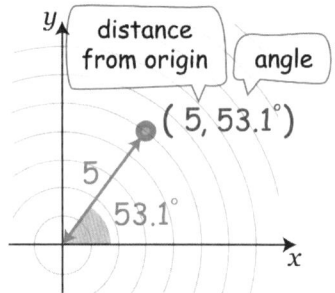

In ①_____ coordinate system, we mark a point by **how far along** and **how far up** it is.

In ②_____ coordinate system, we mark a point by **how far away**, and what **angle** it is.

※ Polar Coordinates

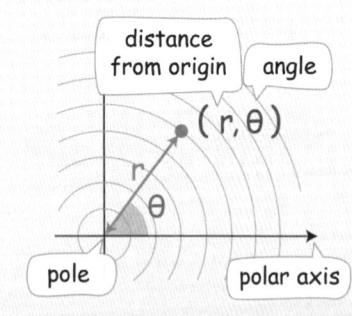

Polar Coordinate is a way to pinpoint where you are on a map or graph by how far away, and at what angle the point is.

$(-r, \theta)$ is the reflection over the pole (origin) of (r, θ)

☺ Vocabulary

Polar axis: The positive x axis

Pole: Origin in polar coordinate (0,0)

Blank : ① Cartesian(=rectangular)   ② polar

358   Mia's Precalculus

EXAMPLE 1. Plot the point having the given polar coordinates.

① $\left(4, 225°\right)$

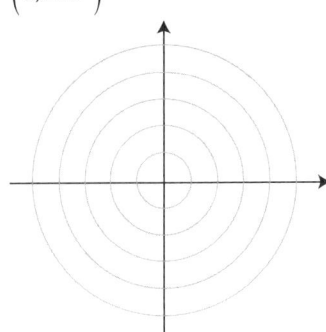

② $\left(-2, -330°\right)$

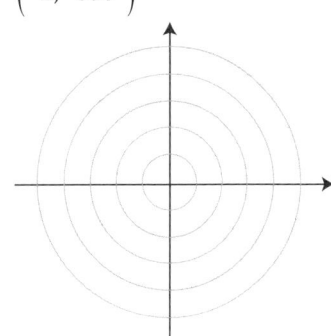

③ $\left(3, \dfrac{7\pi}{4}\right)$

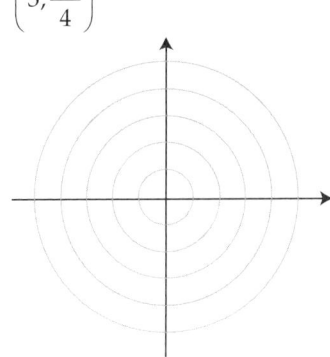

④ $\left(2, -\dfrac{5\pi}{4}\right)$

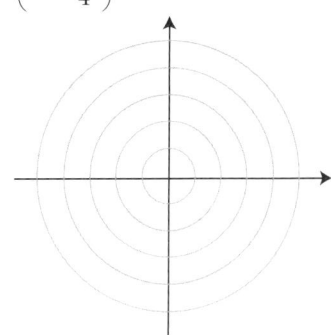

⑤ $\left(2, -\dfrac{5\pi}{6}\right)$

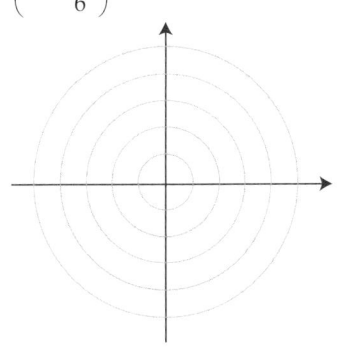

⑥ $\left(1, \dfrac{13\pi}{3}\right)$

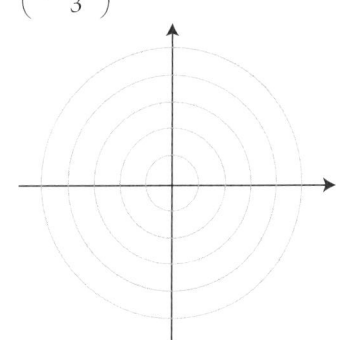

⑦ $\left(-3, \dfrac{11\pi}{6}\right)$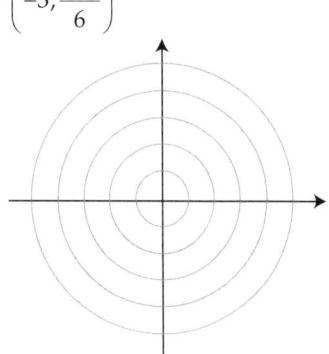

⑧ $\left(-3, 3\pi\right)$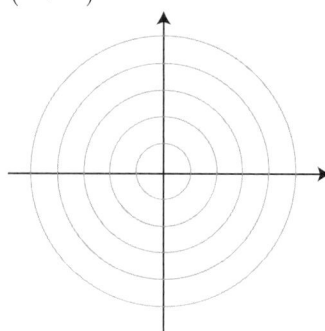

⑨ $\left(-4, -\dfrac{7\pi}{4}\right)$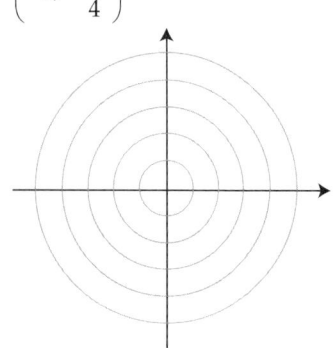

⑩ $\left(-2, -\dfrac{5\pi}{3}\right)$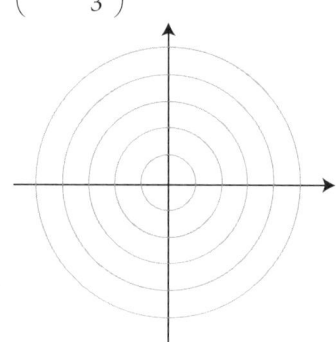

EXAMPLE 2. Locate the given point and write the coordinates in three other ways.

① $\left(3, 60°\right)$

② $\left(4, 90°\right)$

③ $\left(2, \dfrac{5\pi}{6}\right)$

④ $\left(3, \dfrac{\pi}{4}\right)$

2. Convert between Polar to Cartesian $(r, \theta) \Leftrightarrow (x, y)$

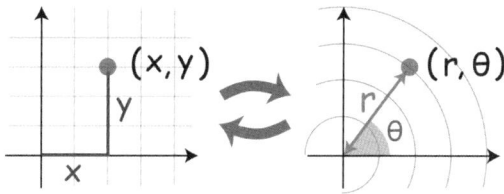

Use the trigonometric Function to find:

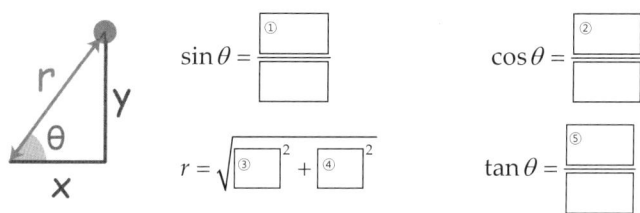

$\sin \theta = \dfrac{\text{①}}{}$ $\cos \theta = \dfrac{\text{②}}{}$

$r = \sqrt{\text{③}^2 + \text{④}^2}$ $\tan \theta = \dfrac{\text{⑤}}{}$

※ Formulas for Polar Coordinates

$$x = r \times \cos\theta \qquad y = r \times \sin\theta$$

$$r = \sqrt{x^2 + y^2} \qquad \tan\theta = \dfrac{y}{x}$$

(remember; $\tan^{-1}$ gives you only the reference angle)

Blank : ① $\dfrac{y}{r}$ ② $\dfrac{x}{r}$ ③ x   ④ y   ⑤ $\dfrac{y}{x}$

EXAMPLE 3. Convert the given polar coordinates of the point to rectangular coordinates.

① $(6, 225°)$

② $(7, 210°)$

③ $\left(-7, \dfrac{5\pi}{3}\right)$

④ $\left(6, \dfrac{5\pi}{4}\right)$

⑤ $\left(3, -\dfrac{\pi}{6}\right)$

EXAMPLE 4. Convert the rectangular coordinates of the point to polar coordinates (r, θ) with r > 0 and $0 \leq \theta < 2\pi$.

① $(-1, 1)$

② $(6, -6\sqrt{3})$

③ $(5\sqrt{3}, 5)$

④ $(4, 0)$

⑤ $(0, -3)$

⑥ $(-2\sqrt{3}, 2\sqrt{3})$

⑦ $(-2, 4)$

⑧ $(-5, 3)$

3. Polar Form → Rectangular Form

We use formulas to convert the equation from polar form to rectangular form.

EXAMPLE 5. Find an equivalent equation in rectangular coordinates.

① $r = 1$

② $r\sin\theta = 10$

③ $r(1+\cos\theta) = 5$

④ $r = \sin\theta$

⑤ $r = 10\sin\theta$

⑥ $r(\cos\theta - \sin\theta) = 3$

⑦ $r = \dfrac{2}{4\sin\theta + 5\cos\theta}$

⑧ $r = -2\csc\theta$

⑨ $r = 3\sec\theta$

EXAMPLE 6. Find an equivalent equation in polar coordinates.

① $y = 7$ 　　　　　　　　　　　　② $x + y = 3$

③ $2x - y = 4$ 　　　　　　　　　　④ $x^2 = 4 - y^2$

⑤ $x^2 - y^2 = 2$ 　　　　　　　　　⑥ $x^2 + 1 = y^2$

⑦ $x^2 + y^2 = 1$

Mia's Precalculus

7.2 Graphs of Polar Equations

1. Polar Graph

A **polar equation** is a curve with an equation of the form

$$r = f(\theta)$$

① _____.

Polar curve has many shapes. For example;

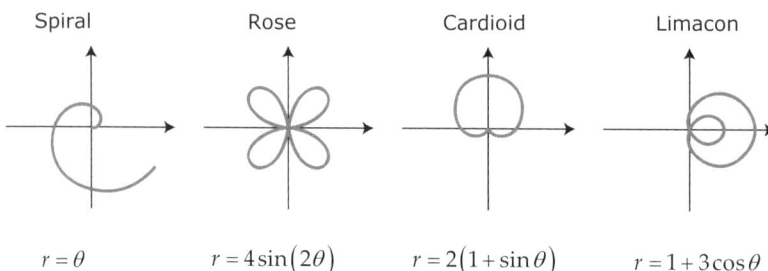

Spiral: $r = \theta$
Rose: $r = 4\sin(2\theta)$
Cardioid: $r = 2(1+\sin\theta)$
Limacon: $r = 1 + 3\cos\theta$

Let's graph some polar equations!

EXAMPLE 1. When $r = 1 + \cos\theta$, fill in the table and graph the polar.

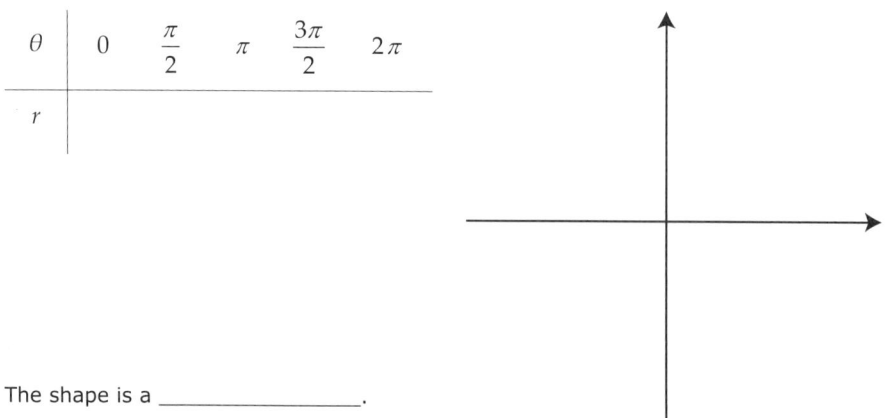

θ	0	$\dfrac{\pi}{2}$	π	$\dfrac{3\pi}{2}$	2π
r					

The shape is a _____.

Blank : ① r = f(θ)

EXAMPLE 2. Graph the polar equations.

① $r = 1 - \sin\theta$

② $r = 1 - \cos\theta$

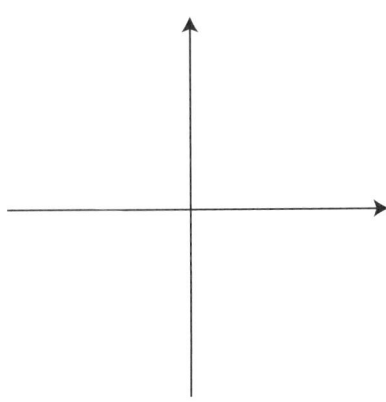
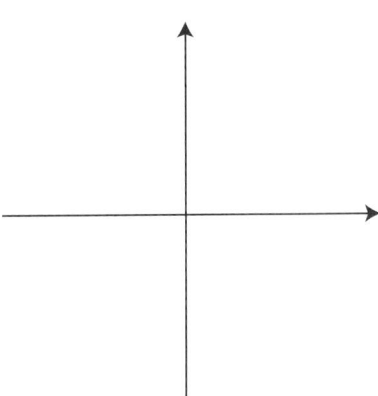

③ $r = 2 + \sin\theta$

④ $r = 3 - 2\cos\theta$

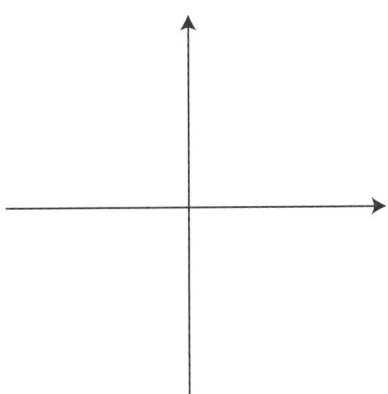
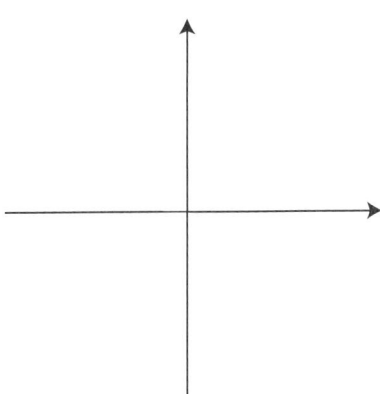

⑤ $r = 2 + 3\cos\theta$

⑥ $r = 2 - 4\sin\theta$

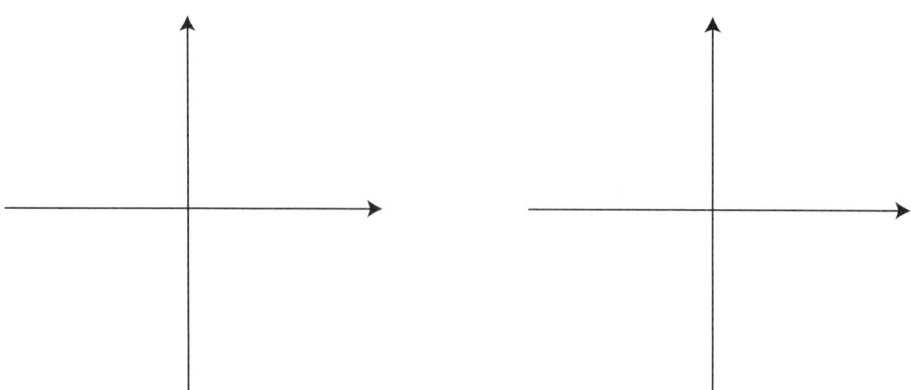

We can notice that

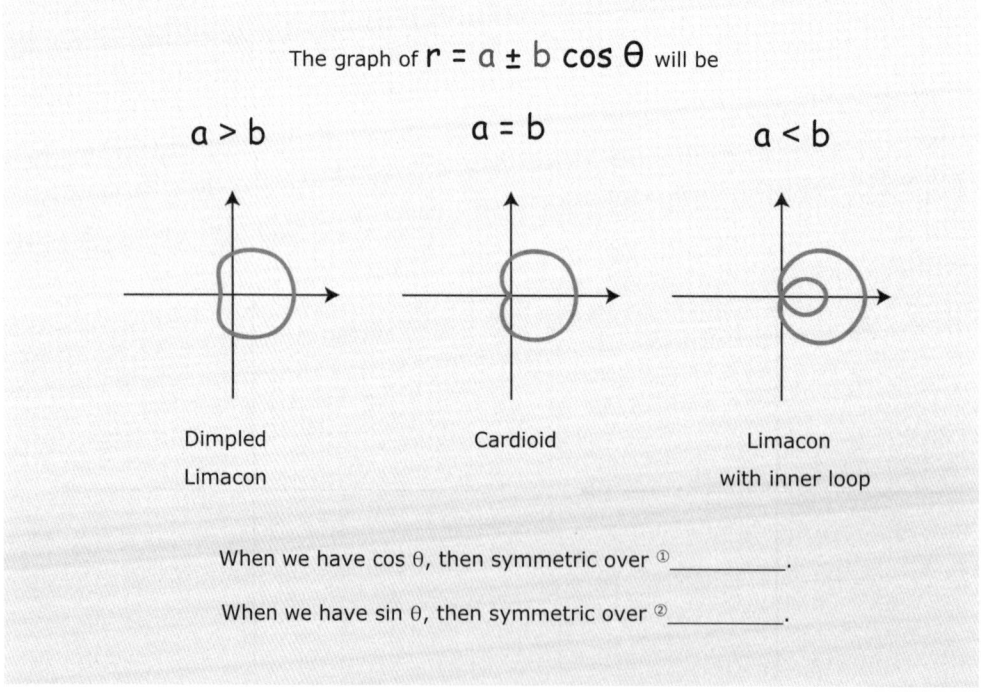

The graph of $r = a \pm b \cos\theta$ will be

a > b — Dimpled Limacon

a = b — Cardioid

a < b — Limacon with inner loop

When we have $\cos\theta$, then symmetric over ①_____.

When we have $\sin\theta$, then symmetric over ②_____.

Blank : ① x axis ② y axis

EXAMPLE 3. When $r = 3\cos 2\theta$ fill in the table and graph the polar.

θ	0	$\dfrac{\pi}{2}$	π	$\dfrac{3\pi}{2}$	2π
r					

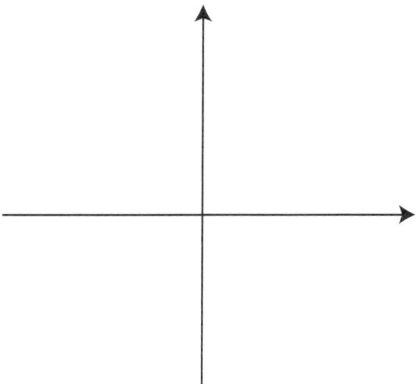

The shape is a _____.

EXAMPLE 4. Graph the polar equations.

① $r = 4\sin 3\theta$ ② $r = 5\sin 2\theta$

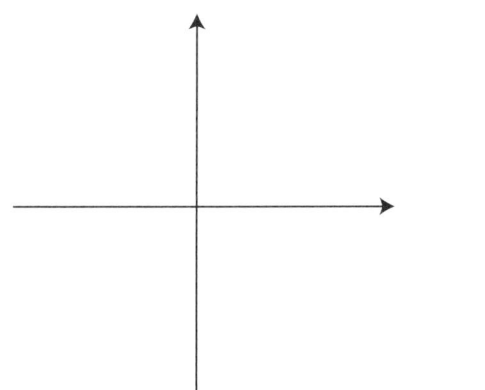
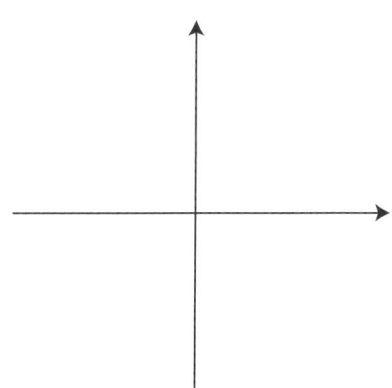

③ $r = 5\sin 4\theta$ ④ $r = 2\cos 3\theta$

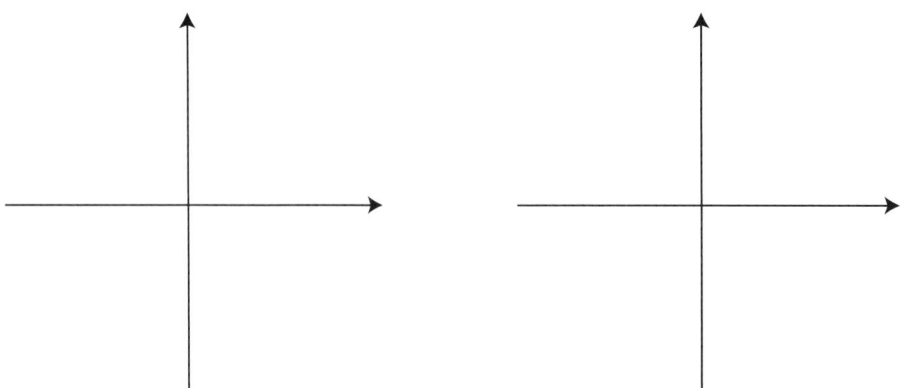

We can notice that

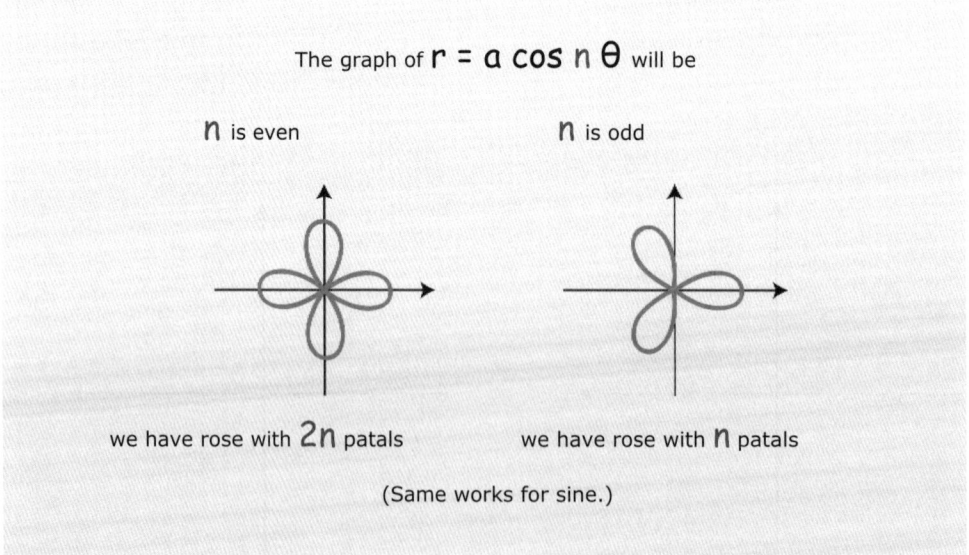

The graph of $r = a \cos n\theta$ will be

n is even — we have rose with $2n$ patals

n is odd — we have rose with n patals

(Same works for sine.)

EXAMPLE 5. Graph $r^2 = 9\sin(2\theta)$ in the polar system.

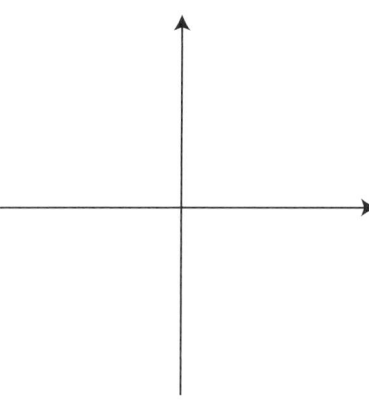

The shape is a _____.

EXAMPLE 6. Graph $r = 2$ in the polar system.

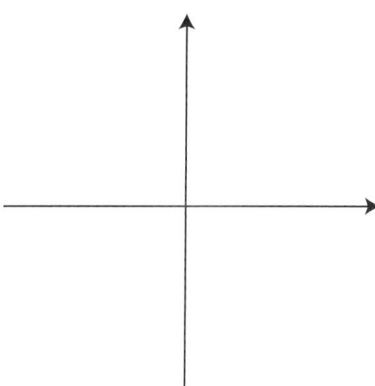

The shape is a _____.

EXAMPLE 7. Graph $r = 2\cos\theta$ in the polar system.

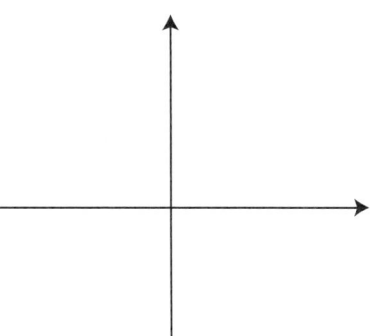

The shape is a _____.

EXAMPLE 8. Graph $r = \theta$ in the polar system.

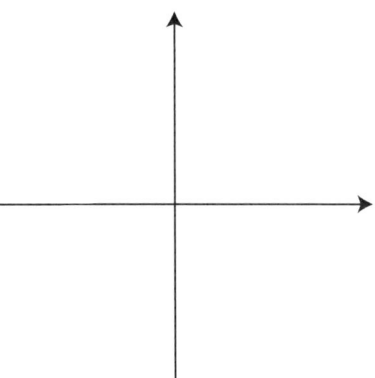

The shape is a _____.

EXAMPLE 9. Graph $r = \sec\theta$ in the polar system.

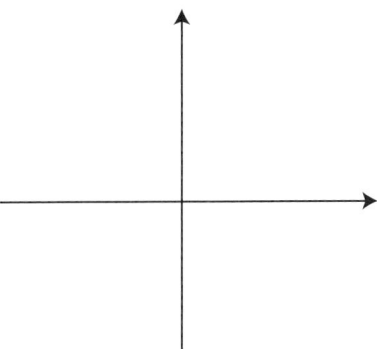

The shape is a _____.

☺ Polar Graph All in One

Shape	Equation	Notes	
Line	$\theta = c$		
Circle	$r = a$	radius is a	
	$r = a\cos\theta$	diameter is a	

Name	Equation	Condition	Graph
Rose	$r = a\cos n\theta$	If n is even, we have **2n** patals.	
		If n is odd, we have **n** patals.	
Cardiod or Limacon	$r = a \pm b\cos\theta$	If $a > b$, then Dimpled Limacon	
		If $a = b$, then Cardioid	
		If $a < b$, then Limacon with inner loop	
Lemniscate	$r^2 = a^2 \cos 2\theta$		
Spiral	$r = \theta$		

※ Tests for Symmetry in Polar Coordinates

If it is $r = f(\sin\theta)$, then it is symmetric over line $\theta = \dfrac{\pi}{2}$ (y-axis).

If it is $r = f(\cos\theta)$, then it is symmetric over polar axis(x-axis).

EXAMPLE 10. Match the polar equation with the graphs.

a) $r = 2 - 3\cos\theta$

b) $r = 8\sin\theta$

c) $r = \theta$

d) $r = 3\sin 4\theta$

e) $r = 8\cos 3\theta$

f) $r = 2 + 2\sin\theta$

I.

II.
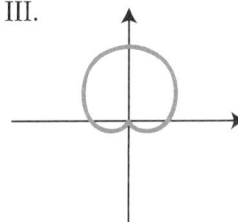

III.
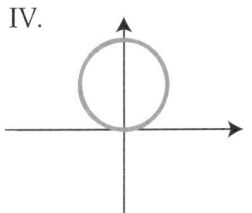

IV.
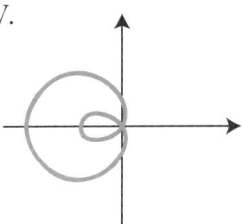

V.
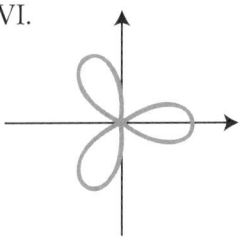

VI.

Mia's Precalculus
7.3 Complex Number and DeMoivre's Thm

1. Complex Number

※ A complex number, z, is a number that can be written in the form $z = a + bi$ (Cartesian form), where a and b are real numbers and $i^2 = -1$:

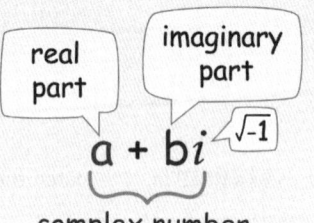

- a is the real part of z.
- bi is the imaginary part of z.
- The complex conjugate of z, written as $z^* = $ ①_____

※ If two complex numbers are equal, their real parts are the same and their imaginary parts are the same.

2. Complex Plane

We are familiar with Cartesian plane:
But where do we put a complex number $3 + 4i$?
We need a new plane!

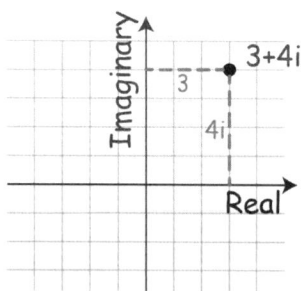

We call this a ②_____ plane or ③_____ diagram:
it is a combination of real and imaginary numbers!

Blank : ① $a - bi$ ② complex   ③ Argand

EXAMPLE 1. Draw the complex number in an imaginary plane.

① $z = 1 - 3i$ ② $z = -4 - 3i$

③ $z = 6i$ ④ $z = -5$

⑤ $z = -2$ ⑥ $z = -7i$

3. Polar Form of Complex Numbers

Complex numbers can be represented in ①_____ form.

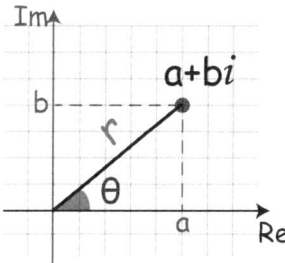

Blank : ① polar

Modulus of z = r = |z| = distance of the complex number from the origin

$$|z| = r = |a+bi| = \boxed{①\ \sqrt{a^2+b^2}}$$

Argument of z = θ = angle in standard postion

$$\tan\theta = \frac{b}{a}$$

(remember; $\tan^{-1}$ only gives you the reference angle)

A complex number can also be described in polar form:

$$z = \boxed{②\ r(\cos\theta + i\sin\theta)} = r\operatorname{cis}\theta$$

※ Polar Form of Complex Number

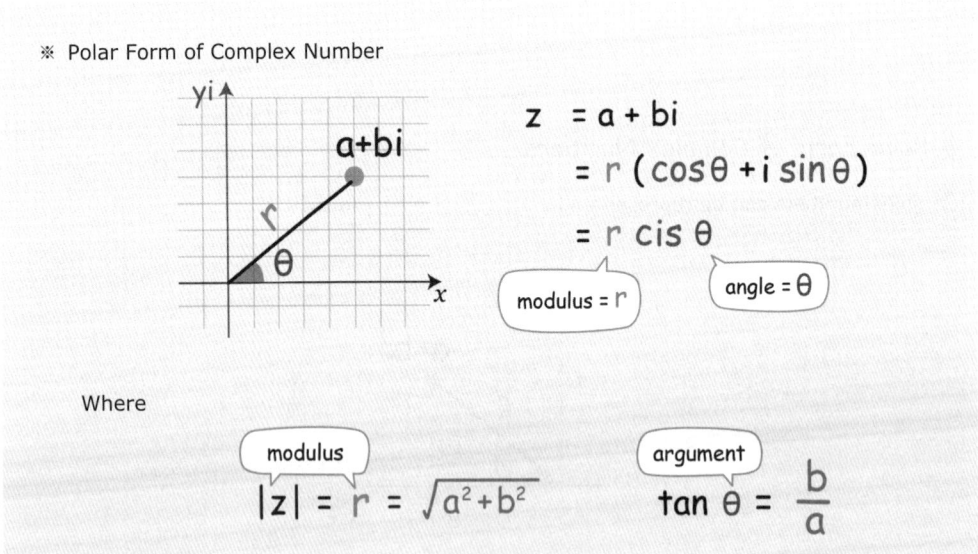

Where

$$|z| = r = \sqrt{a^2+b^2} \qquad \tan\theta = \frac{b}{a}$$

Blank : ① $\sqrt{a^2+b^2}$ ② $r(\cos\theta + i\sin\theta)$

EXAMPLE 2. Use an algebraic method to find the trigonometric form (polar form) with $0 \leq \theta < 2\pi$ for

① $z = 1+i$

② $z = \sqrt{3}-i$

③ $z = -\sqrt{3}i+1$

④ $z = -2+2i$

⑤ $z = -2+3i$

⑥ $z = \sqrt{5}-i$

EXAMPLE 3. Convert into Cartesian form.

⑦ $2\left(\cos 120° + i\sin 120°\right)$

⑧ $3\left(\cos 210° + i\sin 210°\right)$

⑨ $2\left(\cos\dfrac{7\pi}{6} + i\sin\dfrac{7\pi}{6}\right)$

⑩ $3\left(\cos\dfrac{3\pi}{2} + i\sin\dfrac{3\pi}{2}\right)$

⑪ $4cis23\pi$

⑫ $3cis32\pi$

4. Product and Quotient of Complex Numbers

Let $z_1 = r_1(\cos\theta_1 + i\sin\theta_1)$ and $z_2 = r_2(\cos\theta_2 + i\sin\theta_2)$.

Then $z_1 z_2 = r_1(\cos\theta_1 + i\sin\theta_1) r_2(\cos\theta_2 + i\sin\theta_2)$

$= r_1 r_2 (\cos\theta_1 \cos\theta_2 + \boxed{①}$

$+ i(\sin\theta_1 \cos\theta_2 + \boxed{②})$

$= r_1 r_2 (\cos \boxed{③} + i\sin \boxed{④})$

When you multiply two complex numbers in polar form
you multiply their moduli and add their arguments:
When you divide two complex numbers
you divide their moduli and subtract their arguments.

※ Product and Quotient of Complex Numbers

(mupltiply the modulus) (add the angles)

$$z_1 z_2 = r_1 r_2 \operatorname{cis}(\theta_1 + \theta_2)$$

$$\frac{z_1}{z_2} = \frac{r_1}{r_2} \operatorname{cis}(\theta_1 - \theta_2)$$

When multiplying in Polar Form:

⑤_____ the moduli(plural of modulus), ⑥_____ the angles.

Blank : ① $-\sin\theta_1 \sin\theta_2$ ② $\cos\theta_1 \sin\theta_2$ ③ $(\theta_1 + \theta_2)$ ④ $(\theta_1 + \theta_2)$ ⑤ multiply ⑥ add

EXAMPLE 4. Find the product and the quotient of z_1 and z_2 in polar form.

① $z_1 = 2(\cos 40° + i \sin 40°)$
   $z_2 = 4(\cos 20° + i \sin 20°)$

② $z_1 = \cos 120° + i \sin 120°$
   $z_2 = 2(\cos 100° + i \sin 100°)$

③ $z_1 = 2\left(\cos \dfrac{\pi}{5} + i \sin \dfrac{\pi}{5}\right)$
   $z_2 = 3\left(\cos \dfrac{\pi}{10} + i \sin \dfrac{\pi}{10}\right)$

④ $z_1 = 4\left(\cos \dfrac{3\pi}{5} + i \sin \dfrac{3\pi}{5}\right)$
   $z_2 = 4\left(\cos \dfrac{3\pi}{10} + i \sin \dfrac{3\pi}{10}\right)$

⑤ $z_1 = 2 \operatorname{cis} \dfrac{7\pi}{6} \quad z_2 = \dfrac{1}{4} \operatorname{cis} \dfrac{\pi}{3}$

5. De Moivre's Theorem

To square a complex number, multiply it by itself:
- multiply the modulus: modulus × modulus = **modulus ^{2}**
- add the angles: angle + angle = **2 angle** , so we double them.
  Result: square the moduli, double the angle.

And the mathematician *Abraham de Moivre* found it works for any integer exponent n:

※ **De Moivre's Theorem**

$$z^n = r^n(\cos n\theta + i \sin n\theta)$$

modulus = r^n , angle = $n\theta$

EXAMPLE 5. Use De Moivre's Theorem to find the indicated power of the complex number. Write the answers in rectangular form(= a+bi).

① $\left[\sqrt{2}\left(\cos\dfrac{5\pi}{12} + i\sin\dfrac{5\pi}{12}\right)\right]^4$

② $\left[\sqrt{3}\left(\cos\dfrac{5\pi}{18} + i\sin\dfrac{5\pi}{18}\right)\right]^6$

③ $(1-i)^5$

④ $(\sqrt{3}-i)^7$

⑤ $\left(1-\sqrt{3}i\right)^6$ ⑥ $\left(2-2i\right)^5$

⑦ $\left(\sqrt{3}-i\right)^{-6}$

EXAMPLE 6. Simplify the following expression.
$$\frac{(\cos 6A + i\sin 6A)^6 (\cos 3A + i\sin 3A)}{\cos 4A + i\sin 4A}$$

EXAMPLE 7. Evaluate.

$$\frac{(1+i)^{10}}{4i}$$

6. Finding Roots of Complex Numbers

※ Finding nth Roots of a Complex Number

To solve equations of the form $z^n = w$:

① Write w in polar form.

② Let $z = r \text{ cis } \theta$ and apply De Moivre's theorem to get $z^n = r^n \text{ cis } n\theta$.

③ Find r and all possible values of θ.

In general, for a positive integer n, the complex number $z = r \text{ cis } \theta$ has exactly n distinct nth roots given by

$$\sqrt[n]{r}\left(\cos\frac{\theta + 2\pi k}{n} + i\sin\frac{\theta + 2\pi k}{n}\right)$$

where $k = 0, 1, 2, \ldots, n - 1$.

The equation will have n solutions which form a regular polygon with vertices on a circle.

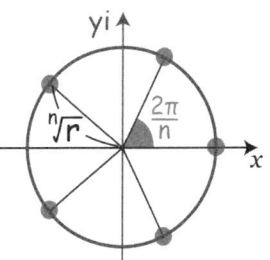

EXAMPLE 8. Find the indicated roots, and graph the roots in the complex plane.

① square roots of $z = 4\sqrt{3} + 4i$.

② cube roots of $z = -1 + i$.

③ cube roots of $z = 3 - 3\sqrt{3}i$.

④ forth roots of $z = -1 - \sqrt{3}i$.

⑤ fifth roots of $z = i$.

⑥ fifth roots of $z = -32$.

Mia's Precalculus
7.4 Parametric Equations

1. Parametric Equations

A **parametric equation** is where the x and y coordinates are both written in terms of another letter.

$$x = f(t), \quad y = g(t)$$

That another letter (usually given the letter t or θ) is called a ①_____.

Finding the Cartesian equation
: Try to eliminate the parameter t or θ by using

② _____ or ③ _____.

Yuna is gliding around on a frozen coordinate plane. At time t (in seconds) Yuna's position on the coordinate plane is given by $(x(t), y(t))$ where

$$x(t) = t^2 - 2t, \quad y(t) = t + 2.$$

If Yuna starts at time t = 0 and stops at time t = 15, she will trace out the parametric curve like the one sketched below.

What is Yuna's position at $t = 0$, $t = 1$, $t = 3$?

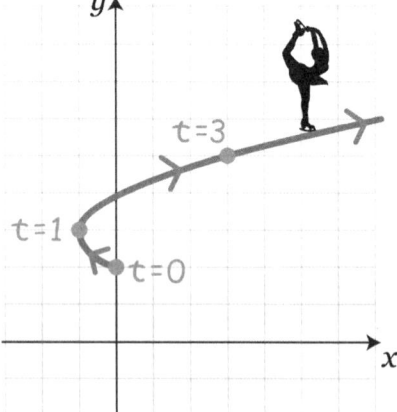

Blank : ① parameter   ② substitution   ③ trig identity

EXAMPLE 1. Identify the graph of the parametric curve

① $x = 1 - 2t, \quad y = 2 - t$

② $x = \dfrac{t}{3}, \quad y = \sqrt{t}$

③ $x = t^2 - 1, \quad y = -t + 4$

④ $x = 3t, \quad y = t^2 - 2$

⑤ $x = 2\cos\theta, y = 3\sin\theta, \ 0 \le \theta \le 2\pi$

⑥ $x = 5\cos\theta, y = 7\sin\theta, \ 0 \le \theta \le 2\pi$

⑦ $x = 2\sec\theta, y = 3\tan\theta, \ 0 \le \theta \le 2\pi$

⑧ $x = \sec\theta, y = \tan\theta, \ 0 \le \theta \le 2\pi$

If we want to graph $x = t^2 - 2t$, $y = t + 2$;

t	x	y
-2	8	0
-1	①	
0	①	
1	-1	3
2	0	4
3	3	5

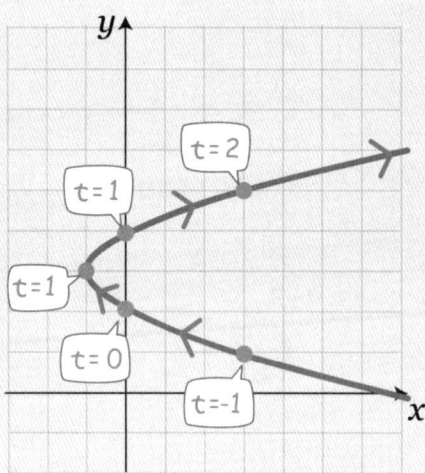

EXAMPLE 2. Sketch the parametric function indicating the orientation. State the domain.

① $x = 3t + 2, y = t + 1$; $0 \leq t \leq 4$

② $x = t - 3, y = 2t^2 + 4$; $t \geq -2$

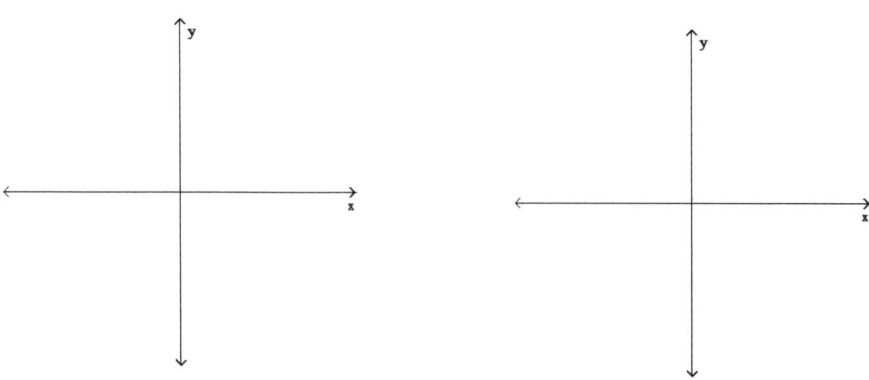

Blank : ① 3, 1   ② 0, 2

③ $x = 1+t,\ y = t^2 - 4t\ ;\ -2 \leq t \leq 2$

④ $x = \sqrt{t},\ y = 3t + 1$

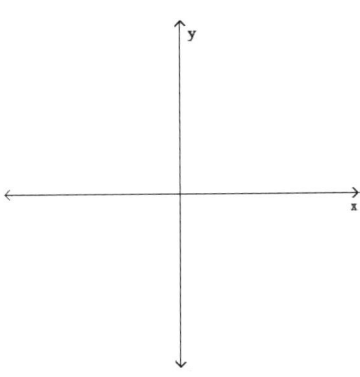

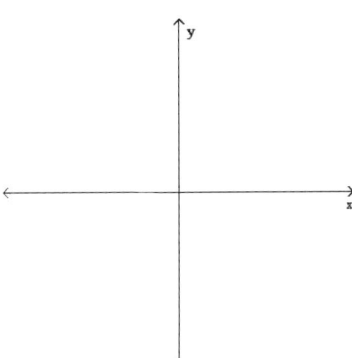

⑤ $x = \sqrt{t-2},\ y = 1-t$

⑥ $x = t^2,\ y = t^4 + 1\ ;\ 0 \leq t \leq 3$

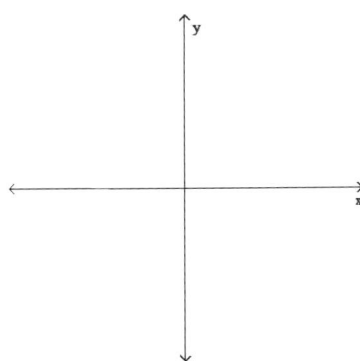

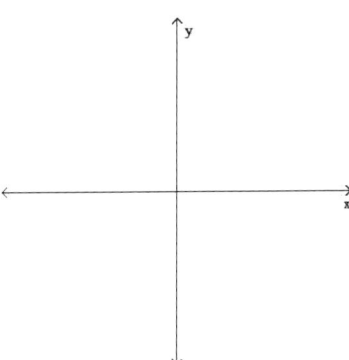

⑦ $x = 2\cos t,\ y = 3\sin t\ ;\ 0 \leq t \leq 2\pi$

⑧ $x = 2\sin t,\ y = \cos t\ ;\ 0 \leq t \leq \dfrac{\pi}{2}$

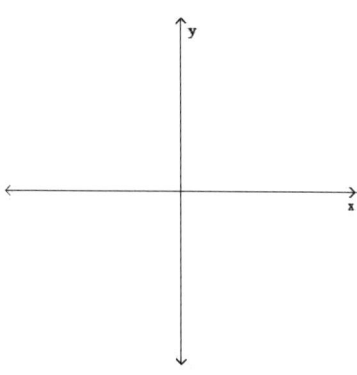
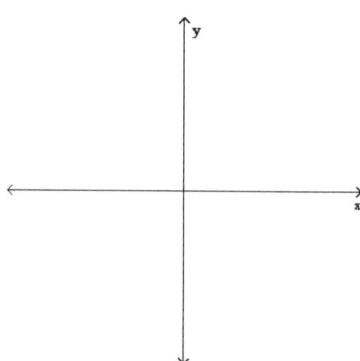

⑨ $x = 2\sin t,\ y = 3\cos t\ ;\ \dfrac{\pi}{2} \leq t \leq \pi$

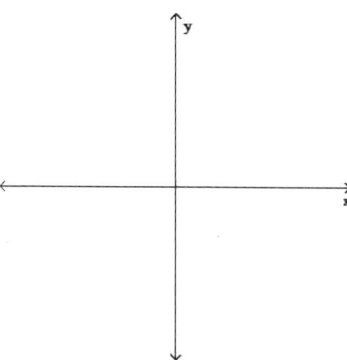

⑩ $x = 2^t$, $y = 2^{-t}$; $t \geq 0$

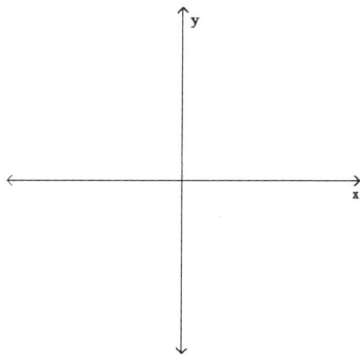

⑪ $x = \sin^2 t$, $y = \sin^4 t$; $0 \leq t \leq \pi$

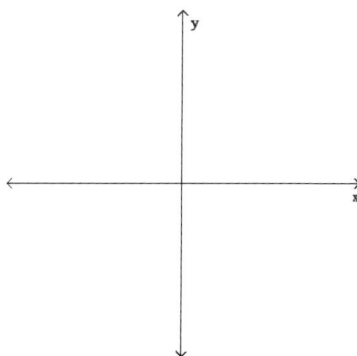

Part 8
Vector

8.1 Vector Basics
8.2 Vectors in Two Dimensions
8.3 The Dot Product
8.4 Three-Dimensional Coordinate
8.5 Vectors in Three Dimensions
8.6 The Cross Product

Mia's Precalculus
8.1 Vector Basics

1. Vector

A **vector** has ①_____ (how long it is) and ②_____:

A **scalar** has only ③_____ (no directions).

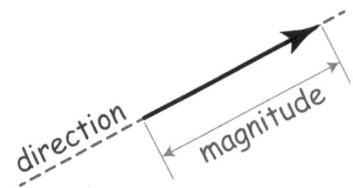

The length of the line shows its *magnitude*
and the arrowhead points in the *direction*.

- Notation : ④_____

- Magnitude notation : ⑤_____

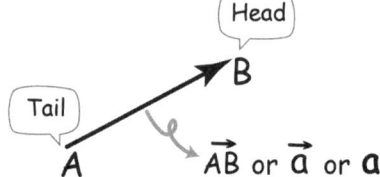

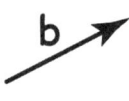

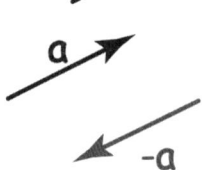

- Opposite vector :
two vectors that have **equal length** and the **opposite direction**.

- Equivalent vectors : $\vec{a} = \vec{b}$
two vectors that have **equal length** and the **same direction**.

Blank : ① magnitude　② direction　③ magnitude　④ $\vec{AB} = \vec{a} = a$　⑤ $|\vec{AB}| = |\vec{a}| = |a|$

2. Direction of Vector

There are three ways to describe a direction of a vector;

In standard position (= to the horizontal = direction angle in vector)

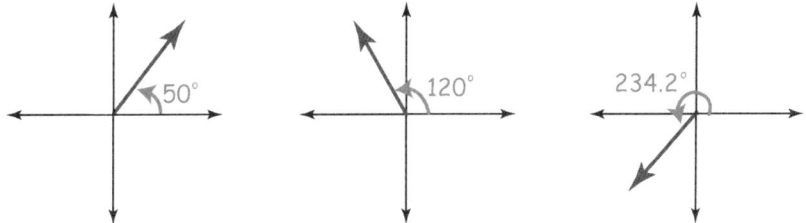

True bearing : The angle in degrees measured clockwise from North.
ex) bearing of 50° : 50° clockwise from North.

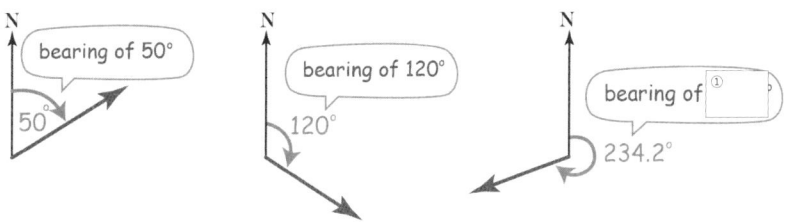

Quadrant bearing: The angle made between a north or south direction and an east or west direction.
North or south is written first, then the angle, then east or west.

ex) S50°W : from south 50° towards the west.

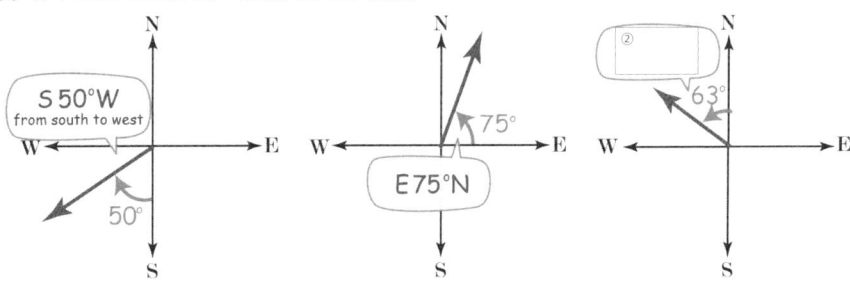

Blank : ① 234.2°　② N63°W

Part 8. Vector 397

EXAMPLE 1. State whether each quantity described is a vector quantity or a scalar quantity. If it is vector, then sketch the vector.

① a boat traveling 20 feet per second at a bearing of 30°

② a ship sailing 30 miles per hour at a bearing of S60°W

③ John pulling a sled with a force of 40 newtons

④ person 12 feet per hour at a bearing of 210°

⑤ a car traveling 60 miles per hour at a bearing of S25°E

⑥ a boat traveling at 15 miles per hour

EXAMPLE 2. Convert the direction into standard position.

① bearing of 240°

② bearing of 145°

③ bearing of W55°N

④ bearing of S65°E

3. Adding two vectors (Resultant of vectors)

We can **add** two vectors in two different ways;

1) "Head to tail" method	2) "Tail to tail" method (Parallelogram Method)
: by simply joining them head-to-tail	: by making a Parallelogram
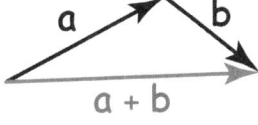	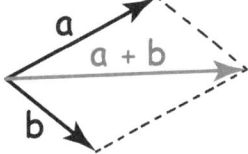

The sum of the vectors is called the ①_____.

Blank : ① resultant

4. Subtracting two vectors

We can also **subtract** one vector from another:
first we reverse the direction of the vector we want to subtract,
then add them as usual:

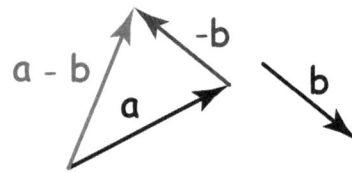

5. Scale Multiplication

When we multiply a vector by a scalar it is called "**scaling**" a vector, because we change how big or small the vector is.

EXAMPLE 3. Use the vectors **a**, **b**, **c** and **d** in the accompanying figure to graph the vector.

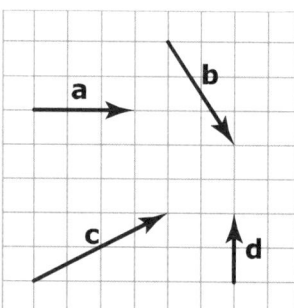

① **b + c**

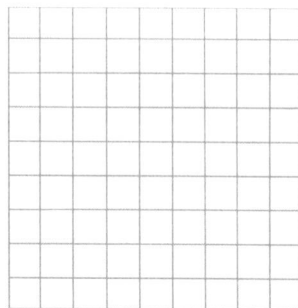

② **3d**

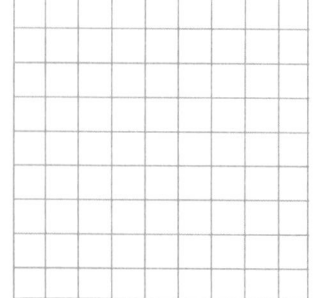

③ 2**b**

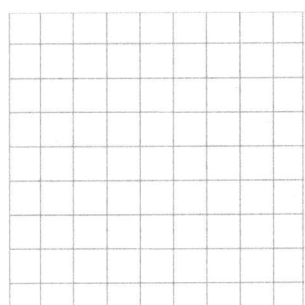

④ **a** + **b**

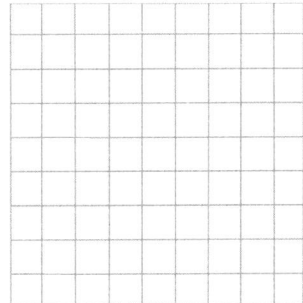

⑤ **c** - **d**

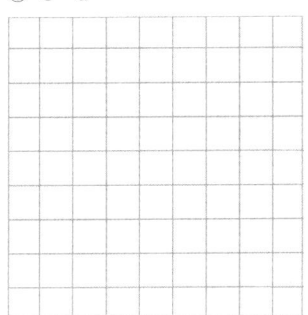

⑥ **b** - **c**

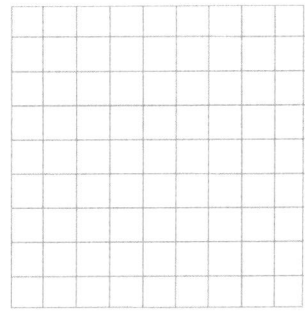

⑦ 2**a** - 3**d**

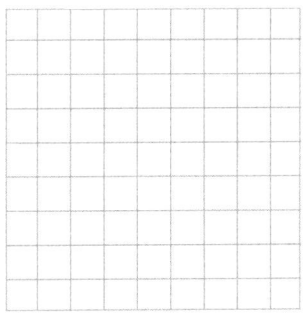

⑧ 2**b** - **c**

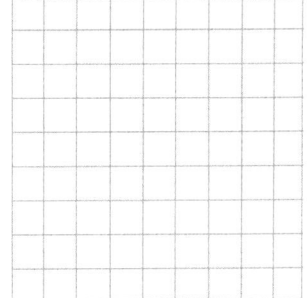

EXAMPLE 4. True or false?

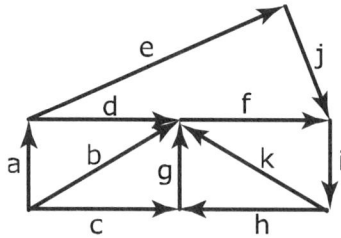

① $a + d = b$

② $c + g = b$

③ $b + g = c$

④ $k + g = h$

⑤ $a + c = b$

⑥ $g + f + i + h = 0$

⑦ $a + e + j + i + h = c$

⑧ $e + j = d + f$

6. Expand Knowledge (Finding Vector Using Sine and Cosine Rule)

> Speed, tension, weight, and force represent the ①_____ of the vector.

EXAMPLE 5. Victor runs with the football at a speed of 5 m/sec due east and throws the ball at a speed of 8 m/sec in the direction N47°E. What is the resultant speed and direction of the ball?

EXAMPLE 6. An airplane flies east for 210km before turning the direction to bearing of 145° and flying for 100km. Find the distance and direction of the plane from its starting point.

Blank : ① magnitude

Mia's Precalculus

8.2 Vectors in Two Dimensions

1. Vectors in the Plane

When we put a vector in a Cartesian coordinate, we can represent a vector using numbers.

A ①_____ vector is a vector that starts at the origin (0, 0).

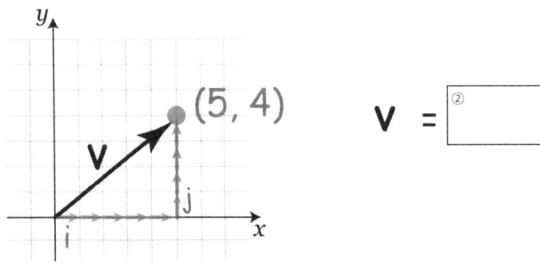

$$v = \boxed{②} = \boxed{③}$$

The vectors i and j are called base vectors with magnitude of 1.

※ Position Vectors

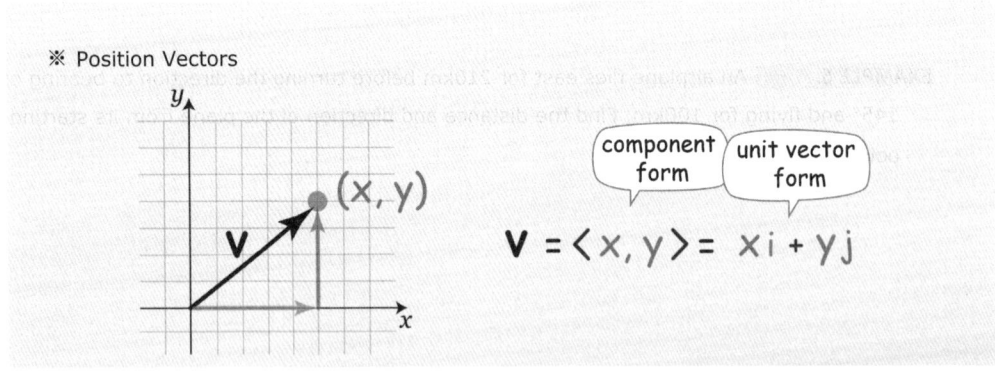

component form / unit vector form

$$v = \langle x, y \rangle = xi + yj$$

Blank : ① position ② <5, 4> ③ 5i+4j

EXAMPLE 1. Write the illustrated vectors in component form and in unit vector form:

①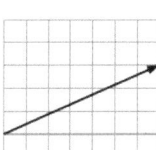

②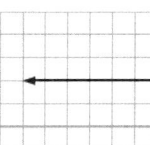

③

④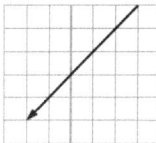

2. Displacement Vector

A displacement vector is a vector between two points.

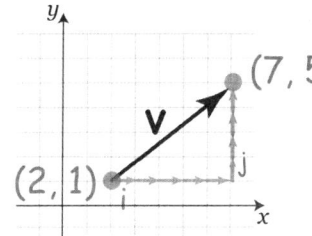

V = ①
  = ②

※ Displacement Vector (Head minus Tail Rule)

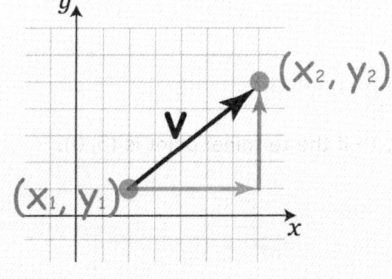

HMT

$V = \langle x_2 - x_1, y_2 - y_1 \rangle$

$= (x_2 - x_1)i + (y_2 - y_1)j$

Blank : ① <5, 4>   ② 5i+4j

EXAMPLE 2. Given points $A(-1, 2)$, $B(3, 4)$, and $C(4, -5)$, find the vector of:

① vector **b**　　　　　　　　　　　② vector **c**

③ C from O　　　　　　　　　　　④ B from O

⑤ $\overrightarrow{AO}$　　　　　　　　　　　⑥ $\overrightarrow{CO}$

⑦ $\overrightarrow{BA}$　　　　　　　　　　　⑧ $\overrightarrow{AC}$

⑨ $\overrightarrow{BC}$　　　　　　　　　　　⑩ B from A

⑪ A from C

EXAMPLE 3. Find the terminal point of $v = 3i - 2j$ if the initial point is $(-2, 1)$.

EXAMPLE 4. Find the initial point of $v = <-3, 1>$ if the terminal point is $(5, 0)$.

3. Vector Algebra

※ Sum Vector of V and U

If vector **v** = <v_1, v_2>, **u** = <u_1, u_2>

$$\mathbf{v} + \mathbf{u} = \langle v_1+u_1, v_2+u_2 \rangle$$

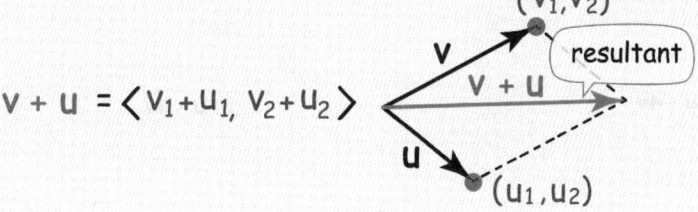

※ Scaling Vector

$$k\mathbf{v} = \langle kv_1, kv_2 \rangle$$

※ Parallel Vectors

Parallel vectors have same direction but different lengths.
Numerically, vectors are parallel if and only if they are *scalar multiples* of each other

If **a** is parallel to **b**, then **a** = k**b**.

EXAMPLE 5. Consider the vector **u** =<2, -1>, **v** =<3, 0>. Find;

① **u** + **v**   ② **u** - **v**

③ 2**u** + 3**v**   ④ -**u** + 4**v**

EXAMPLE 6. Consider the vector $u = 3i - j$, $v = -i + 3j$. Find;

① $u + v$

② $u - v$

③ $-u - 4v$

④ $u - 3v$

※ **Magnitude**

Magnitude is the length of the vector (= distance from head to tail)

Magnitude of $v = <x, y>$ is

$$|v| = \sqrt{x^2 + y^2}$$

(Magnitude of **v**)

※ **Unit Vector in the same direction**

You can find a unit vector **in the same direction** by dividing out the
①_____ of the vector.

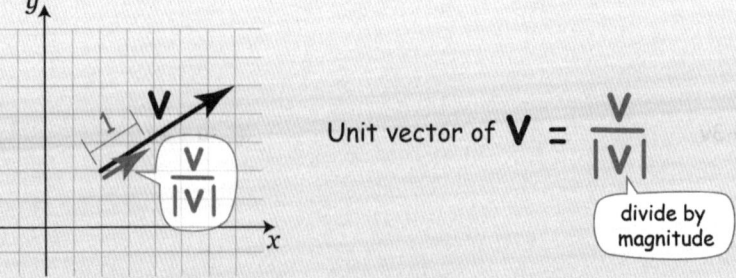

Unit vector of $\mathbf{V} = \dfrac{V}{|V|}$

(divide by magnitude)

Blank : ① magnitude

EXAMPLE 7. Find the magnitude of the given vector and a unit vector in the direction of the given vector.

① **a** = <2, 0>

② $-3i + j$

③ **v** = $5i - 12j$

④ **b** = <-1, 5>

⑤ vector from P = (5, 8) to Q = (6, 9)

⑥ vector from P = (-1, 3) to Q = (2, 7)

4. Horizontal and Vertical Component of Vector

※ Vector using Direction Angle θ

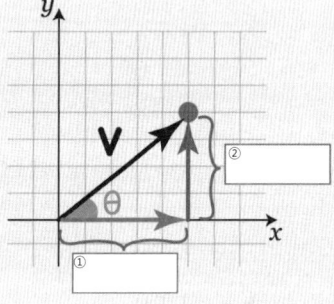

$$\mathbf{v} = \langle |v|\cos\theta, |v|\sin\theta \rangle$$

EXAMPLE 8. Write the vector **v** in the form ai+bj, given its magnitude and the direction.

① $|\mathbf{v}| = 5, \theta = 60°$ ② $|\mathbf{v}| = 3, \theta = 150°$

③ $|\mathbf{v}| = 3, \theta = 240°$ ④ $|\mathbf{v}| = 24, \theta = 225°$

Blank : ① $|v| \cos\theta$ ② $|v| \sin\theta$

※ When v = <x, y> is given,

Magnitude of v
$$|v| = \sqrt{x^2 + y^2}$$

direction angle
$$\tan \theta = \frac{y}{x}$$

EXAMPLE 9. Find the magnitude and direction (in degrees) of each vector, and rewrite the vector with horizontal and vertical components.

① $a = \langle 3, 3 \rangle$

② $b = \langle 1, \sqrt{3} \rangle$

③ $c = -3\sqrt{3}i + 3j$

④ $d = -5i - 5j$

⑤ $e = -i - 5j$

⑥ $f = i - 3j$

5. Expand Knowledge (Finding Vectors using horizontal and vertical components)

EXAMPLE 10. A river flows due east at 3 mph. A boat travels with a speed of 25 mph in the direction N35°W. Find the actual speed and direction of the boat.

EXAMPLE 11. A jet is flying through a wind that is blowing 50 km/h in the direction S46°E. The jet's speed with no wind is 580 km/h with bearing of 240°. What is the true speed and direction of the jet?

Mia's Precalculus

8.3 The Dot Product

1. Dot Products and Angles

You can calculate the dot Product of two vectors in two ways:

1) Dot Product using magnitudes and angle

Where:
  $|u|$ is the magnitude (length) of vector **u**
  $|v|$ is the magnitude (length) of vector **v**
  θ is the angle between **u** and **v**

So we multiply the length of **u** times the length of **v**, then multiply by the cosine of the angle between **u** and **v**.

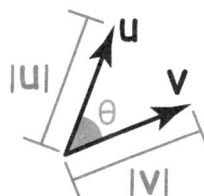

v · **u** = ①

2) Dot Product using coordinates

We multiply the x's, multiply the y's, then add.

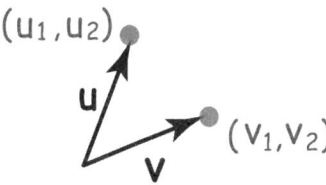

v · **u** = ②

※ Dot (Scalar) Product of Vectors

dot product
v · **u** = $v_1 u_1 + v_2 u_2$
       = $|v| |u| \cos θ$

Blank : ① $|v| |u| \cos θ$ ② $v_1 u_1 + v_2 u_2$

Notice that the scalar product of two vectors is a ①_____ number NOT a vector. ($\mathbf{v} \cdot \mathbf{u} \neq \mathbf{vu}$)

EXAMPLE 1. Find $\mathbf{a} \cdot \mathbf{b}$.

① $\mathbf{a} = \langle 2,4 \rangle$, $\mathbf{b} = \langle 2,5 \rangle$

② $\mathbf{a} = \langle 5,-10 \rangle$, $\mathbf{b} = \langle 6,5 \rangle$

③ $\mathbf{a} = 6i+2j$, $\mathbf{b} = 2i+4j$

④ $\mathbf{a} = 4i+8j$, $\mathbf{b} = -2i+3j$

⑤ $\mathbf{a} = 6j$, $\mathbf{b} = i+4j$

⑥ $\mathbf{a} = -i+2j$, $\mathbf{b} = -j$

⑦ $|\mathbf{a}| = 2$, $|\mathbf{b}| = 3$,
Angle between $\mathbf{a}$ and $\mathbf{b}$ is $\dfrac{2\pi}{3}$

⑧ $|\mathbf{a}| = 3$, $|\mathbf{b}| = 2$,
Angle between $\mathbf{a}$ and $\mathbf{b}$ is $\dfrac{5\pi}{6}$

Blank : ① scalar

2. Angle between two vectors

If v · u = |v||u| cos θ , then cos θ = ① _____.

※ Angle between two vectors

The angle between two Vector **v** = $\langle v_1, v_2 \rangle$ and **u** = $\langle u_1, u_2 \rangle$ is

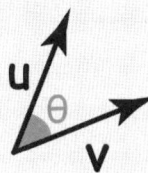 $\cos \theta = \dfrac{\mathbf{v} \cdot \mathbf{u}}{|\mathbf{v}||\mathbf{u}|}$

EXAMPLE 2. Find the angle between the two vectors to the nearest degree.

① **a** = $\langle 2,4 \rangle$, **b** = $\langle 2,1 \rangle$ ② **a** = $\langle 5,-1 \rangle$, **b** = $\langle 0,5 \rangle$

③ **a** = $4i+8j$, **b** = $-2i+j$ ④ **a** = $6i-2j$, **b** = $2i+4j$

⑤ **a** = $6j$, **b** = $i+4j$ ⑥ **a** = $-i+2j$, **b** = $-i$

Blank : ① $\dfrac{\mathbf{v} \cdot \mathbf{u}}{|\mathbf{v}||\mathbf{u}|}$

3. Properties of Dot Product

※ Facts about Dot product

① If vectors **V** and **U** are perpendicular, ①_____

② If vectors **V** and **U** are parallel, ②_____

③   **v · v**   = ③_____

④   (k**v**) **· u**   = ④_____ (k is scalar)

⑤   **v · (a + b)**   = ⑤_____ (distributive)

⑥   **v · u**   = ⑥_____ (commutative)

⑦   **v · u · w**   ⑦(possible/impossible)

EXAMPLE 3. Determine whether the vectors u and v are parallel, orthogonal, or neither.

Orthogonal means perpendicular.

①   **u** = $\langle 10,0 \rangle$, **v** = $\langle 0,-9 \rangle$ ②   **u** = $\langle 7,2 \rangle$, **v** = $\langle 21,6 \rangle$

③   **u** = $i + \sqrt{3}j$, **v** = $i - 2j$ ④   **u** = $2i + 4j$, **v** = $4i - 2j$

Blank : ① v · u = 0   ② v · u = |v||u| ③ $|v|^2$ ④ k(v · u)   ⑤ v · a + v · b   ⑥ u · v   ⑦impossible

⑤ **u** $= 3i+2j$, **v** $=6i+4j$ ⑥ **u** $= \langle 8,4 \rangle$, **v** $= \langle 10,7 \rangle$

⑦ **u** $= \langle 1,-2 \rangle$, **v** $= \langle -4,8 \rangle$

EXAMPLE 4. Find t such that **a** $= \langle 3, 3-2t \rangle$, **b** $= \langle t^2+t, -2 \rangle$ are perpendicular.

EXAMPLE 5.* Given that **a** and **b** are perpendicular vectors such that |**a**| = 5, |**b**| = 3, evaluate

① (2**a** − **b**) · (**a** + 4**b**)

② (**a** + **b**) · (**a** − **b**)

4. The Component of u along v

The **component** of **u** along **v** (or the **component** of **u** in the direction of **v**) is the length along **v** obtained by dropping down a perpendicular line from **u**.

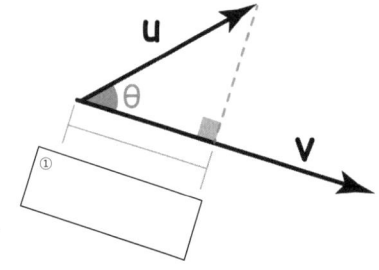

component of **u** along **v**

= ② _____

= $\dfrac{\boxed{③}\,|u|\cos\theta}{\boxed{④}}$

= ⑤ _____

Blank : ① |u| cos θ   ② |u| cos θ   ③ |v| ④ |v| ⑤ $\dfrac{v \cdot u}{|v|}$

※ The **component** of **u** along **v** (the **component** of **u** in the direction of **v**) is

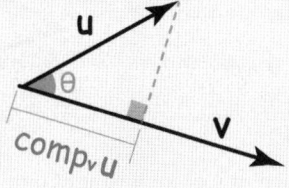

$$\text{comp}_v \mathbf{u} = \frac{\mathbf{u} \cdot \mathbf{v}}{|\mathbf{v}|}$$

EXAMPLE 6. Find the component of **a** along **b**.

① $\mathbf{a} = \langle 2, 4 \rangle$, $\mathbf{b} = \langle 2, 1 \rangle$ ② $\mathbf{a} = \langle 5, -1 \rangle$, $\mathbf{b} = \langle 0, 5 \rangle$

③ $\mathbf{a} = 6i - 2j$, $\mathbf{b} = 2i + 4j$ ④ $\mathbf{a} = 4i + 8j$, $\mathbf{b} = -2i + 2j$

⑤ $\mathbf{a} = i + 4j$, $\mathbf{b} = 6i$ ⑥ $\mathbf{a} = -i + 2j$, $\mathbf{b} = -j$

5. The Projection of u Onto v

The **projection** of **u** along **v** is
vector parallel to **v**
and whose length is the component of **u** along **v**

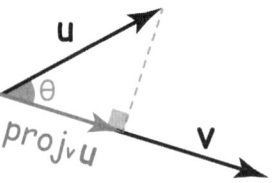

proj$_v$ u = (unit vector in direction of v)(component of u along v)

= ① _____ = ② _____

※ The **projection** of **u** along **v** is

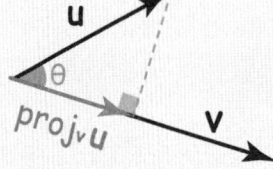

$$\text{proj}_v u = \left(\frac{u \cdot v}{|v|^2}\right) v$$

EXAMPLE 7. Find the projection of **a** onto **b**.

① $a = \langle 2, 4 \rangle$, $b = \langle 2, 1 \rangle$ ② $a = \langle 5, -1 \rangle$, $b = \langle 0, 5 \rangle$

Blank : ① $\dfrac{v}{|v|}\left(\dfrac{v \cdot u}{|v|}\right)$ ② $v\left(\dfrac{v \cdot u}{|v|^2}\right)$

③ **a** = $6i - 2j$, **b** = $2i + 4j$

④ **a** = $4i + 8j$, **b** = $-2i + 2j$

⑤ **a** = $i + 4j$, **b** = $6i$

⑥ **a** = $-i + 2j$, **b** = $-j$

6. Expand Knowledge (Force and Work Problems)

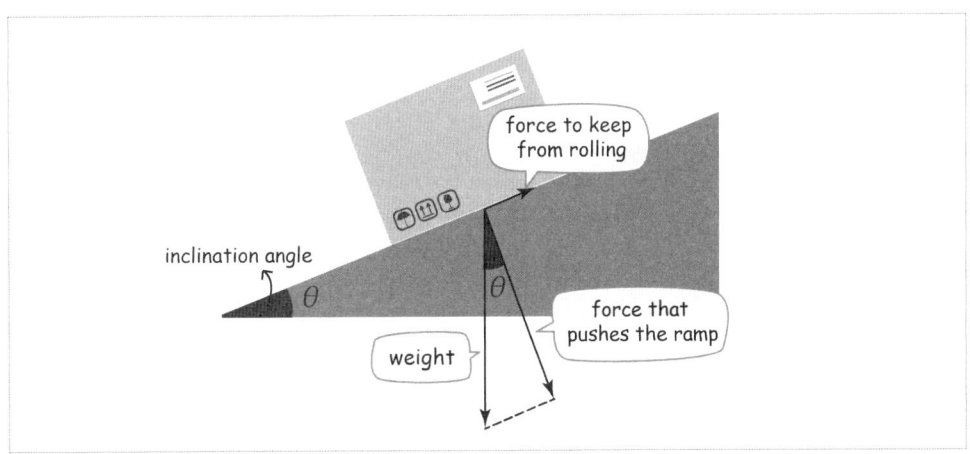

EXAMPLE 8. A 2500 lb car in on a ramp that is inclined 32° to the horizontal. Find the force required to keep it from rolling down the ramp.

EXAMPLE 9. It takes a force of 30 pounds to keep a box from sliding down a ramp that is inclined at 22° from the horizontal.

a) How much does the box weigh?

b) Find the force the box exerts against the ramp.

EXAMPLE 10. A box that weighs 500 lb is placed in an inclined ramp. If a force of 50lb is sufficient to keep the package from sliding, find the angle of inclination of the ramp.

Work = force x distance
Same thing works in vector; Work is dot product of the force vector and the distance vector.

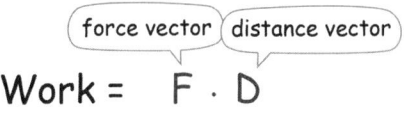

Work = F · D

EXAMPLE 11. The force F = <4, 3> moves the desk 5 ft along the x axis in the positive direction. Find the work done. (Unit of force is in pound)

EXAMPLE 12. The force F = <-1, 3> moves the object from the point (-1, 2) to the point (3, 5). Find the work done. (Unit of force is in pound and unit of distance is in feet)

EXAMPLE 13. A person pushes a car with a force of 100 newtons with the angle 47° as shown. If he moves the car 5m, find the work done.

Mia's Precalculus
8.4 Three-Dimensional Coordinate

1. Three dimensional Coordinate

In 3-dimensional coordinate system,
we use x-, y-, and z-axes.

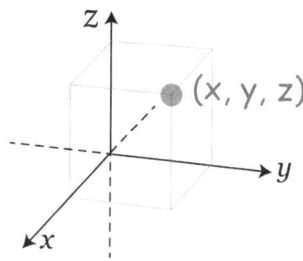

EXAMPLE 1.   Describe or illustrate the following:

① $A(0, 2, 0)$ ② $B(3, 0, 2)$

③ $C(2, 4, 7)$ ④ $D(4, 3, 5)$

⑤ $E(-2, 1, 2)$ ⑥ $F(1, -2, 0)$

⑦ $x = 2$

⑧ $y = 2$

⑨ $z = 1$

⑩ $x + y = 1$

2. Distance and Midpoint

※ Distance Formula in 3-D coordinate

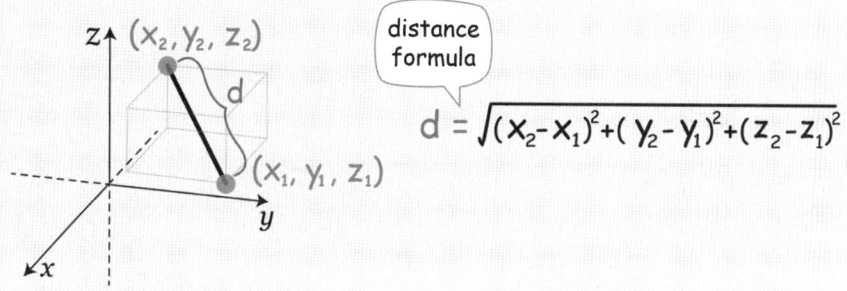

distance formula

$$d = \sqrt{(x_2-x_1)^2+(y_2-y_1)^2+(z_2-z_1)^2}$$

※ Midpoint Formula in 3-D coordinate

Midpoint

$$M = \left(\frac{x_1+x_2}{2}, \frac{y_1+y_2}{2}, \frac{z_1+z_2}{2}\right)$$

EXAMPLE 2. Find the distance and the midpoint of the pair of point, (-1, 3, 5) and (0, -2, 3)

EXAMPLE 3. The distance between two points in space A(2, y, -3) and B(1, -1, 4) is 8. Find the possible values of y.

3. Sphere

The **circle** is all the points (x, y) that are "①_____" away from the center ②_____.

In 3D plane, all the points (x, y, z) that are "r" away from the center (a, b, c) is a ③_____.

※ Equation of Circle and Sphere

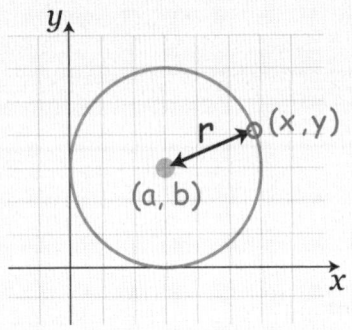

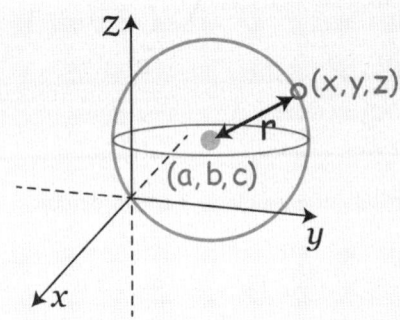

$(x-a)^2 + (y-b)^2 = r^2$
center (a, b)   radius r

: equation of **circle**
with center at (a, b) radius r

$(x-a)^2 + (y-b)^2 + (z-c)^2 = r^2$
center (a, b, c)   radius r

: equation of **sphere**
with center at (a, b, c) radius ④_____

EXAMPLE 4. Describe the graph of the set of points (x, y, z) where

① $x^2 + (y-1)^2 + (z+2)^2 = 36$.   ② $x^2 + (y+2)^2 + z^2 = 8$.

Blank : ① r   ② (a, b)   ③ sphere   ④ r

③ $(x+2)^2 + y^2 + (z+1)^2 = 27$.

EXAMPLE 5. Describe the graph of the set of points (x, y, z) where

① $x^2 + y^2 + z^2 - 10x + 4y + 6z = 11$. ② $x^2 + y^2 + z^2 = 12x - 6z$.

EXAMPLE 6. Describe or illustrate the graph of the set of points (x, y, z) where $x^2 + z^2 = 1$.

Mia's Precalculus

8.5 Vectors in Three Dimensions

1. Vectors in the Plane

1) Position Vector

Vectors also work perfectly well in 3 dimensions.
In 3-dimensional coordinate system, we use x-, y-, and z-axes.

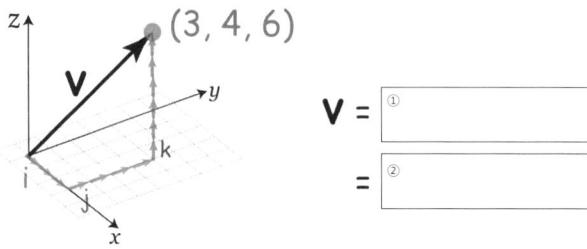

※ Position Vectors

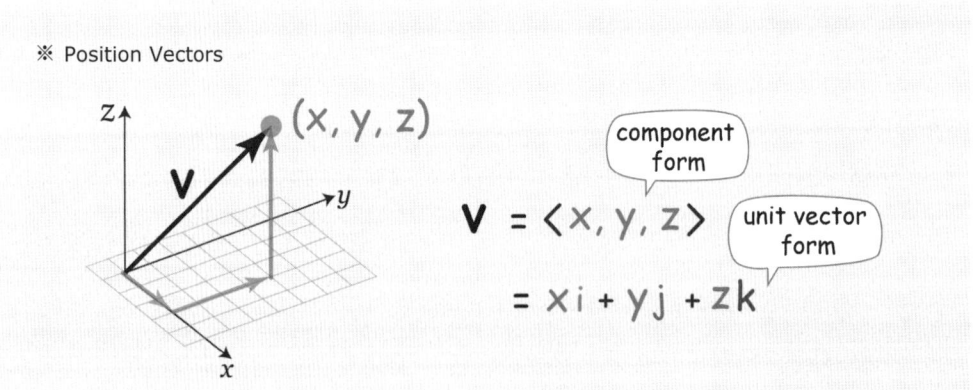

Blank : ① <3, 4, 6>   ② 3i+4j+6k

2) Displacement Vector

A displacement vector is a vector between two points.

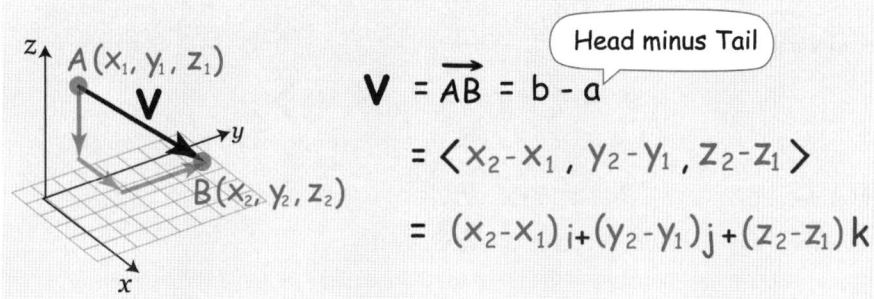

※ Displacement Vector (Head minus Tail)

$$\vec{V} = \vec{AB} = b - a$$
$$= \langle x_2-x_1, y_2-y_1, z_2-z_1 \rangle$$
$$= (x_2-x_1)i + (y_2-y_1)j + (z_2-z_1)k$$

EXAMPLE 1. Given points $A(-1, 2, 0)$, $B(3, 4, 2)$, and $C(4, -5, -2)$, find the vector of:

① B from O ② B from A

③ $\vec{BA}$ ④ $\vec{OC}$

⑤ $\vec{BC}$ ⑥ $\vec{CA}$

EXAMPLE 2. Find the terminal points for vector $w = 4i + 2j - 2k$ given the initial point $(-1, 2, -3)$.

2. Vector Algebra

※ Sum Vector of V and U

$$v \pm u = \langle v_1 \pm u_1, v_2 \pm u_2, v_3 \pm u_3 \rangle$$

※ Scaling Vector

$$kv = \langle kv_1, kv_2, kv_3 \rangle$$

※ Parallel Vectors

Parallel vectors have same direction but different lengths.
Numerically, vectors are parallel if and only if they are *scalar multiples* of each other

If **a** is parallel to **b**, then **a** = k**b**.

※ Magnitude

Magnitude is the length of the vector (= distance from head to tail)
Magnitude of v = <x,y,z> is

Magnitude of **v**

$$|v| = \sqrt{x^2 + y^2 + z^2}$$

※ Unit Vector in the same direction

You can find a unit vector **in the same direction** by dividing out the ①_____ of the vector.

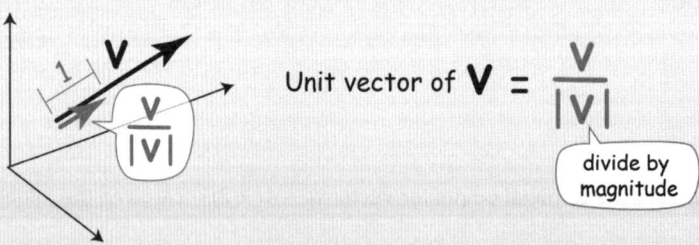

Unit vector of **v** = $\dfrac{v}{|v|}$

divide by magnitude

Blank : ① magnitude

EXAMPLE 3. Consider the vector $u = 3i - j + k, \quad v = -i + 3k$. Find;

① **u + v** ② **u - v**

③ **2u + 3v** ④ **-u + 4v**

EXAMPLE 4. Find r and s given that
$$\mathbf{a} = <2,-1,r> \text{ is parallel to } \mathbf{b} = <s,2,-3>.$$

EXAMPLE 5. Find the magnitude of the given vector and a unit vector **u** in the direction of the given vector.

① **u** = <2, 1, 3> ② $u = -3i + k$

③ $u = 3i - 4k$ ④ $u = 2i + 2j - k$

3. Dot Products and Angles

You can calculate the Scalar Product of two vectors in two ways:

※ Dot (Scalar) Product of Vectors

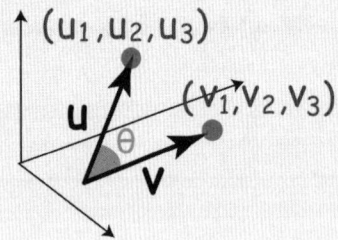

dot product
$$\mathbf{v} \cdot \mathbf{u} = v_1 u_1 + v_2 u_2 + v_3 u_3$$
$$= |\mathbf{v}||\mathbf{u}|\cos\theta$$

Notice that the scalar product of two vectors is a ①_____ number NOT a vector.

※ Angle between two vectors

The angle between two Vector $v = \langle v_1, v_2, v_3 \rangle$ and $u = \langle u_1, u_2, u_3 \rangle$ is

$$\cos\theta = \frac{\mathbf{v} \cdot \mathbf{u}}{|\mathbf{v}||\mathbf{u}|}$$

EXAMPLE 6. For given vector, find
a) $\mathbf{p} \cdot \mathbf{q}$
b) the angle between **p** and **q** in degrees

① $\mathbf{p} = <2, 1, 0>$, $\mathbf{q} = <-1, -3, 1>$ ② $\mathbf{p} = <1, -2, 3>$, $\mathbf{q} = <1, 5, 7>$

Blank : ① scalar

③ **p** = 2*i* + 3*j* − *k*, **q** = −*i* + 2*k*   ④ **p** = <−1, −2, 0>, **q** = <4, 0, −2>

4. Properties of Dot Product

※ Facts about Dot product

① If vectors **V** and **U** are perpendicular, ①_____

② If vectors **V** and **U** are parallel, ②_____

③ **v** · **v** = ③_____
④ (*k***v**) · **u** = ④_____ (*k* is scalar)
⑤ **v** · (**a** + **b**) = ⑤_____ (distributive)
⑥ **v** · **u** = ⑥_____ (commutative)
⑦ **v** · **u** · **w**   ⑦(possible/impossible)

Blank : ① v · u = 0   ② v · u = |v||u| ③ |v|² ④ k(v · u)   ⑤ v · a + v · b   ⑥ u · v   ⑦ impossible

EXAMPLE 7. Determine whether the vectors **u** and **v** are parallel or perpendicular.

① **u** = $2i + 2j - 6k$, **v** = $3i + 3j + 2k$

② **u** = $i + j + k$, **v** = $2i - j - k$

③ **u** = $3i - 2j + 7k$, **v** = $-6i + 4j - 14k$

④ **u** = $2i - 5k$, **v** = $4i - 10k$

EXAMPLE 8. Find the value k for which **a** = $\langle k, 1, 3 \rangle$ and **b** = $\langle 4, k, 3k \rangle$ are;

① parallel each other

② perpendicular each other

5. Expand Knowledge

EXAMPLE 9. *Given points $A = (2, -3, 1)$, $B = (1, -5, -3)$ and $C = (1, -1, -2)$, find the size of $\angle BAC$ in degrees.

EXAMPLE 10. *Use vector methods to determine the measure of $\angle ABC$ in degrees.

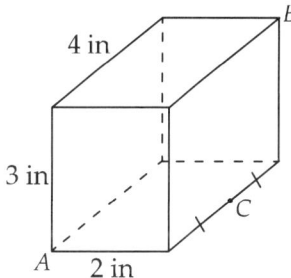

Mia's Precalculus

8.6 The Cross Product

1. Cross Product

☺ Reminder : The determinant of matrix

$\begin{vmatrix} a & b \\ c & d \end{vmatrix} = $ ① _____ $\begin{vmatrix} 2 & 1 \\ 3 & -1 \end{vmatrix} = $ ② _____

(We are going to learn this more in Matrix section!)

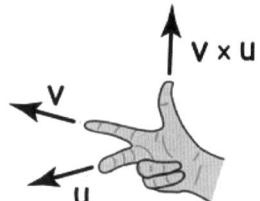

The cross product ③ _____ is a ④ _____ which is perpendicular to both **u** and **v**.

1) Cross Product I

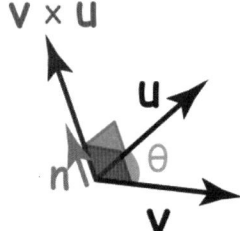

v × u

|**u**| is the magnitude (length) of vector **u**
|**v**| is the magnitude (length) of vector **v**
θ is the angle between **u** and **v**
n is the normal unit vector which is perpendicular to both **u** and **v**

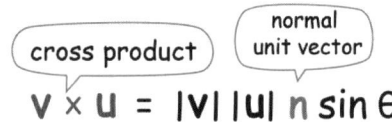

$$v \times u = |v| |u| \, n \sin \theta$$

(cross product) (normal unit vector)

2) Cross Product II

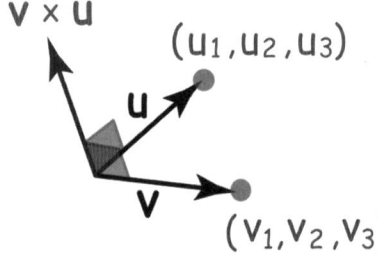

v × u
(u_1, u_2, u_3)
(v_1, v_2, v_3)

cross product

$$v \times u = \langle v_2 u_3 - v_3 u_2,\ v_3 u_1 - v_1 u_3,\ v_1 u_2 - v_2 u_1 \rangle$$

Blank : ① ad − bc   ② 2(-1) − 1(3) = -5   ③ v × u   ④ vector

☺ Easy way to do;

$$\mathbf{v} \times \mathbf{u} = \begin{vmatrix} \oplus & \ominus & \oplus \\ i & j & k \\ v_1 & v_2 & v_3 \\ u_1 & u_2 & u_3 \end{vmatrix}$$

$$= \oplus i \begin{vmatrix} v_2 & v_3 \\ u_2 & u_3 \end{vmatrix} \ominus j \begin{vmatrix} v_1 & v_3 \\ u_1 & u_3 \end{vmatrix} \oplus k \begin{vmatrix} v_1 & v_2 \\ u_1 & u_2 \end{vmatrix}$$

※ Vector (Cross) Product of Vectors

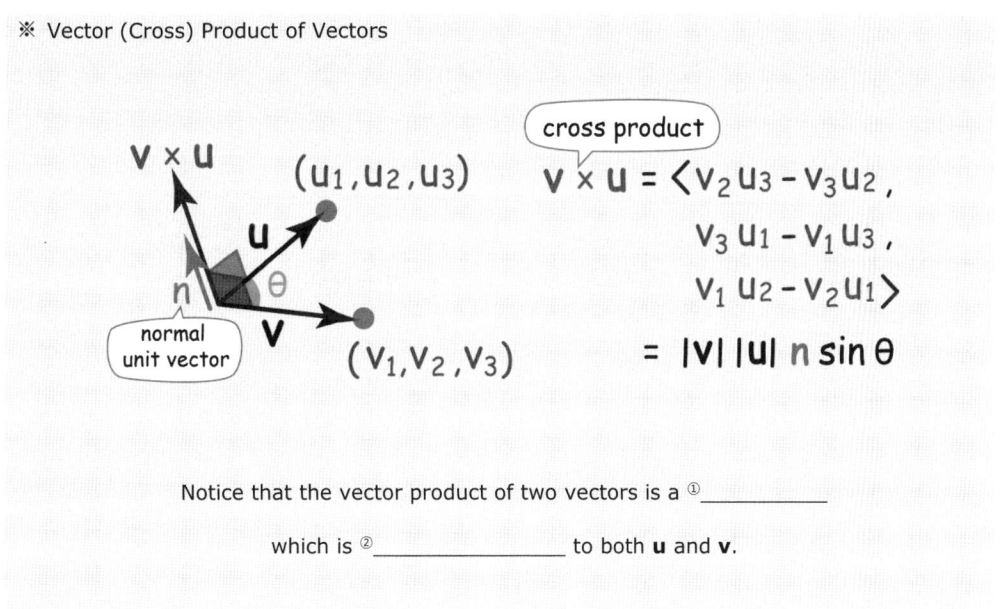

$$\mathbf{v} \times \mathbf{u} = \langle v_2 u_3 - v_3 u_2,\ v_3 u_1 - v_1 u_3,\ v_1 u_2 - v_2 u_1 \rangle$$

$$= |\mathbf{v}||\mathbf{u}|\, \mathbf{n} \sin \theta$$

Notice that the vector product of two vectors is a ①_____ which is ②_____ to both **u** and **v**.

Blank : ① vector   ② perpendicular

EXAMPLE 1. For the given vectors, find;
$$\mathbf{a} = <2,1,-1>, \mathbf{b} = <1,2,0>, \mathbf{c} = <2,0,4>$$

① **a** x **b**   ② **b** x **c**

③ **c** x **a**   ④ **b** x **a**

⑤ **a** · (**b** x **c**)   ⑥ **b** · (**a** x **c**)

EXAMPLE 2. Find a vector perpendicular to both

① **a** = $<1,1,-2>$, **b**= $<-5,1,3>$　　　② **a** = $<1,2,-1>$, **b**= $<1,0,-3>$

EXAMPLE 3. Find a vector that is perpendicular to the plane passing through the three given points.

① A(0, 1, 2), B(-2, 1, -3) C(1, 1, 0)　　　② A(2, 3, -1), B(0, 1, -2) C(1, 2, -2)

EXAMPLE 4. Let $\mathbf{p} = i + j + 3k$ and $\mathbf{q} = i - 3k$.

(a) Calculate $\mathbf{p} \times \mathbf{q}$.

(b) Find a unit vector perpendicular to both $\mathbf{p}$ and $\mathbf{q}$.

2. Properties of the Vector product

※ Facts about vector (cross) product

① $|\mathbf{v} \times \mathbf{u}|$ = ① _____

② If vectors **V** and **U** are parallel, ② _____

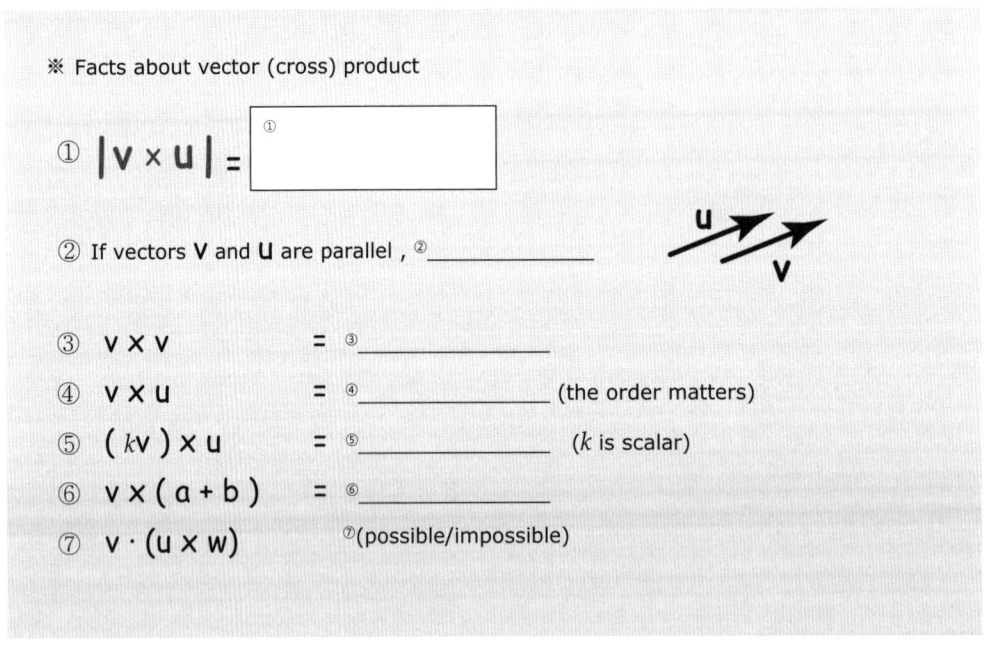

③ $\mathbf{v} \times \mathbf{v}$ = ③ _____

④ $\mathbf{v} \times \mathbf{u}$ = ④ _____ (the order matters)

⑤ $(k\mathbf{v}) \times \mathbf{u}$ = ⑤ _____ (k is scalar)

⑥ $\mathbf{v} \times (\mathbf{a} + \mathbf{b})$ = ⑥ _____

⑦ $\mathbf{v} \cdot (\mathbf{u} \times \mathbf{w})$ ⑦(possible/impossible)

Blank : ① $|\mathbf{v}| |\mathbf{u}| \sin \theta$ ② $\mathbf{v} \times \mathbf{u} = 0$ ③ 0 ④ $-(\mathbf{u} \times \mathbf{v})$ ⑤ $k(\mathbf{v} \times \mathbf{u})$ ⑥ $\mathbf{v} \times \mathbf{a} + \mathbf{v} \times \mathbf{b}$ ⑦ possible

☺ v x u and u x v has opposite direction.

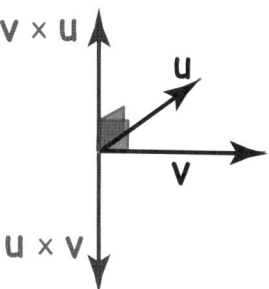

EXAMPLE 5. If $\mathbf{a} = i + 3j + 2k$ and $\mathbf{b} = 2i - 2j$

(a) Find $\mathbf{a} \times \mathbf{b}$ and $\mathbf{b} \times \mathbf{a}$.

(b) find the sine of the angle between $\mathbf{a}$ and $\mathbf{b}$.

EXAMPLE 6.   * Given that $|\mathbf{a}| = 4$, $|\mathbf{b}| = 5$ and that a and b are perpendicular, evaluate $|(2\mathbf{a} - \mathbf{b}) \times (\mathbf{a} + 2\mathbf{b})|$.

3. Area of Parallelogram

To find the area of parallelogram;

2 × area of △ADC

$= 2 \times \frac{1}{2}|v||u|$ ①

$= |v||u|$ ②

$=$ ③

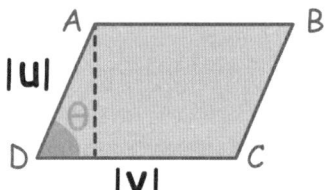

※ The vector product can be used to find the area of some geometrical figures:

$$\text{Area of } \parallelogram = |v \times u|$$

$$\text{Area of } \triangle = \frac{1}{2}|v \times u|$$

where **u** and **v** form two adjacent sides of the shape.

EXAMPLE 7. Find the area of the parallelogram determined by the given vectors.

① **a** = <1,2,−3>, **b** = <1,4,−2>   ② **a** = <0,1,3>, **b** = <2,−4,−2>

Blank: ① $\sin\theta$ ② $\sin\theta$ ③ $|v \times u|$

EXAMPLE 8. Points $A\,(-3, 1, 5)$, $B\,(1, 1, 2)$ and $C\,(1, -2, 7)$ are vertices of a parallelogram ABCD.

(a) Find the coordinates of D.

(b) Find the area of the parallelogram.

4. Volume of a Parallelepiped

Volume of a Parallelepiped
= (Base area) (Height)

= ① _____

= ② _____

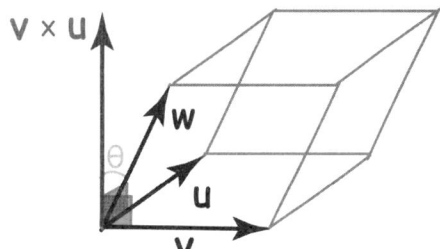

Volume is always positive so we need | |.

※ Volume of a Parallelepiped

The volume of the parallelepiped determined by the vectors **a**, **b**, and **c** is

$$|\,a \cdot (b \times c)\,|$$

Blank : ① $|v \times u|\,|w|\cos\theta$ ② $w \cdot (v \times u)$

EXAMPLE 9. Find the volume of the parallelepiped determined by the vectors

① **a** = <1, 2, 3>, **b** = <3, 2, 1>, **c** = <0, 8, 10>.

② **a** = <0, 2, 3>, **b** = <-1, 2, 4>, **c** = <1, 0, 3>.

☺ ALL in ONE

dot product	cross product
a · b	a x b
The result is a scalar.	The result is a vector.
$|a||b|\cos\theta$	$n|a||b|\sin\theta$
a · b = b · a	a x b = -(b x a)
a · b = 0 when a, b are perpendicular	a x b = 0 when a, b are parallel
a · a = $|a|^2$	a x a = 0

Part 9
Conic Section

9.1 Conic Sections and Parabolas
9.2 Ellipses
9.3 Hyperbolas
9.4 Transformation of Conics
9.5 Rotation of Conics

Mia's Precalculus
9.1 Conic Sections and Parabolas

1. Conic Section

What shape do we have if we cut a cone ..

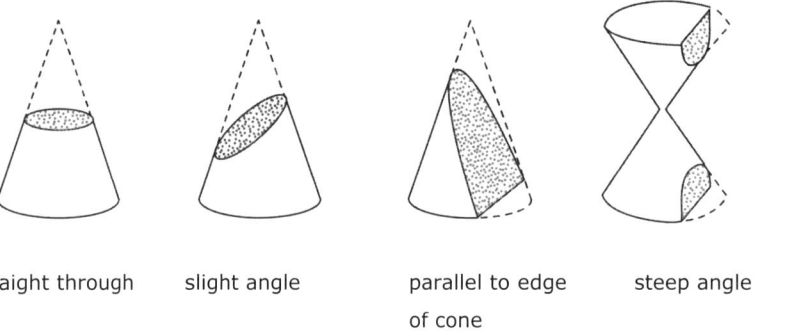

straight through   slight angle   parallel to edge of cone   steep angle

: ① _____   : ② _____   : ③ _____   : ④ _____

These curves are related!

2. Parabola

A ⑤_____ is a curve where any point is at an **equal distance** from a straight line(⑥_____) and a fixed point(⑦_____).

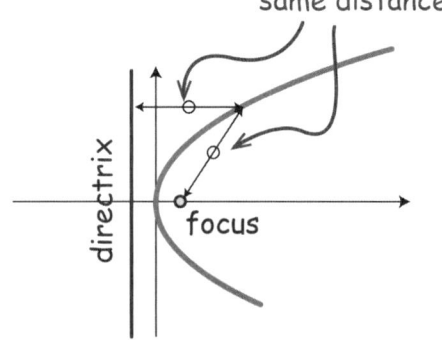

Blank : ① circle   ② ellipse   ③ parabola   ④ hyperbola   ⑤ parabola   ⑥ directrix   ⑦ focus

☺Vocabulary

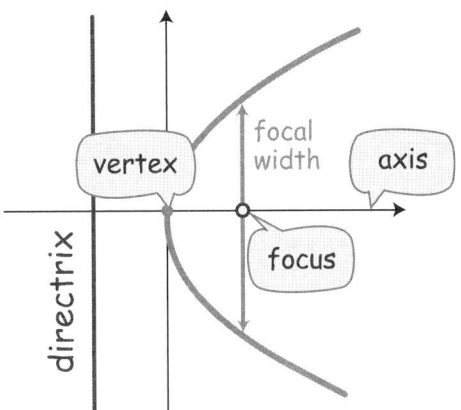

• ① _____ :a fixed point

• ② _____ :a fixed straight line

• ③ _____ : turning point

• ④ _____ of Symmetry

• ⑤ _____ :the distance from the vertex to the focus of the parabola.

• ⑥ _____ (= focal diameter)

:a line that passes through the focus and has endpoints on the parabola.

Blank : ① focus ② directrix ③ vertex ④ axis ⑤ focal length ⑥ focal width

3. Equation of Parabola

A **parabola** is the set of all points in a plane that are equidistant from a fixed line, the directrix, and a fixed point, the focus.

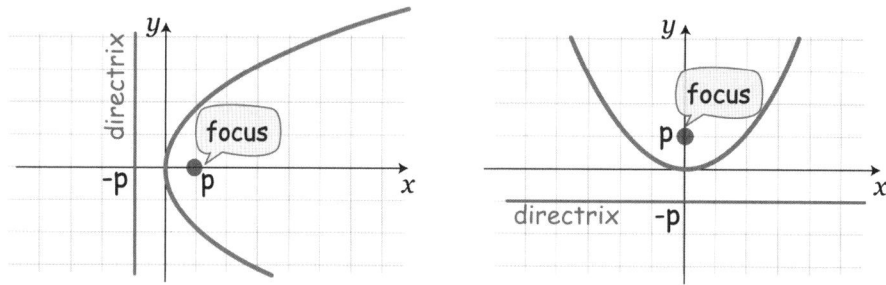

$4px = y^2$ focus x	Formula	$4py = x^2$ focus y
①	..it opens..	up
②	Focus	(0, p)
③	Directrix	y = -p
④	Vertex	(0, 0)
⑤	Axis of Symmetry	y-axis
⑥	Focal length	$|p|$
⑦	Focal width	$|4p|$

Blank : ① to the right ② (p, 0) ③ x = -p ④ (0, 0) ⑤ x axis ⑥ |p| ⑦ |4p|

EXAMPLE 1. Graph the parabola. Label the focus, directrix and focal width.

① $y = \dfrac{1}{4}x^2$

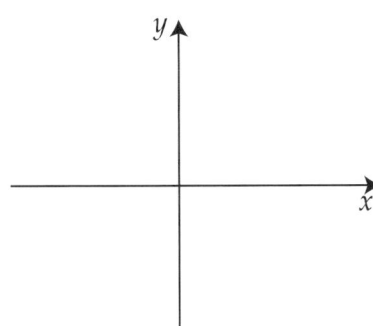

Focus:
directrix:
focal width:

② $16y = x^2$

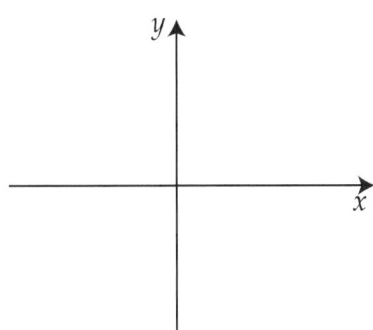

Focus:
directrix:
focal width:

③ $x = 8y^2$

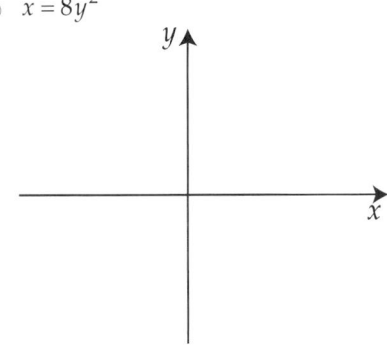

Focus:
directrix:
focal width:

④ $8x = y^2$

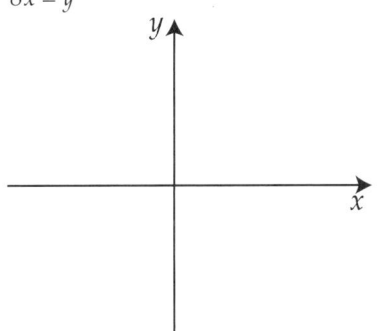

Focus:
directrix:
focal width:

⑤ $y^2 + 6x = 0$

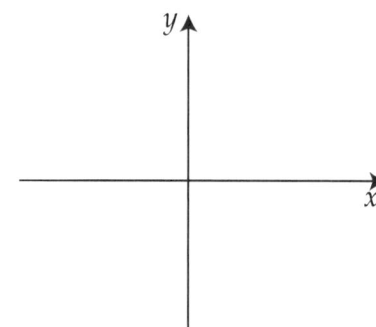

Focus:
directrix:
focal width:

⑥ $0 = x^2 + 16y$

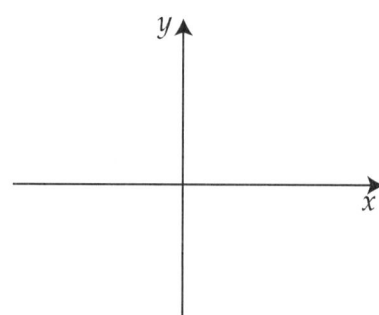

Focus:
directrix:
focal width :

EXAMPLE 2. Find the standard form of the equation for the parabola.

① Vertex at the origin, focus at (0, -2)

② Focus at (0, 3), directrix y = -3

③ Focus at (7, 0), directrix x = -7

④ Vertex at the origin, focus at (-8, 0)

⑤ Vertex at the origin, opens to the right, focal width = 12

⑥ Vertex at the origin, opens downward, focal width = 16

⑦
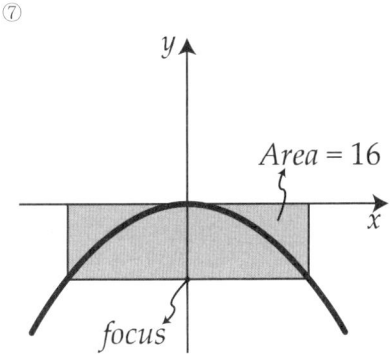

Mia's Precalculus
9.2 Ellipses

1. Ellipses

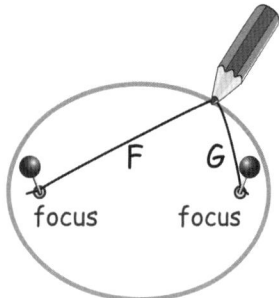

An ①_____ usually looks like a squashed circle.

We can draw an ellipse using a string whose ends are attached to two nails. The pencil is moved all the way around while always keeping the string tight.

(The length of the sting F + G always be the ②_____)

※ Geometric Definition of Ellipse

An **ellipse** is the set of all points (x, y) in a plane, the sum of whose distances from two distinct fixed point (foci) is constant.

☺Vocabulary

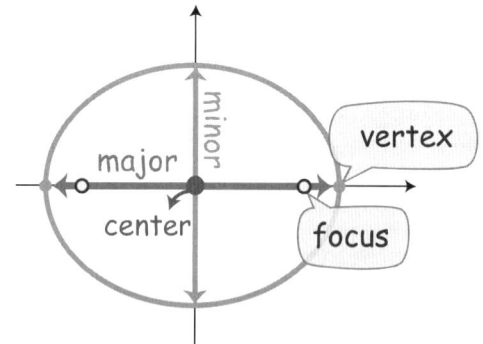

- ③_____ :The points at which an ellipse makes its sharpest turns.

- ④_____ :two fixed points, together they are called ⑤_____.(pronounced "fo-sigh")

- ⑥_____ :the longest diameter (at the widest part of the ellipse).

- ⑦_____ _____ :the shortest diameter(at the narrowest part of the ellipse).

Blank : ① ellipse ② same ③ vertex ④ focus ⑤ foci ⑥ major axis ⑦ minor axis

2. Equation of Ellipses

By placing an ellipse on an x-y plane, the equation of the curve is:

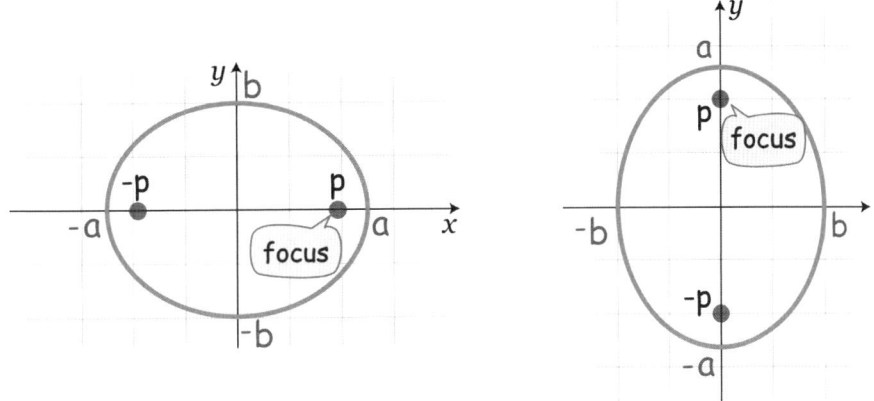

	Standard Equation	
	$\dfrac{x^2}{a^2} + \dfrac{y^2}{b^2} = 1$ (vertex)	$\dfrac{y^2}{a^2} + \dfrac{x^2}{b^2} = 1$ (vertex)
①	center	(0, 0)
②	Foci	(0, ±p)
③	Vertices	(0, ±a)
④	major Axis	|2a|
⑤	minor Axis	|2b|
⑥	Pythagorean Relation	$p = \sqrt{a^2 - b^2}$

Blank : ① (0, 0)　② (±p, 0)　③ (±a, 0)　④ \|2a\|　⑤ \|2b\|　⑥ $p = \sqrt{a^2 - b^2}$

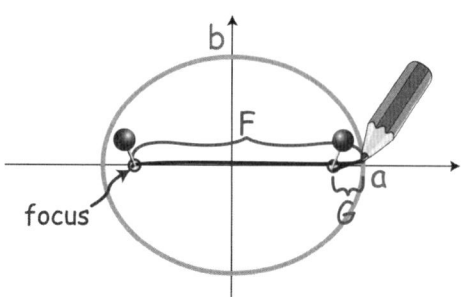

While we are drawing an ellipse if you fixed a pencil on a (=the vertex) *then we can say*

F + G = ①_____

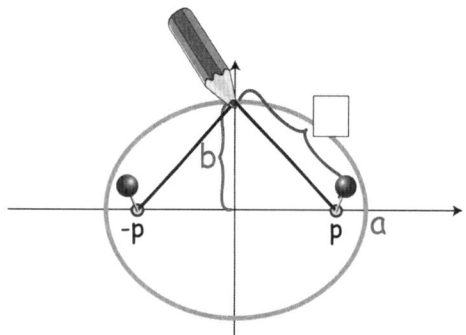

If you fix a pencil on b then we can say

$$p^2 = \boxed{②} - \boxed{③}$$
$$p = \boxed{④}$$

※ Pythagorean Relation in Ellipse (helps to find foci of ellipse)

$$\text{focus } p = \sqrt{a^2 - b^2}$$

3. How to graph Ellipses

EXAMPLE 1. Graph the ellipse. Label the Foci, vertices.

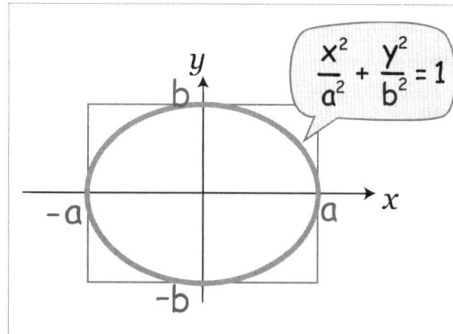

$$\frac{x^2}{a^2} + \frac{y^2}{b^2} = 1$$

i) Mark points a units along x directions from the center and points b units along y directions from the center.

ii) Draw an ellipse through these points

Blank : ① 2a ② a^2 ③ b^2 ④ $\sqrt{a^2 - b^2}$

① $\dfrac{x^2}{16}+\dfrac{y^2}{25}=1$

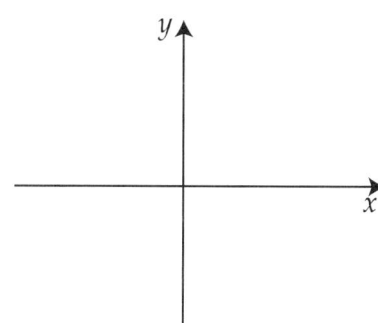

Foci:

Vertices:

② $\dfrac{x^2}{49}+\dfrac{y^2}{3}=1$

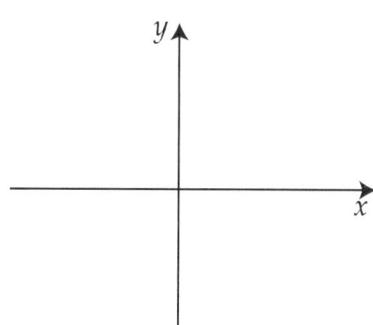

Foci:

Vertices:

③ $4x^2+16y^2=64$

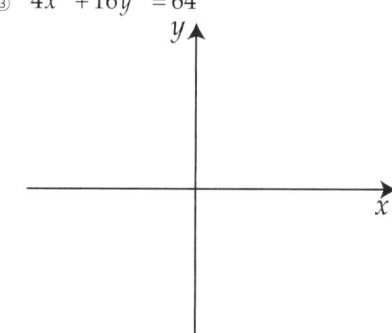

Foci:

Vertices:

④ $16x^2+9y^2=144$

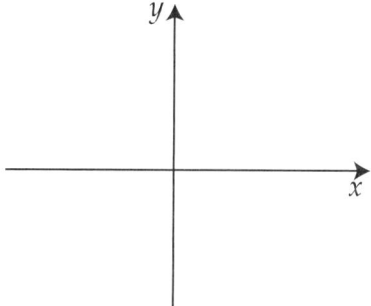

Foci:

Vertices:

⑤ $16x^2 + 4y^2 = 1$

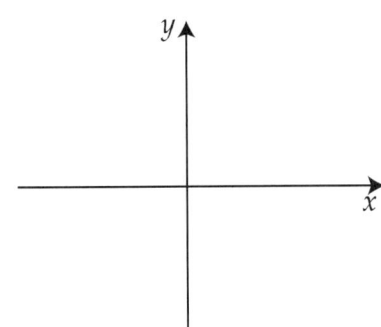

Foci:
Vertices:

⑥ $x^2 + 9y^2 = 1$

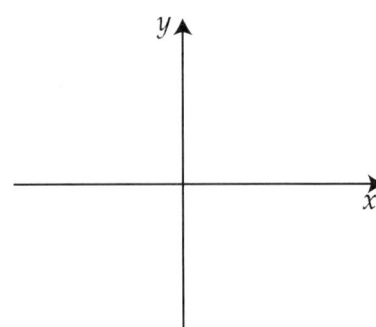

Foci:
Vertices:

⑦ $20y^2 = 5 - 4x^2$

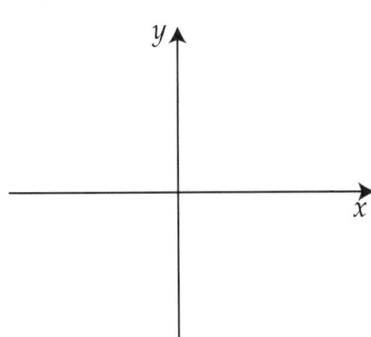

Foci:
Vertices:

EXAMPLE 2. Find the standard form of the equation for the ellipse.

① Vertices at (±10, 0) and foci at (±5 , 0)   ② Vertices at (±4, 0) and foci at (±3 , 0)

③ Major axis is of length 16 and foci at (0, ±2)   ④ Major axis is of length 6 and foci at (0, ±2)

⑤ Minor axis is of length 8 and foci at (±3, 0)   ⑥ Minor axis is of length 10 and foci at (0, ±7)

⑦ Minor axis endpoints (±2, 0), major axis length 22

⑧ An ellipse with intercepts (±3, 0) and (0, ±8), center at origin

Mia's Precalculus

9.3 Hyperbolas

1. Hyperbolas

※ Geometric Definition of Hyperbola

An **Hyperbola** is the set of all points (x, y) in a plane, the difference of whose distances from two distinct fixed point (foci) is constant.

☺Vocabulary

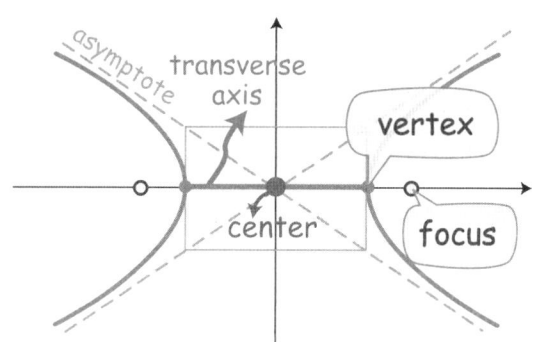

- ①_____ : The points at which an hyperbola makes a turns.

- ②_____ : two fixed points, together they are called ③_____.

- ④_____ axis : line goes through vertex to another vertex

Blank : ① vertex ② focus ③ foci ④ transverse axis

2. Equation of Hyperbolas

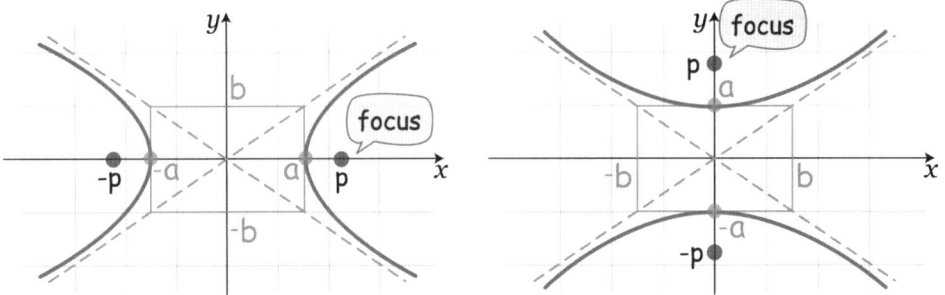

	Standard Equation	
$\dfrac{x^2}{a^2} - \dfrac{y^2}{b^2} = 1$ (vertex)		$\dfrac{y^2}{a^2} - \dfrac{x^2}{b^2} = 1$ (vertex)
①	center	(0, 0)
②	Foci	(0, ±p)
③	Vertices	(0, ±a)
④	Transverse axis	|2a|
⑤	Pythagorean Relation	$p = \sqrt{a^2 + b^2}$
⑥	Asymptotes	$y = \pm \dfrac{a}{b} x$

Blank : ① (0, 0)   ② (±p, 0)   ③ (±a, 0)   ④ |2a| ⑤ $p = \sqrt{a^2 + b^2}$ ⑥ $y = \pm \dfrac{b}{a} x$

☺ Other way of finding Asymptotes

Asymptotes can be found by replacing the 1 by ①_____ :

$$\frac{x^2}{a^2} - \frac{y^2}{b^2} = 1 \rightarrow \frac{x^2}{a^2} - \frac{y^2}{b^2} = 0 \rightarrow y = \boxed{}$$

$$\frac{y^2}{a^2} - \frac{x^2}{b^2} = 1 \rightarrow \frac{y^2}{a^2} - \frac{x^2}{b^2} = 0 \rightarrow y = \boxed{}$$

$\frac{x^2}{a^2} - \frac{y^2}{b^2} = 0$ (switch to 0)

3. How to graph Hyperbolas

EXAMPLE 1. Graph the hyperbola. Label the Foci, vertices, and asymptotes.

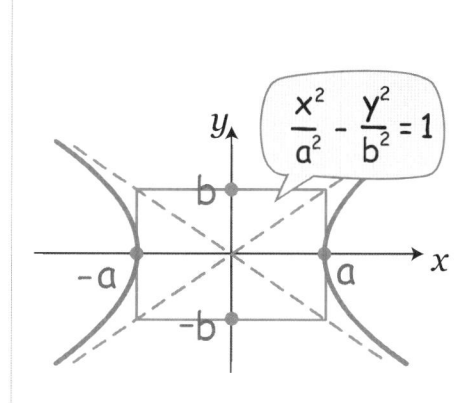

i) Mark points a units along x directions from the center and points b units along y directions from the center.

ii) draw a rectangle and asymptotes as shown

ii) Draw a hyperbola. (shape depends on the first term)

Blank : ① 0   ② $y = \pm \frac{b}{a} x$ ③ $y = \pm \frac{a}{b} x$

① $\dfrac{x^2}{25} - \dfrac{y^2}{36} = 1$

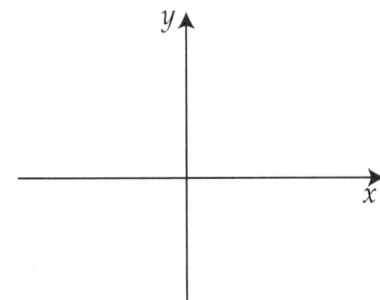

Foci:
Vertices:
Asymptotes:

② $\dfrac{x^2}{16} - \dfrac{y^2}{4} = 1$

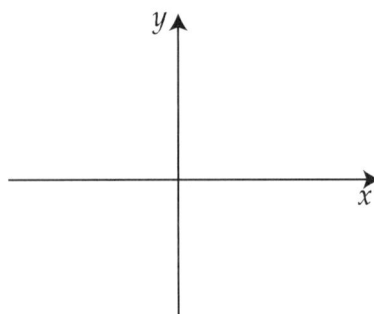

Foci:
Vertices:
Asymptotes:

③ $16y^2 - x^2 = 1$

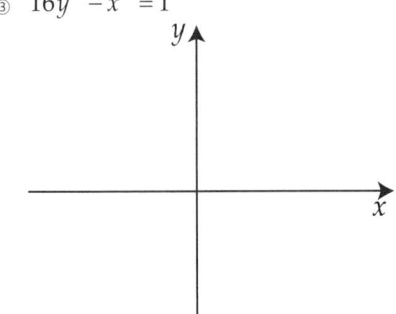

Foci:
Vertices:
Asymptotes:

④ $y^2 - 9x^2 = 1$

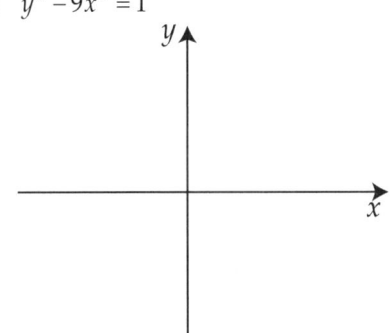

Foci:
Vertices:
Asymptotes:

⑤ $x^2 - 4y^2 = 5$

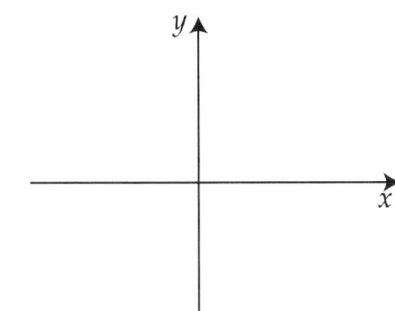

Foci:
Vertices:
Asymptotes:

⑥ $y^2 = 4 + 25x^2$

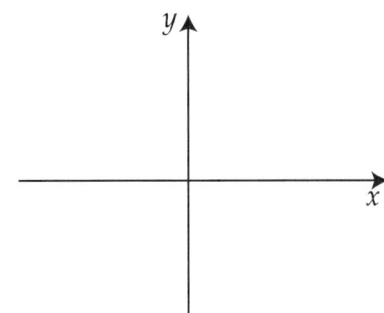

Foci:
Vertices:
Asymptotes:

EXAMPLE 2. Find the standard form of the equation for the hyperbola.

① Vertices at (±2, 0), foci at (±4, 0) ② Vertices at (0, ±4), foci at (0, ±10)

③ Foci at (0, ±9), transverse axis with length 10

④ Foci at (±6, 0), transverse axis with length 4

⑤ Vertices at (0, ±4), asymptotes at $y = \pm\dfrac{2}{5}x$

⑥ Vertices at (±6, 0), asymptotes at $y = \pm\dfrac{2}{3}x$

Mia's Precalculus
9.4 Transformation of Conics

1. Transformation of Conic Sections

☺ Reminder

Find the center of $x^2 + y^2 - 10x + 8y + 16 = 0$.   ① _____

※ Transformation of Conic Sections

$$x \text{ replaced by } x - h$$

$$y \text{ replaced by } y - k$$

then the center $(0, 0)$ is shifted to (h, k)

2. Transformation of Parabola

※ Transformation of Parabola

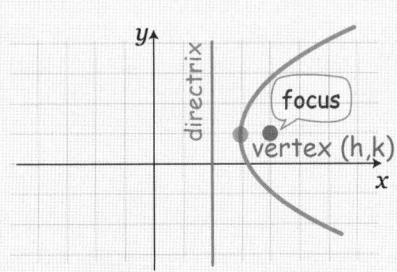
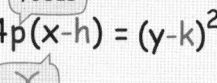
$4p(x-h) = (y-k)^2$

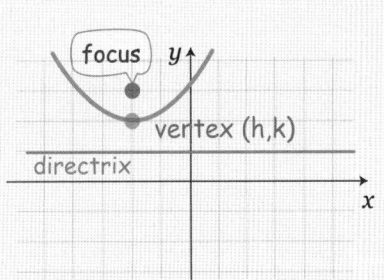
$4p(y-k) = (x-h)^2$

Blank : ① $(x - 5)^2 + (x + 4)^2 = 5^2$, center : (5, -4)

EXAMPLE 1. Find the vertex, foci and directrix of the parabola.

① $(x-2)^2 = 8(y-3)$

② $(y-5)^2 = 16(x+2)$

Vertex:
Focus:
directrix:

Vertex:
Focus:
directrix:

③ $x = -\dfrac{1}{2}(y+7)^2 - 2$

④ $y = -(x-3)^2 - 1$

Vertex:
Focus:
directrix:

Vertex:
Focus:
directrix:

EXAMPLE 2. Find the standard form of the equation for the parabola.

① Focus at (3, -9), directrix x = -1

② Focus at (4, -9), directrix y = -15

③ Vertex at (8, 3), opens upward, focal width = 10

④ Vertex at (1, -4), opens to the left, focal width = 16

3. Transformation of Ellipses

※ Transformation of Ellipse

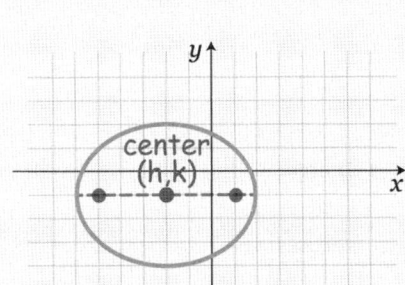

$$\frac{(x-h)^2}{a^2} + \frac{(y-k)^2}{b^2} = 1$$

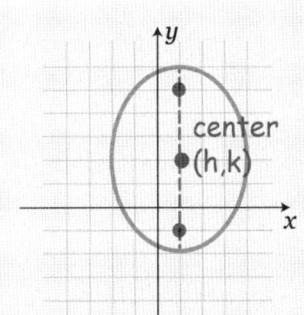

$$\frac{(y-k)^2}{a^2} + \frac{(x-h)^2}{b^2} = 1$$

EXAMPLE 3. Find the center, foci, and vertices of the ellipse.

① $\dfrac{(x+4)^2}{16} + \dfrac{(y-2)^2}{25} = 1$

② $\dfrac{(x-2)^2}{36} + \dfrac{(y+1)^2}{9} = 1$

Center:

Foci:

Vertices:

Center:

Foci:

Vertices:

③ $4(x-2)^2 + 8(y+1)^2 = 2$

④ $4(x+3)^2 + 9(y-2)^2 = 1$

Center:

Foci:

Vertices:

Center:

Foci:

Vertices:

EXAMPLE 4. Find the standard form of the equation for the ellipse.

① An ellipse with foci at (2, 5) and (2, -1); major axis length of 10

② An ellipse with foci at (-1, 1) and (5, 1); major axis length of 10

③ An ellipse with major axis from (-1, -4) to (7, -4); minor axis from (3, -7) to (3, -1).

4. Transformation of Hyperbolas

※ Transformation of Hyperbolas

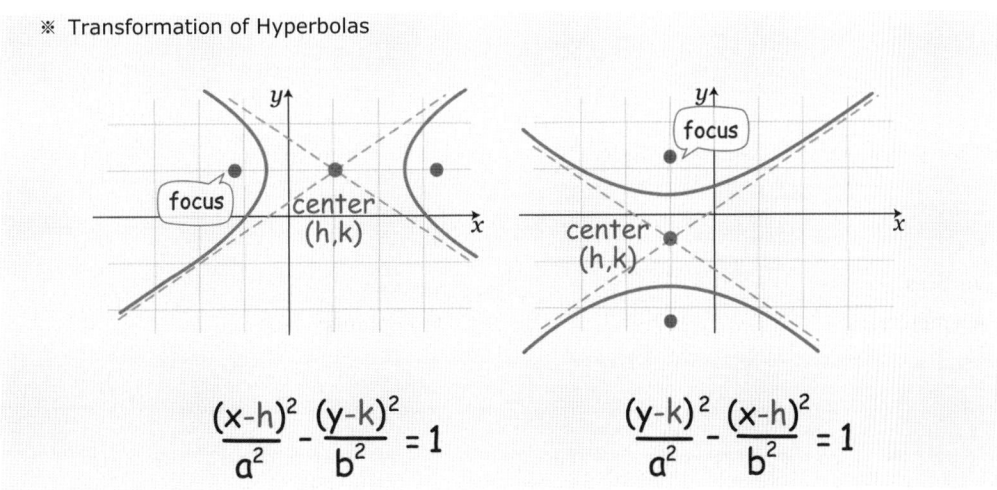

EXAMPLE 5. Find the center, foci, vertices, and asymptotes of the hyperbola.

① $\dfrac{(x+5)^2}{16} - \dfrac{(y-1)^2}{9} = 1$

② $\dfrac{(x+4)^2}{4} - \dfrac{(y+4)^2}{25} = 1$

Center:
Foci:
Vertices:
Asymptotes:

Center:
Foci:
Vertices:
Asymptotes:

③ $4(y-5)^2 - (x-1)^2 = 16$

④ $4(y-3)^2 - (x-4)^2 = 1$

Center:
Foci:
Vertices:
Asymptotes:

Center:
Foci:
Vertices:
Asymptotes:

EXAMPLE 6. Find the standard form of the equation for the hyperbola.

① Center (4, -3), focus (11, -3), vertex (6, -3)

② Center (-2, 5), focus (-2, 12), vertex (-2, 8)

③ Vertices at (7, -2), (5, -2), asymptotes at $y = 4x - 26, y = -4x + 22$

④ Vertices at (-1, 9),(-1, 3), asymptotes at $y - 6 = \pm\dfrac{3}{2}(x+1)$

5. Identifying Conics

$$Ax^2 + Cy^2 + Dx + Ey + F = 0$$

If $AC = 0$, then it is parabola.   (If A or C is 0)

If $AC > 0$, then it is Ellipse.   (If A,C have same sign.)

If $AC < 0$, then it is hyperbola.   (If A,C have different sign.)

EXAMPLE 7. Determine whether the equation represents an ellipse, a parabola, a hyperbola. Then find the vertex (or vertices) and focus(or foci).

① $x^2 + 6x - 4y + 1 = 0$

② $y^2 + 2y - x = 0$

③ $2x^2 + 3y^2 - 8x + 6y + 5 = 0$ ④ $4x^2 + 3y^2 + 8x - 6y = 5$

⑤ $x^2 - y^2 - 2x - 2y - 1 = 0$ ⑥ $y^2 - 4x^2 - 4y - 8x - 4 = 0$

6. Eccentricity of Conic Sections

※ Formula for Eccentricity

Formula for Eccentricity = $\dfrac{p}{a}$

where $p = \sqrt{a^2 - b^2}$ for ellipse, $p = \sqrt{a^2 + b^2}$ for hyperbola, and a is the semi major axis for ellipse, semi transverse axis for hyperbola.

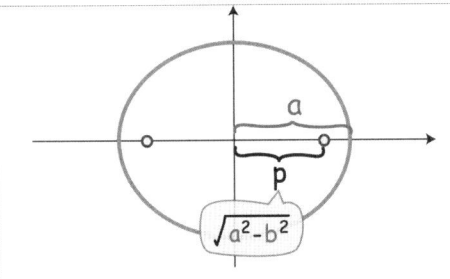	For a ellipse, eccentricity is $\dfrac{\sqrt{a^2 - b^2}}{a}$ (it will be <1)
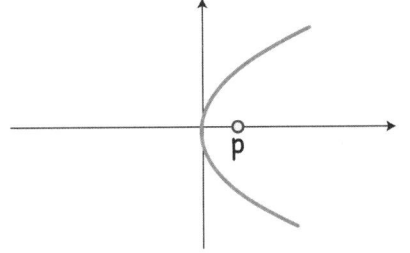	For a parabola, eccentricity is 1.
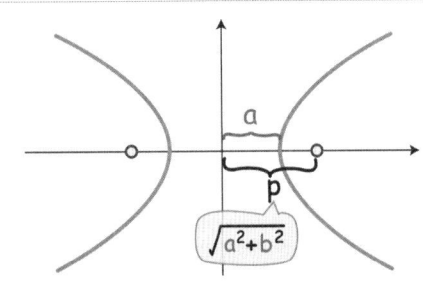	For a hyperbola, eccentricity is $\dfrac{\sqrt{a^2 + b^2}}{a}$ (it will be >1)

Eccentricity shows us how much a conic section (a circle, ellipse, parabola or hyperbola) varies from being 'un'circular.

Larger the eccentricity means Not circular.

At **eccentricity = 0** we get a *circle*
for **eccentricity < 1** we get an *ellipse*
for **eccentricity = 1** we get a *parabola*
for **eccentricity > 1** we get a *hyperbola*.

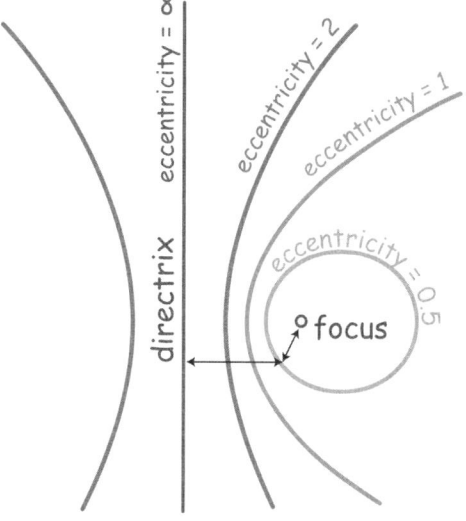

EXAMPLE 8. Identify the eccentricity of each.

① $\dfrac{x^2}{16} - \dfrac{y^2}{9} = 1$

② $\dfrac{x^2}{4} + \dfrac{y^2}{25} = 1$

③ $x = 4y^2$

④ $\dfrac{y^2}{16} - x^2 = 1$

⑤ $\dfrac{(x+2)^2}{4} + \dfrac{(y+2)^2}{16} = 1$

⑥ $\dfrac{(x+1)^2}{4} - \dfrac{(y+2)^2}{9} = 1$

⑦ $\dfrac{(y+1)^2}{16} - \dfrac{x^2}{25} = 1$

⑧ $\dfrac{x^2}{49} + (y+3)^2 = 1$

Mia's Precalculus
9.5 Rotation of Conics

1. Rotation of Conic Sections

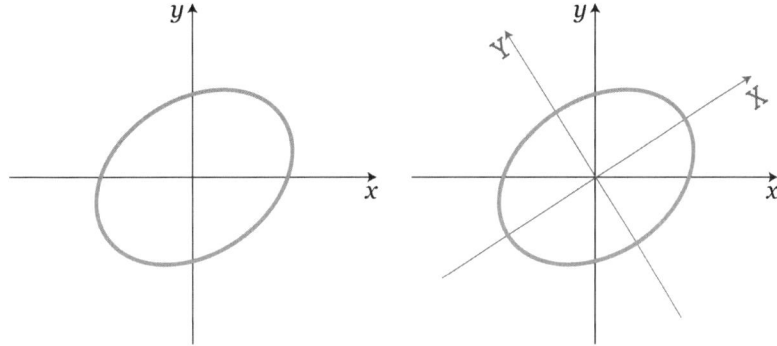

This ellipse has been rotated.

This ellipse will have NEW axis of symmetry at ①_____ and ②_____.

Let's find out the equation of the rotated ellipse.

Let's say we have a point (x, y).

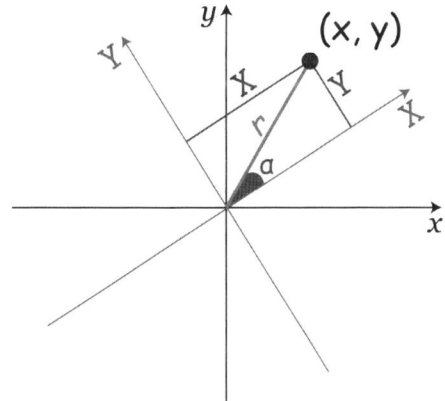

From the figure we can say;

$$X = r \,\boxed{③}$$

$$Y = r \,\boxed{④}$$

Blank : ① X axis ② Y axis ③ $\cos \alpha$ ④ $\sin \alpha$

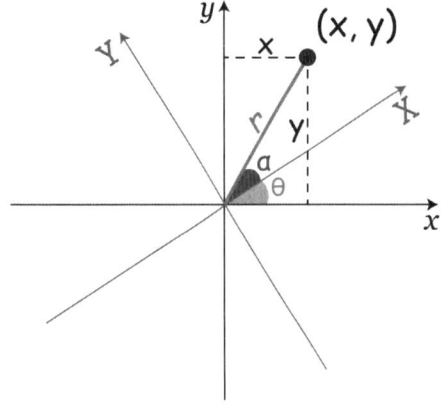

From this figure we can say;

$x = r\cos(\boxed{①})$
$= r(\boxed{②} - \sin\alpha\sin\theta)$
$= \boxed{③} - r\sin\alpha\sin\theta$

$y = r\sin(\boxed{④})$
$= r(\boxed{⑤} + \cos\alpha\sin\theta)$
$= \boxed{⑥} + r\cos\alpha\sin\theta$

If we plug in X, Y, then we can say;

$x = \boxed{⑦}\cos\theta - \boxed{⑧}\sin\theta$
$y = \boxed{⑨}\sin\theta + \boxed{⑩}\cos\theta$

※ Rotation of Axes Formulas

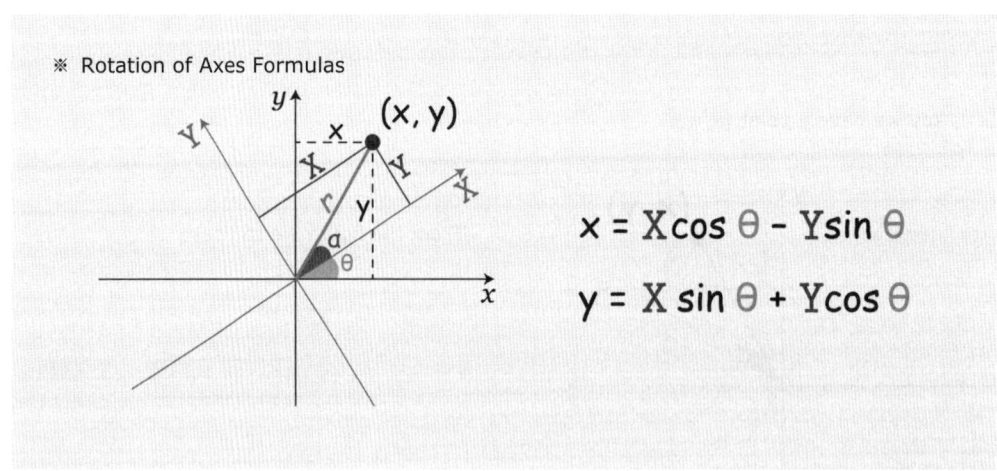

$x = X\cos\theta - Y\sin\theta$
$y = X\sin\theta + Y\cos\theta$

Blank : ① $(\alpha + \theta)$ ② $\cos\alpha\cos\theta$ ③ $r\cos\alpha\cos\theta$ ④ $(\alpha + \theta)$ ⑤ $\sin\alpha\cos\theta$ ⑥ $r\sin\alpha\cos\theta$
⑦ X   ⑧ Y   ⑨ X   ⑩ Y

EXAMPLE 1. Determine the xy-coordinates of the given point if the coordinate axes are rotated through the indicated angle.

① $(X,Y)=(2,-4), \quad \theta=30°$ 　　　　② $(X,Y)=(0,4), \quad \theta=45°$

③ $(X,Y)=(3,-\sqrt{3}), \quad \theta=60°$ 　　　　④ $(X,Y)=(-1,\sqrt{3}), \quad \theta=30°$

EXAMPLE 2. Determine the equation of the given conic in XY-coordinates when the coordinate axes are rotated through the given angle.

① $xy=2, \quad \theta=45°$ 　　　　② $x^2+4y^2=36, \quad \theta=30°$

③ $x^2 + 2y^2 = 14$, $\theta = 60°$

2. Identifying Rotated Conics

If we have xy term then it is a rotated conic.

Rotated..

$$Ax^2 + Bxy + Cy^2 + Dx + Ey + F = 0$$

If discriminant $B^2 - 4AC = 0$, then it is parabola.

If discriminant $B^2 - 4AC < 0$, then it is Ellipse.

If discriminant $B^2 - 4AC > 0$, then it is hyperbola.

And $\cot 2\theta = \dfrac{A - C}{B}$ tell us how much is rotated.

EXAMPLE 3. (a) Use the discriminant to determine whether the graph of the equation is a parabola, an ellipse, or a hyperbola. (b) Rotate the axes so that the new equation has no xy term. (c) Sketch the graph.

① $x^2 + 2xy + y^2 - 8x + 8y = 0$

② $31x^2 + 10\sqrt{3}xy + 21y^2 - 144 = 0$

③ $xy + 16 = 0$

④ $11x^2 + 10\sqrt{3}xy + y^2 - 64 = 0$

Part 10
Matrix and System of Equation

10.1 Systems of Linear Equations in Several Variables
10.2 Algebra of Matrices
10.3 Inverse and Matrix Equation
10.4 Partial Fractions

Mia's Precalculus
10.1 Systems of Linear Equation
in Three Variables

1. Gaussian Method and Systems of Equations

Gaussian method is a method for solving system of linear equations.

Once you have a system of equation, change to **Augmented matrix.**

(∵ Matrix consisting the coefficients and right hand side numbers of the system)

$$\begin{matrix} x - 2y + 3z = 9 \\ -x + 3y = -4 \\ 2x - 5y + 5z = 17 \end{matrix} \longrightarrow \left[\begin{array}{ccc|c} 1 & -2 & 3 & 9 \\ -1 & 3 & 0 & -4 \\ 2 & -5 & 5 & 17 \end{array}\right]$$

Augmented Matrix

Do a row operations to make these three spots 0!
We call it 'Row-Echelon Form'

$$\left[\begin{array}{ccc|c} & & & \\ 0 & & & \\ 0 & 0 & & \end{array}\right]$$

※ Row-Echelon Form

Row Echelon Form

$$\left[\begin{array}{ccc|c} 1 & & & \\ 0 & 1 & & \\ 0 & 0 & 1 & \end{array}\right]$$

※ Rules for Row Operations

① You can switch two rows.

② You can multiply a row by a constant ($\neq 0$)

③ You can add or subtract a row to another row.

Linear system

$$\begin{aligned} x - 2y + 3z &= 9 \\ -x + 3y &= -4 \\ 2x - 5y + 5z &= 17 \end{aligned}$$

Augmented Matrix

$$\longrightarrow \begin{bmatrix} 1 & -2 & 3 & \vdots & 9 \\ -1 & 3 & 0 & \vdots & -4 \\ 2 & -5 & 5 & \vdots & 17 \end{bmatrix}$$

$$\begin{aligned} x - 2y + 3z &= 9 \\ y + 3z &= 5 \\ 2x - 5y + 5z &= 17 \end{aligned}$$

$$\begin{bmatrix} 1 & -2 & 3 & \vdots & 9 \\ 0 & \boxed{①} & & & \\ 2 & -5 & 5 & \vdots & 17 \end{bmatrix} \leftarrow R_1 + R_2$$

$$\begin{aligned} x - 2y + 3z &= 9 \\ y + 3z &= 5 \\ -y - z &= -1 \end{aligned}$$

$$\begin{bmatrix} 1 & -2 & 3 & \vdots & 9 \\ 0 & 1 & 3 & \vdots & 5 \\ 0 & \boxed{②} & & & \end{bmatrix} \leftarrow (-2)R_1 + R_3$$

$$\begin{aligned} x - 2y + 3z &= 9 \\ y + 3z &= 5 \\ 2z &= 4 \end{aligned}$$

$$\begin{bmatrix} 1 & -2 & 3 & \vdots & 9 \\ 0 & 1 & 3 & \vdots & 5 \\ 0 & 0 & \boxed{③} & & \end{bmatrix} \leftarrow R_2 + R_3$$

$$\begin{aligned} x - 2y + 3z &= 9 \\ y + 3z &= 5 \\ z &= 2 \end{aligned}$$

$$\begin{bmatrix} 1 & -2 & 3 & \vdots & 9 \\ 0 & 1 & 3 & \vdots & 5 \\ 0 & 0 & 1 & \vdots & 2 \end{bmatrix} \leftarrow 1/2\, R_3$$

You can use back-substitution to find x and y.

Blank : ① 1 3 5   ② -1 -1 -1   ③ 2 4

EXAMPLE 1. Solve the system by using Gaussian Method.

① $\begin{aligned} x + 2y - z &= -3 \\ -2x - y + z &= 0 \\ 3x + y - 2z &= -1 \end{aligned}$
② $\begin{aligned} x + y + z &= -1 \\ x - y + 3z &= 7 \\ 3x + y + z &= -3 \end{aligned}$

③ $\begin{aligned} 2x + 2y - z &= 2 \\ x - 3y + z &= -28 \\ -x + y &= 14 \end{aligned}$
④ $\begin{aligned} -4x - y - z &= -11 \\ x \quad\quad - z &= 2 \\ 2y + 4z &= 0 \end{aligned}$

2. Gauss-Jordan Method and Systems of Equations

If we put the augmented matrix of a linear system in reduced row-echelon form, then we don't need to back-substitute to solve the system.

※ Row-Echelon Form

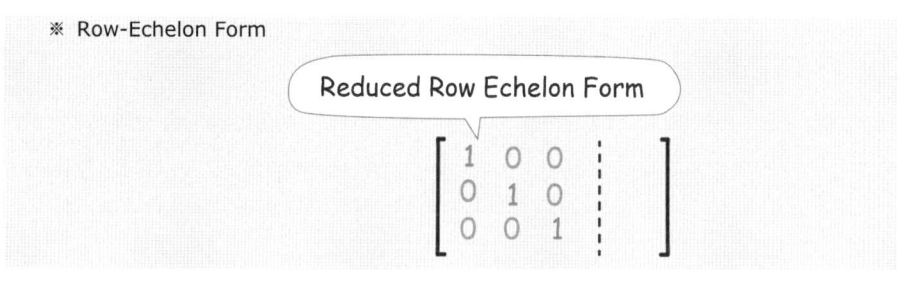

Linear system

$x - 2y + 3z = 9$
$y + 3z = 5$
$z = 2$

Augmented Matrix

$$\begin{bmatrix} 1 & -2 & 3 & | & 9 \\ 0 & 1 & 3 & | & 5 \\ 0 & 0 & 1 & | & 2 \end{bmatrix}$$

$x - 2y + 3z = 9$
$y = -1$
$z = 2$

$$\begin{bmatrix} 1 & -2 & 3 & | & 9 \\ 0 & 1 & 0 & | & \boxed{①} \\ 0 & 0 & 1 & | & 2 \end{bmatrix} \leftarrow R_2 - 3R_3$$

$x - 2y = 3$
$y = -1$
$z = 2$

$$\begin{bmatrix} 1 & -2 & 0 & | & \boxed{②} \\ 0 & 1 & 0 & | & -1 \\ 0 & 0 & 1 & | & 2 \end{bmatrix} \leftarrow R_1 - 3R_3$$

$x = 1$
$y = -1$
$z = 2$

$$\begin{bmatrix} 1 & 0 & 0 & | & \boxed{③} \\ 0 & 1 & 0 & | & -1 \\ 0 & 0 & 1 & | & 2 \end{bmatrix} \leftarrow R_1 + 2R_3$$

Blank : ① -1   ② 3   ③ 1

EXAMPLE 2. Solve the system by using Gaussian Jordan Method.

① $\begin{aligned} x + 2y - z &= -3 \\ -2x - y + z &= 0 \\ 3x + y - 2z &= -1 \end{aligned}$
② $\begin{aligned} x + y + z &= -1 \\ x - y + 3z &= 7 \\ 3x + y + z &= -3 \end{aligned}$

③ $\begin{aligned} 2x + 2y - z &= 2 \\ x - 3y + z &= -28 \\ -x + y &= 14 \end{aligned}$
④ $\begin{aligned} -4x - y - z &= -11 \\ x \quad\quad - z &= 2 \\ 2y + 4z &= 0 \end{aligned}$

3. Type of Solution

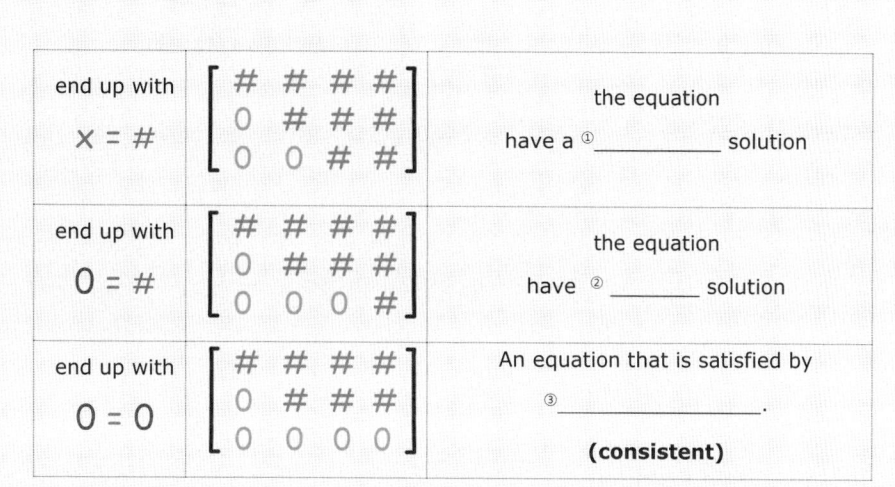

When a system has infinitely many solutions, the general solution involves writing x, y and z in terms of a real parameter t.

Since $ax + by + cz = d$ is a plane in 3 dimensions coordinate, the solution shows us the number of intersection.

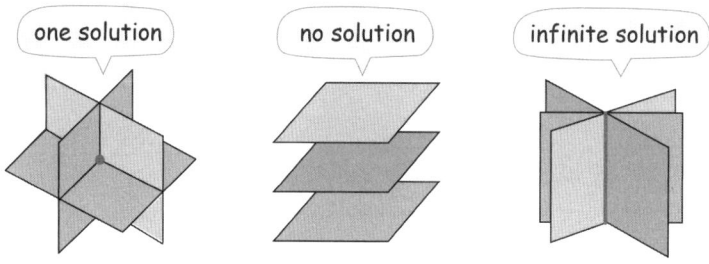

Blank : ① one ② no ③ all real numbers

EXAMPLE 3. Solve the system.

① $\begin{aligned} x+y+z &= 2 \\ y-3z &= 1 \\ 2x+y+5z &= 0 \end{aligned}$

② $\begin{aligned} x+4y-2z &= -3 \\ 2x-y+5z &= 12 \\ 8x+5y+11z &= 30 \end{aligned}$

③ $\begin{aligned} x+y+z &= 7 \\ 3x-2y-z &= 4 \\ x+6y+5z &= 24 \end{aligned}$

④ $\begin{aligned} x-y+3z &= 3 \\ 4x-8y+32z &= 24 \\ 2x-3y+11z &= 4 \end{aligned}$

EXAMPLE 4.

(a) Find the value of k for which the system of equations

$$2x + y + 2z = 4$$
$$6x - y - 6z = 8 \quad \text{is consistent.}$$
$$4x + 6y + 16z = k$$

(b) For the value of k found above, find the general solution of the system.

EXAMPLE 5. Consider the system of equations:
$$x + 2y - 2z = 1$$
$$x - 4y + z = 4$$
$$x + y + kz = a$$

(a) Find the set of values of k for which the system has a unique solution.

(b) Find the value of k and a for which the system has infinitely many solutions.

(c) State the set of values of k and a for which the system has no solutions.

Mia's Precalculus

10.2 Algebra of Matrices

1. Matrix

※ A **Matrix** is an array of numbers (plural: Matrices)

※ Order of Matrix (=Dimension of Matrix = ①_____ of Matrix)

To show how many rows and columns a matrix has we often write

           numbers of ②_____ × numbers of ③_____.

$$2\text{ rows}\left\{\begin{bmatrix} 6 & 4 & 24 \\ 1 & -9 & 7 \end{bmatrix}\right. \overset{3\text{ columns}}{}\quad \begin{bmatrix} 2 & 3 \\ 0 & 4 \\ 3 & -1 \end{bmatrix} \quad \begin{bmatrix} -1 & -3 \\ 2 & 4 \end{bmatrix}$$

        2 X 3   ④_____   ⑤_____

※ Each element is shown by a lower case letter with a "subscript" of row, column:

$$A = \begin{bmatrix} a_{11} & a_{12} & a_{13} \\ a_{21} & a_{22} & a_{23} \end{bmatrix} \qquad a_{rc} \text{ (row, column)}$$

2. Operation of Matrices

※ To **add** or **subtract** two matrices: add the numbers in the matching positions.

$$\begin{bmatrix} 2 & -5 \\ 1 & 9 \end{bmatrix} - \begin{bmatrix} 1 & 3 \\ -2 & -4 \end{bmatrix} = \begin{bmatrix} 1 & -8 \\ 3 & 13 \end{bmatrix} \quad (2-1=1)$$

Blank : ① size   ② row   ③ column   ④ 3 x 2   ⑤ 2 x 2

※ We can **multiply** a matrix **by some value**:

$$3 \times \begin{bmatrix} 1 & 3 \\ -2 & -4 \end{bmatrix} = \begin{bmatrix} 3 & 9 \\ -6 & -12 \end{bmatrix}$$

$3 \times 1 = 3$

EXAMPLE 1. Find the sum or difference of the matrix, if possible.

① $\begin{bmatrix} -1 & 5 \\ 2 & 4 \end{bmatrix} + 2 \begin{bmatrix} 2 & 8 \\ -4 & 5 \end{bmatrix}$

② $\begin{bmatrix} 1 & 5 & 7 \\ -4 & 0 & 5 \end{bmatrix} - 2 \begin{bmatrix} 7 & -1 & 4 \\ -2 & 4 & 4 \end{bmatrix}$

③ $-\begin{bmatrix} 2 & -3 \\ 4 & -1 \\ 8 & 7 \end{bmatrix} - 3 \begin{bmatrix} 0 & 8 \\ 4 & -2 \\ 3 & 4 \end{bmatrix}$

④ $\begin{bmatrix} 1 & 4 & 0 \end{bmatrix} + 2 \begin{bmatrix} 4 \\ -3 \\ 1 \end{bmatrix}$

⑤ $2 \begin{bmatrix} 2 & 3 \\ -8 & 2 \end{bmatrix} + 3 \begin{bmatrix} 2 & 4 \\ 4 & -2 \\ 5 & 7 \end{bmatrix}$

EXAMPLE 2. Solve the equation.

① $\begin{bmatrix} 2 & 6 \\ 3 & 1 \end{bmatrix} + X = \begin{bmatrix} 4 & 7 \\ 0 & 9 \end{bmatrix}$

② $\begin{bmatrix} 0 & 3 & 9 \\ -1 & 5 & -3 \end{bmatrix} - X = \begin{bmatrix} 2 & -11 & 6 \\ 3 & 4 & 8 \end{bmatrix}$

※ But to **multiply** a matrix A **by another matrix B**

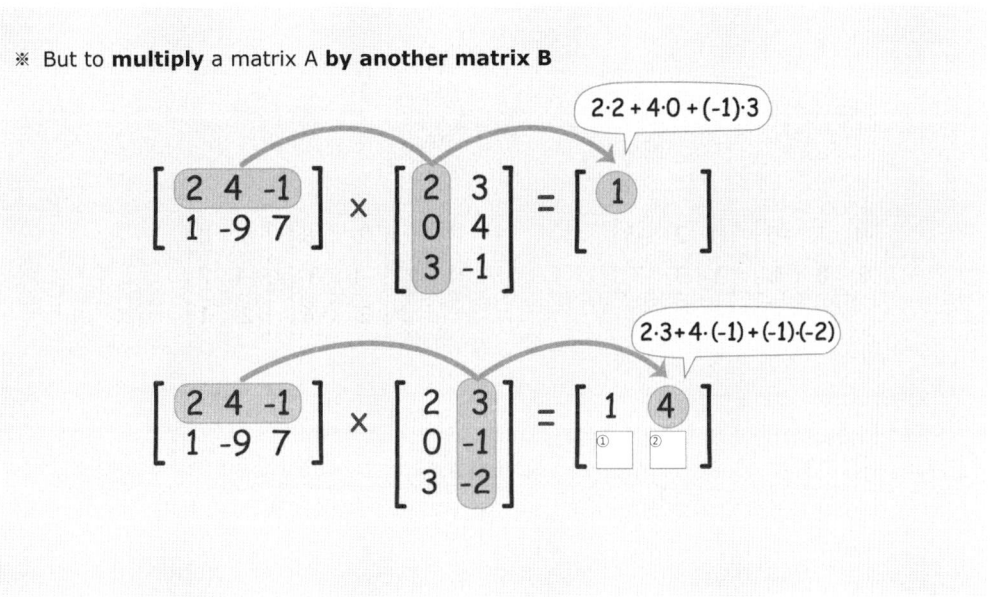

EXAMPLE 3. Find the product, if possible.

① $\begin{bmatrix} -1 & 0 \\ 2 & 4 \end{bmatrix} \times \begin{bmatrix} 2 & 8 \\ -4 & 1 \end{bmatrix}$

② $\begin{bmatrix} -1 & 3 \\ 3 & 2 \end{bmatrix} \times \begin{bmatrix} -2 & 0 \\ -1 & 3 \end{bmatrix}$

Blank : ① 23   ② -2

③ $\begin{bmatrix} -2 & 3 & 5 \end{bmatrix} \times \begin{bmatrix} 0 & 1 \\ -1 & 2 \\ 2 & 3 \end{bmatrix}$ ④ $\begin{bmatrix} 0 & -3 & 1 \\ 5 & -1 & 0 \end{bmatrix} \times \begin{bmatrix} 1 & 2 \\ 0 & 1 \\ 1 & -1 \end{bmatrix}$

⑤ $\begin{bmatrix} 0 & 7 \\ 2 & 1 \end{bmatrix} \times \begin{bmatrix} -4 & 3 & 0 \\ 4 & 2 & -2 \end{bmatrix}$ ⑥ $\begin{bmatrix} -6 & 2 & 9 \end{bmatrix} \times \begin{bmatrix} 4 \\ 0 \\ -3 \end{bmatrix}$

⑦ $\begin{bmatrix} -4 & 1 & -5 \\ 0 & 0 & 4 \end{bmatrix} \times \begin{bmatrix} 0 & 2 & -5 \\ 1 & 3 & 7 \end{bmatrix}$ ⑧ $\begin{bmatrix} 2 & -8 \\ -1 & 3 \\ 2 & -6 \end{bmatrix} \begin{bmatrix} 5 & 0 \\ -1 & 7 \\ 2 & 1 \end{bmatrix}$

※ Product of Matrices

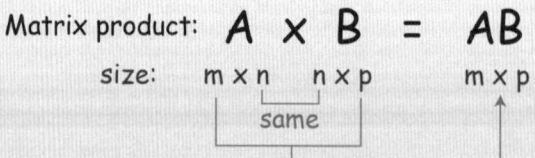

Product of Matrices AB is defined
only when the number of columns in A is equal to the number of rows in B.

EXAMPLE 4. If matrices A, B, C, D and E have dimensions of 2 x 3, 2 x 3, 3 x 2, 2 x 2, and 3 x 3, respectively, what are the dimensions of following operations?

① BA

② AEC

③ BCD

④ $D(A - 3B)$

⑤ $BC + 2D$

⑥ $(AE - B)C$

⑦ $(BC - D)A$

EXAMPLE 5. Which of the following matrices can be multiplied by themselves?

$$A = \begin{bmatrix} 1 & 1 \\ 3 & 1 \\ 1 & 2 \end{bmatrix} \quad B = \begin{bmatrix} 3 & -1 & 1 \\ 1 & -1 & 2 \\ 2 & 1 & -3 \end{bmatrix} \quad C = \begin{bmatrix} 1 & 1 & 4 \end{bmatrix} \quad D = \begin{bmatrix} 1 & 0 \\ 0 & 1 \end{bmatrix}$$

3. Properties of Matrices

✳ Properties of Matrix

$$(AB)C = A(BC) \quad \text{Association Property}$$

$$C(A + B) = CA + CB$$
$$\quad \text{Distributive Property}$$
$$(A + B)C = AC + BC$$

BUT Matrix **Multiplication** is **NOT Commutative**!

$$AB \neq BA$$

EXAMPLE 6. If A and B are two matrices, find $(A+B)^2$.

EXAMPLE 7. If A and B are two matrices, find $(A+B)(A-B)$.

4. Identity Matrix

The "Identity Matrix" is the matrix equivalent of the number "1":

$$I_3 = \begin{bmatrix} 1 & 0 & 0 \\ 0 & 1 & 0 \\ 0 & 0 & 1 \end{bmatrix}$$

3 x 3 Identity Matrix

It is "square" matrix (has same number of rows as columns),
It has 1s on the diagonal and 0s everywhere else.
Its symbol is the capital letter I.

It is a special matrix, because when we multiply by it, the original is unchanged:

$$AI = IA = A$$

EXAMPLE 8. Find the product.

① $\begin{bmatrix} -1 & 0 \\ 2 & 4 \end{bmatrix} \times \begin{bmatrix} 1 & 0 \\ 0 & 1 \end{bmatrix}$

② $\begin{bmatrix} 1 & 0 & 2 \\ 0 & 2 & -4 \\ 3 & -5 & 4 \end{bmatrix} \times \begin{bmatrix} 1 & 0 & 0 \\ 0 & 1 & 0 \\ 0 & 0 & 1 \end{bmatrix}$

5. Expand Knowledge

EXAMPLE 9.* If matrix $A = \begin{bmatrix} 1 & 1 \\ 0 & 1 \end{bmatrix}$, what is A^{55}?

Mia's Precalculus

10.3 Inverse and Matrix Equation

1. Determinant of Matrices

The ①_____ of a matrix is a special number that can be calculated from a **square matrix**.

※ Determinant of 2x2 Matrix:

$$|A| = \begin{vmatrix} a & b \\ c & d \end{vmatrix} = ad - bc$$

Determinant of Matrix A

EXAMPLE 1. Find the determinant.

① $\begin{vmatrix} 7 & 3 \\ 5 & 2 \end{vmatrix}$
② $\begin{vmatrix} 2 & 3 \\ -1 & 2 \end{vmatrix}$

③ $\begin{vmatrix} 4 & 5 \\ -1 & 1 \end{vmatrix}$
④ $\begin{vmatrix} 12 & -7 \\ -4 & 3 \end{vmatrix}$

⑤ $\begin{vmatrix} 2 & 2 \\ 5 & 5 \end{vmatrix}$
⑥ $\begin{vmatrix} 2 & -4 \\ 3 & -6 \end{vmatrix}$

Blank : ① determinant

※ Determinant of 3x3 Matrix:
  We have two ways to do;
  Method 1)

$$|A| = \begin{vmatrix} a & b & c \\ d & e & f \\ g & h & i \end{vmatrix} \begin{matrix} a & b \\ d & e \\ g & h \end{matrix} = aei + bfg + cdh - gec - hfa - idb$$

Method 2)

$$|A| = a\begin{vmatrix} e & f \\ h & i \end{vmatrix} - b\begin{vmatrix} d & f \\ g & i \end{vmatrix} + c\begin{vmatrix} d & e \\ g & h \end{vmatrix}$$

$$= a(ei-fh) - b(di-fg) + c(dh-eg)$$

EXAMPLE 2. Find the determinant.

① $\begin{vmatrix} 1 & -1 & 5 \\ -4 & 2 & -4 \\ -1 & -2 & 3 \end{vmatrix}$

② $\begin{vmatrix} 4 & 1 & 1 \\ 3 & 6 & 1 \\ 2 & 5 & 2 \end{vmatrix}$

③ $\begin{vmatrix} 1 & 2 & 4 \\ 2 & 2 & 5 \\ 1 & 2 & 4 \end{vmatrix}$
④ $\begin{vmatrix} 1 & 0 & 2 \\ 0 & 2 & -4 \\ 3 & -5 & 4 \end{vmatrix}$

EXAMPLE 3. Solve for x

$$\begin{vmatrix} x & x \\ 8 & x \end{vmatrix} = \begin{vmatrix} 7 & -2 & 1 \\ 0 & 3 & -1 \\ 5 & -4 & 2 \end{vmatrix}$$

2. Inverse of Matrices

When you multiply a Matrix by its ①_____ matrix, you get the Identity Matrix.

$$A \times A^{-1} = A^{-1} \times A = I$$

※ Inverse of a Matrix of 2 × 2

$$A^{-1} = \begin{bmatrix} a & b \\ c & d \end{bmatrix}^{-1} = \frac{1}{|A|} \begin{bmatrix} d & -b \\ -c & a \end{bmatrix}$$

switch! negative~
Determinant

$$= \frac{1}{ad-bc} \begin{bmatrix} d & -b \\ -c & a \end{bmatrix}$$

If det $A \neq 0$, then A^{-1} exists

If det $A = $ ②_____ , then A^{-1} does not exist.

EXAMPLE 4. Find the inverse, if it exists, for the matrix.

① $\begin{bmatrix} 5 & 3 \\ 3 & 2 \end{bmatrix}$
② $\begin{bmatrix} 10 & 1 \\ -1 & 0 \end{bmatrix}$

③ $\begin{bmatrix} -5 & -1 \\ 6 & 0 \end{bmatrix}$
④ $\begin{bmatrix} -2 & 4 \\ 4 & -4 \end{bmatrix}$

⑤ $\begin{bmatrix} 4 & -8 \\ 3 & -6 \end{bmatrix}$
⑥ $\begin{bmatrix} -2 & 4 \\ 1 & -2 \end{bmatrix}$

Blank : ① inverse ② 0

※ Inverse of a Matrix of n x n

$$\left[\begin{array}{ccc|ccc} \# & \# & \# & 1 & 0 & 0 \\ \# & \# & \# & 0 & 1 & 0 \\ \# & \# & \# & 0 & 0 & 1 \end{array}\right] \sim \left[\begin{array}{ccc|ccc} 1 & 0 & 0 & \# & \# & \# \\ 0 & 1 & 0 & \# & \# & \# \\ 0 & 0 & 1 & \# & \# & \# \end{array}\right]$$

(left: A, right: A^{-1})

EXAMPLE 5. Find the inverse, if it exists, for the matrix.

① $\begin{bmatrix} 5 & 5 \\ 6 & 1 \end{bmatrix}$
② $\begin{bmatrix} 0 & -2 \\ 2 & 2 \end{bmatrix}$

③ $\begin{bmatrix} 1 & 3 & 2 \\ 1 & 3 & 3 \\ 2 & 7 & 8 \end{bmatrix}$
④ $\begin{bmatrix} 1 & 1 & 1 \\ 2 & 1 & 1 \\ 2 & 2 & 3 \end{bmatrix}$

3. Matrices and Systems of Equations

EXAMPLE 6. You have Matrix A and B, find Matrix X when $AX = B$

EXAMPLE 7. You have Matrix A and B, find Matrix X when $XA = B$

EXAMPLE 8. Solve the system by using the inverse of the coefficient matrix.

① $\begin{aligned} 3x + 5y &= -10 \\ -3x - 6y &= 9 \end{aligned}$

② $\begin{aligned} x + 3y &= -8 \\ -14x - 4y &= -2 \end{aligned}$

③
$$x + 2y + 3z = 7$$
$$x + y + z = -12$$
$$2x + 2y + z = 12$$

inverse of $\begin{bmatrix} 1 & 2 & 3 \\ 1 & 1 & 1 \\ 2 & 2 & 1 \end{bmatrix}$ is $\begin{bmatrix} -1 & 4 & -1 \\ 1 & -5 & 2 \\ 0 & 2 & -1 \end{bmatrix}$

④
$$x + 2y + 3z = 7$$
$$x + y + z = -3$$
$$-x + y + 2z = 9$$

inverse of $\begin{bmatrix} 1 & 2 & 3 \\ 1 & 1 & 1 \\ -1 & 1 & 2 \end{bmatrix}$ is $\begin{bmatrix} 1 & -1 & -1 \\ -3 & 5 & 2 \\ 2 & -3 & -1 \end{bmatrix}$

4. Cramer's Rule

Given that
$$ax + by = p$$
$$cx + dy = q$$

then

$$x = \frac{\begin{vmatrix} p & b \\ q & d \end{vmatrix}}{\begin{vmatrix} a & b \\ c & d \end{vmatrix}} \quad y = \frac{\begin{vmatrix} a & p \\ c & q \end{vmatrix}}{\begin{vmatrix} a & b \\ c & d \end{vmatrix}}$$

(replace with p,q)

EXAMPLE 9. Solve the system by using the cramer's rule.

① $\begin{array}{l} 2x+6y=2 \\ 2x-y=-5 \end{array}$
② $\begin{array}{l} -5x+3y=8 \\ 3x-6y=-30 \end{array}$

Given that $\begin{array}{l} ax + by + cz = p \\ dx + ey + fz = q \\ gx + hy + iz = r \end{array}$

$$x = \frac{\begin{vmatrix} p & b & c \\ q & e & f \\ r & h & i \end{vmatrix}}{\begin{vmatrix} a & b & c \\ d & e & f \\ g & h & i \end{vmatrix}} \quad y = \frac{\begin{vmatrix} a & p & c \\ d & q & f \\ g & r & i \end{vmatrix}}{\begin{vmatrix} a & b & c \\ d & e & f \\ g & h & i \end{vmatrix}} \quad z = \frac{\begin{vmatrix} a & b & p \\ d & e & q \\ g & h & r \end{vmatrix}}{\begin{vmatrix} a & b & c \\ d & e & f \\ g & h & i \end{vmatrix}}$$

Mia's Precalculus
10.4 Partial Fractions

1. Partial Fraction for Proper Fractions

Let's find the "parts" that make the single fraction (the "partial fractions").

① Factor the bottom.

② i) Write one partial fraction for each of those factors

$$\frac{N}{(x-2)(x+3)} = \frac{A}{(x-2)} + \frac{B}{(x+3)}$$

ii) Sometimes you may get a **factor with an exponent,** like $(x+2)^2$

You need a partial fraction for each exponent from 1 up.

$$\frac{N}{(x-2)^2} = \frac{A}{(x-2)} + \frac{B}{(x-2)^2}$$

iii) When you have a **irreducible quadratic binomial factor** (like x^2+3) you need a linear on the numerator.

$$\frac{Cx+D}{x^2+2} \quad \substack{\text{linear factor} \\ \text{irreducible quadratic factor}}$$

③ Multiply through by the bottom so we no longer have fractions

④ Now find the constants A, B, C or D (by substituting the **roots**)

ex) Write in partial fractions.

① $\dfrac{N}{x^2 - 2x - 3}$

② $\dfrac{N}{(x-1)^3}$

③ $\dfrac{N}{x(x^2+1)}$

④ $\dfrac{N}{(x-2)(x+2)^2(x^2+2)}$

⑤ $\dfrac{N}{(x^2+1)^2}$

EXAMPLE 1. Find the values of A, B and C that complete the partial fractions.

① $\dfrac{6}{x^2-9} = \dfrac{A}{x-3} + \dfrac{B}{x+3}$

② $\dfrac{x-8}{x^2-4x} = \dfrac{A}{x} + \dfrac{B}{x-4}$

③ $\dfrac{2x-4}{x(x^2+2)} = \dfrac{A}{x} + \dfrac{Bx+C}{(x^2+2)}$

EXAMPLE 2. Write the partial fraction decomposition of the rational expression.

① $\dfrac{2x-5}{x^2-5x-6}$ ② $\dfrac{x-9}{x^2-9x+20}$

③ $\dfrac{2x^2-x-13}{x(x+1)(x-1)}$ ④ $\dfrac{19x^2-8x-16}{x(x+4)(x-4)}$

⑤ $\dfrac{x+4}{x^3-2x^2+x}$

⑥ $\dfrac{2x^2+x-3}{(x+2)(x+1)^2}$

⑦ $\dfrac{7x^2-2}{(x+1)^3}$

⑧ $\dfrac{4x^2-4x+3}{(x-1)^3}$

⑨ $\dfrac{8x+1}{(x-1)(x^2+x+1)}$

⑩ $\dfrac{3x-2}{x^3-1}$

⑪ $\dfrac{3x^3 + 2x^2}{(x^2+5)^2}$

⑫ $\dfrac{x^2 + 3x - 1}{(x^2+2)^2}$

2. Partial Fraction for Improper Fractions

> If you have improper fraction, then first do long division.

EXAMPLE 3. Write the partial fraction decomposition of the rational expression.

① $\dfrac{x^2 + 2x + 1}{x^2 - 2x}$

② $\dfrac{2x^2 + 5x - 4}{x^2 - x}$

③ $\dfrac{4x^3+12x^2+13x+7}{4x^2+4x+1}$

④ $\dfrac{6x^3+x^2+5x-1}{x^3+x}$

Part 11
Sequence and Series

11.1 Sequence and Sigma Notation
11.2 Arithmetic Sequence and Series
11.3 Geometric Sequence and Series
11.4 Applications of Sequence and Series
11.5 Binomial Expansion
11.6 Mathematical Induction

Mia's Precalculus
11.1 Sequence and Sigma Notation

1. Sequence

※ Sequence: list of numbers which follows a certain rule

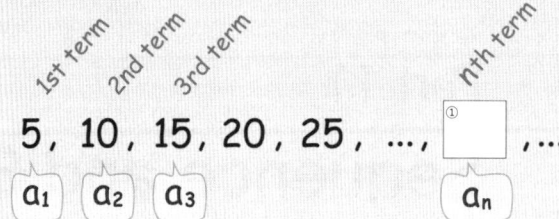

※ The notation for sequences

a_n represents the ② _____ of the sequence a.

(term number n is positive integer)

※ Sequences can be described in two ways:

① **Deductive rules** shows you the nth term formula

(defines how a_n depends on n.)

ex) $a_n = 5n$

② **Recursive rules** shows you the relationship between the terms

ex) $a_n = a_{n-1} + 5,\ a_1 = 5$

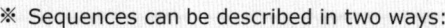

Blank : ① 5n   ② nth term (general term)

EXAMPLE 1. Find the first 4 terms of the sequence.

① $a_n = 3^n + 2$

② $a_n = (-1)^{n+1}(n-2)$

③ $a_n = \dfrac{(-1)^n}{2^{n-1}}$

④ $a_n = \dfrac{n+1}{n}$

⑤ $a_n = 3(a_{n-1} + 2), \ a_1 = 1$

⑥ $b_n = 2b_{n-1} - 1, \ b_1 = 2$

⑦ $a_n = a_{n-1} - a_{n-2}, \ a_1 = 1, \ a_2 = -1$

⑧ $b_n = b_{n-1} + b_{n-2}, \ b_1 = 1, \ b_2 = 3$

⑨ $b_{n+1} = \dfrac{1}{b_n}$, $b_1 = 3$

EXAMPLE 2. Write a general term a_n for the sequence.

① $\dfrac{1}{1}, \dfrac{1}{2}, \dfrac{1}{3}, \dfrac{1}{4}, \ldots$

② $\dfrac{2}{1}, \dfrac{3}{2}, \dfrac{4}{3}, \dfrac{5}{4}, \ldots$

③ $2, 4, 6, 8, 10, \ldots$

④ $-1, 1, -1, 1, \ldots$

⑤ $7, -14, 21, -28, 35, \ldots$

⑥ $1 \cdot 1, 2 \cdot 3, 3 \cdot 5, 4 \cdot 7, \ldots$

☞Usually when you have

$1, -1, 1, -1, 1, \ldots = $ ① ☐   even numbers = ③ _____

$-1, 1, -1, 1, -1, \ldots = $ ② ☐   odd numbers = ④ _____

Blank : ① $(-1)^{n+1}$ ② $(-1)^n$ ③ $2n$ ④ $2n+1$ or $2n-1$

2. Series or Sigma Notation

※ The notation for series

① S_n denotes the sum of the first n terms of the sequence.

$$S_n = a_1 + a_2 + \cdots + a_n$$

② $\sum_{k=m}^{n} a_k$ denotes the sum of the m th term to the n th term, so $S_n = \sum_{k=1}^{n} a_k$.

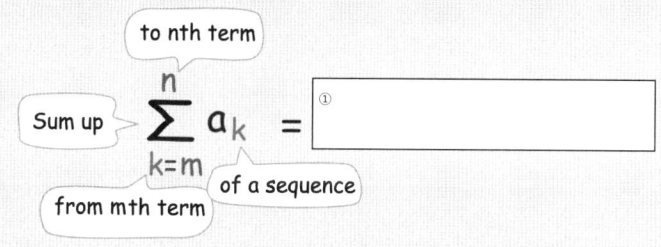

and read "the sum of ②____ from ③_____ to ④_____"

ex) $\sum_{k=2}^{5} a_k = $ ⑤ _____

EXAMPLE 3. Write out the sum.(Do not evaluate.)

① $\sum_{k=1}^{5} 3k$ ② $\sum_{k=5}^{8} k^2$

③ $\sum_{k=0}^{12} \cos \pi k$ ④ $\sum_{k=1}^{\infty} \sin 2$

Blank : ① $a_m + a_{m+1} + \ldots + a_n$ ② a_k ③ mth term ④ nth term ⑤ $a_2 + a_3 + a_4 + a_5$

⑤ $\sum_{k=1}^{3} \dfrac{5^k}{6^{k+1}}$ ⑥ $\sum_{k=0}^{4} \left(\dfrac{5}{4}\right) 2^k$

⑦ $\sum_{k=0}^{\infty} (-1)^k \dfrac{x^{2k}}{(2k)!}$ ⑧ $\sum_{k=1}^{\infty} \dfrac{a^{k+1}}{k}$

EXAMPLE 4. Write the sum using sigma notation, assuming the suggested pattern continues.

① $4+5+6+7$ ② $8+10+12+14+16$

③ $1-3+5-7+9-11$ ④ $\sin\pi + \sin 2\pi + \sin 3\pi + \sin 4\pi + \ldots$

⑤ $64+81+100+121+144$ ⑥ $3^3 + 4^3 + 5^3 + \ldots + 10^3$

⑦ $1 + \dfrac{1}{4} + \dfrac{1}{9} + \dfrac{1}{16} + \ldots$

⑧ $1 + \dfrac{1}{2\sqrt{2}} + \dfrac{1}{3\sqrt{3}} + \dfrac{1}{8} + \ldots$

⑨ $x + x^2 + x^3 + x^4 + \ldots$

EXAMPLE 5. Find the first three partial sums S_1, S_2, S_3 of the sequence, and use the pattern to find S_{20}.

① $a_n = \dfrac{1}{n} - \dfrac{1}{n+1}$

② $a_n = \sqrt{n+1} - \sqrt{n}$

③ $a_n = \log\left(\dfrac{n+1}{n+2}\right)$

3. Expand Knowledge

※ Properties of Sigma Notation (c is a constant)

$$\sum_{k=1}^{n}(a_k \pm b_k) = \sum_{k=1}^{n} a_k \pm \sum_{k=1}^{n} b_k$$

$$\sum_{k=1}^{n} ca_k = c\sum_{k=1}^{n} a_k$$

$$\sum_{k=1}^{n} c = cn$$

EXAMPLE 6. * If $\sum_{k=1}^{100} a_k = 50$ and $\sum_{k=1}^{100} b_k = 30$, then what is;

① $\sum_{k=1}^{100}(2a_k - b_k + 1)$

② $\sum_{k=1}^{100}(-a_k + 3b_k + 2)$

※ Sums of power

$$\sum_{k=1}^{n} k = 1+2+3+\cdots+n = \frac{n(n+1)}{2}$$

$$\sum_{k=1}^{n} k^2 = 1^2+2^2+3^2+\cdots+n^2 = \frac{n(n+1)(2n+1)}{6}$$

$$\sum_{k=1}^{n} k^3 = 1^3+2^3+3^3+\cdots+n^3 = \left(\frac{n(n+1)}{2}\right)^2$$

EXAMPLE 7. * Evaluate.

① $\sum_{k=1}^{10} (k^2 - k)$

② $\sum_{k=1}^{30} (2k+3)$

③ $1+2+3+\ldots+50$

④ $1^2 + 2^2 + 3^2 + \ldots + 30^2$

⑤ $1 \cdot 2 + 2 \cdot 3 + 3 \cdot 4 + \ldots + 50 \cdot 51$

Mia's Precalculus

11.2 Arithmetic Sequence and Series

1. Arithmetic Sequences

※ **Arithmetic Sequence**

An arithmetic sequence has a constant difference, d, between two consecutive terms.

$$a,\ a+d,\ a+2d,\ a+\boxed{①}\,d,\ \cdots,\ \boxed{②}$$

(1st term, 2nd term, 3rd term, 4th term, ..., nth term; each step +d)

where a is the ③_____ term, and d is a ④_____ _____.

General term (nth term): $a_n = a + (n-1)d$ (linear form)
— 1st term: a
— Common difference: $(n-1)d$

Recursive definitions: $a_{n+1} = a_n + d$

EXAMPLE 1. Determine whether the sequence is arithmetic. If it is arithmetic, find the common difference.

① $a_n = 2 + 3(n-1)$ ② $a_n = 5 - 2n$

Blank : ① 3   ② a + (n–1)d   ③ first   ④ common difference

③ $a_n = 2 - 7^{n-1}$

④ $a_n = \dfrac{1}{5n+6}$

⑤ $a_n = \dfrac{n-1}{3}$

⑥ $a_n = 3 + n^2$

EXAMPLE 2. Find the common difference d and the general term (nth term) of given sequence.

① 2, 5, 8, 11, . . .

② 7, 1, -5, -11, . . .

③ $2, \dfrac{5}{2}, 3, \dfrac{7}{2}, \ldots$

④ $8, 8\dfrac{1}{4}, 8\dfrac{1}{2}, 8\dfrac{3}{4}, 9, \ldots$

⑤ $x-1, x-3, x-5, \ldots$

⑥ $2t+1, 2t+7, 2t+13, \ldots$

⑦ $14\sqrt{3}, 19\sqrt{3}, 24\sqrt{3},...$

⑧ $\ln 3, \ln 6, \ln 12, \ln 24,...$

EXAMPLE 3. Find the general term (nth term) of given sequence.
① 6th term is 17, 12th term is 29.   ② 3rd term is 13, 8th term is 38.

EXAMPLE 4.   Find the number of terms in the sequence.
① 3, 5, 7, ..., 37   ② 7, 3, -1, ..., -81

2. Arithmetic Series

To find the arithmetic series;

$$\underbrace{(a) + (a+d) + (a+2d) + \cdots + (a+(n-1)d)}_{\text{first n terms}} = S_n \quad \text{(Sum of the first n terms)}$$

$$a \;+\; a+d \;+\cdots+\; a+(n-2)d + a+(n-1)d = S_n$$

$$\underset{③}{)} \;\boxed{①} \;+ a+(n-2)d + \cdots + \;a+d\; + \;\boxed{②}\; = S_n$$

※ Arithmetic Series

Sum of first n terms: $\;S_n = \dfrac{n}{2}(2a + (n-1)d) = \dfrac{n}{2}(a + a_n)$

(1st term, Common diff, 1st term, last term)

EXAMPLE 5. Evaluate the sum.

① $8 + 6 + 4 + 2 + \cdots$ (10 terms) ② $1 + 4 + 7 + 10 + \cdots$ (20 terms)

Blank : ① $a + (n-1)d$ ② a ③ $+$

③ $3+5+7+9+\ldots+21$

④ $4+8+12+\ldots+400$

⑤ $4+\dfrac{13}{2}+9+\dfrac{23}{2}+\ldots+29$

⑥ $0.5+0.9+1.3+1.7+\ldots+4.1$

⑦ $\sum_{n=1}^{5}(n-4)$

⑧ $\sum_{n=1}^{10}(4n-2)$

⑨ $\sum_{n=4}^{15}(-2n+3)$

⑩ $\sum_{n=10}^{21}(4n-6)$

EXAMPLE 6. The first five terms of an arithmetic sequence are $8, \frac{22}{3}, \frac{20}{3}, 6, \frac{16}{3}, \ldots$.

(a) Which term is equal to zero?

(b) The sum of the first n terms is 50. Find the possible values of n.

3. Expand Knowledge

EXAMPLE 7.* In an arithmetic series, if $S_n = 2n^2 + 3n$, find the first three terms.

EXAMPLE 8. *Find an expression for the sum of the first 20 terms of the series

$$\ln x + \ln x^4 + \ln x^7 + \ln x^{10} + \ldots$$

giving your answer in $\ln x^k$ form. Find k.

Mia's Precalculus
11.3 Geometric Sequence and Series

1. Geometric Sequences

※ **Geometric Sequence**

An geometric sequence has a constant ratio, r, between two consecutive terms:

$$a,\ ar,\ ar^2,\ ar^{①},\ \ldots,\ ^{②}\boxed{}$$

(1st term, 2nd term, 3rd term, 4th term, ×r, ×r, ×r)

where a is the ③_____ term, and r is a ④_____ _____.

General term (nth term): $a_n = ar^{n-1}$ (exponential form) — Common ratio, 1st term

Recursive definitions: $a_{n+1} = a_n r$

EXAMPLE 1. Find the common ratio r and the general term (nth term) of given sequence.

① $2, -1, \dfrac{1}{2}, -\dfrac{1}{4}, \ldots$

② $-\dfrac{1}{4}, \dfrac{1}{2}, -1, \ldots$

Blank : ① 3   ② ar^{n-1} ③ first   ④ common ratio

③ $\sqrt{2},\ 2,\ 2\sqrt{2},\ 4,\ldots$

④ $5, -5, 5, -5,\ldots$

⑤ $x-3,\ -3x+9,\ 9x-27,\ldots$

⑥ $2x,\ 10x,\ 50x,\ldots$

⑦ $x^{a+2}, x^{a+5}, x^{a+8},\ldots$

⑧ $x^{1/3},\ x^{2/3},\ x,\ x^{4/3},\ldots$

⑨ $\ln 2,\ \ln 2^3,\ \ln 2^9,\ \ln 2^{27},\ldots$

⑩ $\sqrt{3},\ \sqrt[3]{3},\ \sqrt[6]{3},\ 1,\cdots$

EXAMPLE 2. Find the general term (nth term) of given sequence.

① 3rd term is $\dfrac{1}{81}$, 9th term is $\dfrac{1}{3}$.

② 7th term is 4, 12th term is 128.

EXAMPLE 3. Find the number of terms in the sequence.

① $\dfrac{3}{4}, \dfrac{3}{2}, 3, 6, \ldots, 192$

② $-6, -12, -24, \ldots, -384$

2. Geometric Series

To find the geometric series;

$$\underbrace{(a)+(ar)+(ar^2)+\ldots+(ar^{n-1})}_{\text{first n terms}} = S_n \quad \text{(Sum of the first n terms)}$$

$$S_n = (a)+(ar)+(ar^2)+\cdots+(ar^{n-1})$$

$$\boxed{\text{③}}\,) \; rS_n = \boxed{\text{①}} + (ar^2)+\cdots+(ar^{n-1})+\boxed{\text{②}}$$

※ Geometric Series

Sum of first n terms: $S_n = \dfrac{a(1-r^n)}{1-r}$ — 1st term a, Common ratio r

EXAMPLE 4. Find the sum of the first n terms of the sequence.

① $4, -16, 64, -256, \ldots$ (6 term)
② $7, -21, 63, \ldots$ (5 term)

Blank : ① ar ② ar^n ③ $-$

536 Mia's Precalculus

③ $\sum_{k=1}^{3}\left(\frac{3}{4}\right)4^k$

④ $\sum_{k=0}^{3}\left(\frac{2}{3}\right)^{k+1}$

⑤ $\sum_{k=0}^{5}10\left(\frac{1}{5}\right)^k$

⑥ $\sum_{k=1}^{4}(0.1)^k$

3. Infinite Geometric Series

A geometric series that does not end is called an **infinite geometric series**.

If the common ratio $|r|\geq 1$(①_____), then the sum ②(diverges/converges).

ex) $1+2+4+8+16+\cdots$

If the common ratio $|r|<1$(③_____), then the sum ④(diverges/converges).

ex) $1+\dfrac{1}{2}+\dfrac{1}{4}+\dfrac{1}{8}+\dfrac{1}{16}+\cdots$

Blank : ① r≤-1 or r≥1   ② diverges   ③ -1<r<1   ④ converges

※ Infinite Geometric Series

For infinite geometric series, if the common ratio $|r|<1$, then the sum converges to $\dfrac{a}{1-r}$.

Sum of infinite terms
$$S_\infty = \sum_{k=1}^{\infty} ar^{n-1} = \dfrac{a}{1-r} \quad \text{when } -1 < r < 1$$

EXAMPLE 5. Determine whether the infinite series is convergent or divergent. If it is convergent, find its sum.

① $1 + \dfrac{1}{2} + \dfrac{1}{4} + \dfrac{1}{8} + \ldots$

② $1 + \dfrac{4}{3} + \left(\dfrac{4}{3}\right)^2 + \left(\dfrac{4}{3}\right)^3 + \ldots$

③ $\dfrac{2}{3} - 2 + 6 - \ldots$

④ $0.5 + 0.25 + 0.125 + \ldots$

⑤ $1 + 1.1 + 1.21 + 1.331 + \ldots$

⑥ $\dfrac{1}{\sqrt{2}} + \dfrac{1}{2} + \dfrac{1}{2\sqrt{2}} + \dfrac{1}{4} + \ldots$

⑦ $\sum_{k=1}^{\infty} 3(0.75)^{k-1}$

⑧ $\sum_{k=2}^{\infty} \left(\dfrac{2}{3}\right)^{k-1}$

⑨ $\sum_{k=0}^{\infty} 2(-0.1)^k$

⑩ $\sum_{k=1}^{\infty} (1.01)^k$

⑪ $\sum_{k=0}^{\infty} \left(-\dfrac{4}{5}\right)^k$

⑫ $\sum_{k=1}^{\infty} 2\left(\dfrac{2}{3}\right)^k$

⑬ $\sum_{k=1}^{\infty} \left(\dfrac{\pi}{2}\right)^k$

EXAMPLE 6. Express the rational number as a fraction of integers.

① 0.66666....

② 0.030303...

③ 0.234234234...

④ 0.2535353...

⑤ 0.1252525...

4. Expand Knowledge

EXAMPLE 7. * The sum of the first 6 terms of a geometric sequence is 6 and the sum to infinity is 12. Find the common ratio.

EXAMPLE 8. * The geometric series $(2-x)+(2-x)^2+(2-x)^3+...$ converges. What values can x take?

EXAMPLE 9. * Where does the number converge to?
$$\sqrt{2},\ \sqrt{2\sqrt{2}},\ \sqrt{2\sqrt{2\sqrt{2}}},\ \sqrt{2\sqrt{2\sqrt{2\sqrt{2}}}},\ ...$$

11.4 Applications of Sequence and Series

Mia's Precalculus

1. 3 Consecutive terms of Sequence

If we have 3 consecutive terms a, b, c;

arithmetic : ①_____

geometric : ②_____

EXAMPLE 1. Given the sequence 2, x, y, 9. If the first three terms form an arithmetic sequence and the last three terms form a geometric sequence, find x and y. ($2 < x < y < 9$)

EXAMPLE 2. The first three terms of a geometric sequence are $2x + 4$, $x + 5$, $x + 1$, where x is a real number.

(a) Find the two possible values of x.

Blank : ① $b - a = c - b$ ② $\dfrac{b}{a} = \dfrac{c}{b}$

(b) Given that it exists, find the sum to infinity of the series.

2. Applications

EXAMPLE 3. A brick patio has the approximate shape of a trapezoid (see figure). The patio has 20 rows of bricks. The first row has 12 bricks and the 20th row has 88 bricks. How many bricks are in the patio?

EXAMPLE 4. A straight bamboo stick of length 300 cm is cut into several pieces. The shortest piece is 1 cm long and the longest piece is 29 cm. If the length of the pieces forms an arithmetic sequence with common difference d, find d.

EXAMPLE 5. *Find the sum of all integers between 1 and 100 which are not multiples of 3.

EXAMPLE 6. A starting salary for a teacher is $25000 and there is an annual increase of 3%.
  (a) How much will the teacher earn in their tenth year?

  (b) How much will the teacher earn in total during a 35-year teaching career?

EXAMPLE 7. A ball is dropped from a height of 3 m. Each time it hits the ground it bounces up to 90% of its previous height.

(a) How high will it bounce after it strikes the ground for the 5th time?

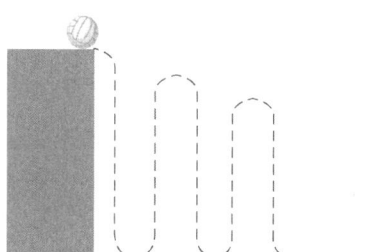

(b) What total distance does the ball travel before it stops bouncing?

EXAMPLE 8. The sides of a square are 16 inches in length. A new square is formed by connecting the midpoints of the sides of the original square, and two of the resulting triangles are shaded (see figure). If this process is repeated infinitely, determine the total area of the shaded region.

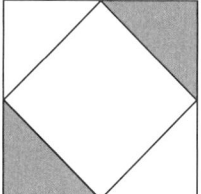 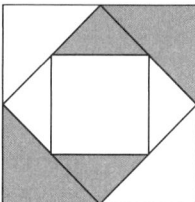 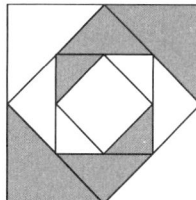 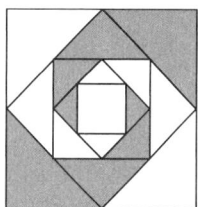

EXAMPLE 9. What fraction of the square is eventually shaded if the indicated shading process continues infinitely?

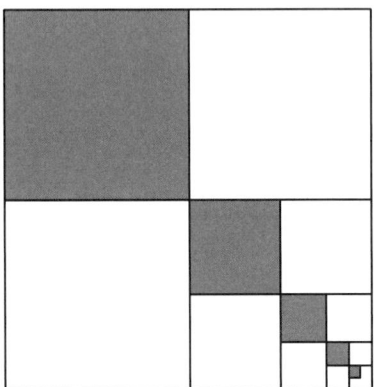

EXAMPLE 10. *An investor deposits $400 at the start of every year in an account that earns interest at the rate of 8% per year, compounded annually. How much will be in the account in the 10th year?

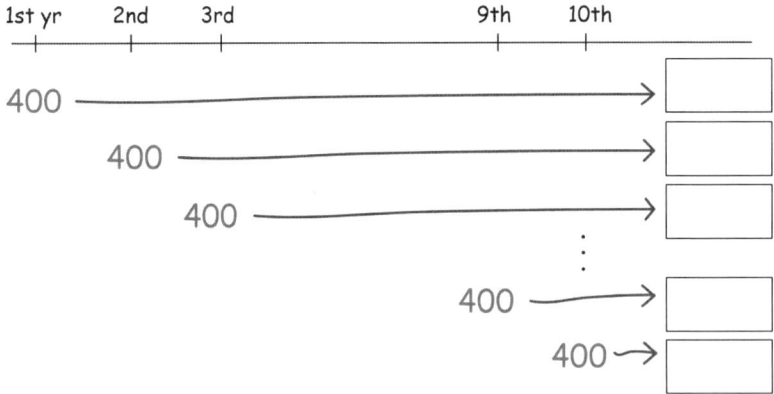

Mia's Precalculus
11.5 Binomial Expansion

1. Binomial Theorem

$$(a+b)^n$$

The **binomial theorem** shows how to calculate a *power of a binomial*.

We already know....

$$(a+b)^0 = 1$$

$$(a+b)^1 = a+b$$

$$(a+b)^2 = a^2 + 2ab + b^2$$

$$(a+b)^3 = a^3 + 3a^2b + 3ab^2 + b^3$$

Let's talk about the patterns here.

1) Patterns of Exponents of a and b

Notice that the

$$(a+b)^3 = a^3 + 3a^2b + 3ab^2 + b^3$$ exponents of a start at ①___ and go *down*

$$= a^3 + 3a^2b + 3ab^2 + b^3$$ exponents of b start at ②___ and go *up*

Blank : ① 3   ② 0

Part 11. Sequence and Series

2) Patterns of Coefficient

$$\begin{array}{cc} 1 & 1 \\ a+b & 1a+1b \\ a^2+2ab+b^2 & 1a^2+2ab+1b^2 \\ a^3+3a^2b+3ab^2+b^3 & 1a^3+3a^2b+3ab^2+1b^3 \end{array}$$

Pascal's Triangle

If we look at just the coefficients, you'll notice that it makes a ① _____ _____!

For $(a+b)^4$, exponents of a starts at ② _____ and go down.

exponents of b starts at ③ _____ and go up.

The coefficient goes ④ _____.

$(a+b)^4 = $ ⑤ _____

EXAMPLE 1. Use Pascal's triangle to Expand.

① $(x+2)^4$ ② $\left(x - \dfrac{2}{x}\right)^4$

Blank : ① pascal's triangle   ② 4   ③ 0   ④ 1, 4, 6, 4, 1   ⑤ $a^4 + 4a^3b + 6a^2b^2 + 4ab^3 + b^4$

③ $(2x-1)^5$ ④ $(3+x)^5$

⑤ $\left(x^2+\dfrac{1}{x}\right)^5$ ⑥ $(4x-3y)^3$

2. Binomial Coefficient

※ Factorial Notation :

$$n! = n \times (n-1) \times \cdots \times 3 \times 2 \times 1$$

It is generally agreed that $0! =$ ①_____ , and $(neg)! =$ ②_____.

※ Combination:

$$\,_nC_r = \binom{n}{r} = \dfrac{n!}{(n-r)!\,r!}$$

Blank : ① 1 (=1!) ② undefined

EXAMPLE 2. Evaluate.

① $6! \times 0!$

② $3! \times 2!$

EXAMPLE 3. Simplify without using a calculator:

① $\dfrac{3!}{6!}$

② $\dfrac{100!}{98!}$

③ $\dfrac{8!}{6! \times 2!}$

④ $\dfrac{7! \times 3!}{9!}$

⑤ $\dfrac{n!}{(n+1)!}$

⑥ $\dfrac{(n+2)!}{n!}$

⑦ $\dbinom{6}{2}$

⑧ $\dbinom{7}{4}$

⑨ $\dbinom{10}{0}$

⑩ $\dbinom{8}{8}$

※ Properties of Combination

$$\binom{n}{r} = \binom{n}{n-r} \qquad \binom{n}{0} = \binom{n}{n} = 1$$

EXAMPLE 4. Write $10 \times 11 \times 12$ as a ratio of two factorials.

EXAMPLE 5. Write $n \times (n-1) \times (n-2)$ as a ratio of two factorials.

3. Binomial Theorem Formula

And it matches to Pascal's Triangle like this:

$$\begin{array}{c} 1 \\ 1a + 1b \\ 1a^2 + 2ab + 1b^2 \\ 1a^3 + 3a^2b + 3ab^2 + 1b^3 \end{array} \qquad \begin{array}{c} \binom{0}{0} \\ \binom{1}{0} \binom{1}{1} \\ \binom{2}{0} \binom{2}{1} \binom{2}{2} \\ \binom{3}{0} \binom{3}{1} \binom{3}{2} \binom{3}{3} \end{array}$$

Pascal's Triangle

For $(a+b)^4$, exponents of a starts at ①_____ and go down.

exponents of b starts at ②_____ and go up.

The coefficient goes ③_____.

(using combination notation)

$(a+b)^4 =$ ④_____

So we can conclude that :

$$(a+b)^n = \underbrace{\binom{n}{0}a^n}_{\text{1st term}} + \underbrace{\binom{n}{1}a^{n-1}b^1}_{\text{2nd term}} + \underbrace{\binom{n}{2}a^{n-2}b^2}_{\text{3rd term}} + \cdots + \boxed{⑤} + \cdots + b^n$$

Now it can all go into one formula:

※ Binomial Theorem

$$(a+b)^n = \sum_{r=0}^{n} \binom{n}{r} a^{n-r} b^r$$

(adds up to same)

EXAMPLE 6. Find the coefficient of the given term from the expansion of ;

① $(2x-1)^8$; term x^3 ② $(2+x)^{10}$; term x^4

Blank : ① 4 ② 0 ③ $\binom{4}{0}, \binom{4}{1}, \binom{4}{2}, \binom{4}{3}, \binom{4}{4}$ ④ $\binom{4}{0}a^4 + \binom{4}{1}a^3b + \binom{4}{2}a^2b^2 + \binom{4}{3}ab^3 + \binom{4}{4}b^4$ ⑤ $\binom{n}{r}a^{n-r}b^r$

③ $(3-2x^2)^6$; term x^8

④ $(x^2-3)^7$; term x^6

⑤ $(x^2+4y)^8$; term $x^{10}y^3$

⑥ $\left(x-3y^3\right)^5$; term x^3y^6

⑦ $\left(2x+\dfrac{1}{x}\right)^{12}$; term x^8

⑧ $\left(x^2+\dfrac{4}{x}\right)^{12}$; term x^{15}

⑨ $\left(x-\dfrac{3}{\sqrt{x}}\right)^4$; term x

EXAMPLE 7. In the expansion of $\left(2x + \dfrac{1}{\sqrt{x}}\right)^9$. Find the constant term.

※ **General Term ($r+1$ th term)**

$$T_{r+1} = \binom{n}{r} a^{n-r} b^r \quad \text{($r+1$ th term)}$$

Careful! r needs to be **1 less than** the term number!

$$(a+b)^n = \binom{n}{0}a^n + \binom{n}{1}a^{n-1}b^1 + \binom{n}{2}a^{n-2}b^2 + \cdots + \binom{n}{r}a^{n-r}b^r + \cdots$$

(1st term, 2nd term, 3rd term, ① term)

EXAMPLE 8. Find the following;

① the 7th term of $\left(3x - \dfrac{1}{x^2}\right)^{10}$.

② the 6th term of $\left(2x - \dfrac{3}{x}\right)^9$.

(in this case r would be ___)

Blank : ① $r+1$

554 Mia's Precalculus

③ the 5th term of $\left(x^2+2y\right)^8$.

4. Expand Knowledge

EXAMPLE 9. * Find the coefficient of x^5 in the expansion of $(x+3)(2x-1)^6$.

EXAMPLE 10. * Find the coefficient of x^5 in the expansion of $(x+2)(x^2+1)^8$.

Mia's Precalculus
11.6 Mathematical Induction

1. Mathematical Induction Proving

There are a lot of ways to prove mathematical expressions or formula.
Mathematical Induction is a special way of proving things.

Let's think about dominos.

In order to get all of the dominoes to fall, two things need to happen:

1) The first domino must fall.
2) The dominos must be setup so that if any single domino falls, then the next one in the line will also fall.

Then ① _____ the dominos will fall.

Mathematical Induction has a similar idea with dominos.

※ Mathematical Induction in Mathematics

- Step1: Show that it is true for the ② _____ **one**. (when n = 1)
- Step2: Show that if ③ _____ **one** is true (n = k)

    then the ④ _____ **one** is true. (n = k+1)

Then **all** will be true!

Blank : ① all ② first ③ any ④ next

ex) Prove that $1+3+5+...+(2n-1)=n^2$ is true for all positive integers n.

Step1) Show it is true for n=1

For _____, the equation will be _____ = _____, which is _____.

Step2) Assume that it is true for n=k

Assume that _____ is _____.

Then, prove that it is true for "n=k+1"

If _____, then

$1+3+5+7+...+(2\boxed{}-1)+(2\boxed{}-1) = \boxed{} + (2k+\boxed{})$

$= k^2 + \boxed{} + \boxed{}$

$= \boxed{}$

The equation is _____ for n=k+1.

Therefore the statement is true for all positive integer, n, by mathematical induction.

1) Induction and Series

EXAMPLE 1. Prove that $1+5+9+...+(4n-3) = n(2n-1)$ is true for all positive integers n.

EXAMPLE 2. Prove that $1\times 3 + 2\times 4 + 3\times 5 + ... + n(n+2) = \dfrac{n(n+1)(2n+7)}{6}$ is true for all positive integers n.

2) Divisibility problems

EXAMPLE 3. The expression $f(n)$ is defined by $f(n) = 7^n - 1$ for all natural numbers n. Prove that $f(n)$ is divisible by 6 for all $n \in N$.

> If an expression is divisible by an integer 6, we can write it as A × 6 for some integer A.

EXAMPLE 4. Prove that $5^n - 2^n$ is evenly divisible by 3 for all positive integers n.

3) Induction and inequalities

EXAMPLE 5. Use induction to show that the inequality $2^n > 6n+1$ holds for all integers $n \geq 5$.

EXAMPLE 6. Use induction to show that the inequality $n! > 2^n$ holds for all integers $n \geq 4$.

Answers

Answers

1. Functions

※ Decimal answers are rounded to the nearest thousandth.

1.1 Quadratic Functions

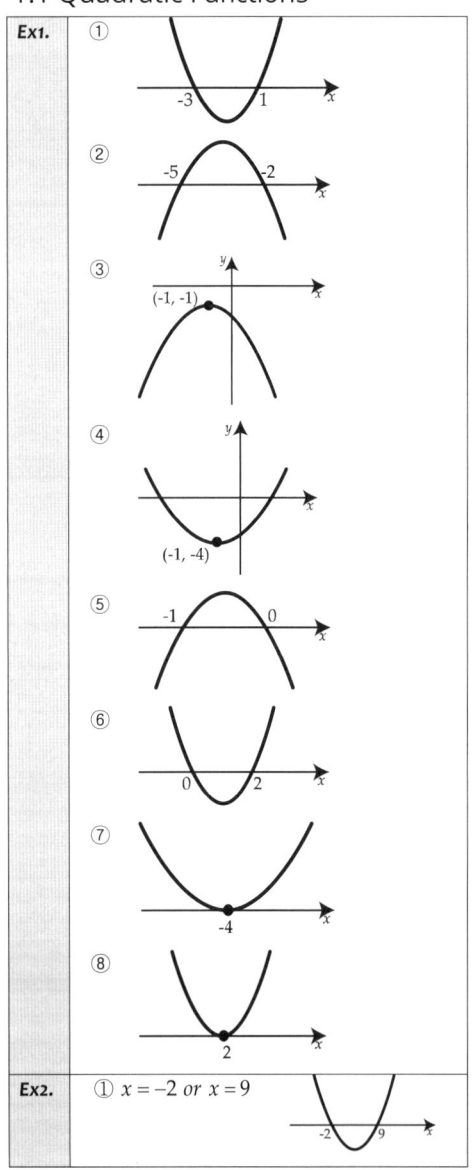

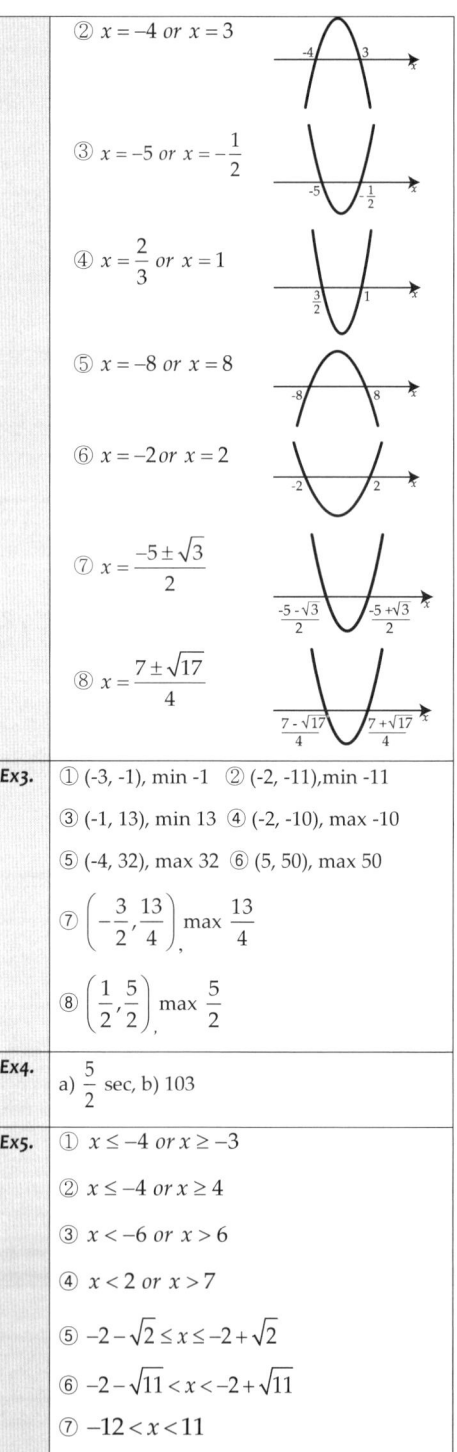

Ex3.	① (-3, -1), min -1 ② (-2, -11), min -11
	③ (-1, 13), min 13 ④ (-2, -10), max -10
	⑤ (-4, 32), max 32 ⑥ (5, 50), max 50
	⑦ $\left(-\dfrac{3}{2}, \dfrac{13}{4}\right)$, max $\dfrac{13}{4}$
	⑧ $\left(\dfrac{1}{2}, \dfrac{5}{2}\right)$, max $\dfrac{5}{2}$

Ex4.	a) $\dfrac{5}{2}$ sec, b) 103

Ex5.	① $x \leq -4 \text{ or } x \geq -3$
	② $x \leq -4 \text{ or } x \geq 4$
	③ $x < -6 \text{ or } x > 6$
	④ $x < 2 \text{ or } x > 7$
	⑤ $-2 - \sqrt{2} \leq x \leq -2 + \sqrt{2}$
	⑥ $-2 - \sqrt{11} < x < -2 + \sqrt{11}$
	⑦ $-12 < x < 11$

562 Mia's Precalculus

	⑧ $-3 \leq x \leq -1$
	⑨ $x < 2$ or $x > 2$ $(x \neq 2)$
	⑩ all real numbers $\mathbb{R}$
	⑪ all real numbers $\mathbb{R}$
	⑫ $x < 4$ or $x > 4$ $(x \neq 4)$
	⑬ $x = 5$
	⑭ no solution
Ex6.	① no real root
	② two distinct real roots
	③ two repeated real roots
	④ two repeated real roots
	⑤ two distinct real roots
	⑥ no real root
Ex7.	$k = \dfrac{1}{8}$
Ex8.	$k \leq -9$ or $k \geq -1$, $k \neq 0$
Ex9.	$(2, 3), (3, 5)$
Ex10.	$m = -2$ or $m = -6$
Ex11.	$k > -5$
Ex12.	$a + 2$
Ex13.	$\dfrac{1}{10^4}$
Ex14.	9
Ex15.	$\dfrac{4}{13}$ hours
Ex16.	14\$

1.2 Function

Ex1.	① Function ② Not a function
	③ Function ④ Not a function
	⑤ Not a function ⑥ Function
	⑦ Not a function ⑧ Not a function
	⑨ Not a function ⑩ Function
	⑪ Function ⑫ Not a function
Ex2.	① $5, 5+4h+h^2, 4+h$
	② $3, 3+2h, 2$
	③ $\dfrac{2}{3}, \dfrac{h+2}{h+3}, \dfrac{1}{3(h+3)}$
	④ $1, \dfrac{1}{h+1}, -\dfrac{1}{h+1}$
	⑤ $\sqrt{3}, \sqrt{3+h}, \dfrac{\sqrt{3+h}-\sqrt{3}}{h}$
Ex3.	① $\mathbb{R}$
	② $\mathbb{R}, x \leq \dfrac{4}{3}$
	③ $\mathbb{R}, x \neq \pm 2$
	④ $\mathbb{R}, x \neq 6$ or -1
	⑤ $\mathbb{R}$
	⑥ $\mathbb{R}$
	⑦ $\mathbb{R}, x \geq -4, x \neq 5$
	⑧ $\mathbb{R}, x \geq 2, x \neq 7$
	⑨ $\mathbb{R}, x > 5$
	⑩ $\mathbb{R}, x > 1$
	⑪ $\mathbb{R}, x \leq -1$ or $x \geq 4$
	⑫ $\mathbb{R}$
	⑬ $\mathbb{R}, -2 < x < 2$
	⑭ $\mathbb{R}, x \neq \pm\sqrt{5}$
	⑮ $\mathbb{R}, x \geq -3, x \neq 2$
	⑯ $\mathbb{R}, x > 3$
Ex4.	① Domain: $(2,5) \cup (5,8)$, Range: $[-1, 4)$
	② Domain: $\mathbb{R}$, Range: $(-\infty, 4]$
	③ Domain: $(-\infty, -4) \cup (-4, 4) \cup (4, \infty)$, Range: $(-\infty, -2] \cup (0, \infty)$
	④ Domain: $(-\infty, 0) \cup (0, \infty)$, Range: $(-\infty, 2) \cup (2, \infty)$

Ex5.	① $y = \dfrac{4-x^2}{2}$, Function
	② $y = \dfrac{1}{x^2-1}$, Function
	③ $y = -2 \pm \sqrt{4-x^2}$, Not a function
	④ $y = \pm 3\sqrt{\dfrac{x^2}{4}-1}$, Not a function
	⑤ $y = \sqrt[3]{x}$, Function
	⑥ $y = \pm\sqrt[4]{x}$, Not a function
Ex6.	$[-1, 2) \cup (2, 3]$
Ex7.	① $f(x) = 4(x-1)^2 + (x-1)$
	② $f(x) = \left(\dfrac{x}{2}\right)^2 - 1$
	③ $f(x) = \ln 2(x+1)$
Ex8.	21

1.3 Analyzing Functions

Ex1.	① even
	② odd
	③ odd
	④ neither
	⑤ even, odd
	⑥ even
	⑦ neither
Ex2.	① even
	② odd
	③ odd
	④ even
	⑤ neither
	⑥ neither
	⑦ even
	⑧ neither

	⑨ odd
	⑩ even
	⑪ odd
	⑫ odd
	⑬ odd
	⑭ neither
Ex3.	① Relative max : 4 (at $x = -4$)
	Relative min : -3 (at $x = 1$)
	② Absolute max : 4 (at $x = -4$)
	Absolute min : none
	③ $(-\infty, -4) \cup (1, 4)$
Ex4.	① 11
	② 2
	③ $-\dfrac{3}{7}$
	④ 1
	⑤ $\dfrac{2\sqrt{3}-3}{3}$
	⑥ $\dfrac{\sqrt{5}-1}{4}$
Ex5.	① odd
	② neither
	③ even
	④ even
	⑤ odd
Ex6.	4

1.4 Piecewise Functions

Ex1. ① Domain: $(-\infty,\infty)$
Range: $(1,\infty)$
Jump Discontinuity

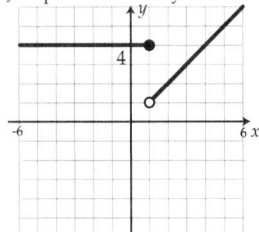

② Domain: $(-\infty,\infty)$
Range: $(-\infty,\infty)$
Continuous

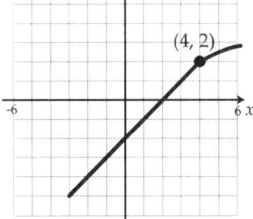

③ Domain: $(-\infty,\infty)$
Range: $(-\infty,0)\cup(0,\infty)$
Removable Discontinuity

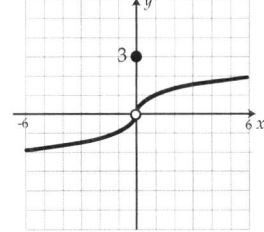

④ Domain: $(-\infty,\infty)$
Range: $(-\infty,0)\cup(0,\infty)$
Removable Discontinuity

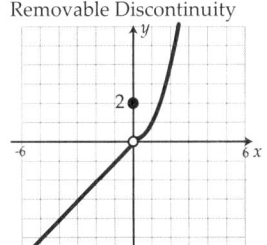

Ex2. ① $f(x)=\begin{cases}-2x-3, & x\leq 0\\ 2, & x>0\end{cases}$

② $f(x)=\begin{cases}1, & x<-2\\ -x+2, & x\geq -2\end{cases}$

③ $f(x)=\begin{cases}1, & x=1\\ \dfrac{1}{2}x-2, & x\neq 1\end{cases}$

④ $f(x)=\begin{cases}-3, & x=0\\ x^2, & x\neq 0\end{cases}$

⑤ $f(x)=\begin{cases}-2, & x\leq -2\\ x, & -2<x\leq 2\\ 2, & x>2\end{cases}$

Ex3. ① $f(0)=2$, $f(1)=2$, $f(3)=3$

② $g(27)=3$, $g(-2)=-\dfrac{1}{2}$, $g(0)=0$

③ $f(-4)=9$, $f(1)=2$, $f(2)=4$

Ex4. $b=2$

Ex5. ① 2
② 3
③ 5
④ −3
⑤ −4
⑥ −7

Ex6. −0.5

Ex7. 7

Ex8. 5

1.5 Transforming Function

Ex1. ①

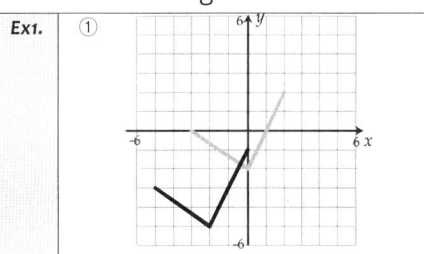

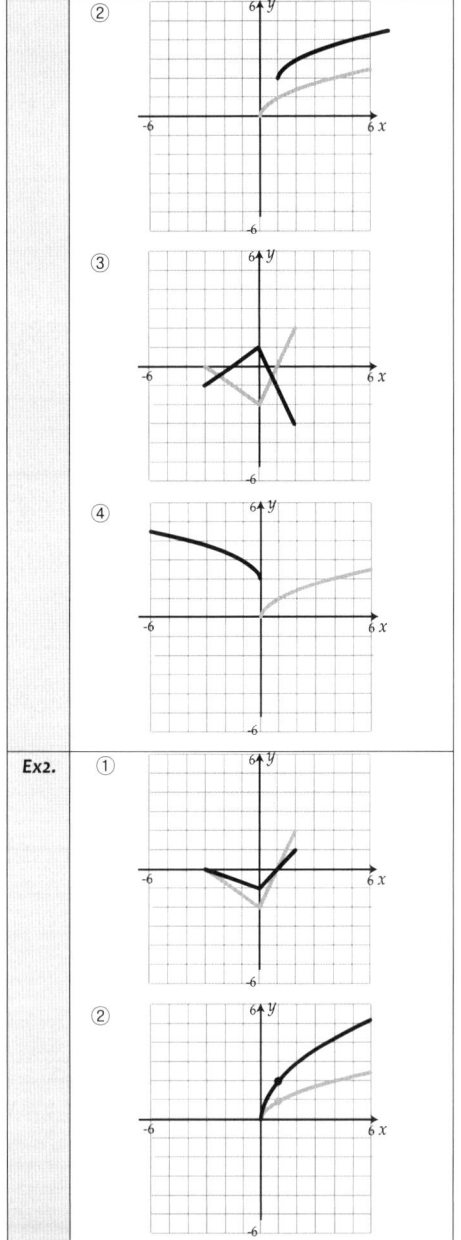
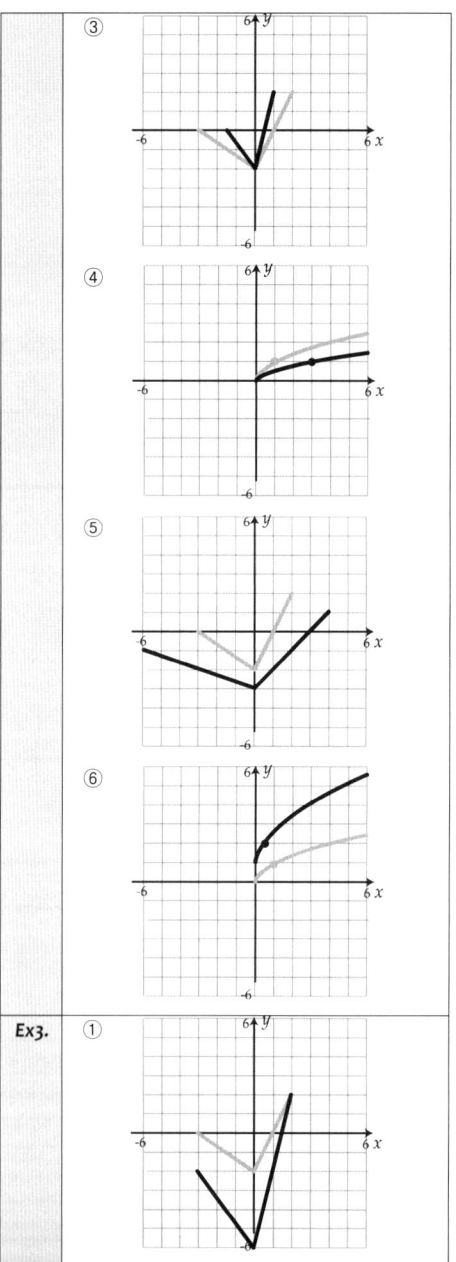

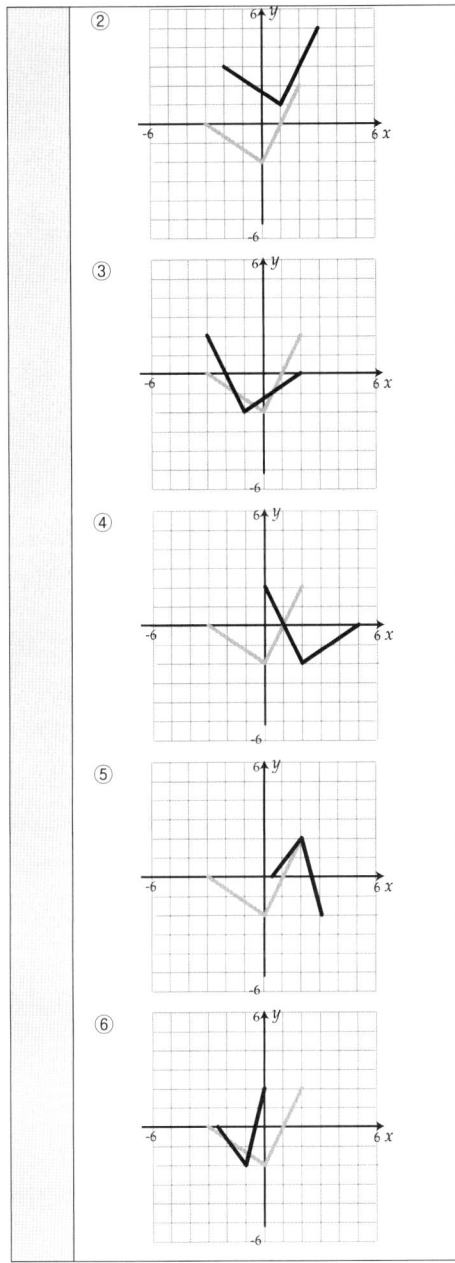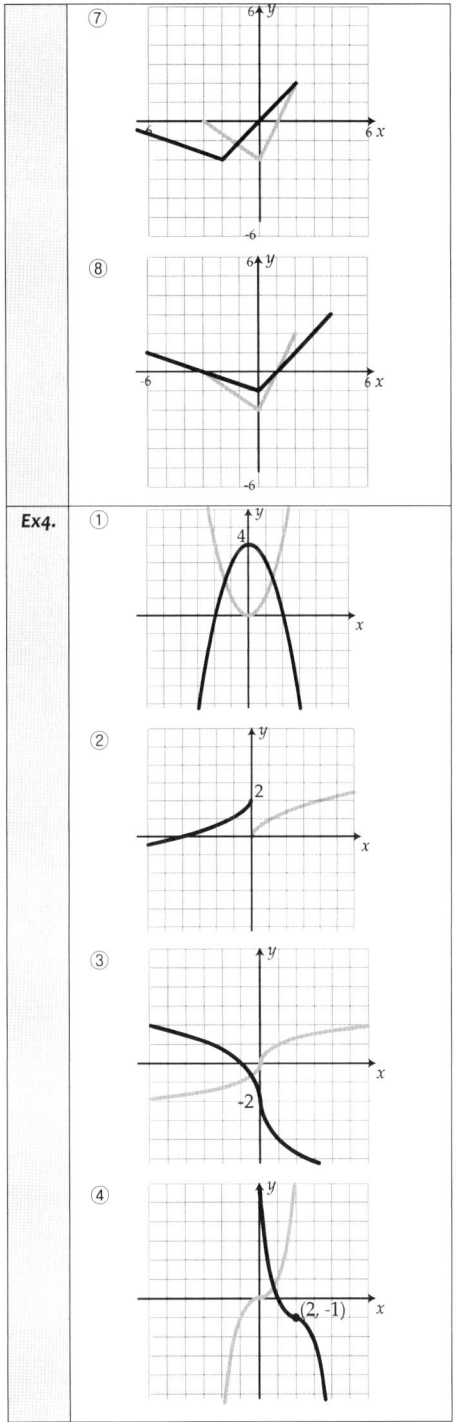

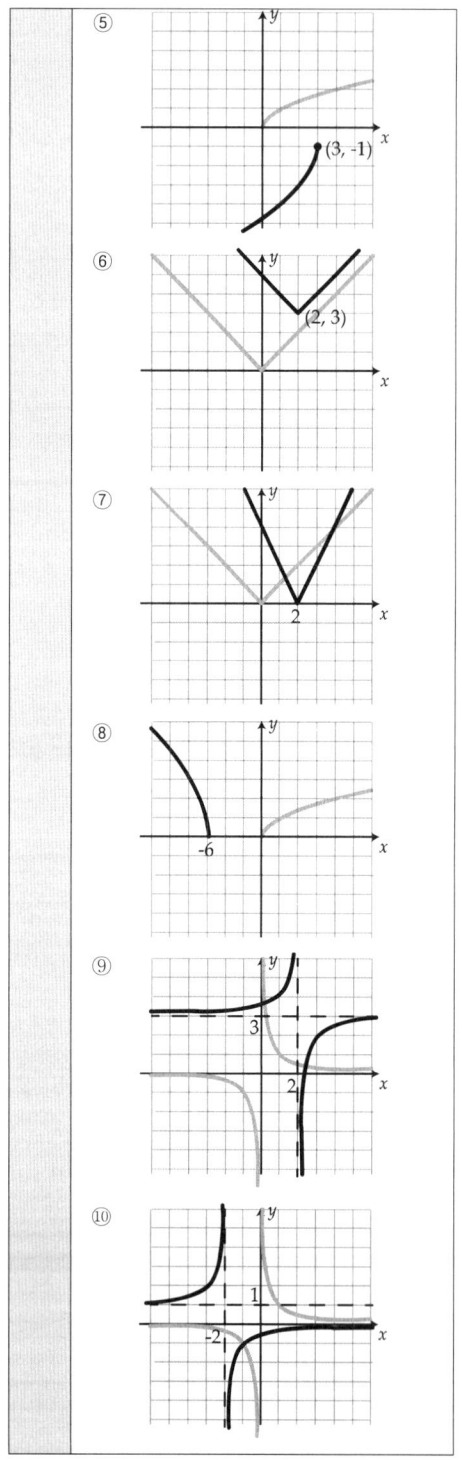
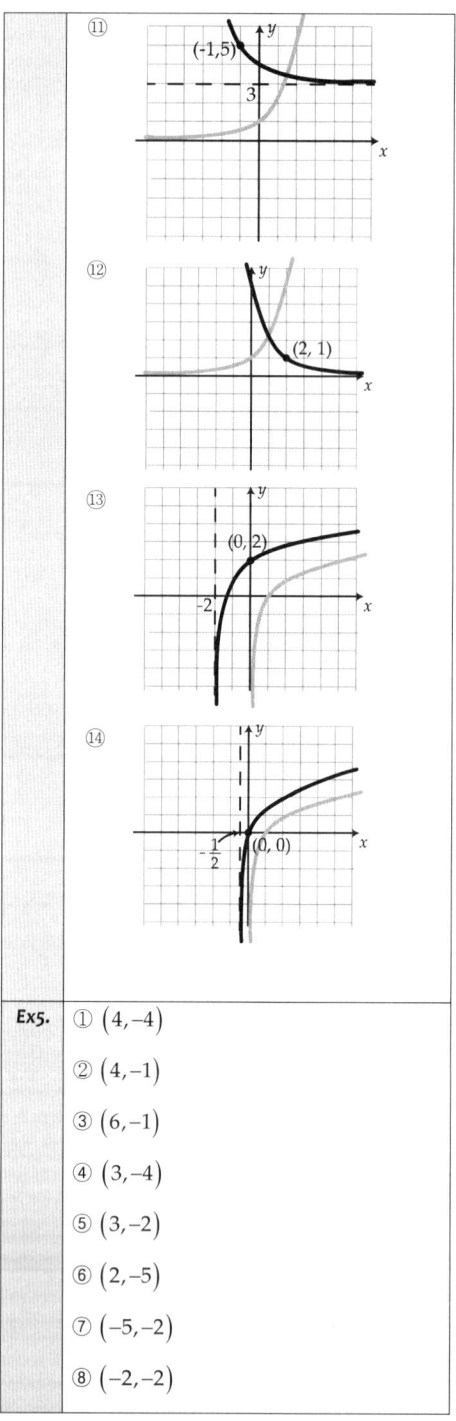

Ex5. ① $(4,-4)$

② $(4,-1)$

③ $(6,-1)$

④ $(3,-4)$

⑤ $(3,-2)$

⑥ $(2,-5)$

⑦ $(-5,-2)$

⑧ $(-2,-2)$

Ex6.

① $f(x) = \begin{cases} x-2, & x \geq 2 \\ 2-x & x < 2 \end{cases}$

② $f(x) = \begin{cases} 2-x, & x \leq 2 \\ x-2, & x > 2 \end{cases}$

③ $f(x) = \begin{cases} 1, & x > 1 \\ -1, & x < 1 \end{cases}$

④ $f(x) = \begin{cases} 1, & x > 0 \\ -1, & x < 0 \end{cases}$

⑤ $f(x) = \begin{cases} x^2 - 3x - 4, & x \leq -1 \text{ or } x \geq 4 \\ -(x^2 - 3x - 4), & -1 < x < 4 \end{cases}$

⑥ $f(x) = \begin{cases} x^2 - x, & x \leq 0 \text{ or } x \geq 1 \\ x - x^2, & 0 < x < 1 \end{cases}$

⑦ $f(x) = \begin{cases} 5, & x \leq 3 \\ 2x - 1, & x > 3 \end{cases}$

Ex7.

①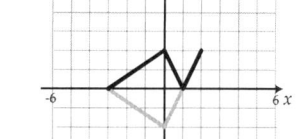

②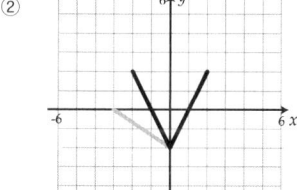

③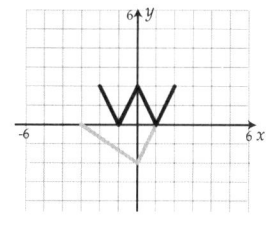

Ex8.

①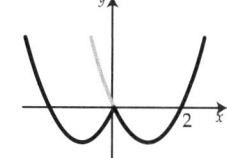

②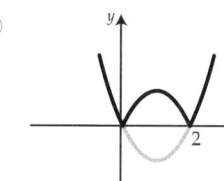

③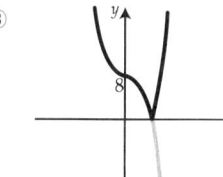

④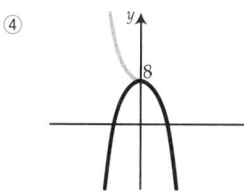

⑤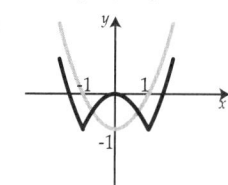

Ex9.

① $y = \sqrt{x+3} - 2$

② $y = \sqrt{x-2} + 7$

③ $y = \frac{1}{2}\sqrt{x} + 3$

④ $y = 2\sqrt{x+1} + 4$

⑤ $y = \sqrt{2x-1}$

⑥ $y = \sqrt{\frac{1}{2}(x+2)} - 1$

⑦ $y = 3\sqrt{-x+2} + 6$

⑧ $y = -2\sqrt{x+2} - 4$

	⑨ $y = -\sqrt{3(x-1)} - 3$
Ex10.	vertical stretch by factor 3 -> shifted left 6 -> shifted down 6
Ex11.	$a = 3$
Ex12.	$k = -\dfrac{1}{4}$
Ex13.	$x = 1, 6, -1, -6$

1.6 Composing Function

Ex1.	① $2\sqrt{x} + 3$
	② $\sqrt{2x+3}$
	③ $4x + 9$
	④ $\sqrt[4]{x}$
	⑤ 3
	⑥ 5
	⑦ $4\sqrt{x} + 9$
Ex2.	① 11
	② 10
	③ 13
	④ 6
Ex3.	① 1
	② 0
	③ 0
	④ 1
Ex4.	① $f(g(x)) = \dfrac{2}{2+3x}$ $D: x \ne 0, -\dfrac{2}{3}$
	$g(f(x)) = \dfrac{2(x+3)}{x}$ $D: x \ne 0, -3$
	② $f(g(x)) = \dfrac{x+4}{2}$ $D: x \ne -4$
	$g(f(x)) = \dfrac{2x}{1+2x}$ $D: x \ne -\dfrac{1}{2}, 0$
	③ $f(g(x)) = \sqrt[4]{1-x}$ $D: x \le 1$

	$g(f(x)) = \sqrt{1-\sqrt{x}}$ $D: 0 \le x \le 1$
	④ $f(g(x)) = (x-2)^{\frac{1}{4}}$ $D: x \ge 2$
	$g(f(x)) = \sqrt{\sqrt{x}-2}$ $D: x \ge 4$
	⑤ $f(g(x)) = x$ $D: x \ge 0$
	$g(f(x)) = |x|$ $D: \mathbb{R}$
	⑥ $f(g(x)) = x - 3$ $D: x \ge 3$
	$g(f(x)) = \sqrt{x^2 - 3}$ $D: x \le -\sqrt{3}$ or $x \ge \sqrt{3}$
Ex5.	※ Answers may vary
	① $g(x) = x^2 + 1$, $f(x) = \sqrt{x}$
	② $g(x) = x^3 + x + 1$, $f(x) = \dfrac{1}{x^2}$
	③ $g(x) = \sqrt{x+1}$, $f(x) = x^2 + 2x + 3$
	④ $g(x) = x - 3$, $f(x) = x^2 + 2x - 5$
Ex6.	$g(x) = 4x - 1$
Ex7.	$f(x) = 4x - 19$
Ex8.	$f(x+1) = \dfrac{2x-1}{3}$
Ex9.	4
Ex10.	$10 + x$
Ex11.	$\dfrac{x}{1-30x}$

1.7 Inverse Function

Ex1.	① One to one function
	② Not a function
	③ just function
	④ just function
	⑤ Not a function
	⑥ One to one function
	⑦ One to one function
	⑧ Not a function

	⑨ just function
	⑩ One to one function
	⑪ Not a function
	⑫ One to one function
Ex2.	① 6
	② 10
	③ 10
	④ 11
	⑤ 3
	⑥ 10
	⑦ 11
	⑧ −4
Ex3.	① −1
	② 1
	③ 0
	④ −2
	⑤ 1
	⑥ $\frac{1}{2}$
	⑦ −4
	⑧ 2
	⑨ −1
	⑩ −1
Ex4.	① $f^{-1} = \frac{x-7}{6}$
	② $f^{-1} = \frac{4}{x}$
	③ $f^{-1} = \frac{\sqrt[3]{2(x-2)}+3}{2}$
	④ $f^{-1} = \left(\frac{x}{2}\right)^3 - 1$
	⑤ $f^{-1} = \sqrt{x-1}$
	⑥ $f^{-1} = -\sqrt{x-1}$
	⑦ $f^{-1} = 2 - \sqrt{x-3}$
	⑧ $f^{-1} = 3 - \sqrt{\frac{x}{2}}$
	⑨ $f^{-1} = \frac{-3x-6}{7x+2}$
	⑩ $f^{-1} = \frac{2x+4}{x+3}$
	⑪ $f^{-1} = \frac{2-3x}{x}$
	⑫ $f^{-1} = \frac{2x}{-x-3}$
Ex5.	① $f^{-1}(x) = \{(0,6), (1,-1), (2,-3), (-5,3)\}$ function
	② $g^{-1}(x) = \{(5,-7), (7,-5), (5,6), (9,-6)\}$ Not a function
Ex6.	Answers may vary
	① $f^{-1} = \sqrt[3]{x} + 2$
	② $f^{-1} = x^2 + 2$
	③ D: $x \geq -2$, $f^{-1} = \sqrt{x+1} - 2$
	④ D: $x \geq 1$, $f^{-1} = \sqrt{x-2} + 1$
	⑤ D: $x \geq -1$, $f^{-1} = x - 1$
	⑥ D: $x \geq -1$, $f^{-1} = \sqrt{x-1} - 1$
Ex7.	① 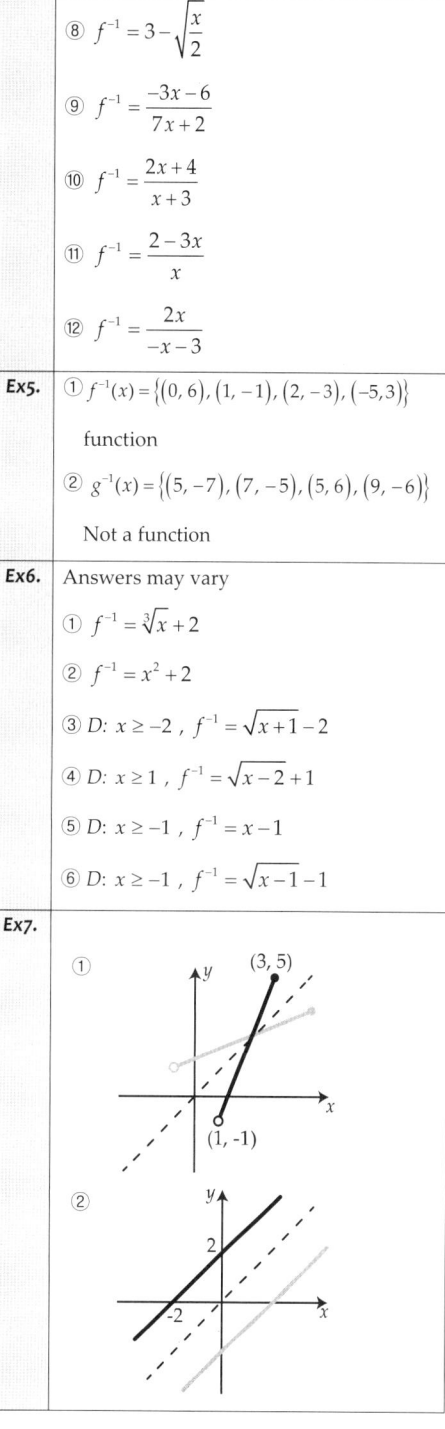 ②

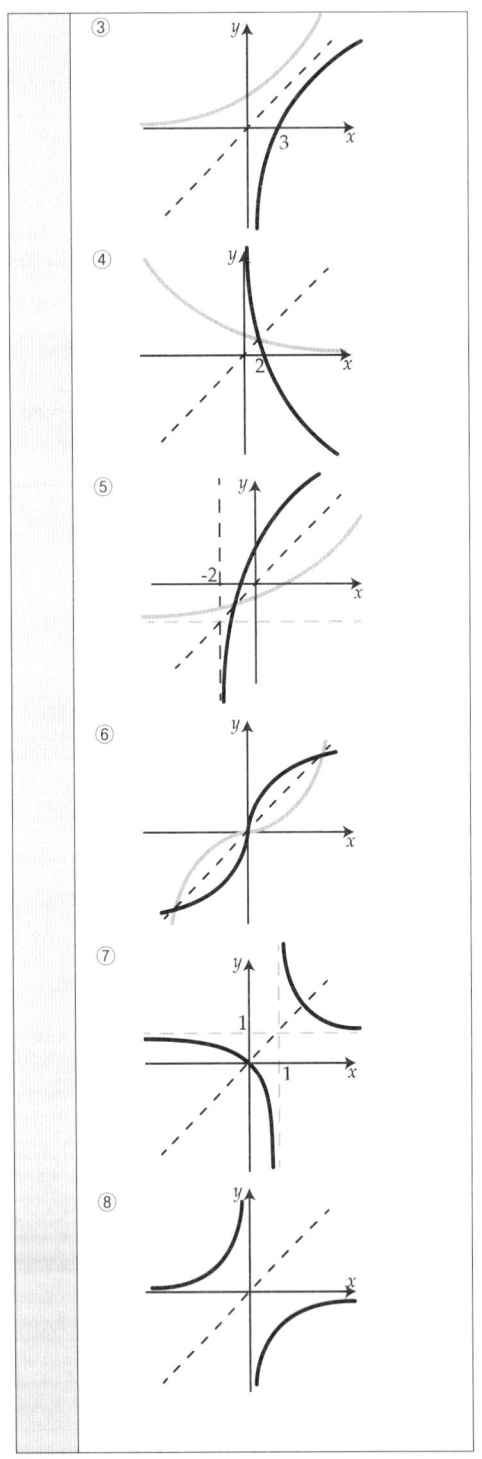

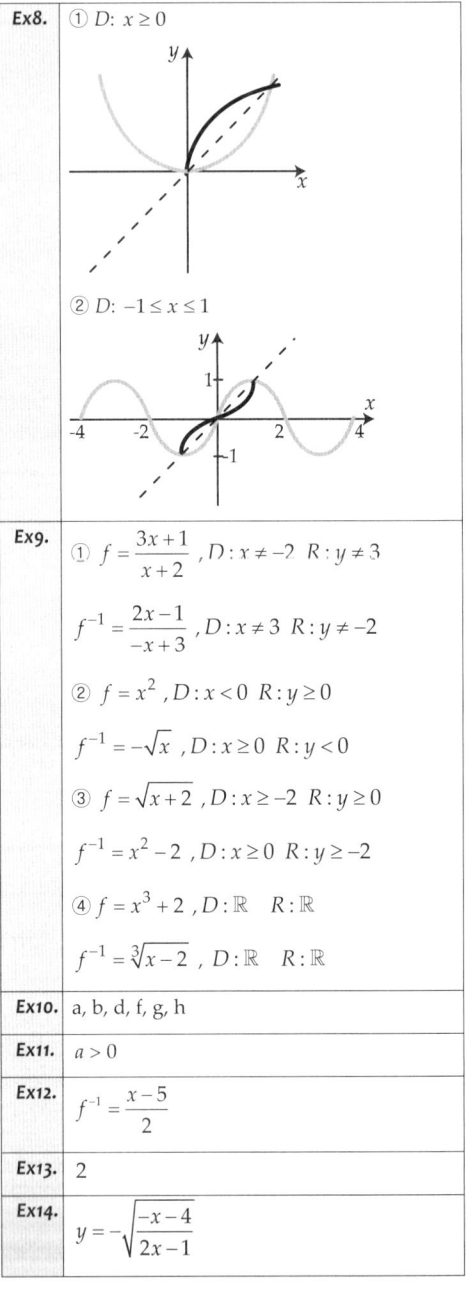

Ex8.	① $D: x \geq 0$
	② $D: -1 \leq x \leq 1$
Ex9.	① $f = \dfrac{3x+1}{x+2}$, $D: x \neq -2$ $R: y \neq 3$ $f^{-1} = \dfrac{2x-1}{-x+3}$, $D: x \neq 3$ $R: y \neq -2$ ② $f = x^2$, $D: x < 0$ $R: y \geq 0$ $f^{-1} = -\sqrt{x}$, $D: x \geq 0$ $R: y < 0$ ③ $f = \sqrt{x+2}$, $D: x \geq -2$ $R: y \geq 0$ $f^{-1} = x^2 - 2$, $D: x \geq 0$ $R: y \geq -2$ ④ $f = x^3 + 2$, $D: \mathbb{R}$ $R: \mathbb{R}$ $f^{-1} = \sqrt[3]{x-2}$, $D: \mathbb{R}$ $R: \mathbb{R}$
Ex10.	a, b, d, f, g, h
Ex11.	$a > 0$
Ex12.	$f^{-1} = \dfrac{x-5}{2}$
Ex13.	2
Ex14.	$y = -\sqrt{\dfrac{-x-4}{2x-1}}$

Answers

2. Polynomial and Rational Functions

2.1 Polynomial Functions

Ex1.	① Polynomial, 4
	② Not a Polynomial
	③ Not a Polynomial
	④ Polynomial, 0
	⑤ Polynomial, 5
	⑥ Polynomial, 1
	⑦ Not a Polynomial
	⑧ Polynomial, 0
Ex2.	① As $x \to -\infty$, $y \to \infty$ As $x \to \infty$, $y \to \infty$
	② As $x \to -\infty$, $y \to \infty$ As $x \to \infty$, $y \to -\infty$
	③ As $x \to -\infty$, $y \to \infty$ As $x \to \infty$, $y \to -\infty$
	④ As $x \to -\infty$, $y \to \infty$ As $x \to \infty$, $y \to \infty$
	⑤ As $x \to -\infty$, $y \to -\infty$ As $x \to \infty$, $y \to -\infty$
	⑥ As $x \to -\infty$, $y \to -\infty$ As $x \to \infty$, $y \to \infty$
Ex3.	①

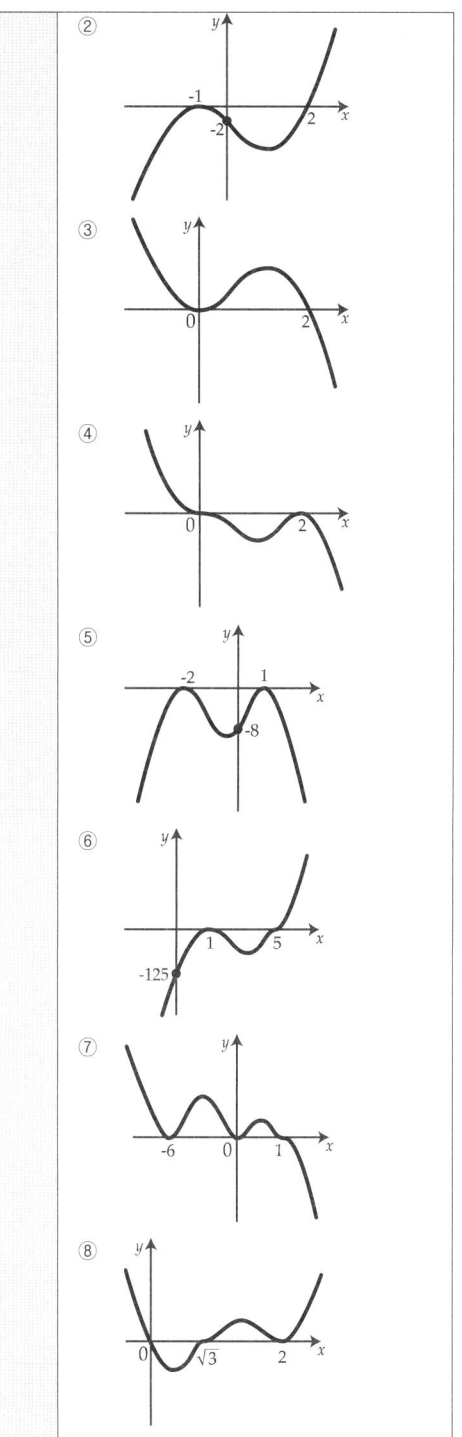

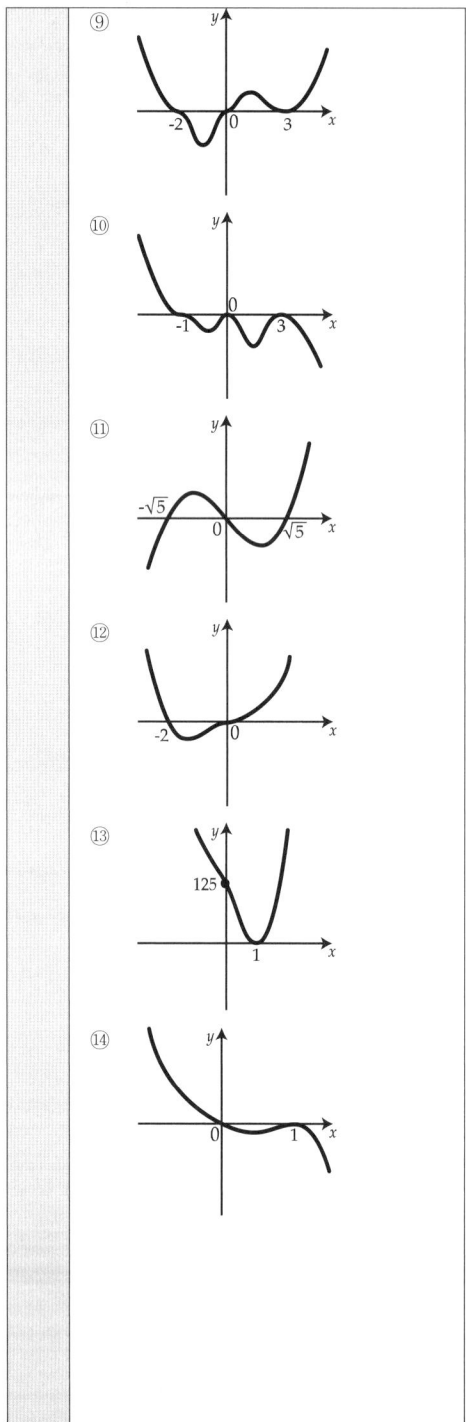
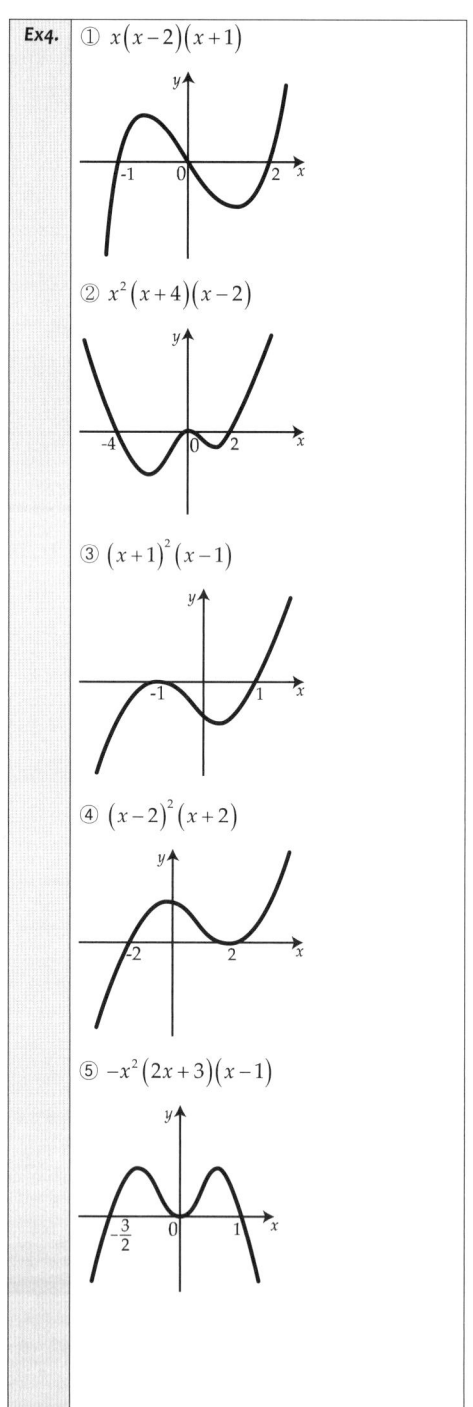

	⑥ $x^2(x+2)(x^2-2x+4)$ 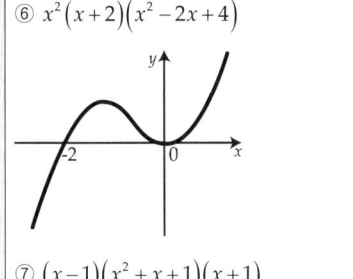 ⑦ $(x-1)(x^2+x+1)(x+1)$ 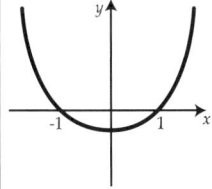
Ex5.	① $2(x+1)(x-3)^2$ ② $-4x^2(x-2)$ ③ $2x^2(x+3)(x+1)$ ④ $-(x+1)(x-2)^3$ ⑤ $-\dfrac{1}{2}x(x-1)(x-3)^3$
Ex6.	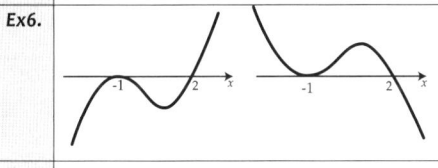
Ex7.	one

2.2 Diving Polynomials

Ex1.	① $x-9+\dfrac{30x-54}{x^2-3}$ ② $x+2+\dfrac{8x-2}{x^2-2x+2}$ ③ $4x^2-20x+100-\dfrac{503}{x+5}$ ④ $3x^2-8x+2+\dfrac{4x-2}{x^2+x+2}$

Ex2.	① x^2-6x+9 ② $3x^2-7x+24-\dfrac{95}{x+4}$ ③ $x^2-2x-4+\dfrac{10}{x+2}$ ④ $5x^2-14x+42-\dfrac{129}{x+3}$ ⑤ $x^3+4x^2+11x+44+\dfrac{166}{x-4}$ ⑥ $2x^3-6x^2-12x-24-\dfrac{40}{x-2}$ ⑦ $x^2+\dfrac{5}{2}x+\dfrac{1}{4}+\dfrac{\tfrac{13}{4}}{2x-1}$ ⑧ $3x^2-\dfrac{1}{2}x+\dfrac{7}{4}+\dfrac{\tfrac{29}{4}}{2x-3}$
Ex3.	① 23 ② 2 ③ 3 ④ 6
Ex4.	① 21 ② 860 ③ $\dfrac{1}{3}$ ④ $\dfrac{49}{64}$
Ex5.	$\dfrac{3}{2}$
Ex6.	① Not Factor ② Factor ③ Factor ④ Not Factor ⑤ Factor
Ex7.	$\dfrac{1}{3}$
Ex8.	2
Ex9.	$q=2$, $p=3$

Ex10.	$a=-4$, $b=0$
Ex11.	-1

2.3 Real Zeros of Poly

Ex1.	① $\pm 1, \pm 2, \pm \dfrac{1}{2}, \pm \dfrac{1}{3}, \pm \dfrac{2}{3}, \pm \dfrac{1}{6}$
	② $\pm 1, \pm 2, \pm 4, \pm 8, \pm \dfrac{1}{2}$
	③ $\pm 1, \pm 2, \pm 4, \pm 8, \pm \dfrac{1}{5}, \pm \dfrac{2}{5}, \pm \dfrac{4}{5}, \pm \dfrac{8}{5}$
	④ $\pm 1, \pm 7, \pm \dfrac{1}{2}, \pm \dfrac{7}{2}, \pm \dfrac{1}{4}, \pm \dfrac{7}{4}$
Ex2.	① pos : 1 , neg : 2, 0
	② pos : 3, 1 , neg : 1
	③ pos : 3, 1 , neg : 0
	④ pos : 4, 2, 0 , neg : 3, 1
Ex3.	$(x-2)(2x-1)(x+3)$
Ex4.	① $(x-2)(x+2)(x+3)$
	② $(x+1)(x+2)(2x-1)$
	③ $(x+1)(2x^2+2x+3)$
	④ $(x-2)(2x^2-3x+3)$
	⑤ $(x+1)^2(x-4)(x+2)$
	⑥ $(x-1)(x+1)(x+3)(x+5)$
Ex5.	① $f(1) = 2-6+1 < 0$
	$f(2) = 16-12+1 > 0$
	According to IVT, there must be a zero in [1, 2]
	② $f(0) < 0$
	$f(1) = 1+5-3 > 0$
	According to IVT, there must be a zero in [0, 1]
	③ $f(0) = 0 < 2$
	$f(2) > 2$
	According to IVT, there must be a x such that f(x) = 2 in [0, 2]
Ex6.	① 3
	② 4

2.4 Fundamental Theorem of Algebra

Ex1.	① real :0 / img : 2
	② real :2 / img : 0
	③ real :3 / img : 0
	④ real :1 / img : 2
	⑤ real :2 (1 repeated) / img : 0
	⑥ real :3 (1 repeated) / img : 0
	⑦ real :2 / img : 2
	⑧ real :0 / img : 6
	⑨ real :1 / img : 4
	⑩ real :4 (1 repeated) / img : 0
Ex2.	① $x = 0, \pm i$
	$x(x+i)(x-i)$
	② $x = 0, \pm 2i$
	$x^2(x+2i)(x-2i)$
	③ $x = -2, \dfrac{-3 \pm \sqrt{7}i}{2}$
	$(x+2)\left(x - \dfrac{-3+\sqrt{7}i}{2}\right)\left(x - \dfrac{-3-\sqrt{7}i}{2}\right)$
	④ $x = 1, 1 \pm \sqrt{2}i$
	$(x-1)(x-1+\sqrt{2}i)(x-1-\sqrt{2}i)$
	⑤ $x = 3, \pm\sqrt{2}i$

	$(x-3)(x-\sqrt{2}i)(x+\sqrt{2}i)$
	⑥ $x = \pm i, \pm 2\sqrt{2}i$
	$(x+i)(x-i)(x+2\sqrt{2}i)(x-2\sqrt{2}i)$
	⑦ $x = \pm 2, \pm 2\sqrt{2}i$
	$(x+2)(x-2)(x+2\sqrt{2}i)(x-2\sqrt{2}i)$
Ex3.	① $x^2 - 2x + 5$ ② $x^2 - 6x + 10$ ③ $x^3 - 2x^2 - 3x + 10$ ④ $x^3 + x^2 + 9x + 9$ ⑤ $x^5 + 2x^4 + 5x^3 + 10x^2 + 4x + 8$
Ex4.	$3, 2+3i$
Ex5.	① sum : 2 / prod : $-\dfrac{5}{2}$ ② sum : -3 / prod : -7 ③ sum : 3 / prod : 1 ④ sum : $\dfrac{7}{2}$ / prod : 1 ⑤ sum : 0 / prod : 36 ⑥ sum : 0 / prod : -1 ⑦ sum : $\dfrac{5}{3}$ / prod : 0 ⑧ sum : -1 / prod : 0
Ex6.	$\dfrac{5}{4}$
Ex7.	$a = -2, b = 45$
Ex8.	$3, 2+3i$
Ex9.	$a = -3$
Ex10.	$b = 12, c = -16$
Ex11.	$x^2 + 6x + 13$
Ex12.	$x^2 - 2x + 49$
Ex13.	$2x^2 - 8x + 15$
Ex14.	$m = \dfrac{1}{2}, k = \dfrac{5}{2}$

2.5 Rational Function

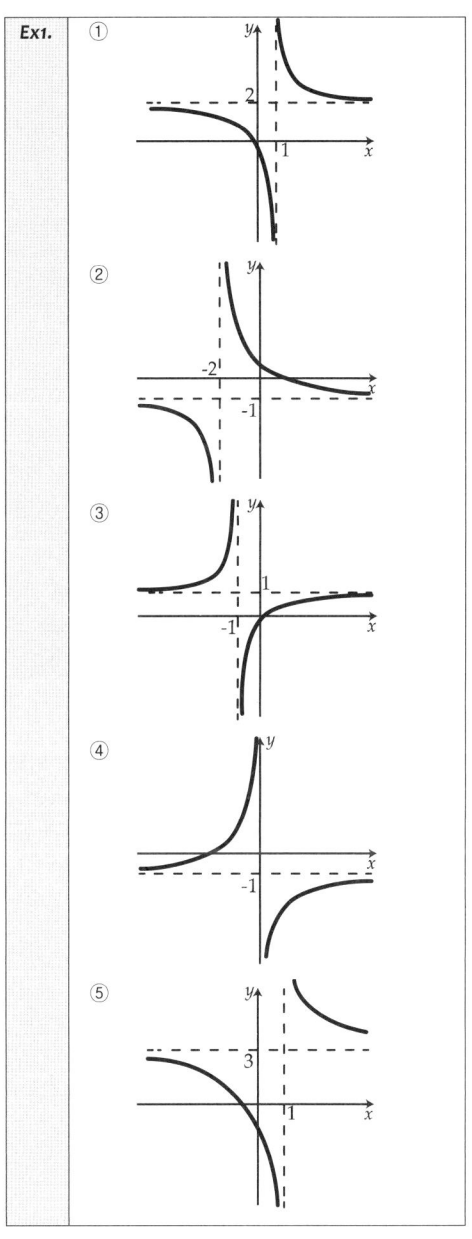

Answers 577

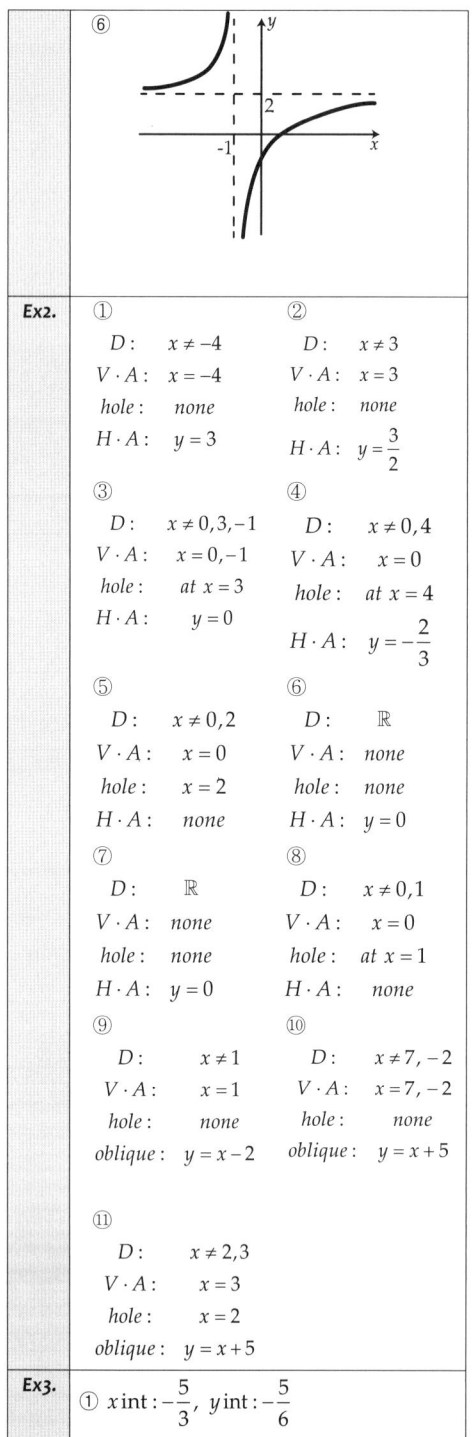
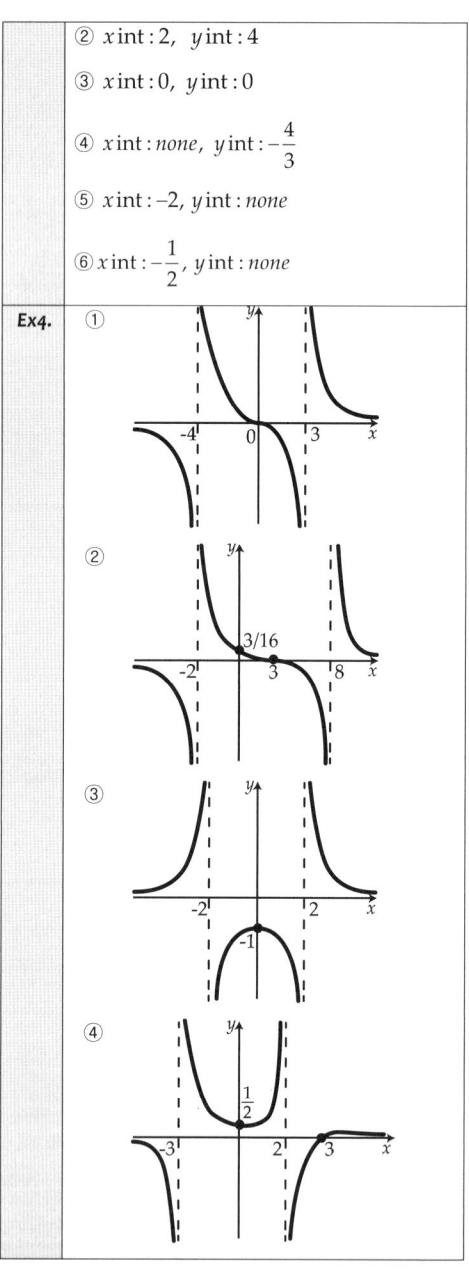

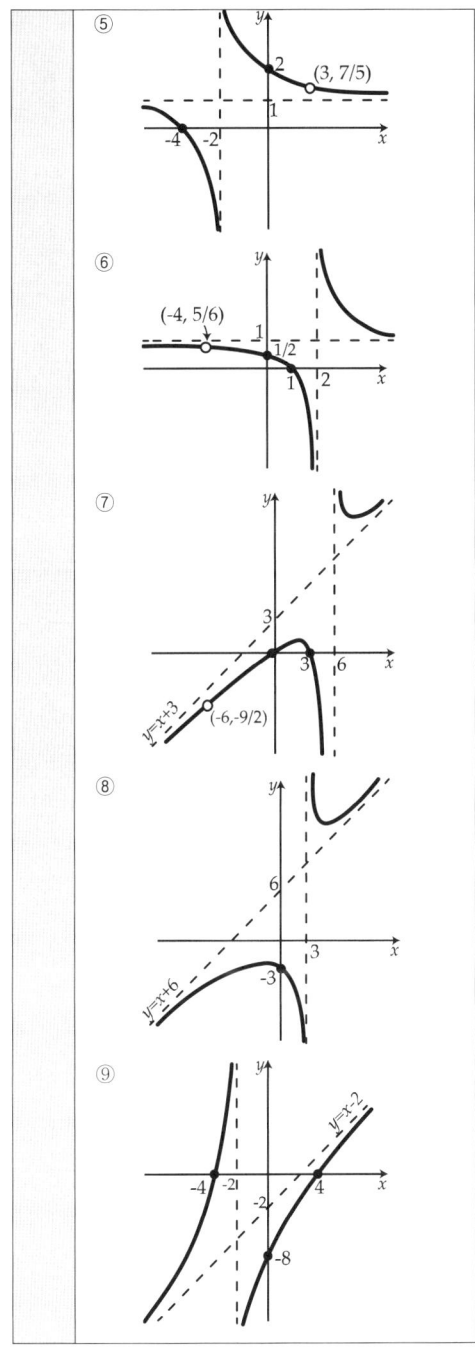
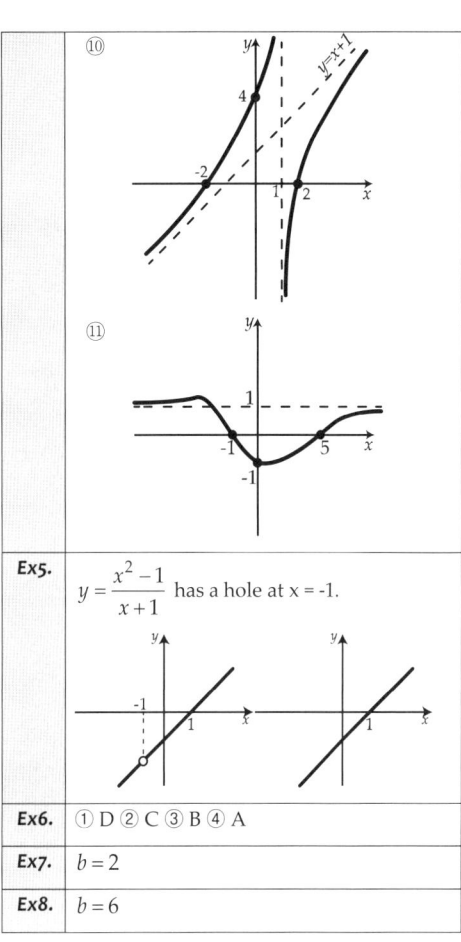

Ex6.	① D ② C ③ B ④ A
Ex7.	$b = 2$
Ex8.	$b = 6$

2.6 Polynomial and Rational Function Inequalities

Ex1.	① $(-3, 3) \cup (5, 7)$
	② $(-\infty, -2] \cup [2, \infty)$
	③ 1
	④ $[-7, -3], x = 0$
	⑤ (i) $(-\infty, -4) \cup (-4, 10)$
	(ii) $(-\infty, -8) \cup (2, 10)$
	⑥ (i) $(0, \infty)$
	(ii) $(-\infty, 0]$

	⑦ (i) $(-\infty, -10], x = 0$ (ii) $[-8, -4] \cup [6, \infty)$ ⑧ (i) $(-\infty, -8] \cup [-2, \infty)$ (ii) $(-9, 0) \cup (0, 5)$
Ex2.	① $(-\infty, -1) \cup (3, 5)$ ② $(-2, 0) \cup \left(\dfrac{1}{2}, \infty\right)$ ③ $(-\infty, -2) \cup (-2, 0) \cup (1, \infty)$ ④ $(-\infty, 0) \cup (0, 2) \cup (3, \infty)$ ⑤ $x = -1, [0, 1], x = 3$ ⑥ $(-\infty, -2] \cup [0, \infty)$ ⑦ $x = -1, [0, \infty)$ ⑧ $(-\infty, 1]$ ⑨ $(-\infty, -3) \cup (-2, 2) \cup (3, \infty)$ ⑩ $(-2, 0) \cup (9, \infty)$ ⑪ $(-6, 0) \cup (0, 6)$ ⑫ $[5, \infty), x = 0$ ⑬ $\left(-8, -\dfrac{5}{2}\right) \cup (2, \infty)$ ⑭ $[-5, -2] \cup [2, \infty)$
Ex3.	① $(-4, -2) \cup (4, \infty)$ ② $(-\infty, 4) \cup (8, \infty)$ ③ $(-\infty, -2] \cup (4, 8) \cup (8, \infty)$ ④ $(-2, 0]$
Ex4.	① $(-\infty, -1) \cup [7, \infty)$ ② $(-\infty, -5) \cup (4, \infty)$ ③ $(-\infty, -6)$ ④ $(-\infty, -9) \cup (10, \infty)$ ⑤ $(-3, -2), x = -1, [3, \infty)$

	⑥ $(-\infty, -1) \cup (-1, 1)$ ⑦ $(-\infty, 1) \cup (3, \infty)$ ⑧ $(7, 12], x = -2, x = 0$ ⑨ $(-\infty, -2) \cup (0, 2)$ ⑩ $(-\infty, -2] \cup [2, \infty)$ ⑪ $[0, 2] \cup (5, \infty)$ ⑫ $(-1, 0) \cup (7, \infty)$ ⑬ $(-\infty, -19] \cup (1, 5)$
Ex5.	$(-4, 0] \cup (4, \infty)$
Ex6.	$x \neq \pm 5$
Ex7.	$(-1, 5)$
Ex8.	$(-\infty, 0] \cup [2, 7]$

Answers

3. Exponential and Log Functions

3.1 Exponential Function

Ex1.
① 1
② 2^{4n-3}
③ $x+y$
④ $\dfrac{1}{x+y}$
⑤ $x^{\frac{3}{4}}$
⑥ $a^{\frac{7}{8}}$
⑦ $a^{\frac{5}{3}}$
⑧ $a^{\frac{1}{2}}$
⑨ $\dfrac{1}{x^{\frac{1}{24}}}$
⑩ $\dfrac{1}{x^{\frac{1}{24}}}$
⑪ $a-b$
⑫ $a-b$

Ex2.
① $2^n \cdot 9$
② $2^3(2^n+1)$
③ $2^n \cdot 12$
④ 2^m
⑤ $(6^x-2)(6^x-9)$
⑥ $(2^x-3)(2^x+2)$
⑦ $(3^x+4)(3^x-1)$
⑧ $(5^x-6)(5^x+1)$
⑨ $(3^x+2^x)(3^x-2^x)$
⑩ $(5-4^x)(5+4^x)$
⑪ 2^n
⑫ 4^n

Ex3.

① $\mathbb{R}$, $y>0$, $y=0$, $(-2, 1)$

② $\mathbb{R}$, $y>0$, $y=0$, 1

③ $\mathbb{R}$, $y>-2$, $y=-2$, $(1, -1)$

④ $\mathbb{R}$, $y<1$, $y=1$

⑤ $\mathbb{R}$, $y<1$, $y=1$

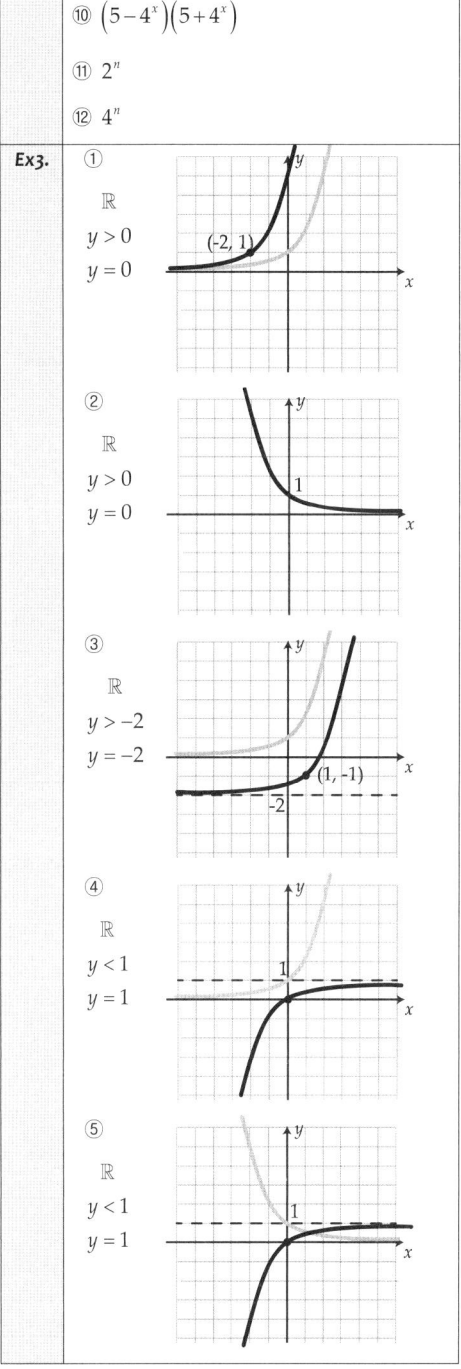

	⑥ $\mathbb{R}$ $y > -2$ $y = -2$	
Ex4.	① $y = 0$	
	② $y = 1$	
	③ $y = -1$	
	④ $y = -3$	

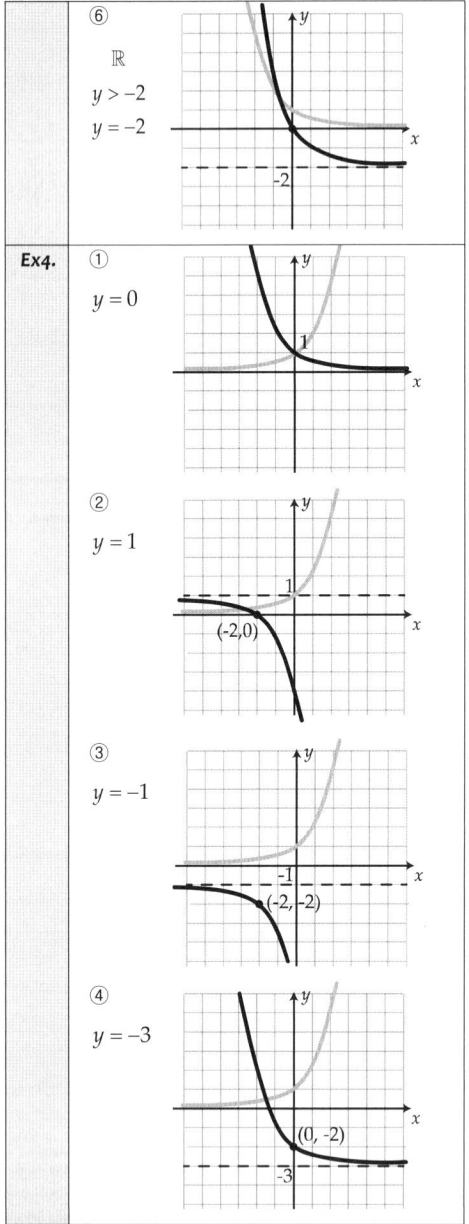

	⑤ $y = -2$
	⑥ $y = 0$
	⑦ $y = -3$
	⑧ $y = 0$
Ex5.	$\dfrac{1}{16}$
Ex6.	80
Ex7.	3
Ex8.	IV, V, VI

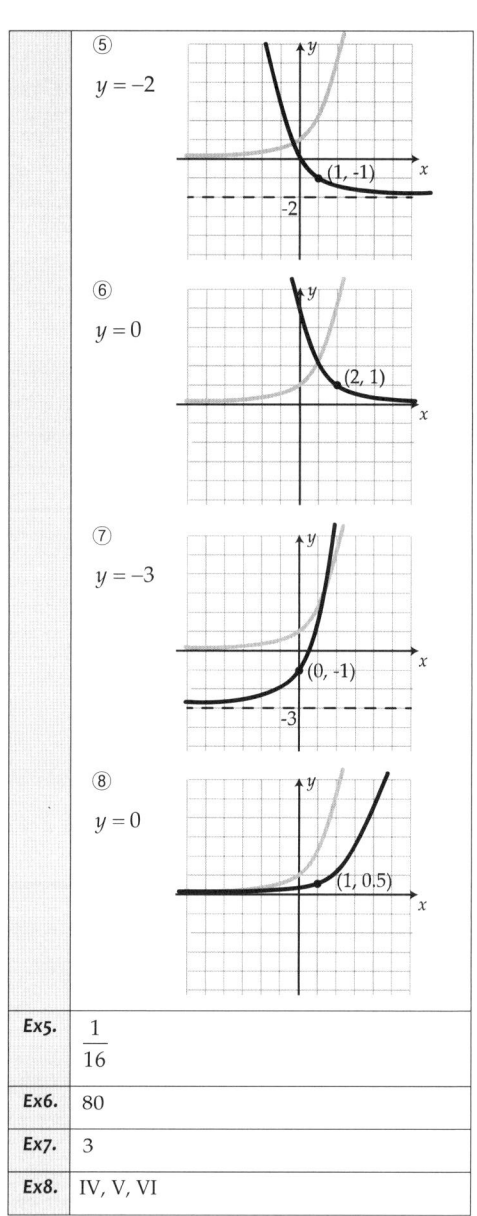

3.2 Compound Interest

Ex1.	① $1000(1+0.09)^8 = \$1992.56$
	② $1000\left(1+\dfrac{0.12}{2}\right)^{3(2)} = \$1418.52$
	③ $14000\left(1+\dfrac{0.14}{12}\right)^{13(12)} = \$85500.53$
	④ $480\left(1+\dfrac{0.09}{4}\right)^{5(4)} = \$749.04$
	⑤ $12000e^{0.06(4)} = \$15254.99$
	⑥ $4000e^{0.005(7)} = \$4142.48$
Ex2.	$2400(1+0.002)^{35} = 2574$
Ex3.	$32000(1-0.0001)^3 = 31990$
Ex4.	$\dfrac{1000}{(1+0.03/2)^3} = \$956.317$
Ex5.	$\dfrac{20000}{e^{0.09}} = \$18278.62$
Ex6.	$\sqrt[3]{2} - 1 = 0.25992\ldots \quad 26\%$

3.3 Logarithmic Function

Ex1.	① 5
	② 5
	③ −2
	④ −2
	⑤ −2
	⑥ −1
	⑦ $\dfrac{1}{2}$
	⑧ $\dfrac{1}{2}$
	⑨ 5
	⑩ $\dfrac{1}{4}$
	⑪ 125
	⑫ 4
	⑬ 6
Ex2.	① $x > -8$
	② $x < 2$
	③ $x < -5 \text{ or } x > \dfrac{1}{2}$
	④ $x < -2 \text{ or } x > -1$
	⑤ $x < -2$
	⑥ $x > -2$
	⑦ $-1 < x < 1$
	⑧ $-2 < x < 1 \text{ or } x > 2$
Ex3.	① 3
	② $\dfrac{1}{2}$
	③ 11
	④ 0
	⑤ 2
	⑥ $\dfrac{1}{5}$
	⑦ −3
	⑧ 6
	⑨ 25
	⑩ $-\dfrac{1}{2}$
	⑪ 4
	⑫ $\dfrac{1}{2}$
	⑬ 1
	⑭ 5
	⑮ kt
	⑯ 2

Ex4.
① $1000 = 10^3$
② $x = \log_5 4000$
③ $\dfrac{1}{8} = e^x$
④ $27 = 3^3$
⑤ $\dfrac{1}{2} = \ln x$
⑥ $x = \log 2$
⑦ $x^y = e^2$
⑧ $2x = \log 5$
⑨ $x^2 - x = \log_2 3$
⑩ $4x^2 = \ln 7$
⑪ $10^y = x^2 - 4x$

Ex5.
① $f^{-1} = \log_2 x + 1$
② $f^{-1} = \log_5 (x-3)$
③ $f^{-1} = \ln\left(\dfrac{x+2}{3}\right)$
④ $f^{-1} = \log \dfrac{x}{3} + 2$
⑤ $f^{-1} = 5^x$
⑥ $f^{-1} = 7^{x-5}$
⑦ $f^{-1} = e^x - 2$
⑧ $f^{-1} = 10^{\frac{x+3}{2}}$
⑨ $f^{-1} = 10^{\frac{x-2}{3}}$
⑩ $f^{-1} = e^{x-1} + 1$
⑪ $f^{-1} = 3^{2(x-2)} + 1$
⑫ $f^{-1} = e^{2x+1} - 2$

Ex6.
① $x = 0$
② $x = -3$
③ $x = 3$
④ $x = 2$
⑤ $x = 1$
⑥ $x = 0$

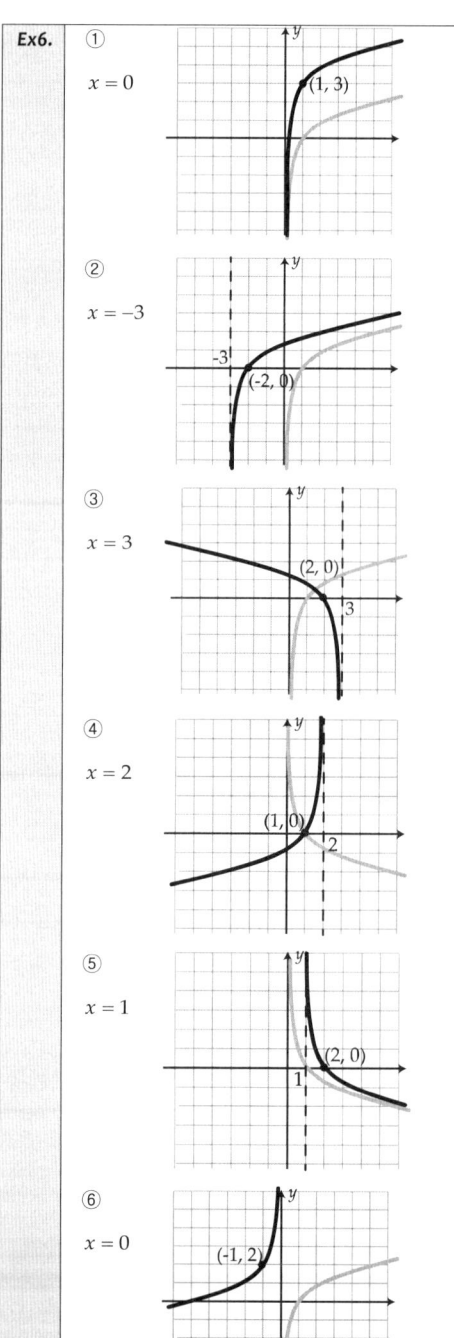

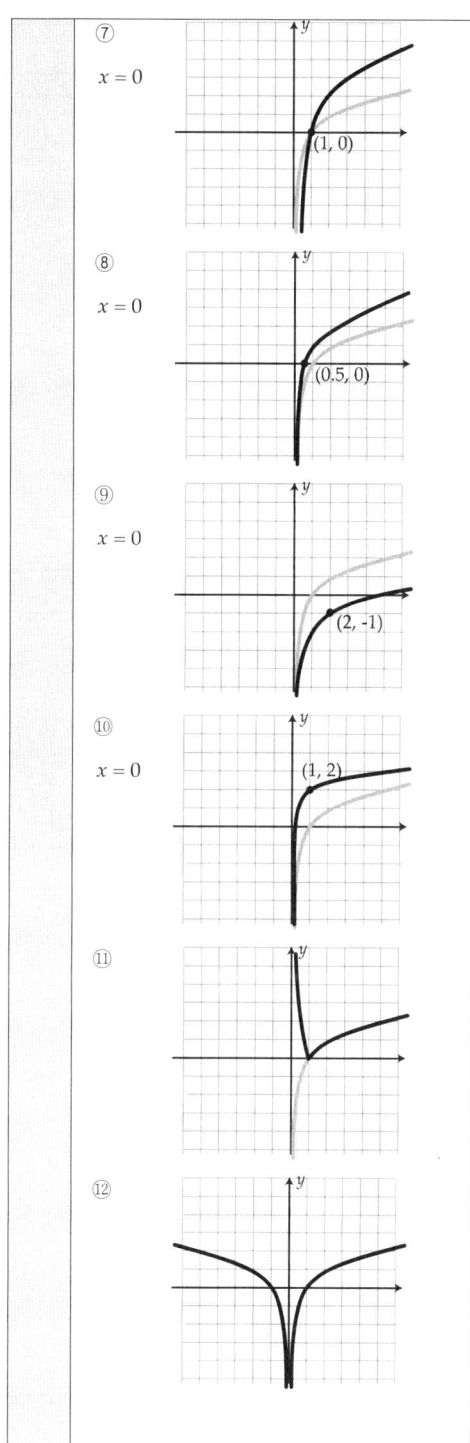

⑦ $x = 0$
⑧ $x = 0$
⑨ $x = 0$
⑩ $x = 0$
⑪
⑫

Ex7.	① 7
	② x^2
	③ 8
	④ 3
Ex8.	$x \geq 3$
Ex9.	$x > 1$
Ex10.	$x > e$
Ex11.	$\log_2 \dfrac{x}{x+1} = y$
Ex12.	1

3.4 Properties of Logarithm

Ex1.	① $\log 30$
	② 1
	③ $\ln \dfrac{16}{3}$
	④ 0
	⑤ $\ln \dfrac{x^2}{y\sqrt{z}}$
	⑥ $\ln \dfrac{xy^2}{z}$
	⑦ $\log \dfrac{2x^3}{y^2}$
	⑧ $\log_5 \dfrac{x^2 y^4}{z^6}$
	⑨ $\log_6 \dfrac{x-1}{x+1}$
	⑩ $\log(x-3)$
	⑪ 2
	⑫ $\dfrac{3}{2}$
	⑬ 2

	⑭ $\dfrac{\log 5}{\log 2}$	
	⑮ $\dfrac{1}{\log 5}$	
	⑯ $\dfrac{\log 8}{\log 5}$	
	⑰ 25	
	⑱ x^3	
	⑲ 36	
	⑳ 2	
	㉑ $\log x^{\frac{3}{2}}$	
	㉒ $\log_2 x^{\frac{5}{6}}$	
Ex2.	① $a+3b$	
	② $3(a+b)$	
	③ $2a+b+\dfrac{1}{3}c$	
	④ $2+\dfrac{1}{2}(a+b)$	
	⑤ $1+2b-\dfrac{1}{2}c$	
	⑥ $\dfrac{1}{2}a-3b-c$	
	⑦ $\dfrac{3a}{2b}$	
	⑧ $\dfrac{a}{2}+\dfrac{b}{4}$	
	⑨ $\dfrac{2c+a}{6(a+b)}$	
	⑩ $\dfrac{b+c}{2a}$	
Ex3.	$\log_{13} 10 - \dfrac{1}{5}\left[2\log_{13} x + 3\log_{13}(4x+1)\right]$	
Ex4.	$\log(x+y)+\log(x-y)$	
Ex5.	6	
Ex6.	III, V, VIII	

Ex7.	$\log_3 2 \cdot \log_3 7$
Ex8.	① vertical stretch by the factor of 2 ② vertical shrink by the factor of $\dfrac{1}{\ln 10}$
Ex9.	① 1 ② 10! ③ 110 ④ 10!
Ex10.	(a) $f^{-1}=\dfrac{e^x}{4}-1$ (b) $y>-1$
Ex11.	$x=1\pm\sqrt{e^y+1}$
Ex12.	$C<D<B<A$
Ex13.	II, III, VII

3.5 Exp and Log Equations and Inequalities

Ex1.	① 24 ② $2+e^{\frac{3}{2}}$ ③ $\dfrac{2}{3^e}+1$ ④ 81 ⑤ 27 ⑥ $\dfrac{8}{7}$ ⑦ 1 ⑧ 4 ⑨ $3^{\frac{4}{3}}$ ⑩ 2^{10}

	⑪ $\dfrac{7}{2}$
	⑫ $\dfrac{5}{4}$
	⑬ 6
	⑭ 1
	⑮ no solution
	⑯ ± 1
	⑰ $\pm\sqrt{3}$
	⑱ 6
	⑲ $10, 1000$
	⑳ $10^{\frac{5}{2}}, 10^{-1}$
	㉑ $8, \dfrac{1}{8}$
	㉒ $10, 10^4$
Ex2.	$x = 3,\ y = 1$
Ex3.	① 3
	② -2
	③ 3
	④ -9
	⑤ $\dfrac{8}{7}$
	⑥ 12
	⑦ $\dfrac{\log 3}{\log 2}$
	⑧ $\dfrac{\log 8}{\log 3} - 1$
	⑨ $\dfrac{\ln 5}{2}$
	⑩ $\dfrac{1 + \ln 7}{3}$
	⑪ $\dfrac{2\log 5 + \log 3}{\log 5 - 3\log 3}$
	⑫ $\dfrac{\log 7 + \log 11}{\log 11 - 2\log 7}$

	⑬ $\dfrac{\log 7}{2\log 7 + \log 2} = \dfrac{\log 7}{\log 98}$
	⑭ $\dfrac{3\log 4}{\log 4 - 2\log 6} = -\dfrac{\log 8}{\log 3}$
	⑮ $\ln 2$
	⑯ $\ln 8,\ \ln 7$
	⑰ $\dfrac{\log 4}{\log 3}\ (= \log_3 4)$
	⑱ $0,\ \dfrac{\log 4}{\log 5}\ (= \log_5 4)$
	⑲ $0,\ \ln 5$
	⑳ $\ln 3$
	㉑ $\dfrac{\ln 4}{2}$
	㉒ $\dfrac{1}{3}\ln\dfrac{1}{2}$
	㉓ $0,\ -3$
Ex4.	$\dfrac{\log(8/5)}{\log 1.06} = 8.066$ years
Ex5.	$\dfrac{\log(124/80)}{4\log\left(1 + \dfrac{0.07}{4}\right)} = 6.315$ years
Ex6.	$\dfrac{\ln 2}{0.03} = 23.105$ years
Ex7.	① $x > \dfrac{\log 3}{\log 2} + 1$
	② $x < \dfrac{\ln 2 - 1}{2}$
	③ $\log 2 < x \le \log 4$
	④ $\log_3 8 \le x < 3$
	⑤ $x < 3$
	⑥ $-1 < x < 3$
	⑦ $0 < x < 2$
	⑧ $\dfrac{1}{2} < x < 1$
	⑨ $-\dfrac{1}{3} < x < 5$

	⑩ $x > e^5$ ⑪ $x \geq e^3$ ⑫ $\sqrt{10} < x < 100$ ⑬ $9 \leq x \leq 27$
Ex8.	$x = 1$, $x = e$, $x = \dfrac{1}{e}$
Ex9.	$x = 1$, $x = 4$
Ex10.	4
Ex11.	10
Ex12.	$3 < x < 4$
Ex13.	$\dfrac{\log 3}{\log 2} \left(= \log_2 3 \right)$

3.6 Exponential Growth and Modeling

Ex1.	① $1078(2)^{\frac{t}{8}}$ (t is in hours) ② $420\left(\dfrac{1}{2}\right)^{\frac{t}{26}}$ (t is in years) ③ $416\left(\dfrac{1}{2}\right)^{\frac{t}{23}}$ (t is in days) ④ $1081(2)^t$ (t is in hours)
Ex2.	(a) $1000(2)^{\frac{t}{3}}$ (b) 32000 (c) $\dfrac{3\log 200}{\log 2} = 22.932$ hrs
Ex3.	$\dfrac{9\log 400}{\log 2} = 77.795$ days

Ex4.	(a) $45\left(\dfrac{1}{2}\right)^{\frac{t}{20}}$ (b) $45\left(\dfrac{1}{2}\right)^{\frac{26}{20}} = 18.276$
Ex5.	$\dfrac{7\log 0.25}{\log 0.5} = 14$ days
Ex6.	$\dfrac{1900 \log 0.3}{\log 0.5} = 3300$ years
Ex7.	(a) $600e^{0.3t}$ (b) $600e^{0.3(10)} = 12051.322$ (c) $\dfrac{\ln(800/6)}{0.3} = 16.310$ hrs (d) 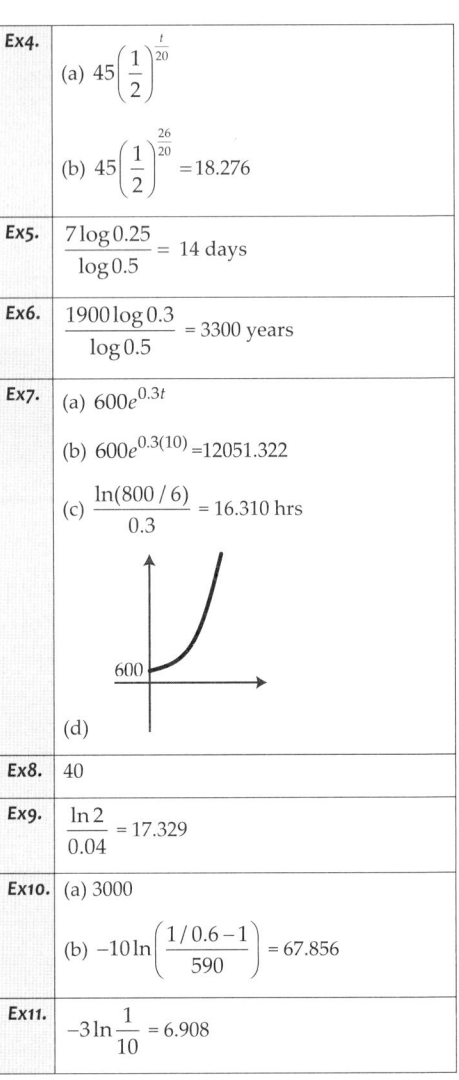
Ex8.	40
Ex9.	$\dfrac{\ln 2}{0.04} = 17.329$
Ex10.	(a) 3000 (b) $-10\ln\left(\dfrac{1/0.6 - 1}{590}\right) = 67.856$
Ex11.	$-3\ln\dfrac{1}{10} = 6.908$

Answers

4. Trigonometry Definition and Graphs

4.1 Angles in Radian

Ex1.
① $\dfrac{\pi}{2}$

② $\dfrac{5\pi}{9}$

③ $-\dfrac{3\pi}{4}$

④ $\dfrac{5\pi}{6}$

⑤ $60°$

⑥ $300°$

⑦ $-240°$

⑧ $-15°$

⑨ $\dfrac{120°}{\pi}$

⑩ $\dfrac{1260°}{\pi}$

Ex2.

①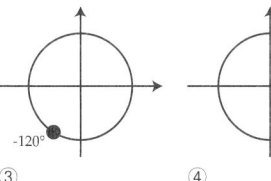

②

③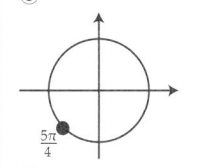

④

⑤

⑥

⑦

⑧

⑨

⑩

Ex3. $\pi - \theta,\ \pi + \theta,\ 2\pi - \theta$

Ex4.

① $480°$; $840°$; $-240°$; $-600°$

② $215°$; $575°$; $-505°$; $-865°$

③ $\dfrac{10\pi}{3}$; $\dfrac{16\pi}{3}$; $-\dfrac{2\pi}{3}$; $-\dfrac{8\pi}{3}$

④ $\dfrac{5\pi}{4}$; $\dfrac{13\pi}{4}$; $-\dfrac{11\pi}{4}$; $-\dfrac{19\pi}{4}$

Ex5.
① $S = 16\pi\, cm$, $A = 96\pi\, cm^2$

② $S = 4\pi\, in$, $A = 20\pi\, in^2$

③ $S = 10\pi\, in$, $A = 60\pi\, in^2$

④ $S = \dfrac{40\pi}{9}\, yd$, $A = \dfrac{160\pi}{9}\, yd^2$

⑤ $S = 3\pi\, m$, $A = 54\pi\, m^2$

⑥ $S = 26\pi\, m$, $A = 312\pi\, m^2$

Ex6.
① $5\ (rad)$

② $\dfrac{9}{5}\ (rad)$

③ $2\ (rad)$

④ $\dfrac{3}{2}\ (rad)$

Ex7.	(a) $5\ cm$
	(b) $10\pi - 10\ cm$
	(c) $20\ cm$
Ex8.	$\dfrac{12}{2+\dfrac{5\pi}{18}} = 4.1773$
Ex9.	175π
Ex10.	① $\dfrac{1}{9}\ rad/\sec$
	② $\dfrac{7}{9}\ cm/\sec$
Ex11.	$48\ in/\sec$
Ex12.	① $20\pi\ rad/\min$
	② $\dfrac{\pi}{3}\ rad/\sec$
Ex13.	$\dfrac{144(60)}{5280}\pi = \dfrac{18}{11}\pi\ mi/hr$
Ex14.	$\dfrac{15}{\pi}\ cm$
Ex15.	$\dfrac{600}{\pi}\ rev/\min$
Ex16.	decreased by 23.2%
Ex17.	$6\pi\ in$
Ex18.	$\dfrac{6\pi}{5}$
Ex19.	$9\sqrt{3} + 24\pi\ m^2$
Ex20.	(a) $12\pi + 12\sqrt{3}$
	(b) $5\pi = small$, $\dfrac{5\pi}{4} = big$

4.2 Trigonometry of Right Triangles

Ex1.	① $\sin\theta = \dfrac{5}{13}\quad \csc\theta = \dfrac{13}{5}$
	$\cos\theta = \dfrac{12}{13}\quad \sec\theta = \dfrac{13}{12}$
	$\tan\theta = \dfrac{5}{12}\quad \cot\theta = \dfrac{12}{5}$
	② $\sin\theta = \dfrac{2}{\sqrt{13}}\quad \csc\theta = \dfrac{\sqrt{13}}{2}$
	$\cos\theta = \dfrac{3}{\sqrt{13}}\quad \sec\theta = \dfrac{\sqrt{13}}{3}$
	$\tan\theta = \dfrac{2}{3}\quad \cot\theta = \dfrac{3}{2}$
	③ $\sin\theta = \dfrac{1}{\sqrt{2}}$
	$\sec\theta = \sqrt{2}$
	$\tan\theta = 1$
	④ $\csc\theta = \sqrt{6}$
	$\cos\theta = \dfrac{\sqrt{30}}{6}$
	$\cot\theta = \sqrt{5}$
	⑤ $\csc\theta = \dfrac{7}{5}$
	$\cos\theta = \dfrac{2\sqrt{6}}{7}$
	$\cot\theta = \dfrac{2\sqrt{6}}{5}$
	⑥ $\sin\theta = \dfrac{24}{25}$
	$\sec\theta = \dfrac{25}{7}$
	$\tan\theta = \dfrac{24}{7}$
Ex2.	① $\dfrac{\sqrt{7}}{4}$
	② $2\sqrt{2}$
	③ $\dfrac{\sqrt{a^2-b^2}}{a}$
	④ $\dfrac{1}{\sqrt{a^2-1}}$
	⑤ $\sqrt{1+a^2}$
Ex3.	① $x = 10\sin\theta$, $y = 10\cos\theta$
	② $x = 9\cos\theta$, $y = 9\sin\theta$
	③ $x = \dfrac{4.5}{\tan\theta}$, $y = \dfrac{4.5}{\sin\theta}$

	④ $x = \dfrac{22}{\sin\theta}$, $y = \dfrac{22}{\tan\theta}$
Ex4.	① $\dfrac{\sqrt{3}}{2}$ ② $\dfrac{\sqrt{2}}{2}$ ③ $\dfrac{\sqrt{2}}{2}$ ④ $\dfrac{\sqrt{3}}{2}$ ⑤ $\sqrt{3}$ ⑥ 1 ⑦ 0 ⑧ $\dfrac{1}{2}$ ⑨ 1 ⑩ $\dfrac{1}{2}$ ⑪ $\dfrac{\sqrt{3}}{3}$ ⑫ 1 ⑬ $\dfrac{2\sqrt{3}}{3}$ ⑭ $\sqrt{2}$ ⑮ $\sqrt{2}$ ⑯ $\sqrt{3}$ ⑰ $\dfrac{\sqrt{3}}{3}$ ⑱ 2
Ex5.	$200\tan 57.6° = 315.150\ ft$
Ex6.	$\dfrac{2}{\tan 15°} = 7.464\ mi$
Ex7.	$25\sin 35° = 14.399\ ft$
Ex8.	height of the building = $500\tan 32° = 312.435\ ft$ length of the flagpole = $500\tan 46° - 500\tan 32° = 205.33\ ft$
Ex9.	$6 + 100\tan 37° = 81.355\ ft$
Ex10.	$1.295\ mi$
Ex11.	$821.534\ ft$

4.3 Trigonometry of Any Angles

Ex1.	① $\sin\theta = \dfrac{5}{13}$ $\cos\theta = \dfrac{12}{13}$ $\tan\theta = \dfrac{5}{12}$ ② $\sin\theta = -\dfrac{24}{25}$ $\cos\theta = \dfrac{7}{25}$ $\tan\theta = -\dfrac{24}{7}$ ③ $\csc\theta = -\dfrac{17}{15}$ $\cos\theta = \dfrac{8}{17}$ $\cot\theta = -\dfrac{8}{15}$ ④ $\csc\theta = -\dfrac{\sqrt{137}}{4}$ $\cos\theta = -\dfrac{11}{\sqrt{137}} = -\dfrac{11\sqrt{137}}{137}$ $\cot\theta = \dfrac{11}{4}$ ⑤ $\sin\theta = -\dfrac{4}{\sqrt{41}} = -\dfrac{4\sqrt{41}}{41}$ $\sec\theta = -\dfrac{\sqrt{41}}{5}$ $\tan\theta = \dfrac{4}{5}$ ⑥ $\sin\theta = \dfrac{1}{\sqrt{2}} = \dfrac{\sqrt{2}}{2}$ $\sec\theta = -\sqrt{2}$ $\tan\theta = -1$
Ex2.	① II ② III ③ IV ④ II

	⑤ I
	⑥ I
	⑦ III
	⑧ IV
Ex3.	① 60°
	② 45°
	③ $\dfrac{\pi}{3}$
	④ $\dfrac{\pi}{3}$
	⑤ $\dfrac{\pi}{6}$
	⑥ $\dfrac{\pi}{4}$
Ex4.	① $-\dfrac{\sqrt{2}}{2}$ ② $-\dfrac{\sqrt{3}}{2}$
	③ $-\dfrac{1}{\sqrt{3}}$ ④ 2
	⑤ $\dfrac{\sqrt{2}}{2}$ ⑥ $\dfrac{1}{2}$
	⑦ $-\dfrac{\sqrt{2}}{2}$ ⑧ $-\dfrac{\sqrt{3}}{3}$
	⑨ $-\dfrac{1}{2}$ ⑩ $-\dfrac{\sqrt{3}}{2}$
	⑪ $\sqrt{2}$ ⑫ $-\sqrt{2}$
	⑬ $\sqrt{3}$ ⑭ $-\dfrac{2\sqrt{3}}{3}$
Ex5.	① $\cos\theta = -\dfrac{3}{5}$
	$\tan\theta = \dfrac{4}{3}$
	② $\sin\theta = \dfrac{2}{\sqrt{53}} = \dfrac{2\sqrt{53}}{53}$
	$\cos\theta = -\dfrac{7}{\sqrt{53}} = -\dfrac{7\sqrt{53}}{53}$

	③ $\sec\theta = -\dfrac{4}{\sqrt{7}} = -\dfrac{4\sqrt{7}}{7}$
	$\tan\theta = -\dfrac{3}{\sqrt{7}} = -\dfrac{3\sqrt{7}}{7}$
	④ $\sin\theta = -\dfrac{1}{\sqrt{5}} = -\dfrac{\sqrt{5}}{5}$
	$\sec\theta = -\dfrac{\sqrt{5}}{2}$
	⑤ $\sin\theta = -\dfrac{12}{13}$
	$\cot\theta = -\dfrac{5}{12}$
	⑥ $\sin\theta = -\dfrac{2\sqrt{6}}{7}$
	$\cot\theta = \dfrac{5}{2\sqrt{6}} = \dfrac{5\sqrt{6}}{12}$
Ex6.	IV
Ex7.	$2\cos\theta$

4.4 Trigonometry in Unit Circle

Ex1.	① $\dfrac{\sqrt{3}}{2}$ ② $-\dfrac{\sqrt{3}}{2}$
	③ $-\dfrac{\sqrt{3}}{2}$ ④ $-\dfrac{\sqrt{2}}{2}$
	⑤ -1 ⑥ $\dfrac{\sqrt{3}}{2}$
	⑦ $-\dfrac{2\sqrt{3}}{3}$ ⑧ $\sqrt{3}$
	⑨ UND ⑩ $-\sqrt{2}$
	⑪ -2 ⑫ $\dfrac{2\sqrt{3}}{3}$
	⑬ 0 ⑭ 0
	⑮ 0 ⑯ 0
	⑰ 0 ⑱ 0

Ex2.	① 0.6 ② −0.6 ③ −0.6 ④ −0.6		⑥	$amp:3 \quad per:\dfrac{2\pi^2}{3}$ $trans: left\ \dfrac{\pi^2}{3},\ down\ 3,\ reflect\ x$ $range: -6 \le y \le 0$
Ex3.	① −0.4 ② −0.4 ③ 0.4 ④ 0.4		Ex3.	① ② ③ ④ ⑤
Ex4.	0			
Ex5.	0			

4.5 Trigonometric Graphs for Sin, Cos

Ex1.	① −1 ② 1 ③ 2 ④ 1
Ex2.	① $amp:4 \quad per:\dfrac{2\pi}{5}$ $trans: left\ \dfrac{\pi}{40},\ up\ 3$ $range: -1 \le y \le 7$
	② $amp:1 \quad per:6\pi$ $trans: right\ 3\pi,\ down\ 1,\ reflect\ x$ $range: -2 \le y \le 0$
	③ $amp:1 \quad per:10\pi$ $trans: left\ 15,\ up\ 2,\ reflect\ x$ $range: 1 \le y \le 3$
	④ $amp:4 \quad per:\pi$ $trans: left\ \dfrac{3\pi}{2},\ down\ 2$ $range: -6 \le y \le 2$
	⑤ $amp:\dfrac{1}{2} \quad per:6$ $trans: right\ \dfrac{3}{5},\ reflect\ x$ $range: -\dfrac{1}{2} \le y \le \dfrac{1}{2}$

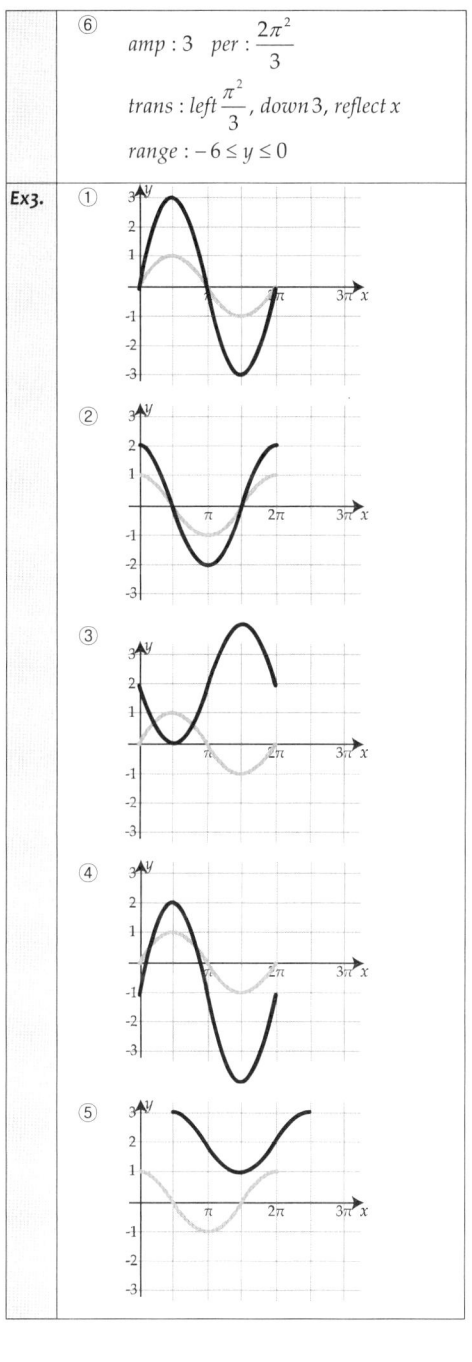

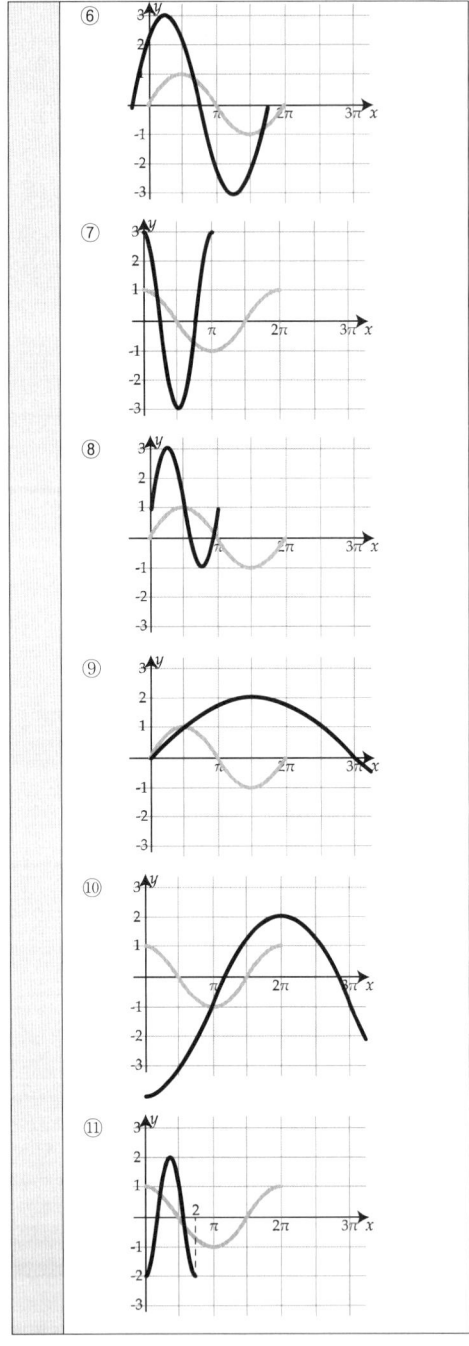

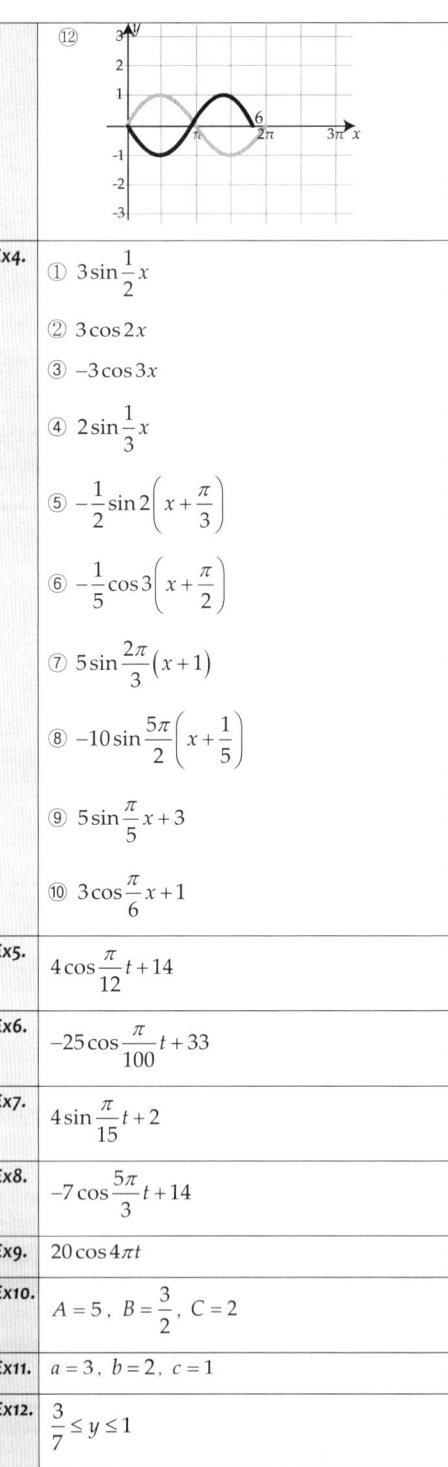

Ex4.	① $3\sin\frac{1}{2}x$
	② $3\cos 2x$
	③ $-3\cos 3x$
	④ $2\sin\frac{1}{3}x$
	⑤ $-\frac{1}{2}\sin 2\left(x+\frac{\pi}{3}\right)$
	⑥ $-\frac{1}{5}\cos 3\left(x+\frac{\pi}{2}\right)$
	⑦ $5\sin\frac{2\pi}{3}(x+1)$
	⑧ $-10\sin\frac{5\pi}{2}\left(x+\frac{1}{5}\right)$
	⑨ $5\sin\frac{\pi}{5}x+3$
	⑩ $3\cos\frac{\pi}{6}x+1$
Ex5.	$4\cos\frac{\pi}{12}t+14$
Ex6.	$-25\cos\frac{\pi}{100}t+33$
Ex7.	$4\sin\frac{\pi}{15}t+2$
Ex8.	$-7\cos\frac{5\pi}{3}t+14$
Ex9.	$20\cos 4\pi t$
Ex10.	$A=5$, $B=\frac{3}{2}$, $C=2$
Ex11.	$a=3$, $b=2$, $c=1$
Ex12.	$\frac{3}{7}\leq y\leq 1$

Ex13.	$\dfrac{3\pi}{4}$
Ex14.	2
Ex15.	per : 6
Ex16.	5

4.6 Trigonometric Graphs for Others

Ex1.	① $per : \dfrac{\pi}{2}$ $\quad trans : right \dfrac{\pi}{8}, up\,1$ ② $per : 4\pi$ $\quad trans : left\,4\pi, up\,3$ ③ $per : 2\pi$ $\quad trans : right\,4, down\,5$ ④ $per : \dfrac{1}{3}$ $\quad trans : right\dfrac{1}{3}$
Ex2.	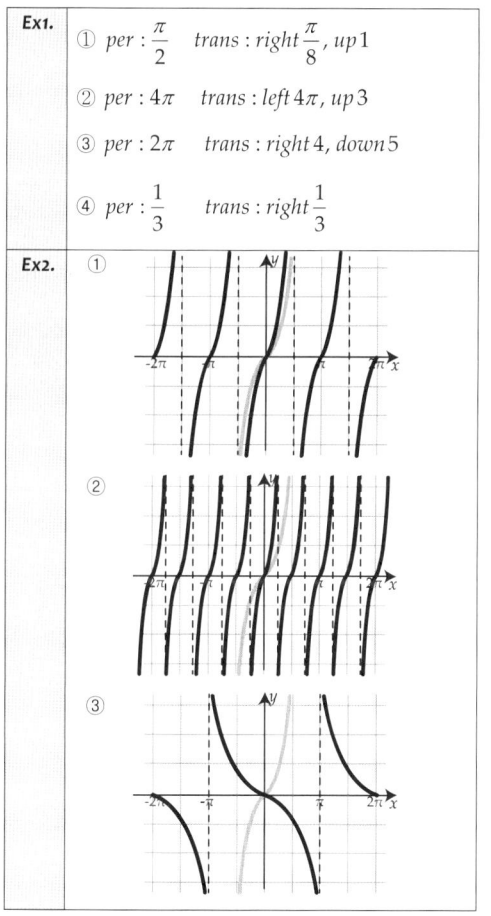
Ex3.	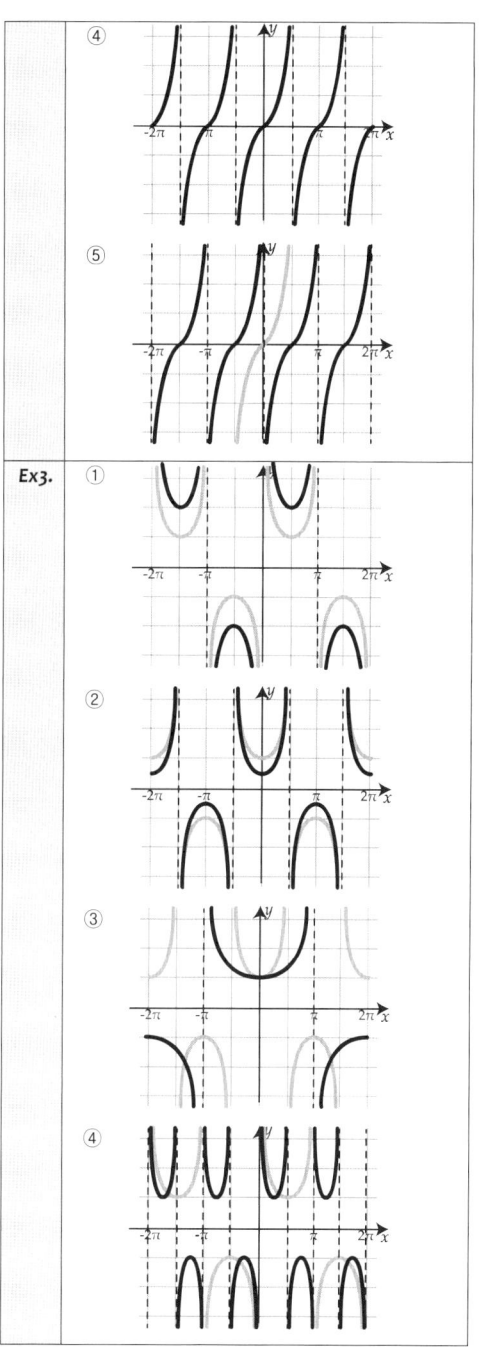

	⑤ 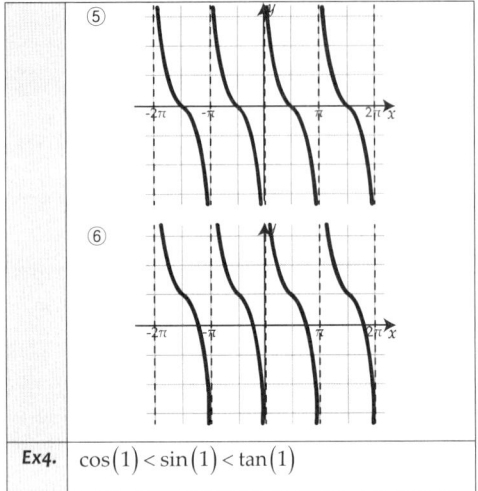 ⑥
Ex4.	$\cos(1) < \sin(1) < \tan(1)$

Answers
5. Trigonometry Identities

5.1 Inverse Trigonometry Function

Ex1.	① 42° ② 77° ③ 25° ④ 65°
Ex2.	$\sin^{-1}\dfrac{12}{40} = 17.458°$
Ex3.	$\tan^{-1}\dfrac{51}{60} = 40.365°$
Ex4.	① $\dfrac{\pi}{6}$ ② $\dfrac{\pi}{6}$ ③ $\dfrac{\pi}{4}$ ④ 0 ⑤ $\dfrac{\pi}{4}$ ⑥ $\dfrac{\pi}{2}$
	⑦ $\dfrac{\pi}{6}$ ⑧ 0 ⑨ $\dfrac{\pi}{6}$ ⑩ $\dfrac{\pi}{3}$ ⑪ $\dfrac{\pi}{4}$ ⑫ $\dfrac{\pi}{4}$ ⑬ $\dfrac{5\pi}{6}$ ⑭ $-\dfrac{\pi}{6}$ ⑮ $-\dfrac{\pi}{3}$ ⑯ $-\dfrac{\pi}{4}$ ⑰ $-\dfrac{\pi}{4}$ ⑱ $\dfrac{2\pi}{3}$
Ex5.	① 0.5 ② 0.2 ③ −0.4 ④ undefined ⑤ undefined ⑥ 0.8 ⑦ 2 ⑧ 3
Ex6.	① $\dfrac{\pi}{6}$ ② $\dfrac{\pi}{3}$ ③ $\dfrac{3\pi}{4}$ ④ $\dfrac{\pi}{3}$ ⑤ $\dfrac{\pi}{3}$ ⑥ $\dfrac{2\pi}{3}$ ⑦ $\dfrac{\pi}{4}$ ⑧ $-\dfrac{\pi}{6}$ ⑨ $\dfrac{\pi}{3}$ ⑩ $-\dfrac{\pi}{3}$ ⑪ $\dfrac{3\pi}{5}$ ⑫ $\dfrac{3\pi}{8}$
Ex7.	① $\dfrac{1}{\sqrt{5}}$ ② $-2\sqrt{2}$ ③ $\dfrac{4}{5}$

	④ $\dfrac{4}{5}$
	⑤ $-\dfrac{12}{5}$
	⑥ $-\dfrac{17}{8}$
Ex8.	① $\dfrac{x}{\sqrt{1-x^2}}$
	② $\sqrt{1-x^2}$
	③ x
	④ x
	⑤ $\dfrac{x}{\sqrt{1-x^2}}$
	⑥ $\dfrac{\sqrt{1+x^2}}{x}$
	⑦ $\dfrac{x}{\sqrt{x^2+5}}$
	⑧ $\dfrac{3}{x}$
	⑨ $\dfrac{2}{\sqrt{x^2+4}}$
Ex9.	① odd
	② neither
	③ odd
Ex10.	① false
	② false
	③ false
Ex11.	① $domain\,[-1,1]\quad range\,[0,1]$
	② $domain\,(-1,1)\quad range\,\mathbb{R}$
	③ $domain\,\mathbb{R}\quad range\,(0,1]$

5.2 Basic Trigonometric Identities

Ex1.	① $\sin x$
	② 1
	③ $\cos u$
	④ $\tan\theta$
	⑤ $\sec\theta$
Ex2.	① $\tan^2 x$
	② $\sin\theta$
	③ $\cot x$
	④ $\sec x$
	⑤ $\tan\theta$
	⑥ -1
Ex3.	① -1
	② 1
	③ 1
	④ 1
	⑤ 1
	⑥ 1
Ex4.	① $-\dfrac{\sqrt{3}}{2}$
	② 0
	③ 0
	④ $-\dfrac{2\sqrt{3}}{3}$
	⑤ $\dfrac{\sqrt{2}}{2}$
	⑥ -1
	⑦ $-\sqrt{3}$
Ex5.	① $\cos x$
	② $\tan x$
	③ 2
	④ 1
	⑤ $\sec x$
	⑥ $\sin\theta$
	⑦ $-\sin x$

	⑧ $\cos x$
	⑨ $\tan x$
	⑩ $\tan x$
	⑪ $\sin x$
Ex6.	$-\dfrac{3}{8}$
Ex7.	$-\dfrac{32}{15}$
Ex8.	$22°$
Ex9.	$\dfrac{89}{2}$

5.3 Verifying Trigonometric Identities

Ex1.

① $\cos^2 x - \sin^2 x$
$= 1 - \sin^2 x - \sin^2 x$
$= 1 - 2\sin^2 x$

② $\dfrac{\csc(-x)}{\sec(-x)} = \dfrac{-\csc x}{\sec x} = \dfrac{-\dfrac{1}{\sin x}}{\dfrac{1}{\cos x}}$
$= -\dfrac{\cos x}{\sin x} = -\cot x$

③ $\left(\dfrac{\sin x}{\cos x} + \dfrac{\cos x}{\sin x}\right)^4 = \left(\dfrac{1}{\sin x \cdot \cos x}\right)^4$
$= \csc^4 x \cdot \sec^4 x$

④ $\dfrac{\cos^2 x}{\sin^2 x} - \cos^2 x = \dfrac{\cos^2 x - \cos^2 x \cdot \sin^2 x}{\sin^2 x}$
$= \dfrac{\cos^2 x(1 - \sin^2 x)}{\sin^2 x} = \dfrac{\cos^2 x \cdot \cos^2 x}{\sin^2 x}$
$= \cot^2 x \cdot \cos^2 x$

⑤ $\dfrac{\cos\theta \cdot \dfrac{\cos\theta}{\sin\theta}}{1 - \sin\theta} - 1 = \dfrac{\dfrac{\cos^2\theta}{\sin\theta}}{1 - \sin\theta} - 1$
$= \dfrac{\dfrac{1 - \sin^2\theta}{\sin\theta}}{\dfrac{1 - \sin\theta}{1}} - 1 = \dfrac{1 + \sin\theta}{\sin\theta} - 1$
$= \csc\theta + 1 - 1 = \csc\theta$

⑥ $\dfrac{\dfrac{\sin x}{\cos x} - \sin x}{\dfrac{\sin x}{\cos x} \cdot \sin x} = \dfrac{\dfrac{\sin x - \sin x \cdot \cos x}{\cos x}}{\dfrac{\sin^2 x}{\cos x}}$

$= \dfrac{\sin x(1 - \cos x)}{\sin^2 x} = \dfrac{\sin x(1 - \cos x)}{1 - \cos^2 x}$

$= \dfrac{\sin x(1 - \cos x)}{(1 - \cos x)(1 + \cos x)}$

$= \dfrac{\sin x}{1 + \cos x} \cdot \dfrac{\tan x}{\tan x}$

$= \dfrac{\sin x \cdot \tan x}{\tan x + \sin x}$

⑦ $\dfrac{\dfrac{1}{\sin x} + \dfrac{1}{\cos x}}{\sin x + \cos x} = \dfrac{\dfrac{\cos x + \sin x}{\sin x \cdot \cos x}}{\dfrac{\sin x + \cos x}{1}}$

$= \dfrac{1}{\sin x \cdot \cos x} = \csc x \cdot \sec x$

⑧ $\dfrac{(\sin x + \cos x)(\sin^2 x - \sin x \cos x + \cos^2 x)}{(\sin x + \cos x)}$

$= 1 - \sin x \cdot \cos x$

⑨ $\dfrac{\cot u - \tan u}{(\cot u + \tan u)(\cot u - \tan u)}$

$= \dfrac{1}{\dfrac{\cos u}{\sin u} + \dfrac{\sin u}{\cos u}} = \dfrac{1}{\dfrac{1}{\sin u \cdot \cos u}}$

$= \sin u \cdot \cos u$

⑩ $\dfrac{(\sin x + \cos x)(\sin x - \cos x)}{(\sin x + \cos x)^2}$

$= \dfrac{(\sin x - \cos x)}{(\sin x + \cos x)}$

$= \dfrac{(\sin x - \cos x)^2}{(\sin x + \cos x)(\sin x - \cos x)}$

$= \dfrac{(\sin x - \cos x)^2}{\sin^2 x - \cos^2 x}$

⑪ $\dfrac{(1 + \sin\theta)^2 + \cos^2\theta}{\cos\theta(1 + \sin\theta)}$

$= \dfrac{1 + 2\sin\theta + \sin^2\theta + \cos^2\theta}{\cos\theta(1 + \sin\theta)}$

$= \dfrac{2(1 + \sin\theta)}{\cos\theta(1 + \sin\theta)} = 2\sec\theta$

⑫ $\dfrac{\csc\theta - \cot\theta + \csc\theta + \cot\theta}{\csc^2\theta - \cot^2\theta}$
$= \dfrac{2\csc\theta}{\csc^2\theta - \cot^2\theta} = 2\csc\theta$

⑬ $\dfrac{(\sec x - 1)(\sec x + 1)}{\tan x(\sec x + 1)}$
$= \dfrac{\sec^2 x - 1}{\tan x(\sec x + 1)}$
$= \dfrac{\tan^2 x}{\tan x(\sec x + 1)} = \dfrac{\tan x}{\sec x + 1}$

⑭ $\dfrac{(1+\sin x)^2}{(1-\sin x)(1+\sin x)} = \dfrac{(1+\sin x)^2}{1-\sin^2 x}$
$= \dfrac{(1+\sin x)^2}{\cos^2 x} = \left(\dfrac{1+\sin x}{\cos x}\right)^2$
$= (\sec x + \tan x)^2$

⑮ $\dfrac{\dfrac{\tan x}{\tan x \cdot \tan y} + \dfrac{\tan y}{\tan x \cdot \tan y}}{\dfrac{1}{\tan x \cdot \tan y} - \dfrac{\tan x \cdot \tan y}{\tan x \cdot \tan y}}$
$= \dfrac{\cot y + \cot x}{\cot x \cdot \cot y - 1}$

⑯ $\dfrac{2 + \dfrac{1}{\sin x \cdot \cos x}}{\dfrac{1}{\sin x \cdot \cos x}} = \dfrac{\dfrac{2\sin x \cdot \cos x + 1}{\sin x \cdot \cos x}}{\dfrac{1}{\sin x \cdot \cos x}}$
$= 1 + 2\sin x \cdot \cos x$
$= \sin^2 x + \cos^2 x + 2\sin x \cdot \cos x$
$= (\sin x + \cos x)^2$

⑰ $\dfrac{\sec^2 x - 1}{1 + \sec x} = \dfrac{(\sec x - 1)(\sec x + 1)}{1 + \sec x}$
$= \sec x - 1 = \dfrac{1}{\cos x} - \dfrac{\cos x}{\cos x}$
$= \dfrac{1 - \cos x}{\cos x}$

Ex2. $\ln|\sec^2\theta - \tan^2\theta| = \ln|1| = 0$

Ex3. $\log_2 \cos x + \log_2\left(\dfrac{(1+\sin x)^2 + \cos^2 x}{\cos x(1+\sin x)}\right)$
$= \log_2 \cos x + \log_2\left(\dfrac{2 + 2\sin x}{\cos x(1+\sin x)}\right)$
$= \log_2 \cos x + \log_2 \dfrac{2}{\cos x}$
$= \log_2 \cos x \cdot \dfrac{2}{\cos x} = 1$

5.4 Sum and difference Identities

Ex1.
① $\dfrac{\sqrt{2}+\sqrt{6}}{4}$

② $\dfrac{\sqrt{6}-\sqrt{2}}{4}$

③ $\dfrac{\sqrt{6}+\sqrt{2}}{4}$

④ $\dfrac{(3+\sqrt{3})^2}{6} = \sqrt{3}+2$

⑤ $-\dfrac{(1+\sqrt{3})^2}{2} = -(\sqrt{3}+2)$

Ex2.
① $\dfrac{\sqrt{3}}{2}$

② $\dfrac{\sqrt{3}}{2}$

③ $-\dfrac{1}{2}$

④ 0

⑤ $-\dfrac{\sqrt{3}}{3}$

⑥ $-\sqrt{3}$

Ex3.
① $\cos x \cdot \cos\dfrac{\pi}{2} - \sin x \cdot \sin\dfrac{\pi}{2} = -\sin x$

② $\sin x \cdot \cos y + \cos x \cdot \sin y$
$+ \sin x \cdot \cos y - \cos x \cdot \sin y$
$= 2\sin x \cdot \cos y$

	③ $\dfrac{\dfrac{\cos x \cdot \cos y - \sin x \cdot \sin y}{\cos x \cdot \cos y}}{\dfrac{\cos x \cdot \cos y + \sin x \cdot \sin y}{\cos x \cdot \cos y}}$ $= \dfrac{1 - \dfrac{\sin x \cdot \sin y}{\cos x \cdot \cos y}}{1 + \dfrac{\sin x \cdot \sin y}{\cos x \cdot \cos y}}$ $= \dfrac{1 - \tan x \cdot \tan y}{1 + \tan x \cdot \tan y}$	
Ex4.	-1	
Ex5.	$\tan 2A$	
Ex6.	① $\dfrac{3 + 4\sqrt{3}}{10}$ ② $\dfrac{3\sqrt{10}}{10}$ ③ $-\dfrac{33}{65}$ ④ $\dfrac{10 + 2\sqrt{5}}{15}$ ⑤ 1 ⑥ $\dfrac{x + x\sqrt{1-x^2}}{\sqrt{1+x^2}}$	
Ex7.	$\dfrac{\pi}{4}$	
Ex8.	$\dfrac{\pi}{4}$	
Ex9.	$\dfrac{8 - 3\sqrt{5}}{15}$	

5.5 Double-Angle Identity

Ex1.	① $\dfrac{\sqrt{3}}{2}$ ② $-\dfrac{1}{2}$ ③ $4\sin 3\alpha \cdot \cos 3\alpha$ ④ $2\sin 5B \cdot \cos 5B$ ⑤ $\cos^2 2A - \sin^2 2A$ $= 2\cos^2 2A - 1 = 1 - 2\sin^2 2A$ ⑥ $2\cos^2 4\beta - 2\sin^2 4\beta$ $= 4\cos^2 4\beta - 2 = 2 - 4\sin^2 4\beta$ ⑦ $\dfrac{2\tan 2C}{1 - \tan^2 2C}$
Ex2.	① $2\sin 2A$ ② $3\sin 4\beta$ ③ $\cos 6\alpha$ ④ $-\cos 4\beta$ ⑤ $-\cos 4\theta$ ⑥ $\cos A$ ⑦ $-2\cos \beta$ ⑧ $\cos 6\theta$ ⑨ $\tan 4\beta$ ⑩ $\tan 2C$
Ex3.	① $\sin 2(2x) = 2\sin 2x \cdot \cos 2x$ $= 2(2\sin x \cdot \cos x)(\cos^2 x - \sin^2 x)$ $= (4\sin x \cdot \cos x)(2\cos^2 x - 1)$ ② $\cos 2(2x) = 2\cos^2 2x - 1$ $= 2(1 - 2\sin^2 x)^2 - 1$ $= 2(1 - 4\sin^2 x + 4\sin^4 x) - 1$ $= 2 - 8\sin^2 x + 8\sin^4 x - 1$ $= 1 - 8\sin^2 x + 8\sin^4 x$

	③ $\dfrac{2\sin x \cdot \cos x + \sin x}{1+(2\cos^2 x - 1) + \cos x}$ $= \dfrac{\sin x(2\cos x + 1)}{\cos x(2\cos x + 1)} = \tan x$
	④ $\tan 2x = \dfrac{2\tan x}{1-\tan^2 x}$ $= \dfrac{\dfrac{2\tan x}{\tan x}}{\dfrac{1}{\tan x} - \dfrac{\tan^2 x}{\tan x}} = \dfrac{2}{\cot x - \tan x}$
Ex4.	$8\cos^4 x - 8\cos^2 x + 1$
Ex5.	① $-\dfrac{240}{289}$ ② $-\dfrac{4\sqrt{6}}{25}$ ③ $-\dfrac{20}{101}$ ④ $-\dfrac{8}{17}$
Ex6.	① $\dfrac{120}{169}$ ② $-\dfrac{527}{625}$ ③ $\dfrac{25}{7}$ ④ $\dfrac{18\sqrt{11}}{55}$ ⑤ $2x\sqrt{1-x^2}$ ⑥ $2x^2 - 1$
Ex7.	① $\dfrac{1}{2}\cos 2x + 2\cos x + \dfrac{3}{2}$ ② $\dfrac{9}{2} - 4\sin x - \dfrac{1}{2}\cos 2x$ ③ $\dfrac{1}{4}\left[\dfrac{3}{2} - 2\cos 2x + \dfrac{1}{2}\cos 4x\right]$ ④ $\dfrac{1}{4}\left[\dfrac{3}{2} + 2\cos 2x + \dfrac{1}{2}\cos 4x\right]$

	⑤ $\dfrac{1}{8} - \dfrac{1}{8}\cos 4x$
Ex8.	$amp : 2$ $per : \pi$
Ex9.	$amp : \dfrac{1}{2}$ $per : \pi$
Ex10.	$\dfrac{7}{5}$
Ex11.	$\dfrac{7}{25}$
Ex12.	$\dfrac{99}{8}$

5.6 Half-Angle and Product-Sum Identities

Ex1.	① $\dfrac{\sqrt{2-\sqrt{2}}}{2}$ ② $\dfrac{\sqrt{2+\sqrt{2}}}{2}$ ③ $-\dfrac{\sqrt{2-\sqrt{2}}}{2}$ ④ $\dfrac{\sqrt{2-\sqrt{3}}}{2}$ ⑤ $\dfrac{\sqrt{2+\sqrt{3}}}{2}$
Ex2.	① $\dfrac{5\sqrt{26}}{26}$ ② $-\dfrac{4}{5}$ ③ $-\dfrac{\sqrt{10}}{10}$
Ex3.	① $2\cos 4\theta \sin \theta$ ② $2\sin 2\theta \cos \theta$ ③ $2\cos 5\theta \cos \theta$ ④ $2\cos 6\theta \cos(-3\theta)$

	⑤ $-2\sin\theta\sin\dfrac{\pi}{2}$	
Ex4.	① $3\left[\sin\dfrac{3\pi}{4}+\sin\left(-\dfrac{\pi}{4}\right)\right]$	
	② $2\left[\sin\dfrac{7\pi}{6}-\sin\left(-\dfrac{\pi}{2}\right)\right]$	
	③ $5(\cos 90°+\cos 60°)$	
	④ $-2[\cos 5x-\cos x]$	
Ex5.	① $\dfrac{\sin(x+y)-\sin(x-y)}{\cos(x+y)+\cos(x-y)}$ $=\dfrac{2\cos x\sin y}{2\cos x\cos y}$ $=\dfrac{\sin y}{\cos y}=\tan y$	
	② $\dfrac{\sin x+\sin 2x+\sin 3x}{\cos x+\cos 2x+\cos 3x}$ $=\dfrac{2\sin 2x\cos(-x)+\sin 2x}{2\cos 2x\cos(-x)+\cos 2x}$ $=\dfrac{\sin 2x(2\cos(-x)+1)}{\cos 2x(2\cos(-x)+1)}=\tan 2x$	

Answers

6. Trig Equations and Geometry Triangles

6.1 Basic Trigonometric Equations

Ex1.	①	i) $\dfrac{5\pi}{4},\dfrac{7\pi}{4}$ ii) $\dfrac{5\pi}{4}+2k\pi,\dfrac{7\pi}{4}+2k\pi$
	②	i) $\dfrac{\pi}{6},\dfrac{11\pi}{6}$ ii) $\dfrac{\pi}{6}+2k\pi,\dfrac{11\pi}{6}+2k\pi$
	③	i) $\dfrac{5\pi}{6},\dfrac{11\pi}{6}$ ii) $\dfrac{5\pi}{6}+2k\pi,\dfrac{11\pi}{6}+2k\pi$
	④	i) $\dfrac{\pi}{4},\dfrac{5\pi}{4}$ ii) $\dfrac{\pi}{4}+2k\pi,\dfrac{5\pi}{4}+2k\pi$
	⑤	i) $\dfrac{\pi}{3},\dfrac{5\pi}{3}$ ii) $\dfrac{\pi}{3}+2k\pi,\dfrac{5\pi}{3}+2k\pi$
	⑥	i) $\dfrac{5\pi}{4},\dfrac{7\pi}{4}$ ii) $\dfrac{5\pi}{4}+2k\pi,\dfrac{7\pi}{4}+2k\pi$
Ex2.	①	i) $\dfrac{\pi}{2}$ ii) $\dfrac{\pi}{2}+2k\pi$
	②	i) $0,\pi,2\pi$ ii) $k\pi$
	③	i) $\dfrac{\pi}{2},\dfrac{3\pi}{2}$ ii) $\dfrac{\pi}{2}+2k\pi,\dfrac{3\pi}{2}+2k\pi$

	④ i) π ii) $\pi + 2k\pi$	
Ex3.	① $x = \sin^{-1}(0.8), \pi - \sin^{-1}(0.8)$ $(0.92729, \pi - 0.92729)$	
	② $x = \tan^{-1}(2.5), \pi + \tan^{-1}(2.5)$ $(1.19028, \pi + 1.19028)$	
	③ $x = \pi - \cos^{-1}(0.3), \pi + \cos^{-1}(0.3)$ $(\pi - 1.2661, \pi + 1.2661)$	
	④ $x = \pi + \sin^{-1}\left(\dfrac{2}{3}\right), 2\pi - \sin^{-1}\left(\dfrac{2}{3}\right)$ $(\pi + 0.72972, 2\pi - 0.72972)$	
	⑤ $x = \pi - \tan^{-1}(2), 2\pi - \tan^{-1}(2)$ $(\pi - 1.10714, 2\pi - 1.10714)$	
Ex4.	① $\dfrac{2\pi}{3}, \dfrac{4\pi}{3}$	
	② $\dfrac{\pi}{3}, \dfrac{2\pi}{3}, 0, \pi, 2\pi$	
	③ $0, \pi, 2\pi, \cos^{-1}\dfrac{2}{3}, 2\pi - \cos^{-1}\dfrac{2}{3}$ $(0.84106, 2\pi - 0.84106)$	
	④ $0, \pi, 2\pi, \dfrac{\pi}{3}, \dfrac{5\pi}{3}$	
	⑤ $\dfrac{\pi}{4}, \dfrac{3\pi}{4}, \dfrac{5\pi}{4}, \dfrac{7\pi}{4}$	
	⑥ $\dfrac{\pi}{3}, \dfrac{4\pi}{3}, \dfrac{2\pi}{3}, \dfrac{5\pi}{3}$	
Ex5.	$\dfrac{5\pi}{6}, \dfrac{11\pi}{6}, \dfrac{17\pi}{6}, \dfrac{23\pi}{6}$	
Ex6.	$\dfrac{\pi}{4}, \dfrac{3\pi}{4}, -\dfrac{\pi}{4}, -\dfrac{3\pi}{4}$	

6.2 More Trigonometric Equations

Ex1.	① $\dfrac{\pi}{6}, \dfrac{5\pi}{6}$	
	② $\dfrac{\pi}{6}, \dfrac{5\pi}{6}, \dfrac{7\pi}{6}, \dfrac{11\pi}{6}$	
	③ $\dfrac{\pi}{4}, \dfrac{3\pi}{4}, \dfrac{5\pi}{4}, \dfrac{7\pi}{4}$	
	④ $\dfrac{\pi}{3}, \dfrac{2\pi}{3}, \dfrac{4\pi}{3}, \dfrac{5\pi}{3}$	
	⑤ $\pi + \sin^{-1}\dfrac{1}{5}, 2\pi - \sin^{-1}\dfrac{1}{5}$	
	⑥ $\dfrac{2\pi}{3}, \dfrac{4\pi}{3}, 0, 2\pi$	
	⑦ $0, \pi, 2\pi$	
	⑧ $\dfrac{\pi}{2}, \dfrac{7\pi}{6}, \dfrac{11\pi}{6}$	
	⑨ $\dfrac{\pi}{4}, \dfrac{5\pi}{4}$	
	⑩ $\dfrac{\pi}{6}, \dfrac{7\pi}{6}$	
	⑪ $0, 2\pi, \dfrac{2\pi}{3}, \dfrac{4\pi}{3}$	
	⑫ $0, \pi, \dfrac{\pi}{3}, \dfrac{5\pi}{3}$	
	⑬ $0, 2\pi$	
	⑭ $\dfrac{\pi}{2}$	
	⑮ $\dfrac{\pi}{2}, \pi$	
Ex2.	① $\dfrac{\pi}{6}, \dfrac{5\pi}{6}, \dfrac{7\pi}{6}, \dfrac{11\pi}{6}$	
	② $\dfrac{5\pi}{18}, \dfrac{7\pi}{18}, \dfrac{17\pi}{18}, \dfrac{19\pi}{18}, \dfrac{29\pi}{18}, \dfrac{31\pi}{18}$	
	③ $\dfrac{\pi}{2}$	
	④ $\dfrac{\pi}{8}, \dfrac{5\pi}{8}$	
	⑤ $\dfrac{\pi}{8}, \dfrac{5\pi}{8}$	
	⑥ $\dfrac{\pi}{12}, \dfrac{5\pi}{12}, \dfrac{13\pi}{12}, \dfrac{17\pi}{12}, \dfrac{\pi}{4}, \dfrac{5\pi}{4}$	
	⑦ $0, \dfrac{\pi}{2}, 2\pi$	

6.3 The Law of Sines

Ex1.	① 15.024 ft
	② 13.987
	③ 1.948 in
	④ 46.509 in
	⑤ 53.823°
	⑥ 59.004°
Ex2.	① 70.48°, 109.52°
	② 58.05°, 121.95°
	③ 27.07°
	④ None
	⑤ None
	⑥ 2.866°
Ex3.	① $B = 20.322°$, $A = 149.68°$ $a = 29.054$
	$B' = 159.68°$, $A' = 10.32°$ $a' = 10.32$
	② None
	③ $B = 20.26°$, $C = 39.73°$ $c = 18.45$
	④ $A = 66.49°$, $C = 53.51°$ $c = 157.82$
	$A = 113.51°$, $C = 6.49°$ $c = 22.18$
Ex4.	$\angle C = 57.697°$, $\angle ADB = 122.302°$
Ex5.	45°
Ex6.	1.295 mi
Ex7.	5.959 km
Ex8.	a) $1 : \sqrt{3} : 2$
	b) $1 : \sqrt{3} : 2$

6.4 The Law of Cosines

Ex1.	① 53.121 mi
	② 20.999 in
	③ 26.998°
	④ 137°
	⑤ 41.06°
	⑥ 43.95°
Ex2.	13.05
Ex3.	81.87° (or 1.4288 rad)
Ex4.	120°
Ex5.	none
Ex6.	38.5 m
Ex7.	28.955°

6.5 Area of Triangle

Ex1.	① $60.22 m^2$
	② $14.772 m^2$
	③ 173.785
	④ 16.356
Ex2.	$\dfrac{5\pi}{6}$
Ex3.	① (a) 15.788, (b) 4.132
	② (a) 30.612, (b) 39.308
	③ (a) 69.297, (b) 333.655
Ex4.	$24\pi - 18\sqrt{3}$
Ex5.	① $6\sqrt{3}$
	② $4\sqrt{35}$
	③ 52.618
Ex6.	2
Ex7.	$r^2 \left(2 - 2\cos\theta - \dfrac{\theta}{2} + \dfrac{\sin\theta}{2} \right)$

Answers

7. Polar coordinate and Complex number

7.1 Polar Coordinates

Ex1.	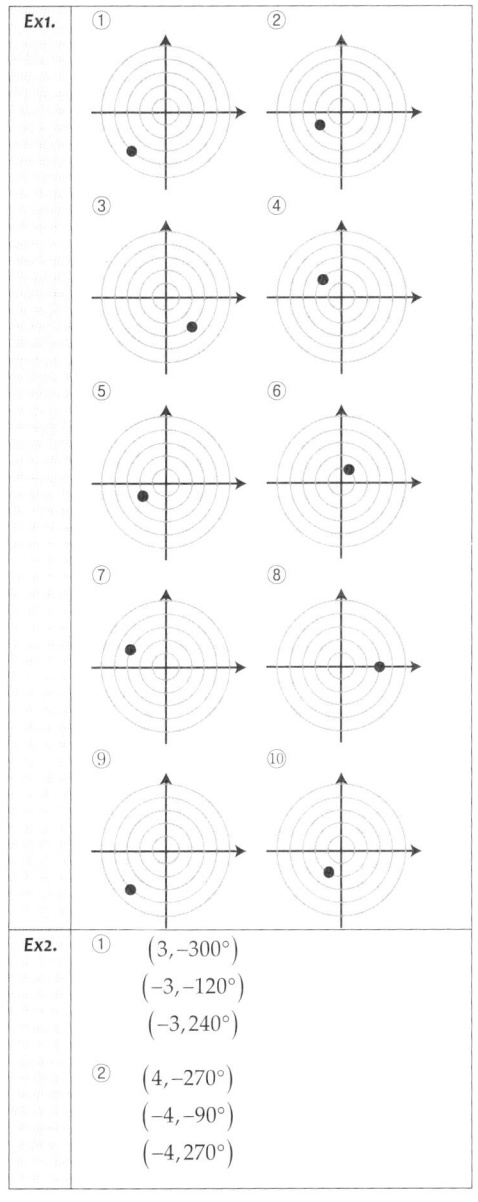
Ex2.	① $(3,-300°)$ $(-3,-120°)$ $(-3,240°)$ ② $(4,-270°)$ $(-4,-90°)$ $(-4,270°)$

	③ $\left(2,-\dfrac{7\pi}{6}\right)$ $\left(-2,-\dfrac{\pi}{6}\right)$ $\left(-2,\dfrac{11\pi}{6}\right)$ ④ $\left(3,-\dfrac{7\pi}{4}\right)$ $\left(-3,-\dfrac{3\pi}{4}\right)$ $\left(-3,\dfrac{5\pi}{4}\right)$
Ex3.	① $\left(-3\sqrt{2},-3\sqrt{2}\right)$ ② $\left(-\dfrac{7\sqrt{3}}{2},-\dfrac{7}{2}\right)$ ③ $\left(-\dfrac{7}{2},\dfrac{7\sqrt{3}}{2}\right)$ ④ $\left(-3\sqrt{2},-3\sqrt{2}\right)$ ⑤ $\left(\dfrac{3\sqrt{3}}{2},-\dfrac{3}{2}\right)$
Ex4.	① $\left(\sqrt{2},\dfrac{3\pi}{4}\right)$ ② $\left(12,\dfrac{5\pi}{3}\right)$ ③ $\left(10,\dfrac{\pi}{6}\right)$ ④ $(4,0)$ ⑤ $\left(3,\dfrac{3\pi}{2}\right)$ ⑥ $\left(2\sqrt{6},\dfrac{3\pi}{4}\right)$ ⑦ $\left(2\sqrt{5},\pi-\tan^{-1}2\right)=\left(2\sqrt{5},2.0344\right)$ ⑧ $\left(\sqrt{34},\pi-\tan^{-1}\dfrac{3}{5}\right)=\left(\sqrt{34},2.601\right)$

Ex5.
① $x^2 + y^2 = 1$
② $y = 10$
③ $\sqrt{x^2 + y^2} + x = 5$
④ $x^2 + y^2 = y$
⑤ $x^2 + y^2 - 10y = 0$
⑥ $x - y = 3$
⑦ $4y + 5x = 2$
⑧ $y = -2$
⑨ $x = 3$

Ex6.
① $r = \dfrac{7}{\sin\theta} = 7\csc\theta$
② $r = \dfrac{3}{\cos\theta + \sin\theta}$
③ $r = \dfrac{4}{2\cos\theta - \sin\theta}$
④ $r^2 = 4$
⑤ $r^2 = 2\sec 2\theta$
⑥ $r^2 = -\sec 2\theta$
⑦ $r^2 = 1$

7.2 Graphs of Polar Equations

Ex1.
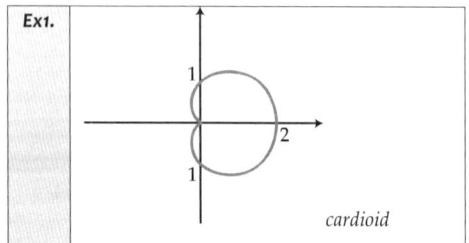
cardioid

Ex2.
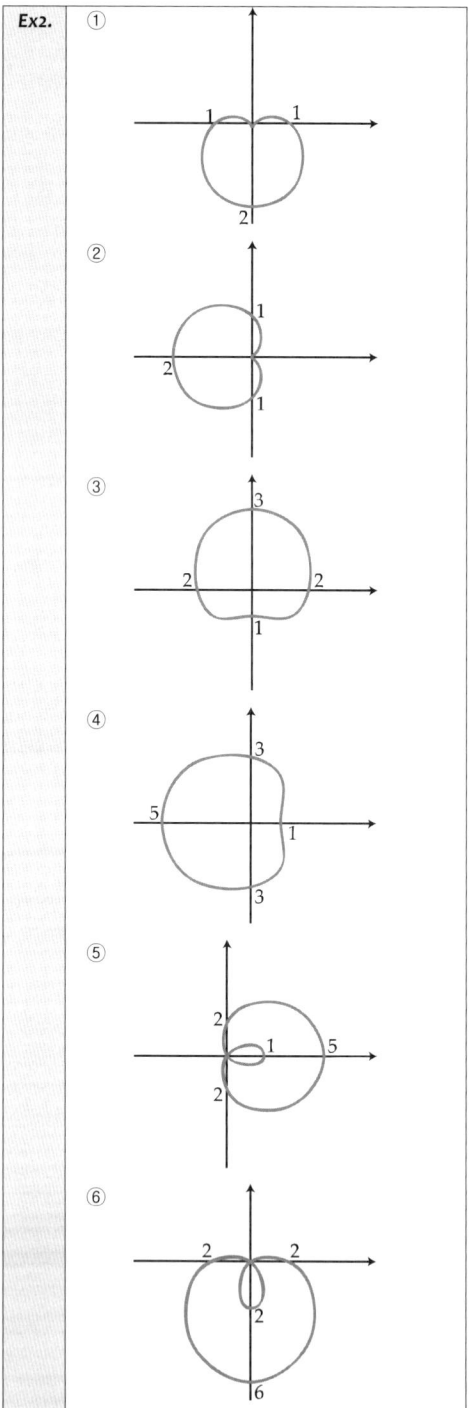

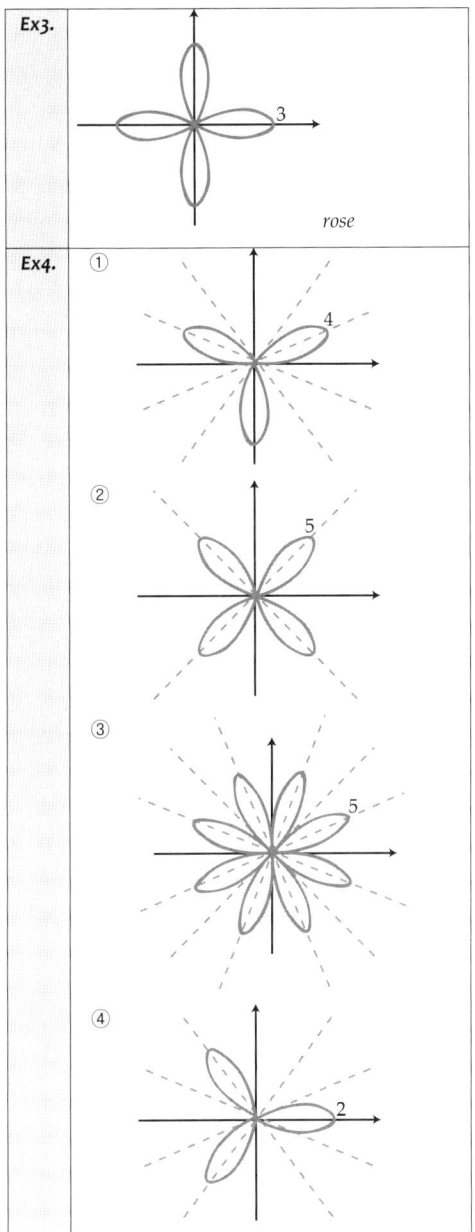
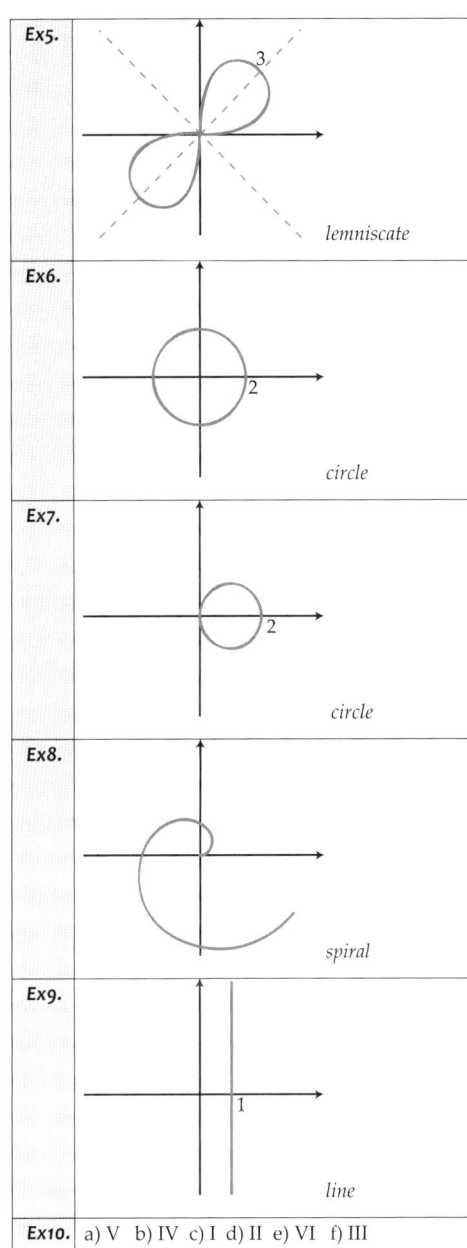

Ex10. a) V b) IV c) I d) II e) VI f) III

7.3 Complex Numbers and De Moivre's Theorem

Ex1.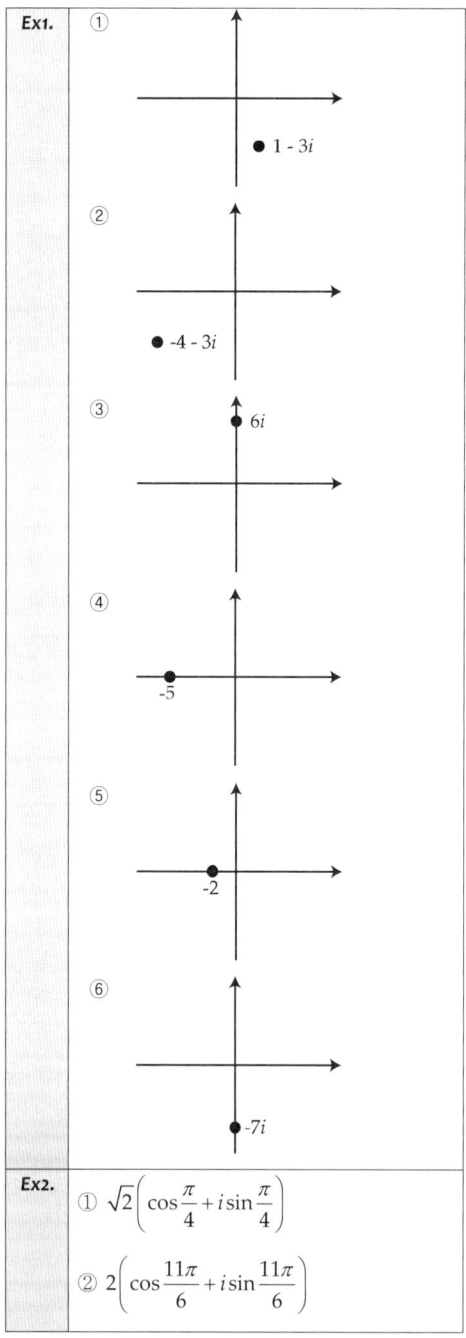

Ex2.
① $\sqrt{2}\left(\cos\dfrac{\pi}{4}+i\sin\dfrac{\pi}{4}\right)$

② $2\left(\cos\dfrac{11\pi}{6}+i\sin\dfrac{11\pi}{6}\right)$

③ $2\left(\cos\dfrac{5\pi}{3}+i\sin\dfrac{5\pi}{3}\right)$

④ $2\sqrt{2}\left(\cos\dfrac{3\pi}{4}+i\sin\dfrac{3\pi}{4}\right)$

⑤ $\pi-\tan^{-1}\dfrac{3}{2}=2.159$

$\sqrt{13}\left(\cos 2.159+i\sin 2.159\right)$

⑥ $2\pi-\tan^{-1}\dfrac{1}{\sqrt{5}}=5.863$

$\sqrt{6}\left(\cos 5.863+i\sin 5.863\right)$

Ex3.
① $-1+\sqrt{3}i$

② $-\dfrac{3\sqrt{3}}{2}-\dfrac{3}{2}i$

③ $-\sqrt{3}-i$

④ $-3i$

⑤ -4

⑥ 3

Ex4.
① $z_1z_2=8\left(\cos 60°+i\sin 60°\right)$

$\dfrac{z_1}{z_2}=\dfrac{1}{2}\left(\cos 20°+i\sin 20°\right)$

② $z_1z_2=2\left(\cos 220°+i\sin 220°\right)$

$\dfrac{z_1}{z_2}=\dfrac{1}{2}\left(\cos 20°+i\sin 20°\right)$

③ $z_1z_2=6\left(\cos\dfrac{3\pi}{10}+i\sin\dfrac{3\pi}{10}\right)$

$\dfrac{z_1}{z_2}=\dfrac{2}{3}\left(\cos\dfrac{\pi}{10}+i\sin\dfrac{\pi}{10}\right)$

④ $z_1z_2=16\left(\cos\dfrac{9\pi}{10}+i\sin\dfrac{9\pi}{10}\right)$

$\dfrac{z_1}{z_2}=\cos\dfrac{3\pi}{10}+i\sin\dfrac{3\pi}{10}$

⑤ $z_1z_2=\dfrac{1}{2}cis\dfrac{3\pi}{2}$

$\dfrac{z_1}{z_2}=8cis\dfrac{5\pi}{6}$

Ex5. ① $2-2\sqrt{3}i$

	② $\dfrac{27}{2} - \dfrac{27\sqrt{3}}{2}i$ ③ $-4+4i$ ④ $-64\sqrt{3}+64i$ ⑤ 64 ⑥ $-128+128i$ ⑦ $-\dfrac{1}{64}$
Ex6.	$\cos 35A + i\sin 35A$
Ex7.	8
Ex8.	※ $cis\theta$ means $\cos\theta + i\sin\theta$ ① $2\sqrt{2}\,cis\dfrac{\pi}{12}, 2\sqrt{2}\,cis\dfrac{13\pi}{12}$ 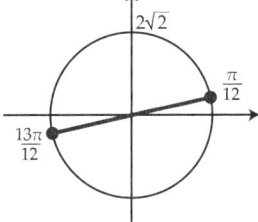 ② $\sqrt[6]{2}\,cis\dfrac{\pi}{4},\ \sqrt[6]{2}\,cis\dfrac{11\pi}{12},\ \sqrt[6]{2}\,cis\dfrac{19\pi}{12}$ 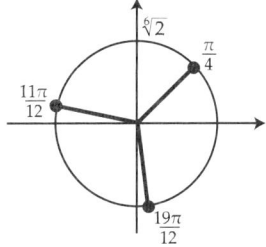 ③ $\sqrt[3]{6}\,cis\dfrac{5\pi}{9},\ \sqrt[3]{6}\,cis\dfrac{11\pi}{9},\ \sqrt[3]{6}\,cis\dfrac{17\pi}{9}$ 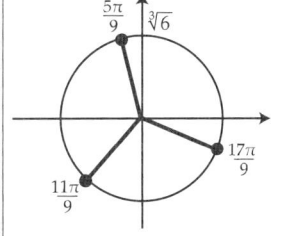

④ $\sqrt[4]{2}\,cis\dfrac{\pi}{3},\ \sqrt[4]{2}\,cis\dfrac{5\pi}{6},\ \sqrt[4]{2}\,cis\dfrac{4\pi}{3},\ \sqrt[4]{2}\,cis\dfrac{11\pi}{6}$

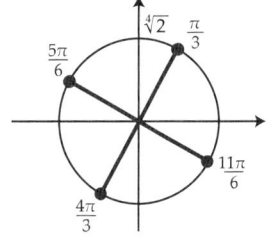

⑤ $cis\dfrac{\pi}{10},\ cis\dfrac{\pi}{2},\ cis\dfrac{9\pi}{10},\ cis\dfrac{13\pi}{10},\ cis\dfrac{17\pi}{10}$

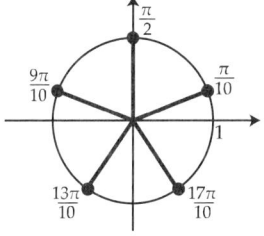

⑥ $2cis\dfrac{\pi}{5},\ 2cis\dfrac{3\pi}{5},\ 2cis\pi,\ 2cis\dfrac{7\pi}{5},\ 2cis\dfrac{9\pi}{5}$

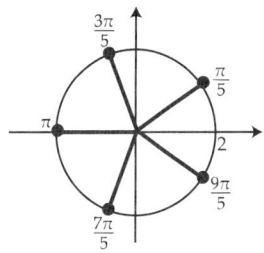

7.4 Parametric Equations

Ex1.	① $x = -3+2y \rightarrow line$ ② $y = \sqrt{3x} \rightarrow radical$ ③ $x = (-y+4)^2 - 1 \rightarrow parabola$ ④ $y = \left(\dfrac{x}{3}\right)^2 - 2 \rightarrow parabola$ ⑤ $\dfrac{y^2}{9} + \dfrac{x^2}{4} = 1 \rightarrow ellipse$ ⑥ $\dfrac{y^2}{49} + \dfrac{x^2}{25} = 1 \rightarrow ellipse$

⑦ $\dfrac{x^2}{4} - \dfrac{y^2}{9} = 1 \to hyperbola$

⑧ $1 + y^2 = x^2 \to hyperbola$

Ex2.

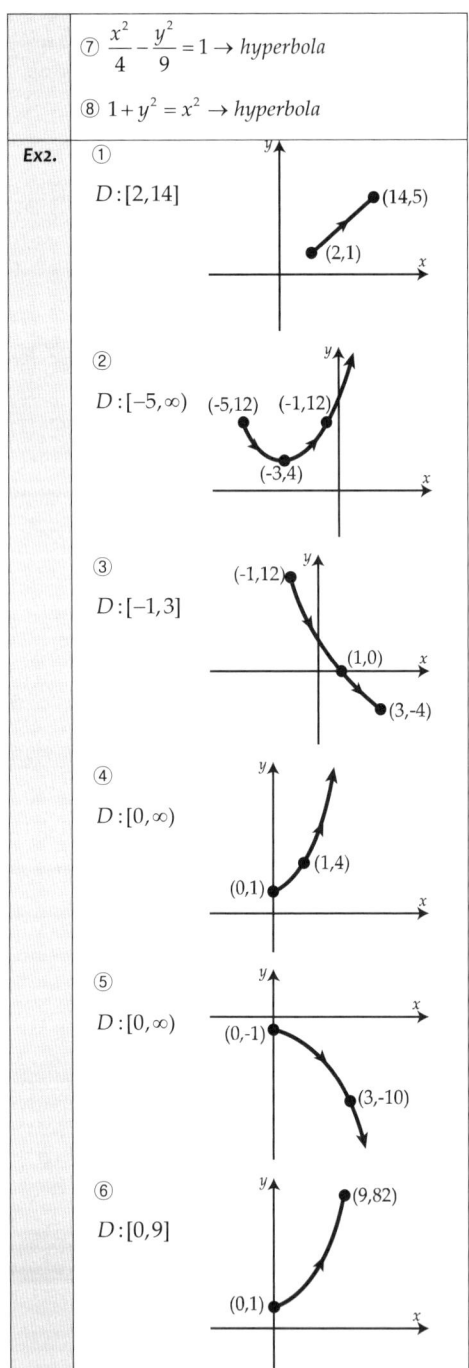

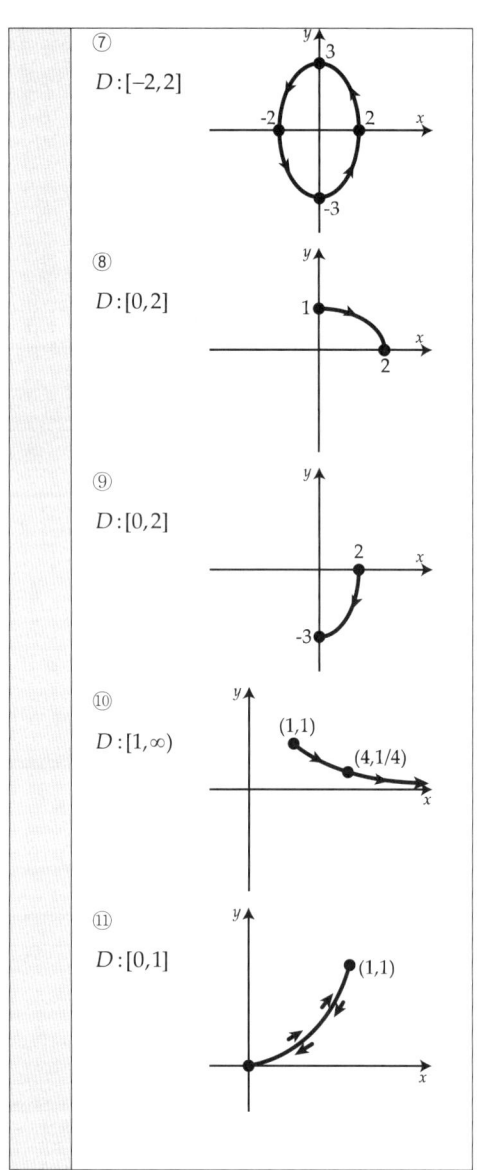

Answers

8. Vector

8.1 Vector Basics

Ex1.	① vector ② vector ③ scalar ④ vector ⑤ vector ⑥ scalar
Ex2.	① 210° ② 305° ③ 125° ④ 335°
Ex3.	
Ex4.	① True ② True ③ False ④ False ⑤ True

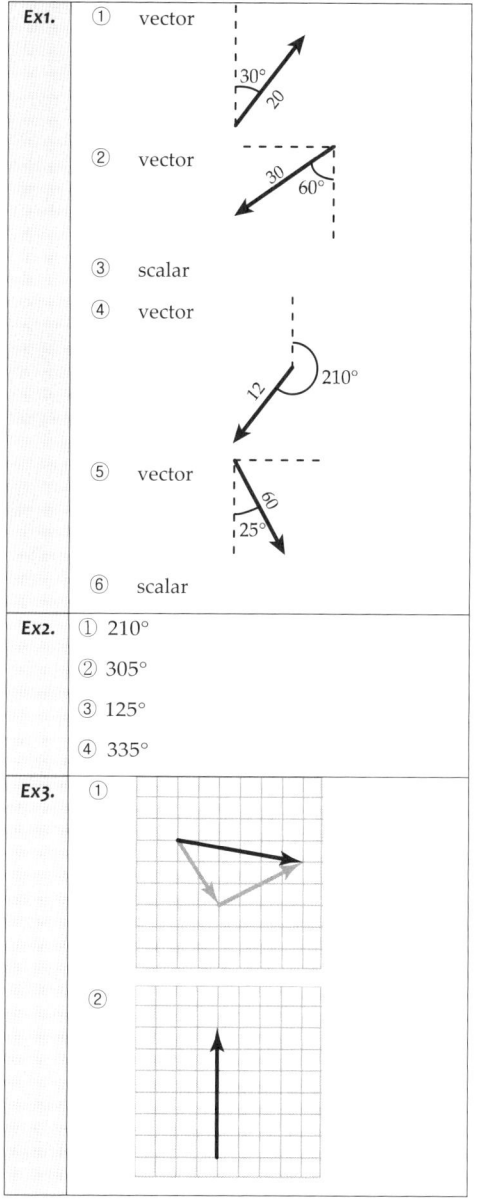
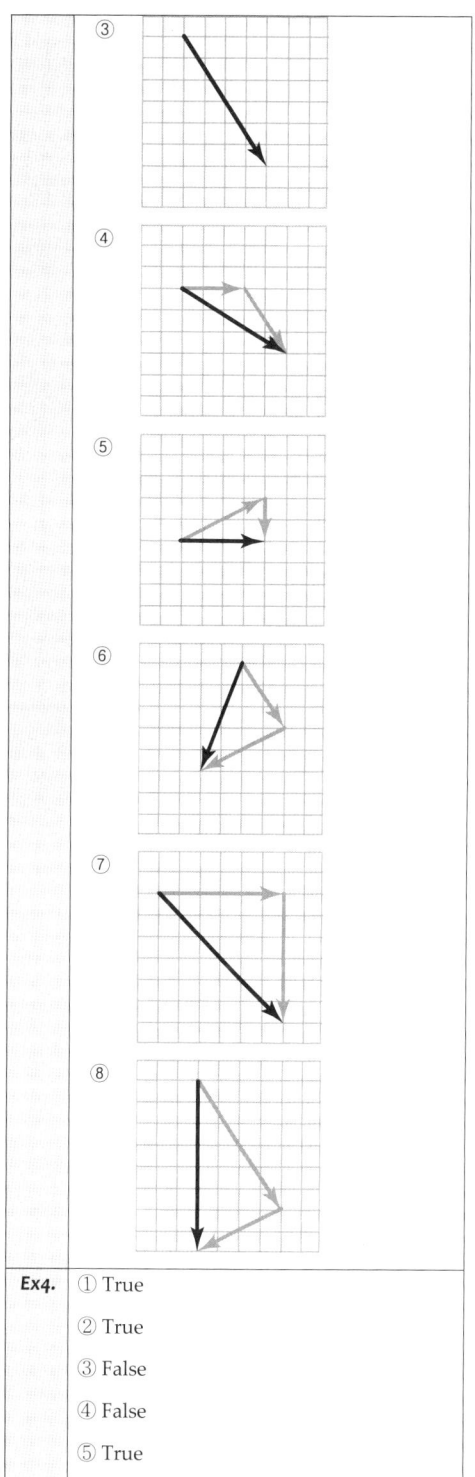

	⑥ True
	⑦ True
	⑧ True
Ex5.	12.145 $m/\sec$ 26.695° to the horizontal
Ex6.	279.625 km in the direction $E17.304°S$

8.2 Vectors in Two Dimensions

Ex1.	① $\langle 7,3 \rangle = 7i+3j$
	② $\langle -6,0 \rangle = -6i$
	③ $\langle 0,6 \rangle = 6j$
	④ $\langle -5,-5 \rangle = -5i-5j$
Ex2.	① $\langle 3,4 \rangle$
	② $\langle 4,-5 \rangle$
	③ $\langle 4,-5 \rangle$
	④ $\langle 3,4 \rangle$
	⑤ $\langle 1,-2 \rangle$
	⑥ $\langle -4,5 \rangle$
	⑦ $\langle -4,-2 \rangle$
	⑧ $\langle 5,-7 \rangle$
	⑨ $\langle 1,-9 \rangle$
	⑩ $\langle 4,2 \rangle$
	⑪ $\langle -5,7 \rangle$
Ex3.	$(1,-1)$
Ex4.	$(8,-1)$
Ex5.	① $\langle 5,-1 \rangle$
	② $\langle -1,-1 \rangle$
	③ $\langle 13,-2 \rangle$
	④ $\langle 10,1 \rangle$
Ex6.	① $2i+2j$
	② $4i-4j$
	③ $i-11j$
	④ $6i-10j$
Ex7.	① $2, \langle 1,0 \rangle$
	② $\sqrt{10}, \left\langle -\dfrac{3\sqrt{10}}{10}, \dfrac{\sqrt{10}}{10} \right\rangle$
	③ $13, \left\langle \dfrac{5}{13}, -\dfrac{12}{13} \right\rangle$
	④ $\sqrt{26}, \left\langle -\dfrac{\sqrt{26}}{26}, \dfrac{5\sqrt{26}}{26} \right\rangle$
	⑤ $\sqrt{2}, \left\langle \dfrac{\sqrt{2}}{2}, \dfrac{\sqrt{2}}{2} \right\rangle$
	⑥ $5, \left\langle \dfrac{3}{5}, \dfrac{4}{5} \right\rangle$
Ex8.	① $\dfrac{5}{2}i+\dfrac{5\sqrt{3}}{2}j$
	② $-\dfrac{3\sqrt{3}}{2}i+\dfrac{3}{2}j$
	③ $-\dfrac{3}{2}i-\dfrac{3\sqrt{3}}{2}j$
	④ $-12\sqrt{2}i-12\sqrt{2}j$
Ex9.	① $\langle 3\sqrt{2}\cos 45°, 3\sqrt{2}\sin 45° \rangle$
	② $\langle 2\cos 60°, 2\sin 60° \rangle$
	③ $\langle 6\cos 150°, 6\sin 150° \rangle$
	④ $\langle 5\sqrt{2}\cos 225°, 5\sqrt{2}\sin 225° \rangle$
	⑤ $180° + \tan^{-1} 5 = 258.69°$ $\langle \sqrt{26}\cos 258.69°, \sqrt{26}\sin 258.69° \rangle$
	⑥ $360° - \tan^{-1} 3 = 288.435°$ $\langle \sqrt{10}\cos 288.435°, \sqrt{10}\sin 288.435° \rangle$
Ex10.	speed = 23.407, 118.975° to the horizontal
Ex11.	speed = 568.254, 214.852° to the horizontal

8.3 The Dot Product

Ex1.	① 24 ② −20 ③ 20 ④ 16 ⑤ 24 ⑥ −2 ⑦ −3 ⑧ $-3\sqrt{3}$
Ex2.	① $\cos^{-1}\dfrac{4}{5} \approx 37°$ ② $\cos^{-1}\left(-\dfrac{1}{\sqrt{26}}\right) \approx 101°$ ③ $\cos^{-1} 0 \approx 90°$ ④ $\cos^{-1}\dfrac{1}{5\sqrt{2}} \approx 82°$ ⑤ $\cos^{-1}\dfrac{4}{\sqrt{17}} \approx 14°$ ⑥ $\cos^{-1}\dfrac{1}{\sqrt{5}} \approx 63°$
Ex3.	① orthogonal ② parallel ③ neither ④ orthogonal ⑤ parallel ⑥ neither ⑦ parallel
Ex4.	$t = -3, \dfrac{2}{3}$
Ex5.	① 14 ② 16
Ex6.	① $\dfrac{8\sqrt{5}}{5}$ ② −1 ③ $\dfrac{2\sqrt{5}}{5}$
	④ $2\sqrt{2}$ ⑤ 1 ⑥ −2
Ex7.	① $\left\langle \dfrac{16}{5}, \dfrac{8}{5} \right\rangle$ ② $\langle 0, -1 \rangle$ ③ $\left\langle \dfrac{2}{5}, \dfrac{4}{5} \right\rangle$ ④ $\langle -2, 2 \rangle$ ⑤ $\langle 1, 0 \rangle$ ⑥ $\langle 0, 2 \rangle$
Ex8.	$1324.798\,lb$
Ex9.	a) $80.084\,lb$ b) $74.253\,lb$
Ex10.	$5.739°$
Ex11.	$20\,lb \cdot ft$
Ex12.	$5\,lb \cdot ft$
Ex13.	$340.999\,newton \cdot meter$

8.4 Three-Dimensional Coordinate

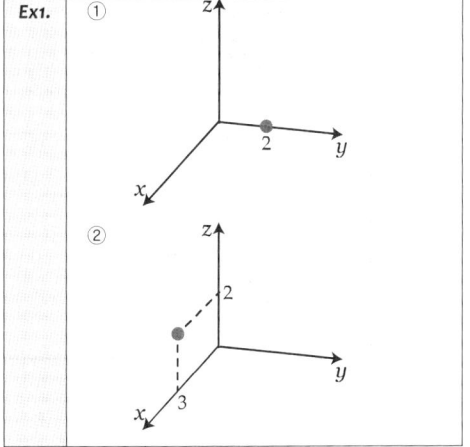

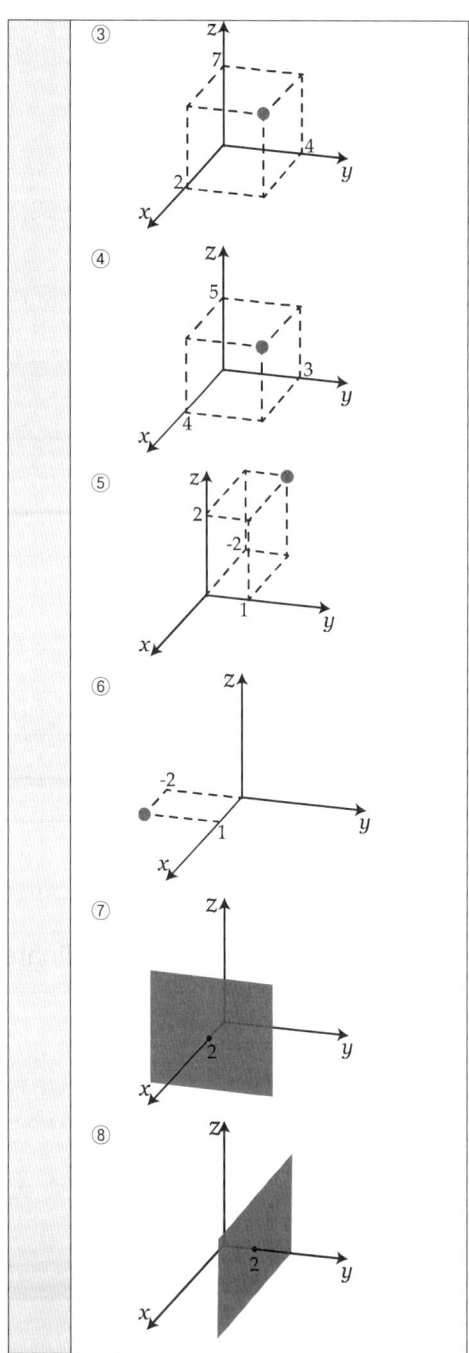

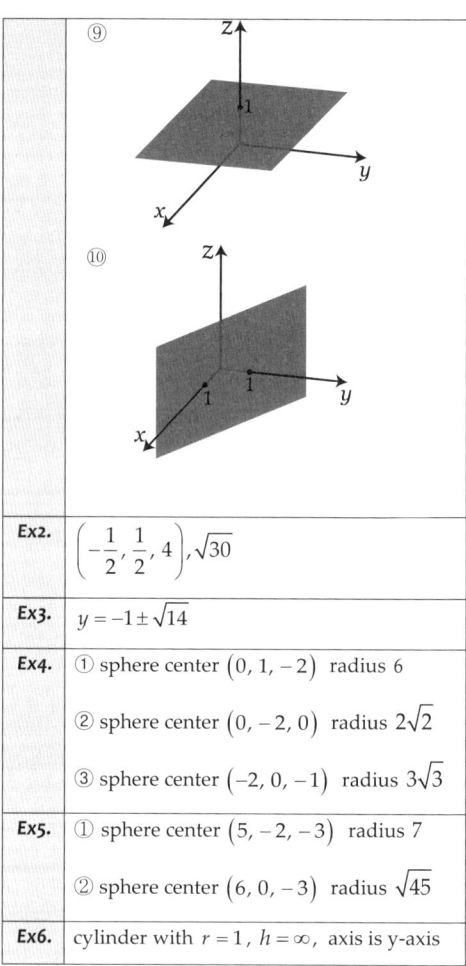

Ex2.	$\left(-\dfrac{1}{2}, \dfrac{1}{2}, 4\right), \sqrt{30}$
Ex3.	$y = -1 \pm \sqrt{14}$
Ex4.	① sphere center $(0, 1, -2)$ radius 6 ② sphere center $(0, -2, 0)$ radius $2\sqrt{2}$ ③ sphere center $(-2, 0, -1)$ radius $3\sqrt{3}$
Ex5.	① sphere center $(5, -2, -3)$ radius 7 ② sphere center $(6, 0, -3)$ radius $\sqrt{45}$
Ex6.	cylinder with $r = 1$, $h = \infty$, axis is y-axis

8.5 Vectors in Three Dimensions

Ex1.	① $\langle 3, 4, 2 \rangle$ ② $\langle 4, 2, 2 \rangle$ ③ $\langle -4, -2, -2 \rangle$ ④ $\langle 4, -5, -2 \rangle$ ⑤ $\langle 1, -9, -4 \rangle$ ⑥ $\langle -5, 7, 2 \rangle$

Ex2.	$(3, 4, -5)$
Ex3.	① $\langle 2, -1, 4 \rangle$ ② $\langle 4, -1, -2 \rangle$ ③ $\langle 3, -2, 11 \rangle$ ④ $\langle -7, 1, 11 \rangle$
Ex4.	$s = -4$, $r = \dfrac{3}{2}$
Ex5.	① $\left\langle \dfrac{2\sqrt{14}}{14}, \dfrac{\sqrt{14}}{14}, \dfrac{3\sqrt{14}}{14} \right\rangle$ ② $\left\langle -\dfrac{3\sqrt{10}}{10}, 0, \dfrac{\sqrt{10}}{10} \right\rangle$ ③ $\left\langle \dfrac{3}{5}, 0, -\dfrac{4}{5} \right\rangle$ ④ $\left\langle \dfrac{2}{3}, \dfrac{2}{3}, -\dfrac{1}{3} \right\rangle$
Ex6.	① a) -5, b) $\cos^{-1}\left(-\dfrac{5}{\sqrt{55}}\right) = 132.392°$ ② a) 12, b) $\cos^{-1}\left(\dfrac{12}{\sqrt{14}\sqrt{75}}\right) = 68.264°$ ③ a) -4, b) $\cos^{-1}\left(-\dfrac{4}{\sqrt{70}}\right) = 118.56°$ ④ a) -4, b) $\cos^{-1}\left(-\dfrac{2}{5}\right) = 113.578°$
Ex7.	① perpendicular ② perpendicular ③ parallel ④ parallel
Ex8.	① $k = \pm 2$ ② $k = 0$
Ex9.	$\theta = \cos^{-1}\left(\dfrac{9}{\sqrt{21}\sqrt{14}}\right) = 58.339°$
Ex10.	$28.89°$

8.6 The Cross Product

Ex1.	① $2i - j + 3k$ ② $8i - 4j - 4k$ ③ $-4i + 10j + 2k$ ④ $-2i + j - 3k$ ⑤ 16 ⑥ -16
Ex2.	① $5i + 7j + 6k$ (or $-5i - 7j - 6k$) ② $-6i + 2j - 2k$ (or $6i - 2j + 2k$)
Ex3.	① $9j$ ② $i - j$
Ex4.	(a) $-3i + 6j - k$ (b) $\left\langle -\dfrac{3\sqrt{46}}{46}, \dfrac{6\sqrt{46}}{46}, -\dfrac{\sqrt{46}}{46} \right\rangle$
Ex5.	(a) $a \times b = 4i + 4j - 8k$, $b \times a = -4i - 4j + 8k$ (b) $\dfrac{\sqrt{42}}{7}$
Ex6.	100
Ex7.	① $\sqrt{69}$ ② $2\sqrt{35}$
Ex8.	(a) $(-3, -2, 10)$ (b) 25
Ex9.	① 24 ② 8

Answers
9. Conic Section

9.1 Conic Sections and Parabolas

Ex1.

① Focus: $(0, 1)$
directrix: $y = -1$
f width: 4

② Focus: $(0, 4)$
directrix: $y = -4$
f width: 16

③ Focus: $\left(\dfrac{1}{32}, 0\right)$
directrix: $x = -\dfrac{1}{32}$
f width: $\dfrac{1}{8}$

④ Focus: $(2, 0)$
directrix: $x = -2$
f width: 8

⑤ Focus: $\left(-\dfrac{3}{2}, 0\right)$
directrix: $x = \dfrac{3}{2}$
f width: 6

⑥ Focus: $(0, -4)$
directrix: $y = 4$
f width: 16

Ex2.

① $-8y = x^2$
② $12y = x^2$
③ $28x = y^2$
④ $-32x = y^2$
⑤ $12x = y^2$
⑥ $-16y = x^2$
⑦ $-8y = x^2$

9.2 Ellipses

Ex1.

① Foci: $(0, \pm 3)$
Vertices: $(0, \pm 5)$

② Foci: $(\pm\sqrt{46}, 0)$
Vertices: $(\pm 7, 0)$

③ Foci: $(\pm 2\sqrt{3}, 0)$
Vertices: $(\pm 4, 0)$

④ Foci: $(0, \pm\sqrt{7})$
Vertices: $(0, \pm 4)$

⑤ Foci: $\left(0, \pm\dfrac{\sqrt{3}}{4}\right)$
Vertices: $\left(0, \pm\dfrac{1}{2}\right)$

616 Mia's Precalculus

⑥ Foci: $\left(\pm\dfrac{2\sqrt{2}}{3}, 0\right)$ Vertices: $(\pm 1, 0)$

⑦ Foci: $(\pm 1, 0)$ Vertices: $\left(\pm\dfrac{\sqrt{5}}{2}, 0\right)$

Ex2.
① $\dfrac{x^2}{100} + \dfrac{y^2}{75} = 1$

② $\dfrac{x^2}{16} + \dfrac{y^2}{7} = 1$

③ $\dfrac{x^2}{60} + \dfrac{y^2}{64} = 1$

④ $\dfrac{x^2}{5} + \dfrac{y^2}{9} = 1$

⑤ $\dfrac{x^2}{25} + \dfrac{y^2}{16} = 1$

⑥ $\dfrac{x^2}{25} + \dfrac{y^2}{74} = 1$

⑦ $\dfrac{x^2}{4} + \dfrac{y^2}{121} = 1$

⑧ $\dfrac{x^2}{9} + \dfrac{y^2}{64} = 1$

9.3 Hyperbolas

Ex1.
① Focus: $(\pm\sqrt{61}, 0)$ Vertices: $(\pm 5, 0)$ Asymptotes: $y = \pm\dfrac{6}{5}x$

② Focus: $(\pm 2\sqrt{5}, 0)$ Vertices: $(\pm 4, 0)$ Asymptotes: $y = \pm\dfrac{1}{2}x$

③ Focus: $\left(0, \pm\dfrac{\sqrt{17}}{4}\right)$ Vertices: $\left(0, \pm\dfrac{1}{4}\right)$ Asymptotes: $y = \pm\dfrac{1}{4}x$

④ Focus: $\left(0, \pm\dfrac{\sqrt{10}}{3}\right)$ Vertices: $(0, \pm 1)$ Asymptotes: $y = \pm 3x$

⑤ Focus: $\left(\pm\dfrac{5}{2}, 0\right)$ Vertices: $(\pm\sqrt{5}, 0)$ Asymptotes: $y = \pm\dfrac{1}{2}x$

⑥ Focus: $\left(0, \pm\dfrac{2\sqrt{26}}{5}\right)$ Vertices: $(0, \pm 2)$ Asymptotes: $y = \pm 5x$

Ex2.
① $\dfrac{x^2}{4} - \dfrac{y^2}{12} = 1$

② $\dfrac{y^2}{16} - \dfrac{x^2}{84} = 1$

③ $\dfrac{y^2}{25} - \dfrac{x^2}{56} = 1$

④ $\dfrac{x^2}{4} - \dfrac{y^2}{32} = 1$

⑤ $\dfrac{y^2}{16} - \dfrac{x^2}{100} = 1$

⑥ $\dfrac{x^2}{36} - \dfrac{y^2}{16} = 1$

9.4 Transformation of Conics

Ex1.
① Vertex: $(2, 3)$
Focus: $(2, 5)$
directrix: $y = 1$

② Vertex: $(-2, 5)$
Focus: $(2, 5)$
directrix: $x = -6$

③ Vertex: $(-2, -7)$
Focus: $\left(-\dfrac{5}{2}, -7\right)$
directrix: $x = -\dfrac{3}{2}$

④ Vertex: $(3, -1)$
Focus: $\left(3, -\dfrac{5}{4}\right)$
directrix: $y = -\dfrac{3}{4}$

Ex2.
① $8(x-1) = (y+9)^2$

② $12(y+12) = (x-4)^2$

③ $10(y-3) = (x-8)^2$

④ $-16(x-1) = (y+4)^2$

Ex3.
① Center: $(-4, 2)$
Foci: $(-4, 5), (-4, -1)$
Vertices: $(-4, 7), (-4, -3)$

② Center: $(2, -1)$
Foci: $(2 \pm 3\sqrt{3}, -1)$
Vertices: $(8, -1), (-4, -1)$

③ Center: $(2, -1)$
Foci: $\left(\dfrac{5}{2}, -1\right), \left(\dfrac{3}{2}, -1\right)$
Vertices: $\left(2 \pm \dfrac{\sqrt{2}}{2}, -1\right)$

④ Center: $(-3, 2)$
Foci: $\left(-3 \pm \dfrac{\sqrt{5}}{6}, 2\right)$
Vertices: $\left(-\dfrac{7}{2}, 2\right), \left(-\dfrac{5}{2}, 2\right)$

Ex4.
① $\dfrac{(x-2)^2}{16} + \dfrac{(y-2)^2}{25} = 1$

② $\dfrac{(x-2)^2}{25} + \dfrac{(y-1)^2}{16} = 1$

③ $\dfrac{(x-3)^2}{16} + \dfrac{(y+4)^2}{9} = 1$

Ex5.
① Center: $(-5, 1)$
Foci: $(0, 1), (-10, 1)$
Vertices: $(-1, 1), (-9, 1)$
Asymptotes: $y - 1 = \pm \dfrac{3}{4}(x + 5)$

② Center: $(-4, -4)$
Foci: $(-4 \pm \sqrt{29}, -4)$
Vertices: $(-2, -4), (-6, -4)$
Asymptotes: $y + 4 = \pm \dfrac{5}{2}(x + 4)$

③ Center: $(1, 5)$
Foci: $(1, 5 \pm 2\sqrt{5})$
Vertices: $(1, 7), (1, 3)$
Asymptotes: $y - 5 = \pm \dfrac{1}{2}(x - 1)$

④ Center: $(4, 3)$
Foci: $\left(4, 3 \pm \dfrac{\sqrt{5}}{2}\right)$
Vertices: $\left(4, \dfrac{7}{2}\right), \left(4, \dfrac{5}{2}\right)$
Asymptotes: $y - 3 = \pm \dfrac{1}{2}(x - 4)$

Ex6.
① $\dfrac{(x-4)^2}{4} - \dfrac{(y+3)^2}{45} = 1$

② $\dfrac{(y-5)^2}{9} - \dfrac{(x+2)^2}{40} = 1$

	③ $(x-6)^2 - \dfrac{(y+2)^2}{16} = 1$
	④ $\dfrac{(y-6)^2}{9} - \dfrac{(x+1)^2}{4} = 1$
Ex7.	① parabola Vertices: $(-3, -2)$ Focus: $(-3, -1)$
	② parabola Vertices: $(-1, -1)$ Focus: $\left(-\dfrac{3}{4}, -1\right)$
	③ Ellipse Vertices: $(2 \pm \sqrt{3}, -1)$ Foci: $(3, -1), (1, -1)$
	④ Ellipse Vertices: $(-1, 3), (-1, -1)$ Foci: $(-1, 2), (-1, 0)$
	⑤ hyperbola Vertices: $(2, -1), (0, -1)$ Foci: $(1 \pm \sqrt{2}, -1)$
	⑥ hyperbola Vertices: $(-1, 4), (-1, 0)$ Foci: $(-1, 2 \pm \sqrt{5})$
Ex8.	① $\dfrac{5}{4}$
	② $\dfrac{\sqrt{21}}{5}$
	③ 1
	④ $\dfrac{\sqrt{17}}{4}$
	⑤ $\dfrac{\sqrt{3}}{2}$
	⑥ $\dfrac{\sqrt{13}}{2}$
	⑦ $\dfrac{\sqrt{41}}{4}$

	⑧ $\dfrac{4\sqrt{3}}{7}$

9.5 Rotation of Conics

Ex1.	① $(2+\sqrt{3}, 1-2\sqrt{3})$
	② $(-2\sqrt{2}, 2\sqrt{2})$
	③ $(3, \sqrt{3})$
	④ $(-\sqrt{3}, 1)$
Ex2.	① $X^2 - Y^2 = 4$
	② $7X^2 + 6\sqrt{3}XY + 13Y^2 = 144$
	③ $7X^2 + 2\sqrt{3}XY + 5Y^2 = 56$
Ex3.	① parabola $\theta = 45°$ $X^2 + 4\sqrt{2}Y = 0$ 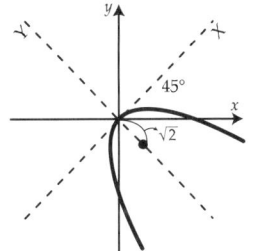
	② Ellipse $\theta = 30°$ $\dfrac{X^2}{4} + \dfrac{Y^2}{9} = 1$ 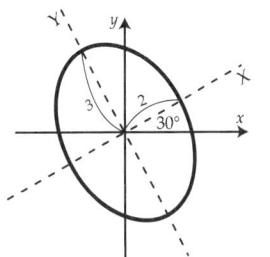

③ hyperbola
$\theta = 45°$
$\dfrac{Y^2}{32} - \dfrac{X^2}{32} = 1$

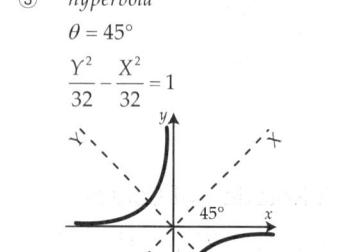

④ hyperbola
$\theta = 30°$
$4X^2 - Y^2 = 16$

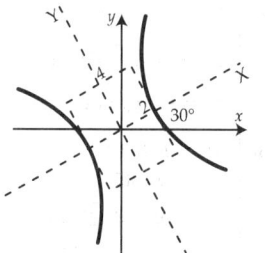

Answers
10. Matrix and System of Equation

10.1 Systems of Linear Equations in Several Variables

Ex1.	① $x = 2$, $y = -1$, $z = 3$
	② $x = -1$, $y = -2$, $z = 2$
	③ $x = -6$, $y = 8$, $z = 2$
	④ $x = 3$, $y = -2$, $z = 1$
Ex2.	① $x = 2$, $y = -1$, $z = 3$
	② $x = -1$, $y = -2$, $z = 2$
	③ $x = -6$, $y = 8$, $z = 2$
	④ $x = 3$, $y = -2$, $z = 1$
Ex3.	① No Solution
	② $x = 5 - 2t$, $y = -2 + t$, $z = t$
	③ $x = \dfrac{-t + 18}{5}$, $y = \dfrac{4t - 17}{-5}$, $z = t$
	④ No Solution
Ex4.	(a) $k = 12$
	(b) $x = \dfrac{t+3}{2}$, $y = 1 - 3t$, $z = t$
Ex5.	(a) $k \neq -\dfrac{3}{2}$
	(b) $k = -\dfrac{3}{2}$, $a = \dfrac{3}{2}$
	(c) $k = -\dfrac{3}{2}$, $a \neq \dfrac{3}{2}$

10.2 Algebra Of Matrices

Ex1.	① $\begin{bmatrix} 3 & 21 \\ -6 & 14 \end{bmatrix}$
	② $\begin{bmatrix} -13 & 7 & -1 \\ 0 & -8 & -3 \end{bmatrix}$
	③ $\begin{bmatrix} -2 & -21 \\ -16 & 7 \\ -17 & -19 \end{bmatrix}$
	④ Impossible
	⑤ Impossible
Ex2.	① $\begin{bmatrix} 2 & 1 \\ -3 & 8 \end{bmatrix}$
	② $\begin{bmatrix} -2 & 14 & 3 \\ -4 & 1 & -11 \end{bmatrix}$
Ex3.	① $\begin{bmatrix} -2 & -8 \\ -12 & 20 \end{bmatrix}$
	② $\begin{bmatrix} -1 & 9 \\ -8 & 6 \end{bmatrix}$
	③ $\begin{bmatrix} 7 & 19 \end{bmatrix}$
	④ $\begin{bmatrix} 1 & -4 \\ 5 & 9 \end{bmatrix}$
	⑤ $\begin{bmatrix} 28 & 14 & -14 \\ -4 & 8 & -2 \end{bmatrix}$
	⑥ $\begin{bmatrix} -51 \end{bmatrix}$
	⑦ Impossible
	⑧ Impossible
Ex4.	① Impossible
	② 2×2
	③ 2×2
	④ 2×3
	⑤ 2×2
	⑥ 2×2
	⑦ 2×3
Ex5.	B, D

Ex6.	$A^2 + AB + BA + B^2$
Ex7.	$A^2 - AB + BA - B^2$
Ex8.	① $\begin{bmatrix} -1 & 0 \\ 2 & 4 \end{bmatrix}$
	② $\begin{bmatrix} 1 & 0 & 2 \\ 0 & 2 & -4 \\ 3 & -5 & 4 \end{bmatrix}$
Ex9.	$\begin{bmatrix} 1 & 55 \\ 0 & 1 \end{bmatrix}$

10.3 Inverse and Matrix Equation

Ex1.	① -1
	② 7
	③ 9
	④ 8
	⑤ 0
	⑥ 0
Ex2.	① 32
	② 27
	③ 0
	④ -24
Ex3.	$x = -1 \text{ or } 9$
Ex4.	① $\begin{bmatrix} 2 & -3 \\ -3 & 5 \end{bmatrix}$
	② $\begin{bmatrix} 0 & -1 \\ 1 & 10 \end{bmatrix}$
	③ $\begin{bmatrix} 0 & \frac{1}{6} \\ -1 & -\frac{5}{6} \end{bmatrix}$
	④ $\begin{bmatrix} \frac{1}{2} & \frac{1}{2} \\ \frac{1}{2} & \frac{1}{4} \end{bmatrix}$
	⑤ Inverse does not exist (determinant is 0)
	⑥ Inverse does not exist (determinant is 0)

Ex5.	① $\begin{bmatrix} -\dfrac{1}{25} & \dfrac{1}{5} \\ \dfrac{6}{25} & -\dfrac{1}{5} \end{bmatrix}$
	② $\begin{bmatrix} \dfrac{1}{2} & \dfrac{1}{2} \\ -\dfrac{1}{2} & 0 \end{bmatrix}$
	③ $\begin{bmatrix} -3 & 10 & -3 \\ 2 & -4 & 1 \\ -1 & 1 & 0 \end{bmatrix}$
	④ $\begin{bmatrix} -1 & 1 & 0 \\ 4 & -1 & -1 \\ -2 & 0 & 1 \end{bmatrix}$
Ex6.	$X = A^{-1}B$
Ex7.	$X = BA^{-1}$
Ex8.	① $\begin{bmatrix} x \\ y \end{bmatrix} = \begin{bmatrix} -5 \\ 1 \end{bmatrix}$
	② $\begin{bmatrix} x \\ y \end{bmatrix} = \begin{bmatrix} 1 \\ -3 \end{bmatrix}$
	③ $\begin{bmatrix} x \\ y \\ z \end{bmatrix} = \begin{bmatrix} -67 \\ 91 \\ -36 \end{bmatrix}$
	④ $\begin{bmatrix} x \\ y \\ z \end{bmatrix} = \begin{bmatrix} 1 \\ -18 \\ 14 \end{bmatrix}$
Ex9.	① $x = -2, y = 1$
	② $x = 2, y = 6$

10.4 Partial Fractions

Ex1.	① $A = -1, B = -1$
	② $A = 2, B = -1$
	③ $A = -2, B = 2, C = 2$
Ex2.	① $\dfrac{1}{x-6} + \dfrac{1}{x+1}$
	② $\dfrac{5}{x-4} - \dfrac{4}{x-5}$
	③ $\dfrac{13}{x} - \dfrac{5}{x+1} - \dfrac{6}{x-1}$
	④ $\dfrac{1}{x} + \dfrac{10}{x+4} + \dfrac{8}{x-4}$
	⑤ $\dfrac{4}{x} - \dfrac{4}{x-1} + \dfrac{5}{(x-1)^2}$
	⑥ $\dfrac{3}{x+2} - \dfrac{1}{x+1} - \dfrac{2}{(x+1)^2}$
	⑦ $\dfrac{7}{x+1} - \dfrac{14}{(x+1)^2} + \dfrac{5}{(x+1)^3}$
	⑧ $\dfrac{4}{x-1} + \dfrac{4}{(x-1)^2} + \dfrac{3}{(x-1)^3}$
	⑨ $\dfrac{3}{x-1} + \dfrac{-3x+2}{x^2+x+1}$
	⑩ $\dfrac{1}{3(x-1)} + \dfrac{-\dfrac{1}{3}x+\dfrac{7}{3}}{x^2+x+1}$ $\left(= \dfrac{1}{3(x-1)} + \dfrac{-x+7}{3(x^2+x+1)}\right)$
	⑪ $\dfrac{3x+2}{x^2+5} + \dfrac{-15x-10}{(x^2+5)^2}$
	⑫ $\dfrac{1}{x^2+2} + \dfrac{3x-3}{(x^2+2)^2}$
Ex3.	① $1 - \dfrac{1}{2x} + \dfrac{9}{2(x-2)}$
	② $2 + \dfrac{4}{x} + \dfrac{3}{x-1}$
	③ $x+2 + \dfrac{2}{2x+1} + \dfrac{3}{(2x+1)^2}$
	④ $6 - \dfrac{1}{x} + \dfrac{2x-1}{x^2+1}$

Answers
11. Sequence and Series

11.1 Sequences and Sigma Notation

Ex1.	① 5, 11, 29, 83 ......
	② $-1, 0, 1, -2$ ......
	③ $-1, \dfrac{1}{2}, -\dfrac{1}{4}, \dfrac{1}{8}$ ......
	④ $2, \dfrac{3}{2}, \dfrac{4}{3}, \dfrac{5}{4}$ ......
	⑤ 1, 9, 33, 105 ......
	⑥ 2, 3, 5, 9 ......
	⑦ $1, -1, -2, -1$ ......
	⑧ 1, 3, 4, 7 ......
	⑨ $3, \dfrac{1}{3}, 3, \dfrac{1}{3}$ ......
Ex2.	① $a_n = \dfrac{1}{n}$
	② $a_n = \dfrac{n+1}{n}$
	③ $a_n = 2n$
	④ $a_n = (-1)^n$
	⑤ $a_n = (-1)^{n+1} 7n$
	⑥ $a_n = n(2n-1)$
Ex3.	① $3 + 6 + 9 + 12 + 15$
	② $5^2 + 6^2 + 7^2 + 8^2$
	③ $\cos 0\pi + \cos \pi + \cos 2\pi + \cdots + \cos 12\pi$
	④ $\sin 2 + \sin 2 + \cdots\cdots$
	⑤ $\dfrac{5}{6^2} + \dfrac{5^2}{6^3} + \dfrac{5^3}{6^4}$
	⑥ $\dfrac{5}{4} + \dfrac{5}{4}(2) + \dfrac{5}{4}(2)^2 + \dfrac{5}{4}(2)^3 + \dfrac{5}{4}(2)^4$
	⑦ $-\dfrac{x^2}{2!} + \dfrac{x^4}{4!} - \dfrac{x^6}{6!} + \cdots\cdots$
	⑧ $a^2 + \dfrac{a^3}{2} + \dfrac{a^4}{3} + \cdots\cdots$
Ex4.	① $\sum_{k=4}^{7} k$
	② $\sum_{k=4}^{8} 2k$
	③ $\sum_{k=1}^{6} (-1)^{k+1}(2k-1)$
	④ $\sum_{k=1}^{\infty} \sin k\pi$
	⑤ $\sum_{k=8}^{12} k^2$
	⑥ $\sum_{k=3}^{10} k^3$
	⑦ $\sum_{k=1}^{\infty} \dfrac{1}{k^2}$
	⑧ $\sum_{k=1}^{\infty} \dfrac{1}{k\sqrt{k}}$
	⑨ $\sum_{k=1}^{\infty} x^k$
Ex5.	① $S_1 = \dfrac{1}{2}$ $S_2 = \dfrac{2}{3}$ $S_3 = \dfrac{3}{4}$ $S_{20} = \dfrac{20}{21}$
	② $S_1 = \sqrt{2} - 1$ $S_2 = \sqrt{3} - 1$ $S_3 = \sqrt{4} - 1$ $S_{20} = \sqrt{21} - 1$

	③ $S_1 = \log \frac{2}{3}$ $S_2 = \log \frac{2}{4}$ $S_3 = \log \frac{2}{5}$ $S_{20} = \log \frac{1}{11}$	
Ex6.	① 170 ② 240	
Ex7.	① 330 ② 1020 ③ 1275 ④ 9455 ⑤ 44200	

11.2 Arithmetic Sequences

Ex1.	① Arithmetic, $d = 3$ ② Arithmetic, $d = -2$ ③ Not arithmetic ④ Not arithmetic ⑤ Arithmetic, $d = \frac{1}{3}$ ⑥ Not arithmetic
Ex2.	① $d = 3$, $a_n = 2 + (n-1)3 = 3n - 1$ ② $d = -6$, $a_n = 7 + (n-1)(-6) = -6n + 13$ ③ $d = \frac{1}{2}$, $a_n = 2 + (n-1)\frac{1}{2} = \frac{1}{2}n + \frac{3}{2}$ ④ $d = \frac{1}{4}$, $a_n = 8 + (n-1)\frac{1}{4}$ ⑤ $d = -2$, $a_n = (x-1) + (n-1)(-2)$ ⑥ $d = 6$, $a_n = (2t+1) + (n-1)6$ ⑦ $d = 5\sqrt{3}$, $a_n = 14\sqrt{3} + (n-1)5\sqrt{3}$ ⑧ $d = \ln 2$, $a_n = \ln 3 + (n-1)\ln 2$

Ex3.	① $7 + (n-1)2$ ② $3 + (n-1)5$
Ex4.	① $n = 18$ ② $n = 23$
Ex5.	① -10 ② 590 ③ 120 ④ 20200 ⑤ $\frac{363}{2}$ ⑥ 23 ⑦ -5 ⑧ 200 ⑨ -192 ⑩ 672
Ex6.	(a) 13th term (b) $n = 10$ or 15
Ex7.	5, 9, 13
Ex8.	$k = 590$

11.3 Geometric Sequences

Ex1.	① $r = -\frac{1}{2}$, $a_n = 2\left(-\frac{1}{2}\right)^{n-1}$ ② $r = -2$, $a_n = -\frac{1}{4}(-2)^{n-1}$ ③ $r = \sqrt{2}$, $a_n = \sqrt{2}\left(\sqrt{2}\right)^{n-1} = \left(\sqrt{2}\right)^n$ ④ $r = -1$, $a_n = 5(-1)^{n-1}$ ⑤ $r = -3$, $a_n = (x-3)(-3)^{n-1}$ ⑥ $r = 5$, $a_n = 2x(5)^{n-1}$

	⑦ $r = x^3$, $a_n = x^{a+2}\left(x^3\right)^{n-1} = x^{a+3n-1}$
	⑧ $r = x^{\frac{1}{3}}$, $a_n = x^{\frac{1}{3}}(x^{\frac{1}{3}})^{n-1} = (x^{\frac{1}{3}})^n$
	⑨ $r = 3$, $a_n = 3^{n-1}\ln 2$
	⑩ $r = 3^{-\frac{1}{6}}$, $a_n = 3^{\frac{1}{2}}\left(3^{-\frac{1}{6}}\right)^{n-1} = 3^{\frac{2}{3}-\frac{1}{6}n}$
Ex2.	① $a_n = \frac{1}{243}\left(\sqrt{3}\right)^{n-1}$ or $\frac{1}{243}\left(-\sqrt{3}\right)^{n-1}$
	② $a_n = \frac{1}{16}(2)^{n-1} = 2^{n-5}$
Ex3.	① $n = 9$
	② $n = 7$
Ex4.	① $\frac{4\left(1-(-4)^6\right)}{1-(-4)} = -3276$
	② $\frac{7\left(1-(-3)^5\right)}{1-(-3)} = 427$
	③ $\frac{3(1-4^3)}{1-4} = 63$
	④ $\frac{\frac{2}{3}\left(1-\left(\frac{2}{3}\right)^4\right)}{1-\frac{2}{3}} = \frac{130}{81}$
	⑤ $\frac{10\left(1-\left(\frac{1}{5}\right)^6\right)}{1-\frac{1}{5}} = 12.4992$
	⑥ $\frac{0.1\left(1-(0.1)^4\right)}{1-0.1} = 0.1111$
Ex5.	① 2
	② Diverge
	③ Diverge
	④ 1
	⑤ Diverge
	⑥ $\sqrt{2}+1$

	⑦ 12
	⑧ 2
	⑨ $\frac{20}{11}$
	⑩ Diverge
	⑪ $\frac{5}{9}$
	⑫ 4
	⑬ Diverge
Ex6.	① $\frac{2}{3}$
	② $\frac{1}{33}$
	③ $\frac{234}{999}$
	④ $\frac{251}{990}$
	⑤ $\frac{124}{990}$
Ex7.	$\pm\sqrt[6]{\frac{1}{2}}$
Ex8.	$1 < x < 3$
Ex9.	2

11.4 Apps of Sequence and Series

Ex1.	$x = 4$, $y = 6$
Ex2.	(a) $x = 7$ or -3
	(b) 54
Ex3.	1000
Ex4.	$\frac{28}{19}$
Ex5.	3367
Ex6.	(a) $25000(1.03)^9 = 32619.33\$$
	(b) $\frac{25000(1-1.03^{35})}{1-1.03} = 1511552.045\$$

Ex7.	(a) $3(0.9)^5 = 1.77147$ (b) 57
Ex8.	128
Ex9.	$\dfrac{1}{3}$
Ex10.	$\dfrac{400(1-1.08^{10})}{1-1.08} = 5794.63\$$

11.5 Binomial Expansion

Ex1.	① $x^4 + 8x^3 + 24x^2 + 32x + 16$ ② $x^4 - 8x^3 + 24 - \dfrac{32}{x^2} + \dfrac{16}{x^4}$ ③ $32x^5 - 80x^4 + 80x^3 - 40x^2 + 10x - 1$ ④ $243 + 405x + 270x^2 + 90x^3 + 15x^4 + x^5$ ⑤ $x^{10} + 5x^7 + 10x^4 + 10x + \dfrac{5}{x^2} + \dfrac{1}{x^5}$ ⑥ $64x^3 - 144x^2y + 108xy^2 - 27y^3$
Ex2.	① 720 ② 12
Ex3.	① $\dfrac{1}{120}$ ② 9900 ③ 28 ④ $\dfrac{1}{12}$ ⑤ $\dfrac{1}{n+1}$ ⑥ $(n+2)(n+1)$ ⑦ 15 ⑧ 35 ⑨ 1 ⑩ 1
Ex4.	$\dfrac{12!}{9!}$

Ex5.	$\dfrac{n!}{(n-3)!}$
Ex6.	① −448 ② 13440 ③ 2160 ④ 2835 ⑤ 3584 ⑥ 90 ⑦ 67584 ⑧ 14080 ⑨ 54
Ex7.	672
Ex8.	① $17010x^{-8}$ ② $-489888x^{-1}$ ③ $1120x^8y^4$
Ex9.	−336
Ex10.	28

11.6 Mathematical Induction

Ex1.	For $n=1$, $1 = 1[2(1)-1]$, which is true. Assume that $1+5+9+\cdots+(4k-3) = k(2k-1)$ is true. For $n = k+1$, $1+5+9+\cdots+(4k-3)+(4(k+1)-3)$ $= k(2k-1)+(4k+1)$ $= 2k^2 - k + 4k + 1$ $= 2k^2 + 3k + 1$ $= (k+1)(2k+1)$ $= (k+1)(2(k+1)-1)$ So it is true for $n = k+1$. Therefore the statement it true by mathematical induction.

Ex2.	For $n=1$, $1\times 3 = \dfrac{1(1+1)(2(1)+7)}{6}$, which is true. Assume that $1\times 3+2\times 4+\ldots+k(k+2) = \dfrac{k(k+1)(2k+7)}{6}$ is true. For $n=k+1$, $1\times 3+2\times 4+\ldots+k(k+2)+(k+1)(k+3)$ $= \dfrac{k(k+1)(2k+7)}{6} + \dfrac{6(k+1)(k+3)}{6}$ $= \dfrac{(k+1)[k(2k+7)+6(k+3)]}{6}$ $= \dfrac{(k+1)[2k^2+13k+18]}{6}$ $= \dfrac{(k+1)(k+2)(2k+9)}{6}$ $= \dfrac{(k+1)[[(k+1)+1][2(k+1)+7]]}{6}$ So it is true for $n=k+1$. Therefore the statement it true by mathematical induction.		$f(k+1) = 5^{k+1} - 2^{k+1}$ $= 5\cdot 5^k - 2\cdot 2^k$ $= 5\cdot(2^k+3A) - 2\cdot 2^k$ $(\because 5^k = 2^k+3A)$ $= 5\cdot 2^k + 15A - 2\cdot 2^k$ $= 3\cdot 2^k + 15A$ $= 3(2^k+5A)$ $= 3B$ Since $f(k+1)$ is divisible by 3, it is true for $n=k+1$. Therefore the statement it true by mathematical induction.
Ex3.	For $n=1$, $f(1)=7^1-1=6$ is divisible by 6. Assume that $f(k) = 7^k-1 = 6A$ where A is positive integer. For $n=k+1$, $f(k+1) = 7^{k+1} - 1$ $= 7\cdot 7^k - 1$ $= 7(6A+1) - 1$ $(\because 7^k = 6A+1)$ $= 42A + 7 - 1$ $= 42A + 6$ $= 6(7A+1)$ $= 6B$ Since $f(k+1)$ is divisible by 6, it is true for $n=k+1$. Therefore the statement it true by mathematical induction.	Ex5.	For $n=5$, $2^5 > 6(5)$ which is true. Assume that $2^k > 6k+1$ is true. For $n=k+1$, $2^{k+1} = 2\cdot 2^k$ $> 2(6k+1) = 12k+2 = 6k+6k+2$ $(\because 2^k > 6k+1)$ $> 6k+7 = 6(k+1)+1$ $(\because 6k+2 > 7 \text{ for } k\geq 5)$ Since $2^{k+1} > 6(k+1)+1$, it is true for $n=k+1$. Therefore the statement it true by mathematical induction.
Ex4.	For $n=1$, $f(1)=5^1-2^1=3$ is divisible by 3. Assume that $f(k) = 5^k-2^k = 3A$ where A is positive integer. For $n=k+1$,	Ex6.	For $n=4$, $4! > 2^4$ which is true. Assume that $k! > 2^k$ is true. For $n=k+1$, $(k+1)! = (k+1)\cdot k!$ $> (k+1)\cdot 2^k$ $(\because k! > 2^k)$ $> 2\cdot 2^k = 2^{k+1}$ $(\because k+1 > 2 \text{ for } k\geq 4)$ Since $(k+1)! > 2^{k+1}$, it is true for $n=k+1$. Therefore the statement it true by mathematical induction.